# Harder than War

# Harder than War

## Catholic Peacemaking in Twentieth-Century America

### PATRICIA MCNEAL

**Rutgers University Press**

*New Brunswick, New Jersey*

Library of Congress Cataloging-in-Publication Data

McNeal, Patricia F.
    Harder than war : Catholic peacemaking in twentieth-century
America / Patricia McNeal.
        p.   cm.
    Includes bibliographical references and index.
    ISBN 0-8135-1739-7 (cloth) — ISBN 0-8135-1740-0 (pbk.)
    1. Peace—Religious aspects—Catholic Church—History—20th
century.   2. Catholic Church—Doctrines—History—20th century.
I. Title.
BX1795.P43M36   1992
261.8'73'09730904—dc20                                    91-16814
                                                          CIP

British Cataloging-in-Publication information available

*For my sons,*
Patrick and Mark,
*and their generation,*
*that they may be peacemakers*

# Contents

# Preface

THIS BOOK BEGAN TWENTY years ago when I wrote my doctoral dissertation, "The American Catholic Peace Movement, 1928–1972." During
the intervening years three significant changes took place that led me to
update my research and write a more comprehensive study of American Catholic peacemaking in the twentieth century.

The first change took place in 1983 when the American Catholic
hierarchy began to assume an important role in American public life
by issuing pastoral letters that addressed society's main social problems.
By explicitly stating the church's moral position and values, the hierarchy hoped not only to educate its members but also to occupy a central
place in the public discourse about public policy in the United States,
and thus to make a distinctive contribution to the life of a pluralistic
society. The pastoral that received the greatest press coverage and discussion was *The Challenge of Peace: God's Promise and Our Response*.
In this document, the Catholic hierarchy fully embraced the legitimacy of Catholic peacemakers who rejected the just war doctrine and
looked to the Gospels as the source of their pacifist and nonviolent
positions.

The second change was the historical study of the Vietnam War. A
plethora of books on Vietnam filled the marketplace and a new field of
study was created. Two recent political studies of the antiwar movement of the Vietnam era—Charles DeBenedetti and Charles Chatfield, *An American Ordeal: The Antiwar Movement of the Vietnam
Era*, and Melvin Small, *Johnson, Nixon, and the Doves*—made me
acutely aware of how significant and distinctive a force religion was in
the American Catholic peace movement when compared with the
broader antiwar movement. Though Catholic pacifists were always

attempting to stop a war or the threat of a war, they were also trying to respond to Christ's call to be peacemakers and to bring forth a peacemaking response from the institutional church.

The final change was the rise of neoconservatism following the election of Ronald Reagan to the U.S. presidency and the election of Pope John Paul II to the papacy. The continual military buildup and displays of force and intervention in our government's foreign policy and the continual retrenchment from Second Vatican Council reforms on the part of important Vatican leaders have created a climate wherein the "neoconservatives" whose right-wing politics are more important than their Christian beliefs are now heralded as "the best and the brightest" in the American Catholic church. This book attempts to set the historical record straight about American Catholic peacemakers.

The purpose of this study is to document the growth of pacifism, nonviolence, and nuclear pacifism within the American Catholic community and assess their impact on the church and the nation. Support for pacifism among American Catholics is a relatively new phenomenon. Catholic pacifism that opposed all war did not emerge in the United States until the 1930s when Dorothy Day, cofounder of the Catholic Worker movement, proclaimed it. Prior to Day's proclamation, those Catholics who opposed war based their opposition on the just war doctrine. Among Roman Catholics the pacifism of the primitive Christian church, like other features of the radical Gospel, largely disappeared with the Age of Constantine. The just war doctrine with subsequent modifications remained the dominant Catholic position on war from its formulation by Augustine until the Second Vatican Council. In 1983, the National Conference of Catholic Bishops in the document *The Challenge of Peace* established pacifism, nonviolence, and nuclear pacifism as well as the just war doctrine as valid positions for Catholics in the United States to hold. The document stated: "We believe the two perspectives support and complement one another, each preserving the other from distortion."[1]

Dorothy Day was the one person most responsible for the shift in American Catholic thought away from the just war doctrine toward pacifism. By the end of World War II, she had added to the Catholic theological agenda the concepts of pacifism, conscientious objection, and nuclear pacifism. Although she did not articulate a theological rationale for these positions—this would evolve in the writings of

Thomas Merton—she did not hesitate to proclaim her pacifism as a moral response generated by the teaching of the Gospel. Her witness challenged the church's theology.

The military tactics of obliteration and atomic bombing during World War II also challenged the relevance of the just war doctrine to modern warfare. These military tactics violated the just war principle of proportionality and the principle of "double effect," which applied to the killing of noncombatants. The tensions between pacifists who contend that the just war doctrine is no longer relevant to modern warfare, and the just war theorists, who contend it is the only moral criteria available to address government decision makers on public policy issues of war and peace, is a dominant theme in the history of American Catholic peacemaking.

The first official Catholic peace organization in the United States (1927) was the Catholic Association for International Peace (CAIP), an elitist lay organization under clerical leadership and financially supported by the American hierarchy. Working independently of the broader American peace movement, CAIP operated out of an internationalist vision that opposed interwar isolationism and sought to awaken in Catholics a sense of collective responsibility as well as support for a world organization. This view depended on a concert of power in the political realm, the degree of collective cooperation among nations determining the type of security that could be devised to prevent war. The CAIP looked to the nation state as the arbiter and authority on issues of war and peace. Its approach to war issues emphasized the political and moral responsibilities of the decision maker to use power, but with normative restraints as delineated in the just war doctrine.

Unlike CAIP, Day and the members of the Catholic Worker movement emphasized the individual and not the state. Day believed that "at a time of war, the coercive power of the state reached its zenith."[2] She saw a nation's decision to declare war as the most extreme opposition to active love and the Gospel message of peace. Day believed that peace depended on the actions of individuals and not nations or world organizations; her internationalism resided in human solidarity and the doctrine of the Mystical Body of Christ whereby the action of each individual affected every other individual. To be consistent with the Worker ideal, Day believed a pacifist response was necessary. Thus, she opposed the draft and the Catholic Worker was the only Catholic group that assisted Catholic conscientious objectors.

Though the differences between CAIP and Day's Catholic Worker movement were great, both witnessed to the inseparable link between justice and peace in the Catholic tradition. Both were self-consciously Catholic and aimed to reconstruct America on the principles of social and economic justice. These domestic concerns for creating a just order led into international issues, particularly those of war and peace.

In the 1950s, Catholic pacifism moved to a new level with the incorporation of the theory of Gandhian nonviolence. Robert Ludlow wrote of the compatibility of Catholic pacifism and nonviolence and Ammon Hennacy showed Catholic Workers how to practice nonviolence. Pacifism opposed all war, but nonviolence provided a way to posit actions for peace and a way to address public policy issues never before available in pacifism. During the Vietnam War, Catholic Workers such as David Miller and Tom Cornell burned their draft cards and moved nonviolence to resistance by this practice of civil disobedience. Daniel and Philip Berrigan escalated that resistance when they destroyed draft files. Later these brothers used the same model of resistance when they symbolically poured blood over and hammered nuclear weapons to awaken the national conscience to the life-ending effects of nuclear warfare.

Dorothy Day, through the Catholic Worker movement, became the midwife in the formation of Catholic pacifist peace organizations such as PAX and the Catholic Peace Fellowship during the Vietnam War. The focus of PAX was to lobby the church to officially recognize both conscientious objection and selective conscientious objection as valid positions for Catholics to hold. The Catholic Peace Fellowship focused on draft counseling and worked with the broader antiwar movement. Its members became leaders in the Catholic Resistance. In 1972, Dorothy Day and the Catholic Worker were present when PAX gave birth to Pax Christi-USA. This organization would not be a solely pacifist organization, but would attract mainline Catholics, members of the American hierarchy, and just war theorists under its umbrella. Members of these groups cooperated with the broader peace movement in the United States and their main focus became opposition to nuclear warfare and nuclear weapons. These were the Catholic peacemakers who were able to proclaim the Gospel message of peace even when their nation proclaimed war.

The major conclusion of this study is that Catholic peacemakers had the greatest impact not on the government but on the institutional church. In 1971, the American hierarchy judged that the Vietnam war was not a "just war." For the first time in the United States, and possibly in history, a national hierarchy announced as unjust a war being waged by its own nation. In the 1983 peace pastoral *The Challenge of Peace*, the leaders of the institutional church condemned the use of nuclear (and conventional) weapons of indiscriminate effect even in retaliation. Though the church still clung to the just war doctrine and believed it alone offered a mediating language with which to address the nation on public policy, on the individual level, the church for the first time officially recognized and embraced its members who in conscience were pacifists, nuclear pacifists, practitioners of Gospel nonviolence and nonviolent resistance, conscientious objectors, and selective conscientious objectors.

The historical record reveals clearly the effectiveness of the moral witness of the American Catholic peace movement on its hierarchy and mainline Catholics. The record also reveals the ineffectiveness of their witness on the policies of the U.S. government on war and peace issues. This ineffectiveness is also characteristic of church policy makers who operated out of the just war ethic. But members of the American Catholic peace movement would be justified in asking "Who has been politically effective?" Americans continue to reap personal benefits from the war machine while at the same time apologizing for its existence. Perhaps the greatest contribution of the American Catholic peace movement is its message that peacemaking requires great personal sacrifice and a religious commitment that can sustain an individual in face of political ineffectiveness—peacemaking is harder than war.

One cannot complete a study of this magnitude without expressing the sincerest gratitude to the many people who made it possible. In the first place I wish to thank all those workers in the American Catholic peace movement who gave their time and support during interviews, especially Daniel and Philip Berrigan and Bishop Thomas Gumbleton. James Forest shared his memories, library, and correspondence with me. Thomas Cornell did the same, and together we loaded my car with boxes of Catholic Peace Fellowship material to take to the archives at the University of Notre Dame to begin its collection. James Douglass gave me his private collection of statements and correspondence relating to his work at the Second Vatican Council. Carol and Jerome Berrigan were most gracious in their concern and hospitality and allowed me access to their basement archives on Daniel and Philip Berrigan. Gordon C. Zahn, professor of sociology at the University of Massachusetts, aided portions of this study with a critical reading and valuable insights. I also want to thank Carole Roos for helping me to write a better book and Delores Fain, secretary at the Cushwa Center at the University of Notre Dame, for her technical assistance.

There were others who also assisted me, particularly the archivists at the Catholic University of America, Marquette University, the University of Notre Dame, and the Peace Collection at Swarthmore College. Financial assistance for travel was provided by grants from Indiana University at South Bend. And I am most grateful to faculty and staff at the Institute for International Peace Studies at the University of Notre Dame, which granted me a Visiting Faculty Fellowship to complete the book.

I also want to thank Professor Allen F. Davis of Temple University who directed my doctoral dissertation almost twenty years ago. Above all I want to thank my husband, Jay P. Dolan, who has constantly encouraged, supported, and helped me to complete this work.

# Harder than War

# 1

# Origins of the Catholic Peace Movement

On 5 April 1917, the day before the U.S. Congress declared war, James Cardinal Gibbons, speaking on behalf of the Catholic hierarchy and the American Catholic church, proclaimed that, "In the present emergency it behooves every American citizen to do his duty and uphold the hands of the President . . . in the solemn obligations that confront us. The primary duty of a citizen is loyalty to country. This loyalty is exhibited by an absolute and unreserved obedience to his country."[1] In pledging the loyalty of American Catholics to the nation Gibbons was reaffirming a tradition of Catholic "patriotism in war-time." This tradition, wrote one historian, "has been a hallmark of the American Catholic community," evident since the earliest days of the nation.[2] It was reinforced by a reaction to the anti-Catholicism prevalent in Protestant America and supported on a theological level by the just war doctrine.

As members of an immigrant church, Catholics in the United States continually sought to dispel the label of foreigners put on them by American nativists.[3] Their enthusiastic support of the nation's wars "has remained one of the most frequently used, if not logical retorts to answer any aspersions on Catholic loyalty to American principles."[4] The general antipathy of the American people for Catholicism was rooted in the virulent anti-Catholicism of the Protestant Reformation and strengthened periodically by waves of immigration, during which between 1790 and 1920 approximately 9,395,000 Catholic immigrants arrived in the United States. In response to the needs of this immigrant population, the church hierarchy was largely concerned with domestic rather than international issues. Church leaders had to turn their attention to building up the institution—churches, schools, and other organizations for

1

the spiritual welfare of the people. This domestic concern was influenced by Catholic social doctrine that emerged at the end of the nineteenth century when Pope Leo XIII, in response to problems posed by the industrial revolution, wrote the encyclical, *Rerum Novarum*, "On the Condition of the Working Man" (1891). The principal issues addressed in the document were "the role of government in society and the economy, the right of laborers to organize, the principle of a just wage, and a Christian critique of both capitalism and socialism."[5] *Rerum Novarum* was not a blueprint for the reform of the world, but "a broad theological and philosophical framework of social analysis" which exhibited not only concern for the individual but for the general welfare of society.[6] Though American Catholics were mainly attracted to Leo XIII's message relating to the reconstruction of the domestic order, the pope had also expressed a new attitude toward peace in *Rerum Novarum*. His central concern was for a new international order in which peace was based on justice and love rather than on military defense, and he called for a reevaluation of the justice of defensive wars in a technological world. He also asked Christians to follow Peter's call to obey God above humans, beginning a new era in which the church would declare independence from any particular social order for the first time since Constantine.[7] Though Catholics in the United States paid little attention to his international message before and during World War I, in the aftermath of the war, American Catholic reformers attempting to reconstruct the domestic order became involved in international issues. In addition, subsequent popes with their emphasis on rights, justice, and order strengthened the connection between justice and peace issues in Catholic social doctrine during the twentieth century. By the Second Vatican Council, the development of Catholic social doctrine had led the international hierarchy to call for a new theology of peace after questioning the adequacy of the just war tradition in the church's teaching.

The previous acceptance by the church of the just war doctrine as normative made legitimate the Catholic acceptance of the state's decisions pertaining to issues of war and peace. The just war doctrine has a long history in the church, originating with Ambrose and Augustine in the fourth century. At that time the pacifism of the early church was complicated by the conversion of Constantine and his transformation of the Roman Empire into a Christian state. According to Augustine, the father of the just war doctrine, every society seeks peace but may have to wage war to preserve that peace. Since Christians live in society, they are bound to share society's responsibilities, possibly including participation in war. However, Christians' motives for their participation would be different from those of pagans in that they wage war to establish peace and their defense of their earthly city is secondary to their fulfillment of the divine will.

During the Middle Ages, Thomas Aquinas refined the doctrine with such great precision that his formulation has remained the traditional interpretation. The just war doctrine presupposes that war is a rational and moral activity when it is governed by rules justifying the resort to violence and the nature of the violent force. Though the doctrine admits a variety of interpretations developed by both Catholic and Protestant theologians, the core of its teaching lists several conditions for going to war. First, war must be declared by a competent authority. Then, there must be a just cause for engaging in war; that is, a grave wrong to be corrected or right to be defended. Third, the likely beneficial results of a war must outweigh the evil results, the so-called principle of proportionality. The fourth condition states that war must be waged only as a last resort, after all peaceful means have been exhausted. Fifth, war must be waged with the right intention; that is, a war can be fought legitimately only if its purpose is to achieve a just end, not the uncharitable activities which usually accompany war.

The conditions for waging war are, first, that the means used are proportional to the likelihood of achieving just ends. And second, that no matter how militarily effective, no means can be employed that is immoral in itself. This last prohibition would apply to the killing of noncombatants. However, according to the principle of the double effect, an attack in which civilians were killed could be morally permissible if the intended object of the attack had been a legitimate military target that could not be dealt with in any other way, and the deaths of the civilians were incidental to the intention of the attacker.[8]

In the just war doctrine the presumption of justice is granted to the state as is all responsibility for war. The state thereby becomes the decision maker for all individual consciences. Where the individual disagrees with the state, the burden of proof rests with the individual.

With this understanding, American Catholics expressed their patriotism through military service and the hierarchy did not hesitate in supporting the government's position in World War I.

The outbreak of this war provided the Catholic hierarchy with an opportunity to demonstrate its patriotic Americanism. In support of President Woodrow Wilson's crusade "to make the world safe for democracy," they formed the National Catholic War Council. Founded in August 1917, it functioned throughout the war "as a highly effective medium in almost every phase of Catholic participation in the war effort, from providing material assistance to chaplains serving with the troops to acting as an official agency designated by President Wilson to promote the war-loan drives."[9]

A few months after World War I ended in Europe, the American bishops issued their first pastoral statement since 1884. This document, entitled *Lessons of War* and issued in September 1919, urged the United States to accept its unique role to "restore peace and order" according to "principles of reasonable liberty and of Christian civilization." In effect, the hierarchy condoned the war as a crusade and like many Americans they were now looking toward the reconstruction of American society.[10]

The success of the war council as a national coordinating agency for the church persuaded its supporters, principally, Bishop Peter J. Muldoon of the Diocese of Rockford, Illinois, to continue its operation after the war as a way for the church to maintain a national focus. The name was changed to the National Catholic Welfare Council (NCWC) and its headquarters was in the nation's capital. It became the primary agency to coordinate and promote Catholic interests and activities at a national level. Though there was initial opposition from some bishops who feared the council would limit their autonomy and authority, NCWC did succeed in providing the church with the type of national organization it needed and gave the bishops a national consciousness that taught them to think about issues that transcended local diocesan concerns.

The council originally had five departments: education, lay activities, press, missions, and social. But the one department "that has probably impinged more than any other on the national consciousness is the Social Action Department."[11] In 1920, the American Catholic hierarchy selected John A. Ryan to direct the new department, which was primarily concerned with social reform at home. However, under Ryan's leadership, social justice was linked for the first time to the broader international interests of war and peace.

John A. Ryan was the oldest of eleven children. Born in 1869 to Irish immigrant parents, he lived his youth in the small farming community of Vermillion, Minnesota. Ryan later acknowledged that his upbringing provided him with "an interest and love of economic justice, as well as political justice."[12] After ordination to the priesthood in 1898, Ryan went to the Catholic University of America to study moral theology. For completion of his degree, he wrote a doctoral dissertation entitled A Living Wage: Its Ethical and Economic Aspects. When it was published in 1906 Ryan began to receive public attention. At the time he was professor of moral theology at St. Paul's Seminary in St. Paul, Minnesota, and was writing articles on social reform for Catholic publications and giving many lectures. He was also mingling freely with reform groups not associated with the Catholic church. In 1915, Ryan returned to Catholic University as a professor and continued to teach there until his forced retirement in 1939. In 1916, he wrote another major book, Distributive Justice: The Right and Wrong of Our Present Distribution of Wealth, which provided a synthesis of his ethics and economics. In his position as director of NCWC's Social Action Department, he gradually emerged as the principal architect of Catholic social concern. At his death in 1945 he was still the dominant American Catholic social theorist.[13]

The genius of Ryan was his ability to merge Catholic social thought with the American current of reform. The basis for this merger was natural law tradition.[14] Pope Leo XIII had positioned the natural law at the foundation of Catholic social ethics in his encyclical, Rerum Novarum. Ryan took this aspect of papal social thought and applied it to the American economic and industrial environment. From this basic principle flowed Ryan's emphasis on a living wage, the importance of labor unions, and the need of the state to intervene and effect change in the social order. This positive role for the state in Catholic social theory did not mean an absolute trust in a particular government or administration that necessarily led to endorsing policy. Rather the natural law provided a language that allowed discussion of the morality of public policy in a pluralistic society.

After World War I the Catholic bishops wanted to present their own program for reconstruction of American society and set up their own committee to draft a document. The priest John O'Grady, secretary of the Committee on Reconstruction, had the responsibility to produce such a plan. He turned to John A. Ryan, who at the time was writing his own program of reconstruction. O'Grady begged him for it and in February 1919 it appeared as the "Bishops' Program of Social Reconstruction." Without a doubt it was "the most forward-looking social document ever to have come from an official Catholic agency in the United States."[15]

Avid criticism of the 1919 statement did occur. Some segments of the Catholic community labeled it as "partisan, pro-labor union, or socialistic propaganda."[16] Nevertheless, it pointed the direction toward which many Catholics were moving in the years after World War I. One visible omission in this quest for social reform was the international issue of war and peace.

As was evidenced in World War I, Catholics were eager to prove their loyalty to the United States, and in seeking social reform they never challenged the place of the nation in the international community. Raised in an immigrant community, Catholic reformers were also not inclined to challenge the country's basic social system. They wanted reform, but only within the boundaries of the accepted American tradition. They looked to the government for help, not to criticize it. Thus, it was inevitable that one of the last issues Catholic reformers would confront was the responsibility of the United States in war and for peace. Moreover, the just war tradition worked against any consideration of this issue.

Ryan typified this acceptance in World War I when he wrote in his autobiography that "I acquiesced in the declaration of war because I assumed that the President and Congress were in a better position than I to make the right decision."[17] Like Ryan's system of social ethics, the just war had its basis in the natural law tradition. For Ryan the state was necessary, and its authority was both real and binding. This did not, however, mean that the state is above the law or that the state is the final arbiter of right and wrong. According to Ryan the state stands under the law and must be judged according to the principles of natural law.[18]

During World War I, however, Ryan was greatly influenced by the proposals of Pope Benedict XV (1914–1922) for ending World War I and reestablishing international order and peace. During his pontificate, Benedict XV was faced with the full impact of world war and its aftermath of hatred and destruction. A former papal diplomat, Benedict XV opposed war in any form and rejected the theory of the just war as historically outmoded and theologically inadequate. He earned the title Pontiff of Peace.

Pope Benedict XV was more in line with the humanist peace tradition within the church, which he expressed in his direct moral appeal to individual conscience, than to the internationalist tradition that emerged after the Council of Trent and was promulgated with qualification by Leo XIII. The internationalists placed their hopes for peace on the diplomatic efforts and military balances of Europe's governments. Benedict XV issued the encyclical *Ad Beatissimum* at the outbreak of World War I. The encyclical outlined the causes of war and the methods for attaining peace. For Benedict XV the causes of war were lack of mutual love, disregard for authority, class war, and gross materialism; the path to peace embraced the Beatitudes and Christ's command that "you love one another as I have loved you." He called for a peace without victory and an end to hostilities, prophetically reminding the belligerents that true Christians must make the first offer of peace. "He was as close to a pacifist as any pope since Benedict XII during the Hundred Years War."[19]

Although the messages of Leo XIII and Benedict XV did not persuade the majority of Catholics nor Ryan to question the decisions of their government, Ryan was greatly influenced by the rejection of Benedict XV's proposal for ending World War I and reestablishing peace, which was sent to the belligerents on 14 August 1917. In responding to the international crisis Ryan established himself as the foremost advocate of the League of Nations. Ryan gave one of the first talks in support of the league at a meeting of the Knights of Columbus in Louisville in December 1918, five months before the covenant of the league was written into the Treaty of Versailles. In May 1919, he stated that the league was "the only means in sight to save the people of Europe from experiences perhaps worse than those of war."[20]

Ryan addressed his most urgent appeals for the league to Catholic bishops, whom he hoped would provide leadership on the issue; he also appealed to editors of the Catholic press because he believed that "the Catholic press was never more than 'spasmodic and half-hearted' in applying principles of Catholic political ethics to international questions."[21]

After 1920, other individuals also identified with the Social Action Department of NCWC took up the cause. Their aim was not to criticize the actions of the government, but rather to encourage it to move toward establishing an international organization that would assure peace. Although the leadership in the Social Action Department was primarily concerned with social reform at home, they attempted for the first time to link their quest for a domestic order of social justice to an international order based on social justice. The Catholic tradition, after all, had always stressed the inseparable link between justice and peace.

Catholic spokespersons for the league often met bitter popular opposition. Charles Fenwick, a Bryn Mawr professor and a nationally known Catholic, spoke out in favor of the league before Catholic audiences in the East and Midwest. Reinforcing his talks with quotations from Augustine, Thomas Aquinas, and the popes, he found that

> not only were Irish Catholics upset because of the failure of President Wilson to do anything about the independence of Ireland, but that German Catholics felt that Germany was being choked to death by the loss of needed territory like the busy Rhine, the iron and coal of the Saar and Alsace-Lorraine, the valuable mines of Silesia and reparations that would last until 1987. Italian Catholics were incensed at the loss of Fiume.

Fenwick also reluctantly admitted that he "never won a single debate, or converted a single audience."[22] Similar experiences were related by Francis McMahon, a professor at the University of Notre Dame, who was met with the charge that the league "was invented by Wilson and taken to Geneva, the ancient city of Calvin, to make it anti-Rome." Others told him that "its instigators were the international Masons." Another charge against the league, McMahon reported, was "its failure to include the Vatican in its organization."[23]

A closely related crusade that attracted Ryan in the 1920s was international peace through disarmament. Not historically literate, Ryan was, nevertheless, well informed on matters within his own memory and he understood European problems, especially economic ones. He gave particular attention to the excessive burden the war debt placed on the German people; he believed this would be a source of continuing threat to world peace.[24] In 1928, Ryan appeared before the House Naval Affairs Committee as a representative of the Church Peace Union, an interdenominational group, to oppose the construction of new capital warships. The *Buffalo Catholic Union and Times* did not approve and demanded to know "How long, O! Lord! would Catholics have to put up with the intrusions of Father Burke and Dr. Ryan into political questions in the discussion of which they have no authority to speak except for their own ill-formed and ill-considered convictions?"[25] Ryan also applauded the Treaty of Locarno, the Kellogg Pact, and the World Court.

In 1922, while visiting England, Ryan met a British peace advocate, Joseph Keating, S.J., from whom he learned about England's Catholic Council for International Peace. After returning to the United States, Ryan discussed with some of his friends the idea of founding a similar Catholic peace organization. He received support from Robert Mc-Gowan and from Carlton J. H. Hayes of Columbia. Worth M. Tippy, Charles S. Macfarland, and especially Sidney L. Gulick, all of the Federal Council of Churches for Prevention of War, urged him to organize a peace movement among Catholics.[26] Frederick J. Libby, executive secretary of the National Council for the Prevention of War (NCPW) was also urging Ryan forward. Ryan at this time was serving on the board of the NCPW. These men propelled Ryan into a territory that Catholics had not entered. The popes had spoken vigorously for peace; the bishops had echoed them. But there it ended. Ryan did not exaggerate in 1925 when he said, "he could tell the whole story of American Catholic peace sentiment in a fraction of the sixteen hundred words that the *NCWC Bulletin* wanted him to write."[27]

The diversity of positions later evidenced in the 1930s by these individuals who had counseled Ryan in the formation of a Catholic peace movement reveal how loosely related peace societies were in the 1920s. In 1922, Ryan did not want to start an American Catholic peace movement, but he did want to form a group of Catholics who could serve as a pressure group to lobby for significant legislation on issues of war and peace in Congress.[28] Ryan's primary focus was the issue of social action, yet he did agree with the judgment of Bishop Peter J. Muldoon, episcopal chair of the Social Action Department, that "the department was not doing enough to educate Catholics on world affairs. It concentrated on domestic social justice alone."[29] Another priest, Joseph Burke, C.S.P., finally pushed Ryan in the direction of organizing a peace group among Catholics. He suggested that Ryan and his assistant, Raymond McGowan, also a priest, "get leading Catholics together at the 28th Annual Eucharistic Congress to be held in Chicago in 1925," and together they could begin to discuss the issue of international peace.[30]

The proposed meeting of fifty Catholic leaders took place following the close of the congress. The assembled group did not draw up any specific plans, but expressed a desire to meet again and established an organizing committee headed by Colonel P. H. Callahan of Louisville, Kentucky. The next conference took place in Cleveland on 6 October 1926; here a committee system was adopted to study, report upon, and help promote Catholic understanding and action on problems of world peace. An organizational meeting was then scheduled for April 1927, at the Catholic University of America in Washington, D.C.[31]

For this meeting Ryan was to chair the subcommittee on international ethics and prepare a working paper for discussion. His final product drew substantially from *The Church and War* by Franziskus Stratmann, O.P.; Stratmann believed no modern war could be just. Ryan's pamphlet became the principal manifesto of the new association when it was published in 1927 with the title *International Ethics.* This report rejected Stratmann's pacifist position, but attempted to limit the characterization of a just war and warned of the need for caution in invoking force. Ryan stated that "righteousness would surely not be protected if wicked men were permitted to have a monopoly on physical coercion."

With the problem of creating a Catholic group in mind, the subcommittee noted: "Justice requires a state to promote peace for the sake of its own members, while charity obliges it to pursue the same ends for the welfare of both itself and other nations. These duties rest not only upon governments, but upon peoples, particularly upon those persons and organizations which can exert influence upon public opinion and upon political rulers."[32] This 1927 meeting realized the goal of a Catholic peace organization: It adopted a constitution, elected officers, and chose a name, the Catholic Association for International Peace (CAIP). Its motto was that of Pope Pius XI's reign, "The Peace of Christ in the Kingdom of Christ." It was the first Catholic peace organization in American history.

> The Association did not look for mass support, but planned to seek to educate Catholics and non-Catholics on the Catholic point of view on international affairs, as drawn from what the Holy Fathers, the Bishops of the United States, and Catholic scholars had said on the principles of attaining world peace through justice and charity. [33]

Studies were to be made by experts and reports published on the principles of peace and their application to current issues. In addition, the association would promote annual conferences, lectures, and study circles to present Catholic opinion on subjects relating to international morality. CAIP was allotted office space in the NCWC headquarters in Washington as an independent branch of the Social Action Department and was given the use of NCWC facilities, including the news service.

In attempting to analyze the ideology, structure, and tactics of CAIP, it is impossible to separate the association from NCWC's Social Action Department because of the central roles of Ryan and McGowan in both organizations. During this period, Ryan's reputation as "American Catholicism's foremost social reformer" enabled him to link American Catholics and liberal, progressive groups. [34] McGowan, however, assumed primary responsibility for CAIP's organization and vision. [35] Both men believed that "highly trained laymen and laywomen would join priests in furnishing the material for the program of education for and the actual re-creation of the social order. Catholics should remake social institutions by gaining positions of power in business organizations and civil life." [36] Thus, the structure of CAIP was elitist from the beginning though it intended to reach the general population of the laity.

People invited to participate in the formation of CAIP and later to serve on its committees were leaders from church, business, military, and university life. Bishop Thomas J. Shahan, rector of the Catholic University of America, was elected honorary president of CAIP. The first secretary was Francis Riggs who served but a short time before he left to become chief of police in Puerto Rico. Other prominent people in the early activities of the organization were Parker T. Moon and

Carlton J. H. Hayes of Columbia Univesrity; John LaFarge, S.J., editor of *America*; Francis Haas of Grand Rapids, later bishop of that diocese; Marie Carroll, librarian of the World Peace Foundation; Vincent Ferrer, O.P., of Rosary College; Archbishop Robert E. Lucey of San Antonio, then a priest of the Archdiocese of Los Angeles; and George Shuster, editor of *Commonweal* and later president of Hunter College.[37] These prominent and influential people belonged to an institutional world of decision making that spoke in political terms of compromise and mediation.[38]

The CAIP's focus was on peace education. Because it was part of the official church bureauracy, NCWC, the association "was to eschew anything like direct action."[39] Its relationship with the NCWC favored the organizational approach of issuing statements from the top of the hierarchical structure rather than working directly with people at a grass-roots level. As a result, CAIP conducted its best work through its pamphlets, which it distributed to its members and existing Catholic organizations. Its campaign of peace education was most effective, not in preventing war but in instructing people in the value of internationalism.

The key organizational component of CAIP was the committee. These were formed to present "a united front against isolationist mentality,"[40] and expressed the internationalist viewpoint of CAIP. The association developed a concept of internationalism that was based on the desire for cooperation among individual nations through a world organization that would mobilize the moral and physical resources of the great majority of nations against aggression. This view depended on a concert of power in the political realm. The degree of collective cooperation among nations would determine the type of security that could be devised to prevent war. CAIP, therefore, was a proponent of collective security and supported America's entrance into the League of Nations and the World Court. After 1937, they would support President Franklin D. Roosevelt's advocacy of collective security.

As early as 1930, the Ethics Committee issued a pamphlet on *The Causes of War* which argued that the primary cause of illegal warfare was the action of "unmoral" states. An unmoral state was defined as one dominated by excessive nationalism and aggressive materialism. In CAIP the major critic of excessive nationalism was Carlton J. H. Hayes, whose pamphlet *Patriotism, Nationalism and the Brotherhood of Man* stated that Catholics were all too quick to subordinate their loyalty to Catholic principles to those of nationalism, chauvinism, and antiforeignism. He went on to argue that there was no basic difference between the selfishness of America's political and economic policy and that of other nations. He did point out, however, that fascism and Nazism were the twentieth century's most extreme forms of virulent nationalism and that such political philosophies were unacceptable to the Catholic church since they exalted the state as the supreme and exclusive object of the individual's loyalty.

The association also attacked aggressive materialism. In its economic reports aggressive materialism was cited as a major source of discord and distrust among nations. In a 1938 report, *World Trade Patterns*, it demonstrated that the economic life of the world was moving, not toward a just distribution of the goods of nature, but toward divisive ideological political blocs of economic control. This was true of all forms of government, democratic, fascist or communist with the most blatant example being Germany's domination of eastern Europe. Like other conservative peace groups, CAIP in 1937 urged that a World Economic Conference be held to remedy the economic ills that seriously contributed to Europe's major troubles. The proposed guiding principle for the conference was the "reaffirmation of the moral unity of mankind and that an injustice done to one nation is an injustice done to all."[41]

Prominent in CAIP's international position was the legitimacy of just war. In 1932, Cyprian Emmanuel, chair of the Ethics Committee, wrote a pamphlet, *The Ethics of War*, presenting the conditions of a just war for the moral nations of the twentieth century. The criteria for such a justifiable war included the basic conditions of the just war doctrine.[42] Since it adopted the just war doctrine, CAIP was able to endorse the Stimson doctrine and the Geneva Disarmament Conference. It also supported the denunciation of Nazism, the revision of neutrality legislation, and ultimately the acceptance of World War II as a just war.

The person most responsible for coordinating the work of CAIP was Elizabeth Sweeney, secretary of the association. Sweeney had previously been a secretary in NCWC's Social Action Department. Extremely competent as a secretary, she was an active member of many Catholic organizations and knowledgeable on the workings of Washington, D.C. One of her principal accomplishments was directing publication of twenty-eight pamphlets between 1928 and 1938. The funds needed to publish these pamphlets were donated by member institutions such as Mount St. Joseph's College, Rosary College, and Rosemont College.[43] CAIP also received contributions from organizations that sympathized with the association's principles and work, such as the National Catholic Welfare Conference (NCWC), National Council of Catholic Men (NCCM), National Council of Catholic Women (NCCW), National Federation of Catholic College Students (NFCCS), and Newman Club Federations.

CAIP's first effort in disseminating peace education material consisted of distributing pamphlets to already existing discussion groups in the hope that groups would focus on the issue of international peace and ultimately to become members of CAIP. Elizabeth Sweeney applied this tactic when she was invited to address the annual convention of NCCW in 1933 on the topic of international peace. After her address, NCCW adopted the topic as the discussion theme for the year and CAIP pamphlets were then used as source material in dioceses throughout the United States.[44]

CAIP also worked with existing nondenominational organizations in order to recruit new members. In Los Angeles, Robert Lucey, a Catholic priest, established an active branch of CAIP out of the existing League of Nations Association. After Lucey left the diocese in 1932, Mary Workman, an active member in the parish, attempted to coordinate activities, but without strong clerical leadership, the group became increasingly less active.[45]

On the college level, CAIP devoted most of its energies to Catholic institutions. As early as 1928, Elizabeth Sweeney proposed to facilitate the distribution of CAIP material to peace study groups in Catholic colleges. Two years later the executive committee suggested that all Catholic colleges should encourage student participation in peace programs on Armistice Day. The first program CAIP organized was at the College of Notre Dame of Maryland; it was led by Elizabeth Morrissey, a member of CAIP on the college faculty.[46] In the early 1930s, more than 150 Catholic colleges adopted Peace Week Programs. There were attempts to initiate CAIP chapters on every campus, but there was also an alternative policy of affiliating with existing clubs, such as the Student Mission Crusade, the Catholic Action Movement, or the International Relations Club.[47] Affiliate members were then organized into geographic units known as Student Peace Federations. In 1936, the association sponsored two Student Peace Federation Conferences modeled on CAIP's annual conference.[48] The Middle Atlantic colleges met at St. Elizabeth College in New Jersey and the Middle Western colleges met at Rosary College in River Forest, Illinois.

During the 1930s, CAIP faced the question of whether or not the Reserve Officers Training Corps (ROTC) programs, which began to emerge on Catholic campuses, were compatible with its mission. In 1931, only three Catholic universities had an ROTC program: Boston College, Fordham University, and Georgetown University. All three colleges offered it as an elective and the total number of students involved was 1,169.[49] However, by 1937 many more Catholic universities had adopted the program. CAIP saw no basic conflict with the ROTC mainly because of its just war presupposition and its commitment to collective security.

CAIP also tried to bring the message of peace to the secondary and elementary levels of education.[50] That such a need existed was obvious from the results of a study made by Monsignor Maurice Sheehy, *National Attitudes in Children*, published by CAIP. The study, which surveyed elementary and high school students in the large metropolitan centers of thirty states and Puerto Rico, revealed the consciousness of racial or national differences among children and youth. This study was supplemented two years later by a pamphlet, *Peace Education in the Curriculum of the Schools*, written by Monsignor J. M. Wolfe of Dubuque, Iowa, chair of the Peace Education Committee, which called for a new curriculum that would present a broad, comprehensive program for cultivating "peace mindedness" among young people.

CAIP attempted to gain support for its principles in Congress through lobbying tactics. In 1933, when Congress voted on the Arms Embargo Bill, ten Catholic Democrats and all seven Catholic Republicans voted against the bill. Members of the association were distraught because five of these legislators were on the sponsoring committee of the annual conference of CAIP which had just met and endorsed the Arms Embargo Bill.[51] Such voting patterns of Catholic legislators suggest that the CAIP had little influence in persuading members of Congress to follow its recommendations. Differences between CAIP and Catholic legislators continued throughout the 1930s.

The CAIP urged its members to work within the framework of all existing organizations devoted to the cause of peace in the world, but it did little more than send pamphlet material upon request or provide a speaker for a peace rally. Some individual members did serve on national committees of various peace organizations. Ryan had served several years on NCPW's executive board. When the board in 1933, over Ryan's repeated protests, decided to intervene between the government in Mexico and the Catholic church, he resigned. President Roosevelt had instituted a "good neighbor" policy toward Latin America during the height of Mexico's anticlericalism, which resulted in antagonism between his administration and the Catholic church. Some American Catholics made Josephus Daniels, the newly appointed U.S. ambassador to Mexico, the scapegoat in their attempt to pressure the Roosevelt administration into meddling in the internal affairs of Mexico in support of the church. Between 1932 and 1936, "it was the most severe strain imposed on the generally harmonious relationship between Roosevelt and American Catholics."[52]

Thus it was the "Mexican question" and not pacifism that led to Ryan's resignation from NCPW. In his autobiography, Ryan admits that he was aware that many of the members of NCPW were pacifist, but it did not cause him any "unpleasant complications" in the years he was with them. Ryan goes on to say that it would have caused his resignation in 1939 when the council took a strong stand against President Roosevelt's recommendation to Congress to lift the embargo on the sale of arms in favor of Great Britain and France and again when they fought against the program for national defense adopted by Congress in 1940. Ryan's main criticism of NCPW was that they had become "hopelessly isolationist."[53] In his autobiography he writes, "Because I still have faith and hope in world peace through international action, and because I still believe that the precepts of the moral law bind nations as well as individuals, I reject and detest isolationism under any and every guise."[54]

CAIP's relations with peace organizations outside the United States were similar with those at home. To establish contact with Europe, Elizabeth Sweeney, as early as June 1929, wrote on behalf of CAIP to Franziskus Stratmann, head of the German Catholic Union for Peace, who in turn urged the need to prepare the way for an international peace conference. Stratmann held that no modern war could be a just war and also urged that war service and military service be declared an absolute contradiction of the teachings of Christ and of the Catholic church.[55] From this position he urged Sweeney to contact Joseph Clayton in England who had written on peace for the English Dominican periodical *Blackfriars*, the Polish Jesuit Graf Rostoworowski, Professor Ude of Graz University, Professor Keller of Freiburg University, and the War Resisters' International. CAIP, however, gave little cooperation beyond publishing a pamphlet called *Catholic Peace Organizations in Europe*. It also worked with the Carnegie Endowment for International Peace in publishing for American readers a five-hundred page work on internationalism and Catholicism. The work, *The Catholic Tradition of the Law of Nations*, was written by John Eppstein under the auspices of the Catholic Council for International Relations of Great Britain.

By 1937 CAIP's internationalism had resulted in opposition to neutrality legislation. CAIP contended that the Neutrality Act made no distinction between the aggressor nation and its victim.[56] In 1938, it reiterated its position by objecting to the "narrow conception of national interest upon which [the] Neutrality Act was based—[an] attitude of washing our hands of responsibility in present crime—[and it was] concerned primarily not with the prevention of war but with [the] avoidance of its consequences."[57] This paved the way for the CAIP to embrace wholeheartedly Roosevelt's move away from neutrality toward collective security.

The only stumbling block in this process for the CAIP was the Spanish Civil War and the ensuing debate between 1937 and 1939 over the Embargo Act. During this time President Roosevelt did not advocate a change in the Neutrality Act of 1937 and a lifting of the Embargo Act. Yet, in his "Quarantine Speech" at Chicago on 5 October 1937 he discarded the doctrine of neutrality for the United States and espoused the idea of collective security—the cardinal principle of internationalism. Despite this, he never lifted the embargo. Like Roosevelt CAIP was also ambiguous. It seemed logical by 1937 that CAIP was ready to reject strict neutrality but the American bishops and the "official" church statements from the NCWC came out in support of Franco in Spain and were against the repeal of the embargo, which would favor the Loyalists. Because of CAIP's close relationship with the NCWC, it chose to remain silent rather than confront the position of the "official" church.

Ryan, however, spoke out on the issue when he joined a group of 174 Catholic laymen and clergymen to defend the American church's support of the insurgents in the Spanish Civil War. The group issued a statement that insisted on the right of revolution against a government that made persecution of the church an integral part of its program. Ryan made no apologies about signing the statement. He had no affection for fascism and he believed the coming struggle in Europe would be between communism and democracy rather than between democracy and fascism. Even though this view set him off from most liberal opinion in America, he reminded himself that where religion was involved, liberals were likely to be "muddleheaded."[58]

After Franco's victory in Spain in 1939, such a conflict of loyalties would never again confront CAIP. Because the "official" church opposed Nazism, CAIP was able to speak out against strict neutrality when it touched on the German situation.

The shift of CAIP from support of neutrality legislation to endorsing collective security reflected the transformation taking place among other non-pacifist peace groups such as the Carnegie Endowment for International Peace, the Church Peace Union, the World Alliance for International Friendship through the Churches, and the League of Nations Association. All these organizations rallied around the concept of collective security and formed the Non-Partisan Committee for Peace Through the Revision of the Neutrality Law. Through this organization and others, the non-pacifist peace groups prepared the nation for war by emphasizing collective security rather than a position of neutrality. As a spokesperson for the committee in late 1939 Ryan expressed the consensus of the group when he stated in a radio broadcast that all Americans were "morally obliged to do all they reasonably can to defeat Hitler and Hitlerism."[59]

By 1940, Ryan was firmly convinced of his position on war and Hitler. In an article that appeared in *Commonweal* and was reprinted as a pamphlet *The Right and Wrong of War*, he wrote:

> The extreme pacfist position, that war as such is always wrong because it involves violence, does not deserve formal discussion. With the position of some recent Catholic authorities, that in our day war is practically never justified because of its awful consequences, I have considerable sympathy; but if Hitler and his government intend to

substitute paganism for Christianity not only in Germany but in foreign territories which they have annexed in the last two years and if they are aiming at world domination, then I have no hesitation in saying that a successful war against this immoral Nazi program would be the lesser evil. In other words, such a war would be justified, despite the enormous ensuing destruction of life and property.[60]

When the United States declared its formal participation in World War II, CAIP unhesitatingly continued the Catholic tradition of patriotism in wartime.

When bombs came down on Pearl Harbor, Catholic debate of foreign policy ceased. The isolationism CAIP had tried to combat disappeared among American Catholics. The historian, George Q. Flynn, in his book *Roosevelt and Romanism*, contends that there was a moral clarity reflected in the American Catholic conscience on World War II, which had little to do with politics and everything to do with theology. A study of the statements of Catholic leaders concerning World War II, according to Flynn, reveals that Catholics believed Hitler was a demonic force in history and the United States held a special place in God's plan of creation that placed God on their side during the war. These two religious assumptions, states Flynn, combined with the dominant teaching of the just war doctrine, turned the war effort into a moral crusade to promote a world of liberty and goodness. Catholics might have put some qualifications on their commitment, realizing that to identify God with any nation was a heresy in doctrine. Yet, Flynn contends that there were no such reservations voiced by Catholic spokespersons. Catholic leaders and their flocks had been trained to think in religious terms, thus it is understandable that they could "be lifted out of history and into a morality play."[61] By approaching the war as a moral crusade, Flynn concludes that Catholic leaders were left with an atrophy of their ethical feelings concerning the objects, tactics, and strategy of the conflict. They had become one with the Roosevelt administration in the attempt to win the just war.

Prior to World War II, CAIP never claimed a membership of more than five hundred.[62] However, because of the prestige of its members, especially John A. Ryan, the ideals of the association reached a wide audience. CAIP's identification with NCWC opened the doors to all other recognized Catholic organizations. Most of the work was coordinated by Elizabeth Sweeney who labored to help CAIP attain the goals of its constitution: "To further accord, with the teachings of the Church, the 'Peace of Christ in the Kingdom of Christ' through the preparation and dissemination of studies applying Christian teaching to international life."

While CAIP claimed to be the "official" peace organization within the Catholic church, other movements representing alternative perspectives on war and peace issues began to emerge in the 1930s. These movements also traced their roots back to the social question, the principal concern of Catholics between the two great wars. The financial crash of 1929 and the ensuing depression focused the concern of Americans on social issues and more than one citizen devised a plan for rebuilding the nation. Among those was Charles E. Coughlin, a Catholic pastor in Royal Oak, Michigan, who gained national prominence through his weekly radio program.[63]

Coughlin's strength was his personality, which he conveyed in his powerful oratory over the radio. He attracted thousands of listeners, the majority of whom lived in Eastern and Midwestern cities. Many became members of his organization, the Christian Front. In his addresses, this "shepherd of discontent" was able to put into words the fears and frustrations of his listeners.

Coughlin was not a peacemaker. He was both a demagogue and an ardent nationalist who believed that the United States was synonymous with Christendom; anything that sapped the strength of this "Christian Commonwealth" had to be eradicated. To this end, capitalism and communism, in Coughlin's opinion the two main evils of the 1930s depression, had to be eradicated from American society. By 1938, his belief in the threat of "international jewry" reinforced his views on capitalism and communism. In his opinion, jewry advanced the evils of capitalism and communism and all three forces threatened the "Christian Commonwealth" both from within and without. An equally passionate isolationism reinforced Coughlin's view of America's place in the world community.

Surfacing during the years of the Great Depression as a social reformer, Coughlin eventually emerged for some Catholics as a spokesperson against World War II. Anything that diverted the energies of the nation away from its reconstruction was to be opposed, and World War

II did just that. Coughlin's main concern was not peace but war as a threat to the Christian nation, America. He remained firm in his isolationism and his opposition to the war became a moral crusade.

One might legitimately ask why Coughlin is being mentioned in a study of the Catholic peace movement. The reason is that Coughlin opposed the participation of the United States in World War II. He did not identify himself with any of the existing peace groups, though at times he found himself standing with them on a particular issue. More significantly, Coughlin's stance against America's entry into World War II represented a new departure in American Catholicism. By challenging America's participation in the war, Coughlin broke with the Catholic tradition of wartime patriotism. However, his motives were not rooted in a concern for peace. Coughlin was an isolationist who challenged the role of the state in this particular war because he believed that American participation would support the wrong side—a side that in his opinion was dominated by British capitalists and Russian communists, and therefore was inconsistent with his view of America as the new Christendom. Thus, despite his extreme nationalism, Coughlin challenged the role of the U. S. government, and some of his followers, members of the Christian Front, even became conscientious objectors.

The third group of Catholics who addressed themselves to the issues of war and peace was centered in the Catholic Worker movement. Founded in 1933 in New York City, it was unique in the history of American Catholicism, being fundamentally a movement of Catholic lay people. Moreover, the Catholic Worker held a position of pacifism and thus became the first Catholic group in the United States to follow this ideal. Like Coughlin and the social actionists of the CAIP, the Catholic Worker first emerged as a group of people concerned about the social reconstruction of America.

The co-founders of the Catholic Worker movement were Peter Maurin and Dorothy Day. Maurin was a French peasant who had abandoned the Christian Brothers to join Le Sillon, a lay movement whose goal was to Christianize modern democracy. Becoming disillusioned with the Sillon movement and seeking to escape the draft in France, he immigrated to Canada in 1909. These experiences had helped to form Maurin's philosophy of Christian personalism. He believed that at the core of Christianity was personal responsibility that the chaotic conditions of modern society destroyed. Each person could affirm his or her personal responsibility by integrating the spiritual and material aspects of life through active participation in the political, economic, and social concerns of the world. If each individual Christian pursued this course, a restoration of unity in the Christian world would result.[64] Wanting to share his vision, Peter Maurin became a peripatetic teacher, who eventually made his way to the United States.

Dorothy Day was by occupation a journalist. After dropping out of college for financial reasons, she was involved with radical movements such as the Industrial Workers of the World and with communism; she was also a feminist.[65] As soon as Day heard Maurin speak, she quit her job as a journalist with the sole desire to join Maurin in building the Catholic Worker movement. As Dorothy Day herself was to say many times of Peter Maurin, "He was my master and I was his disciple."[66]

Dorothy Day managed to find concrete ways of embodying Maurin's ideas. First, she began a newspaper, the *Catholic Worker*, that sold for a penny a copy. She also opened a House of Hospitality on Mott Street in New York City where workers and intellectuals could meet and hold "round-table discussions." Later, she began a farm commune in Easton, Pennsylvania. As the Catholic Worker movement spread beyond New York, the concept of a newspaper, a house of hospitality, and a fascination with the simplicity of the rural life continued to define the movement.

The Catholic Worker movement was not an organization but rather a gathering of diverse people. Those who joined (actually more a matter of self-identification and working with others in the movement) were cosmopolitan scholars and reformers who, unlike members of CAIP, identified themselves with the disinherited.[67] They embraced a life-style of voluntary poverty and focused their attention on economic and social changes that were consistent with the goals of Christian personalism. While these people did not wait for clerical leadership, the Catholic Worker was recognized by the church hierarchy, and the Archdiocese of New York requested its members to accept a chaplain. The founders did so, but the chaplain stayed very much in the background. Dorothy Day, then as always, followed the directives of her church superiors, but the Catholic Worker movement was never dependent upon the institutional church or any other organization for financial support. Voluntary contributions provided what monetary assistance was necessary.

Because of the depression, Catholic Workers focused all their energies on ways to relieve human suffering and to remedy the injustices of American society. They based their program of social reconstruction on Christian personalism and upon Pope Leo XIII's injunction in *Rerum Novarum* to "go to the workingman, especially to the poorest of them." Catholic Workers favored a new economic system to replace what they viewed as a decadent capitalism. Though steeped in the thought of American and European social and liturgical thinkers, they centered the core of their beliefs on the Gospel, showing their love for God by carrying out the corporal and spiritual works of mercy.[68] Thus, in their call for a new social order members favored direct action aimed at countering the evils of industrial society and demanded an unbloody revolution. An explicit concern for peace was not apparent in the early days of the Catholic Worker, but as Dorothy Day was to say before the outbreak of World War II: "For eight years we have been opposing the use of force—in the labor movement, in the class struggle, as well as in the struggles between countries. . . . By working for a better social order in our own country, by working for the 'tranquillity in order' which is the definition of peace, we are working for peace."[69] The Catholic Worker saw the incidents of aggression during the 1930s and the world's response to them as power politics. In its view the League of Nations and the concept of collective security to prevent war seemed to fail each successive test. Thus, the movement developed and acted upon a pacifist rationale.

This pacifist position became explicit at the time of the Spanish Civil War. The Catholic establishment was decidedly pro-Franco, but the Catholic Worker did not support his cause and condemned every aspect of Franco's revolt. In doing this the *Catholic Worker* stated that it was adopting a position of strict neutrality, yet by remaining neutral, it was already in opposition to the mainstream of Catholics in the United States. The paper printed the message of love and Christian pacifism: "Love your enemies; do good to them that hate you, and pray for them that persecute and calumniate you."[70]

The *Catholic Worker* was not the only Catholic publication to profess neutrality during the Spanish Civil War. *Commonweal*, a monthly magazine published by Catholic lay people, and the diocesan paper, the *Echo*, in Buffalo, New York, were neutral during the Spanish Civil War. The *Echo*, also professed pacifism. These are the only known Catholic publications to adopt positions similar to the *Catholic Worker* during this war.

By 1935, the distribution of the movement's newspaper had increased to 110,000 copies and it was also appearing in England and Australia.[71] The paper consistently opposed efforts to involve the United States in war and provided clear statements of its peace position interspersed with articles on the popes' messages on peace, on the morality of war, and on conscription. It denounced Roosevelt's foreign policy and opposed preparedness measures. It urged Catholic Workers not to manufacture munitions and, later, not to purchase defense bonds. Individual Catholic Workers also joined demonstrations and boycotts, appeared before Congressional hearings and attempted to organize Catholic pacifists in resistance to conscription.

Strict neutrality became for the Workers the only viable way to prevent America's entrance into World War II. This stance clearly revealed the ideological differences between the Catholic Worker and CAIP. Ironically, the Catholic Worker found itself aligned with Coughlin in advocating strict neutrality, although Catholic Workers were internationalists (not in CAIP terms of world government, but in religious terms of human solidarity and the Mystical Body of Christ) and the Coughlinites were isolationists. The differences and similarities that emerged among Catholics over the issue of neutrality legislation were identical to those found among all pacifist groups, all advocates of collective security, and all isolationists during the 1930s. Once America entered the war, the pacifist rationale of the Catholic Worker logically required its members to reject participation in the war as a means of resolving the conflict. This was also true of all pacifist peace groups.

The Catholic Worker had little direct cooperation with other groups during the 1930s,[72] although the articles in its newspaper provided some cooperation. In December 1934, the *Catholic Worker* ran an ad for CAIP and it utilized the NCWC news service on items relating to peace. As late as 1939 in its October editorial, the newspaper asked:

> How many Catholics know that in Washington we have a Catholic Association for International Peace . . . , an association which is

headed by Most Reverend Edwin V. O'Hara, Bishop of Kansas City? Among the vice presidents there are many friends of the Catholic Worker. . . . It is absolutely necessary that our groups and cells and as many of our readers as possible should write and obtain literature that is available and form study groups to prepare themselves for the work of peace.

The *Catholic Worker's* pages also praised the work of the Women's International League for Peace and Freedom (WILPF) and the National Council for the Prevention of War.[73] The paper often used resource material from the National Council for the Prevention of War.

In its attempt to offset the influences of anti-Semitism and anti-communism among American Catholics, the *Catholic Worker* also touched on issues crucial to peace. Peter Maurin argued in his newspaper articles that "America is big enough to find a refuge for persecuted Jews." Dorothy Day stated that the Catholic Worker "defended Jews during times of stress."[74] And in 1939 the newspaper reported Archbishop Stritch of Chicago as decrying "the slanders and untruths being printed about the Jews" and his condemnation of the anti-Semitism of Coughlin and the Christian Front.[75]

The Catholic Worker's founders deplored red-baiting as much as anti-Semitism. Day was convinced by her early association with communists "that often the Communist more truly loves his brother, the poor and oppressed, than many so-called Christians."[76] In July 1937, the *Catholic Worker* replied to Coughlin's charge that its members were communists by contending that the movement was not communistic and affirming that the only true "international" was the Catholic church.[77]

The founders were also aware of the great fear of communism and saw it often as the real motive behind Catholic statements on war and peace issues. In October 1936, the Catholic Worker agreed to cooperate with John Noll, bishop of Fort Wayne, in his anticommunist drive, but explained its participation by stating that "it joined mainly because it believed that man was not subject to the state but to Christ and that this message should be delivered to the leaders of all nations not just the communist leaders." The *Catholic Worker* opposed peace groups controlled by communists such as the American League Against War and Fascism, on the grounds that these groups still advocated class war.[78] People interested in these groups were advised to contact the Catholic Worker for more information and urged Catholics to start their own peace groups so that communists would not be the only ones claiming to work for peace.

The pages of the *Catholic Worker* in 1936 pleaded with bankers not to lend money to nations at war.[79] It opposed the cash-and-carry clause of the Neutrality Act of 1937 because it "only served to line up Fascist against Democratic powers."[80] It also admitted, with the defeat of the Ludlow Resolution in the House by only twenty-one votes, that there was no way left for the American people to prevent a presidential declaration of war. This position remained constant and in 1939 the *Catholic Worker* opposed the lifting of the Arms Embargo and declared that the United States "should not export arms to any country in peace or at war."[81]

As the situation in Europe worsened, the *Catholic Worker's* position remained clear and consistent, and like other pacifist peace groups in America it supported the Keep America Out of War campaign after 1939. Increasingly it turned to the needs of its own constituents, particularly to the needs of Catholic conscientious objectors. Pearl Harbor was anticlimatic. President Roosevelt had already won approval to extend American military and economic goods to the Allies, had accepted an anti-German naval commitment in the Atlantic, and had removed most of the fetters from neutrality legislation.[82] Unable to alter national legislation and defeated in their demands for strict neutrality, the *Catholic Worker* remained faithful to its pacifism and refused to support the war when it was finally declared.

The Catholic Worker movement like CAIP and Coughlin was led into the arena of war and peace through its concern for social justice. By moving to the left on the political spectrum in America, the Catholic Worker stepped out of the whole intellectual and social ethos of Americanism. Strengthened by deep religious faith, the movement gradually worked out a stance of pacifism, but any degree of intellectual sophistication concerning this position would not be reached until after World War II. The significance of the Catholic Worker for American Catholic history in the 1930s is that it provided a pacifist alternative to war.

The internationalism of CAIP, on the other hand, left the association with no alternative to war once it was declared. Ryan and his associates wished to achieve world peace through social justice, and the greatest strength of their approach to international problems was their economic interpretation and their clear recognition of the necessity of worldwide planning and control. In the absence of a strong international organization and with no ethic but the just war doctrine, CAIP ended up acknowledging the state as its final decision maker in matters of war. For all the association's opposition to extreme nationalism and to the Coughlin hysteria, CAIP accepted the decisions of its nation for international ends. In the face of Hitlerism its way to peace was through war.

Despite Coughlin's moral crusade against political evils, he was unable to stop the United States from entering World War II. Coughlin was not against participation in war; he believed that America was fighting on the wrong side in this particular war and therefore men should not fight. The irony of this stance is that Coughlin was mainly condemned for his extreme nationalism, yet, at the time of World War II, he stood in opposition to his nation.

The structure and tactics of all three Catholic groups influenced and attracted as members portions of the American Catholic public. CAIP, the "official" Catholic peace organization, attracted middle- and upper-class Catholics, and once war was declared reflected the majority opinion, not only of Catholics, but of all Americans. Coughlin's demagogic approach appealed to the lower class and the more disaffected members of society in his offer to raise their standard of living by rooting out evil. The Catholic Worker attracted those Catholics seeking an intensified life-style of commitment to the Gospel message of "love of neighbor." In all three groups only the Catholic Worker offered a life-style and a supportive community that enabled its members to provide a Christian witness to peace, an alternative to the American way of life.

Neither Coughlin nor the Catholic Worker was able to influence national legislation to the extent of maintaining strict neutrality, even though minor victories were achieved, such as the 1939 delay of the lifting of the arms embargo during the Spanish Civil War. The defeat of strict neutrality and the United States entrance into World War II cancelled out the minor victories. Coughlinites and the Catholic Worker, together with all isolationist and pacifist groups during the 1930s, could not determine national legislation. CAIP's move to collective security in national legislation placed it in the victorious camp of the Roosevelt administration and ultimately in the midst of World War

II. The belief that Hitler had to be stopped, even by war, was a greater cause than the maintenance of peace. In this case, CAIP was no different than the other peace groups that advocated collective security.

The diversity in American Catholicism's quest for peace represented by these three groups contradicts the generally accepted view of a united Catholic front on the issues of war and peace. The three positions of pacifism, internationalism, and isolationism provided the basis for ideological diversity among Catholics as well as among all Americans during the 1930s. The major difference between Catholics and other Americans was that Catholics reinforced these positions with a Catholic theological rationale.

Until the 1930s, the just war doctrine had been the normative ethical position in American Catholicism. With the appearance of the Catholic Worker movement this tradition was challenged for the first time in American history by the earlier Christian tradition of pacifism. After the war, the ethical stance of pacifism became more widespread among Catholics and as a result the just war doctrine considerably less acceptable.[83] The demagogic rhetoric of the crusader Charles Coughlin has disappeared and one reason for its demise was its emphasis on hatreds and negativism rather than on positive ethical values. Though CAIP continued to publish pamphlets and issue statements on war and peace, it had little impact on the Catholic peace movement after the opening of World War II.

The group that would provide the American Catholic peace witness during World War II and for the next forty years would be the Catholic Worker. In order to understand the place of pacifism within the Catholic Worker movement and its impact on the American Catholic church it is necessary to know more fully the thought and action of Dorothy Day. Through the Catholic Worker, she offered a new direction in the American Catholic peace movement and launched what she described as a "permanent revolution" in American Catholicism.[84]

# 2

## Dorothy Day

### *Mother of American Catholic Pacifism*

PRIOR TO THE TWENTIETH CENTURY, pacifist in the United States was a term with a broad connotation and was applicable to anyone advocating international cooperation for peace. The definition narrowed with World War I and came to be "malevolently" applied to anyone who would not support even a "war to end war."[1] The government further narrowed the definition in its selective service legislation to include only those opposed to "war in any form." It was this definition that provided the legal recognition of conscientious objection in the United States during World War II.

Among Roman Catholics the pacifism of the primitive Christian church, like other features of the radical Gospel, largely disappeared with the Age of Constantine. Only in the twentieth century did American Catholics rediscover this heritage in their attempt to address contemporary issues of war and peace. The first American Catholic to challenge the accepted just war teaching was Dorothy Day. Perhaps, because she was a convert to Catholicism, she did not initially confront the just war tradition or offer an intellectual critique; she merely proclaimed her pacifism.[2]

Dorothy Day was born in Brooklyn Heights 8 November 1897 the daughter of John I. Day, a sportswriter. Essentially a conservative, John Day attempted to combine respectability with journalism. The Days were an austere Scotch-Irish Presbyterian family and Dorothy found the coldness of their family life unsatisfying. "There was never any kissing in our family, and never a close embrace," she wrote years later. "There was only a firm and austere kiss from my mother every night. . . . We were like most Anglo-Saxons."[3]

Unable to embrace her parents, Day embraced the poor and the oppressed. As a young girl in Chicago, where her father was a sports editor of *Inter Ocean*, she began reading radical literature, the Russian Kropotkin especially. Initially unaffected by World War I, she entered the University of Illinois at Urbana on a scholarship which she supplemented by caring for children and doing house work. During her two years at college, formal academic disciplines did not capture her interest, she missed classes and disdained the customary patterns of college social mixing. She read everything by Dostoevsky, who impressed her profoundly, along with the works of Gorky and Tolstoy and she became preoccupied with poverty, misery, and the class war, eventually joining the campus Socialist club. As she put it, "I was in love with the masses."

Leaving college in 1916 because of academic dissatisfaction and financial need, Dorothy Day moved with her family to New York, where her father had taken a job on the *Telegraph*. Soon after they arrived she went to work as a reporter and columnist on the Socialist *Call*. Her father's disapproval led her to rent a room on Cherry Street, in the slums of the lower East Side, and never again did she live with her family. Day believed "her father's greatest unhappiness came from her ideas which he thought were subversive and dangerous to the peace of the country."[4]

On her own at nineteen, Day spent the next two years in the tumult of Greenwich Village life. While on the job at the *Call*, she reported on and often participated in strikes, picket lines, peace meetings, and antiwar demonstrations. She also joined the Industrial Workers of the World, because she shared its anarchistic verve and distrust of Marx. In April 1917, Day left the *Call* and went to work for the Anti-Conscription League before joining the staff of the radical *Masses*, which folded by the end of the year due to enforcement of wartime postal censorship. She worked at various jobs during the winter of 1917–1918, one of which was with the *Liberator*. She left Greenwich Village early in 1918 to begin nurses training at King's County Hospital in Brooklyn, after deciding that the step was not contrary to her pacifist principles. In her autobiography, *The Long Loneliness*, Day reflected on her pacifism during World War I and cryptically wrote "I was pacifist in what I considered an imperialist war though not pacifist as a revolutionist."[5]

During these years Day did have brief moments when she experienced religion. In 1917, she joined sixty other women to protest the treatment of imprisoned suffragists. Though as a radical Day never intended to vote, she and others were arrested for their demonstration of support and when they refused bail they were sentenced to thirty days in the Occoquain Prison. While in jail, an attendant brought her a Bible, and she read it. The Psalms comforted her, yet she decided that the comfort received from religion was a sign of weakness.[6] In 1918, at the Golden Swan saloon, she first heard Catholic poet Francis Thompson's "The Hound of Heaven" recited from memory by friend Eugene O'Neill. Many mornings, after staying up all night with Village friends, she attended early morning Mass at Saint Joseph's Church on Sixth Avenue. At King's County Hospital she attended Sunday Mass on a regular basis. Despite these religious experiences, at this point in her life, Day can best be seen as "an old-time native American radical who reflected the strong but nondoctrinaire dissent against the corporate capitalist state that existed in the United States."[7]

While at the hospital Day fell in love with Lionel Moise, a former *Kansas City Star* reporter and moved in with him shortly after the November 1918 Armistice. The war had ceased but Day's personal struggle had just begun. She proceeded to spend the next seven years of her life pursuing unsuccessful and often tragic personal relationships that ended in suicide attempts, an abortion, a marriage, and a divorce. Day tried to keep these seven years of her life hidden and never spoke of them.

During these years, Day spent her time between New York and Chicago, working as a reporter, a proofreader, a librarian, and even as a clerk at Montgomery Ward's. She still managed to write, and in 1923 A. & C. Boni published her first novel. It was about life in the Village and very autobiographical. Though it was not very successful, the publisher sold it to Hollywood on the strength of the name, *The Eleventh Virgin*. Day, however, did receive a payment of $2,500 for her novel which she used to buy a cottage on the shore of Raritan Bay, at Huguenot, Staten Island.[8] A few months later she began to live with Forster Battingham, a young biology instructor. She continued to view herself as a writer. Within a year her second novel, *What Price Love?* was bought by the Bell Syndicate for newspaper serialization.

On 3 March 1927 she gave birth to her daughter Tamar. She was happy though Tamar's father was not. Battingham wondered what point there was to bringing another person into a world of hopelessness and injustice. In her autobiography, Day tells how the birth of her child compelled her to become a Catholic.

> Forster had made the physical world come alive for me and had awakened in my heart a flood of gratitude. The final object of this love and gratitude was God. No human creature could receive or contain so vast a flood of love and joy as I felt after the birth of my child. With this came the need to worship and adore. I had heard many say they wanted to worship God in their own way and did not need a Church in which to praise Him. . . . But my very experience as a radical, my whole make-up, led me to want to associate myself with others, with the masses, in praising and adoring God. Without even looking into the claims of the Catholic Church, I was willing to admit that for me she was the one true Church.[9]

This choice on Day's part meant that she would have to leave her mate, who was deeply irreligious and found all that he needed in nature. Her choice of Catholicism also meant parting with her lifelong radical friends. In some aspects, Day's choice is not entirely incomprehensible. She ultimately seemed to be searching for something that her past experiences had not satisfied. She had never been attracted to the intellectual life; she had found the class-conflict interpretation of Marx inadequate to explain the plight of the masses; and one-issue causes such as women's rights did not long hold her attention. Journalism and writing were still her profession, but she did not view herself as very successful in these areas. Her conversion signified a belief in a deeper reality. This belief was so strong that she was willing to leave all for it.

Day first had her daughter Tamar baptized. Then on 28 December 1927, Dorothy Day was baptized a Catholic in the Church of Our Lady, Holy Christians, in Totenville, Staten Island. The action was almost wholly mechanical. There was no consolation. For the next five years, Day explored her faith, raised her daughter, wrote, worked for a short time for the Fellowship of Reconciliation, and at times did manual labor jobs. She also traveled to Hollywood, to Mexico City, and to Florida to visit her mother—but always returned to New York. Then, while on a writing assignment for *America* and *Commonweal* to cover the Washington hunger march, she noted the total absence of the church's presence on behalf of the poor and knew that somewhere the faith that she had embraced had been turned aside from its true historic mission. She was aware of a frequent dichotomy between the doctrinal ideals of Catholicism and their implementation by church members, and in her autobiography she wrote that she "loved the Church for Christ made visible. Not for itself, because it was so often a scandal to me."[10]

After the hunger march was over Day went to the National Shrine at the Catholic University and prayed that she would discover how the mission of the church could become vital. As she knelt there she also realized that "after three years of Catholicism my only contact with active Catholics had been through articles I had written for one of the Catholic magazines. Those contacts had been brief, casual. I still did not personally know one Catholic layman."[11] Now, this was all to change. Day wrote, "When I returned to New York, I found Peter Maurin—Peter, the French peasant, whose spirit and ideas will dominate . . . the rest of my life."[12]

Maurin's message, whether oral or written, was essentially that of Catholic radicalism. He believed that "the most traditional Catholicism was of supreme social relevance to modern humanity, and that it was only necessary to 'blow the dynamite' of that ancient church to set the whole world afire."[13] His vision was antithetical to liberalism, which is dependent on the changing currents of history and the doctrine of progress. His vision was also unlike liberalism because he did not accept the state as the primary source of community that holds together the change and flow of the material world. And finally, Maurin rejected technology as the means of assuring progress in the world. In place of the liberal myths of nation state, technology, and progress, Maurin drew extensively on the central teaching of orthodox Catholicism and posited the Garden of Eden, the Fall, the light of the Beatitudes, the darkness of oblivion, sacred community, and sinful alienation as central to his social vision. Thus, the radical ideal of Peter Maurin was rooted not in the material world but in the realm of the spirit. His goals would be achieved at the end of time—with the second coming of Christ. Thus, the vision was eschatological and therefore beyond history. It demanded that history submit to it and not the reverse.[14]

Besides this eschatological view of history, the other distinctive feature Maurin presented to Dorothy Day was personalism. "The personalist idea holds that the primacy of Christian love should be brought from its position of limbo where human affairs are concerned and infused into the process of history. The central fact of existence should not be process, with men holding on in whatever spot they found most tolerable, love should redeem process itself. Faith in love is the ultimate reality."[15] This concept of personalism—coupled with a view of freedom that meant the capacity of an individual to turn from tyranny of sense toward the spirit—involved suffering and even tragedy. It basically meant that individuals would reenact in their own lives the mystery of the crucifixion of Christ.

Peter Maurin saw the expression of personalism in individuals who embraced voluntary poverty and at the cost of personal sacrifice performed the works of mercy proclaimed in the Beatitudes. Maurin believed the individual should daily practice the corporal works of feeding the hungry, clothing the naked, and sheltering the shelterless.

Personalism rather than political analysis appealed greatly to Dorothy Day. She had been attracted in vain to political groups such as Socialists and the Industrial Workers of the World in hopes of finding solutions to the plight of the poor. In Christian personalism the solution resided with the individual and was not dependent on historical circumstances. Victory also was assured because of a power beyond history—Christ. Day's commitment to pacifism would be founded in "a matrix of personalism, which called for a heightened sense of personal responsibility for one's neighbors and involvement in struggles for justice on their behalf."[16] It would be Dorothy Day's activism combined with Christian personalism that would keep the Catholic Worker movement embroiled in the messy affairs of society rather than only writing or talking about them.

Maurin was careful to point out what he believed to be the greatest enemies to attaining the Worker ideal in contemporary America: nationalism and capitalism. According to him, the nation had become the symbol of community and had put too much of its use to the ends of competitive power. He opposed capitalism because of its glorification of struggle. He believed capitalists were always in pursuit of their own aggrandizement and used the nation for their own imperialist ends. Maurin did not believe that there was anything new in his analysis of the twin enemies, but he did believe that his solution was new. The Worker ideal presented a viable alternative to the American way of life.

It was the twin enemies of nationalism and capitalism that led Day to apply to herself the term "Catholic anarchist."[17] She did this during the 1930s when the authority of the federal government had become almost sacred to millions of people who perceived the New Deal to be the one and only hope to solve society's ills. Day's anarchism, on the other hand, meant increased reponsibility of one person for another, of the individual to the community along with a much lessened sense of obligation to or dependence on the "distant and centralized state."[18]

Maurin had no blueprint for the decentralization and simplification of American society. The Worker ideal was all very vague and, at best, all he could offer were a few general principles.[19] Yet, these general principles were all that Dorothy Day needed to begin her work. According to William Miller, Day's biographer, "What Peter Maurin did for Dorothy was to reorient her vision from the object to the subject, from collectivisim to Christian personalism. He also provided her with something she had not had—an understanding of the meaning of the Church and her position in it."[20]

Dorothy Day believed that the Worker ideal was a positive Christian alternative and that it should be made available to every individual who desired it. For this to occur, it was first necessary to present the ideal to others. Day's first effort was related to what she knew how to do best—start a newspaper. She entitled it the *Catholic Worker* to announce a Catholic presence and concern for the poor and oppressed in opposition to communists and other radicals who were identified with the poor and oppressed. The publication of the first issue caused Maurin to disappear for a month. He had wanted the paper to devote itself exclusively to the printing of his own essays which appeared under the title of Easy Essays. Day had different ideas and wanted a broader focus on current issues by many contributors. Peter eventually returned.[21]

Day also managed to find other ways of carrying out Maurin's vision. She opened a House of Hospitality on Mott Street in New York City where roundtable discussions between workers and intellectuals occurred. She raised enough money to buy land to start a farming commune in hope of achieving a simplified way of life in contrast to the dehumanizing aspects of the capitalist economy. These three endeavors—the paper, the House of Hospitality, and the farm—provided visibility, place, and work for individuals who also desired to embrace the Worker ideal. The main work of Catholic Workers was administering food, clothing, and shelter to the poor. Since Maurin spent most of his time on the road trying to spread his vision to others, Day was left to direct, order, and maintain the Catholic Worker. Under her leadership Workers not only performed the corporal works of mercy but also began to spend much time protesting the dehumanizing aspects of nationalism and capitalism through their newspaper, by participation in strikes, and by demonstrations against social injustice.

Within a few years of the founding of the Catholic Worker movement, it became evident that it was not the depression, but war that was the major crisis confronting Americans. The *Catholic Worker* stated that "during a time of war the nation state was invested with all the marks of power in the form of military might. At a time of war, the coercive power of the state reached its zenith."[22] A nation's decision to declare war was thus the ultimate question to be faced by the individual. For Day, war was the most extreme opposition to active love, the antithesis of the radical Christian vision she had embraced. Having been opposed to war before her conversion to Catholicism, she now clearly saw that the Gospel message was peace. For Day the only alternative to violence was nonviolence or what she called Catholic pacifism. Her emphasis was on the individual and not the state. She would not cooperate with the state in any way concerning the issue of war. In opposition to war Day brought together the personalism and anarchism of the Worker ideal of love. In this sense her Catholicism enhanced her pacifism of old and placed it within a revolutionary context. As historian Mel Piehl stated, "After 1945, it was the issue of pacifism that most effectively represented the Catholic Worker's gospel idealism."[23]

Peter Maurin never reached the point of making his pacifism a pronouncement. As a young man in France, in November 1898 he had been called to military duty, and he served as a soldier in the 142nd Infantry Regiment of Mende at Lodeve until the following September. According to Marc Ellis, Maurin's most recent biographer, "This was a disturbing, perhaps even transformative experience for him, for his superiors and his brother Celestin confirmed that he strongly objected to military service. The organization of people toward a dubious end undoubtedly disturbed him. His background as a peasant, with its lack of emphasis on nationhood, and as a Brother, with its emphasis on the poor, clashed with the assertion of national aspirations and protection of wealth bound up with the military."[24] Maurin received an honorable discharge and was placed in the reserve. The reserve called him back for two short periods in 1904 and 1907. Maurin's continuing involvement with the military was undoubtedly a major factor in his decision in 1909 to immigrate to Canada where there was no conscription.

There is no clear explanation of why Maurin would not proclaim pacifism. In his Easy Essays he often pointed to the evil and futility of war. John C. Cort, a young Catholic Worker of the 1930s wrote that "Dorothy says that Peter was a pacifist, but I don't recall seeing anything he ever wrote or hearing anything he ever said that supports that. The subject didn't seem to interest him, or else he didn't feel confident enough to challenge the traditional Catholic view that there are just wars and there are unjust wars."[25] Eileen Egan, who knew both founders of the Catholic Worker movement, wrote that "On the subject of the Spanish Civil War, Maurin did not speak out, though he made it clear that his way was the Franciscan way, a way that excluded violence. For a man intent on finding 'concordance,' the confrontation of the Worker movement with modern war, and the bitter criticism it evoked, was hard to bear. 'Perhaps silence would be better for a time than to continue our opposition to war,' he said to Dorothy Day as World War II began. 'Men are not ready to listen.' "[26]

Maurin's reluctance, however, did not prevent Day as editor of the *Catholic Worker* from announcing that pacifism was the paper's position. She viewed pacifism as a part of the total vision that was presented to her by Peter Maurin. The Catholic Worker was a total way of life and to be consistent with the Worker ideal during a time of war, Day believed a pacifist response was necessary, flowing naturally and perhaps supernaturally from the total Worker ideal. As early as October 1933, the newspaper stated that its "delegates" would "be among those present at the United States Congress Against War" and they would be representing 'Catholic Pacifism.' " Since this was the first such collective statement in American history of a group of Catholics, they well knew that they scarcely represented more than themselves.

In 1933 the only American Catholic peace activity came from semiofficial CAIP. The leaders of CAIP disdained mass organization and antiwar action, preferring instead the more genteel peace activities of lobbying, lecturing, and publication prevalent in America before World War I. In Europe, on the other hand, World War I had produced the German Catholic *Friendensbund* and the French *Ligue pour la Paix*. Associated with these mass organizations was a small but influential group of intellectuals and theologians who urged the church to declare herself unequivocally against war. The best known were Father Johannes Ude of Graz University and the German Dominican Franziskus Stratmann. Within the first year of the *Catholic Worker* publication, Stratmann's works, particularly *The Church and War*, were favorably reviewed and quoted in the paper.[27] What was meant by American Catholic pacifism in terms of an intellectual rationale was still undefined.

Catholic Worker pacifism derived from Dorothy Day's personal commitment. In the late 1930s, some of Day's followers were able to elaborate her basic conviction about Catholic pacifism in an attempt to develop a Catholic case against war. The first of these were Paul Hanly Furfey, William Callahan, and Arthur Sheehan. Furfey, a pacifist priest and educator from the Catholic University of America as well as a friend of the movement, foreshadowed the theological rationale that would eventually form the basis of Catholic Worker pacifism in an article he wrote for its newspaper in 1935. He based the antiwar case on the Gospel counsel of perfection. The article centered on an imaginary debate between Christ and a patriot. Furfey based the theological principle for pacifism in the debate, not on the just war theory but on the Christian's calling to a kingdom of love and peace that takes precedence over one's calling to obedience to the state. He urged abandonment of the "Constantinian Compromise" with the war-making state and a return to the eschatological pacifist vision of the early saints and Church Fathers. This was the first statement that reflected a pacifism based on the Gospel message of peace, and with it the American Catholic peace movement mothered by Dorothy Day was born.

Because of the dominance of the just war theory in the Catholic tradition, it was logical for Catholics to attempt to apply it to pacifism. The first theoretician of the just war rationale for Catholic Worker pacifism was young Bill Callahan, managing editor of the paper during much of the decade. In December 1935 he gave a talk to the Catholic

Social Club of Brooklyn entitled "Catholics Should be Conscientious Objectors in Time of War."[28] Then, in October 1936 he announced through the *Catholic Worker* "the formation of a Catholic organization of conscientious objectors." Four months later the group was named PAX and Bill Callahan became its director. The logic of the group was based on the presupposition that the war in question was not just.

Catholic pacifism, however, did not become a central issue of the Catholic Worker movement until the Spanish Civil War, 1936–1939. When the war erupted in July 1936, Dorothy Day proclaimed pacifism and neutrality in the pages of the *Catholic Worker*.

> Poor blood-drenched Spain is the most talked about subject to-day. . . . Who is right and who is wrong? We are inclined to believe that the issue is not so clear cut as to enable either side to condemn the other justifiably. . . .
>
> Our main concern is that the "members of Christ tear one another." . . .
>
> Spain doesn't need favorable publicity for the rebels. She doesn't need condemnation of the loyalists. What she needs is the prayers of the rest of the Mystical Body. Please to God that Members stop hating each other. . . .
>
> The *Catholic Worker* makes this appeal to its readers: Forget your anger. Let your indignation die. Remember only that the Body is rent asunder, and the only solution is Love.[29]

Ironically, the issue of pacifism was overshadowed by anti-Communism. American Catholics had found a rallying point for their anti-Communism in the war. Thus, it was not the *Catholic Worker's* voicing of Dorothy Day's position of pacifism and refusal to take sides in the war that raised the ire of American Catholics, but her refusal to support Franco against the Communists. In the *Catholic Worker's* attempt to offer a Catholic counteropinion to the "propaganda in favor of Franco and rebel Spain," it provoked the strongest reaction against the *Catholic Worker* since its inception.

The experience of the Spanish Civil War inspired Arthur Sheehan to attempt to clarify the meaning of Catholic pacifism by examining the application of the just war criteria to modern warfare. Sheehan used evidence from the Spanish Civil War to show that in modern war each side typically asserted the complete justice of their cause. He argued that modern warfare could not be waged according to the traditional criteria, particularly those concerning pure intentions and the protection of noncombatants. The vast destructive capability of technological weaponry guaranteed that no side could pursue self-defense without perpetuating a great moral evil, a violation of the just war principle of proportionality. Because of modern technological warfare no war could be just, and pacifism was the only option.[30] As a just war pacifist, Sheehan provided the rationale that other Catholic Workers reiterated when defending their position as just war pacifists. Dorothy Day and other Catholic Workers, however, did not look to the just war doctrine, but to the Gospel message of peace for the basis of their pacifism. Thus, debate among Catholic Workers continued on the topic. A clearer analysis of Catholic pacifism based on the Gospel message of peace would not emerge until the outbreak of World War II. Even then the issue of Catholic pacifism would be initially blurred by historical interpretaions of the causes of war and justifications for conscientious objection.

The Catholic Worker's preoccupation with the twin enemies of nationalism and capitalism influenced their interpretation of the cause of World War II. The *Catholic Worker* contended that wars were the work of the big capitalists. In its interpretation that World War II resulted from a conspiracy of high finance, the *Catholic Worker* was joined by the followers of Charles Coughlin and by a notable member of the American hierarchy, Archbisop John T. McNicholas of Cincinnati. But McNicholas and the Coughlinites added the proposition that it was also of Communist inspiration. When the war did break out, the *Catholic Worker* continued to insist that it was a repetition of 1914. It gave its position in a front page statement: "We Are to Blame for New War in Europe."

Peter Maurin believed that the combination of external competition for markets and internal protection of industry had led to the increasing power of the state and the hostility of England and Germany in World War I. This war had ushered in the era of finance capitalism and had resulted not in the establishment of democracy but its antithesis: Marxism in Russia, fascism in Italy, and Nazism in Germany. The world depression in 1929, according to Maurin, had ushered in the last watershed, state capitalism. This decline symbolized the triumph of a secular world guided by self-interest over a religious world once guided by tradition. The end of cultural and religious tradition involved in the decline devalued the individual because the economic, political, and military systems left fewer avenues for the individual to recognize and follow the soul's longing for eternity. Maurin saw World War II as a continuation of the historical forces of capitalism and nationalism.[31]

Maurin's historical interpretation of World War II had a profound effect on Dorothy Day's pacifist rationale. Through 1939, Day and the *Catholic Worker* had used history-based arguments to justify Worker pacifism. This was understandable because the just war tradition had taught Catholics to distinguish between a just war and an unjust war in history. By late 1940, however, it became evident that World War II was not a repetition of World War I and that Catholic pacifism could not be based on the just war tradition whose criteria were themselves based on the actions of a nation in the objective material world. Day realized she had to turn to the spiritual realm beyond history and look to the Gospel message of peace and the individual's conscience as the basis of decision making concerning issues of war and peace.

By 1940, Dorothy Day believed that the Worker's pacifist position had to be put to the test of close theological analysis. She also knew that she was not equipped to provide such reasons herself, and increasingly relied on John Hugo, a young Pittsburgh priest, for spiritual direction. In a note to Day, Hugo wrote: "No doubt [pacifism] is all clear to you; but then you have not tried to work it out doctrinally. If you knew no theology, it would probably be simpler to make a solution. Yet the decision must be based on doctrine. Pacifism must proceed from truth, or it cannot exist at all. And of course this attack on conscription is the most extreme form of pacifism."[32]

John Hugo attempted to answer Day's challenge with a series of articles in the *Catholic Worker* which were reprinted in pamphlet form under the title *Weapons of the Spirit*. In the introduction Hugo began by rejecting the just war tradition and positing the Gospel law, which he believed modern war negated. "While I believe that war may be just, at any rate in theory," he said, "I am also convinced that it is not Christ's way." He then stated that Christ's way is based on faith and love and this sets it above man's way, which is based on reason. The individual is called to live out Christ's love particularly during a time of war. Hugo, like Maurin, contended that modern war is capitalistic and imperialistic. Hugo invited the individual to embrace spiritual means—prayer, fasting, and penance—to overcome the evil of war. Though he never used the word pacifism in his writing, he did invite the individual to live "the more perfect" life in Christ and reject all war. He also stressed the devotions of the Rosary and the Sacred Heart as spiritual aids for those who sought to live the more perfect life.

Dorothy Day's view of nationalism and capitalism as twin enemies had led her to an incorrect interpretation of the cause of World War II, but the Gospel message and Christian personalism would not let her err in her spiritual conviction of pacifism —of that she was convinced. But the cost of such witness to Dorothy Day and the Catholic Worker movement was great. Her pronouncement of pacifism caused dissension among members of the movement across the country. The Chicago House of Hospitality in particular was not pacifist. This house, with John Cogley as editor, had been publishing its own newspaper, the *Chicago Catholic Worker*, which did not reflect the pacifist position of the New York paper. At the St. Francis House of Hospitality in Seattle, the Workers stopped distributing the *Catholic Worker* because it was filled almost entirely with pacifism and instead distributed the *Chicago Catholic Worker*. In June 1940, Dorothy Day sent a letter to all Workers concerning the issue of pacifism.

> We know that there are those who are members of 'Catholic Worker' groups throughout the country who do not stand with us in this issue. We have not been able to change their views through what we have written in the paper, or by letters, or by personal conversation. They wish still to be associated with us, to perform the corporal works of mercy.

" 'And that,' she said, 'was all right.' But there had been other cases when some associated with the movement had taken it on themselves to suppress the paper. In such instances she felt it would be necessary for those persons to disassociate themselves from the movement."[33] By the end of 1942 sixteen of the houses or one half of them had been closed.[34] Dorothy Day even admitted in the May 1942 issue of the *Catholic Worker*, that she had been accused of splitting the movement from top to bottom by her pacifism.

As the war progressed the issue that involved Catholic Workers more than anything else was the draft. Dorothy's pacifism made her an advocate of total resistance to the draft. She believed the individual should not cooperate in any way with the U. S. government concerning the draft. Moreover, her respect for the individual, the heart of Christian personalism, enabled her to reach out and assist all men, regardless of their degree of resistance, who became conscientious objectors (COs) in World War II.[35] Thus, it was the Catholic Worker movement alone, among all American Catholic groups, that offered assistance to individuals who conscientiously objected to World War II.

Prior to Pearl Harbor, the Catholic press opposed conscription or the draft. Archbishop McNicholas even urged men to become conscientious objectors. In March 1938, he issued a pastoral letter that recommended the formation of "A Mighty League of CO's." The *Catholic Worker* published the full text of the letter. McNicholas also denounced the 'war makers' who were advancing the present capitalistic system and who "did not deserve the name of patriots."[36]

This statement coming from a member of the Catholic hierarchy, encouraged the members of PAX to redouble their efforts.[37] Through a regular monthly column in the *Catholic Worker*, PAX attempted to secure signatures to support a Catholic's right to conscientious objection. Moreover, they dared to print a box in the *Catholic Worker* urging men not to register for the draft. The government chose to ignore this legal offense; the Catholic ecclesiastical authorities did not. They thought Dorothy Day and the *Catholic Worker* "had gone too far" and Day was called to the New York Chancery and told, "Dorothy you must stand corrected." She remarked that:

> I was not quite sure what that meant, but I did assent, because I realized that one should not tell another what to do in such circumstances. We had to follow our own consciences, which later took us to jail; but our work in getting out the paper was an attempt to arouse the consciences of others, not to advise action for which they were not prepared.[38]

PAX was active until 1940 when military conscription became imminent. By that time, Bill Callahan had left the Catholic Worker and Arthur Sheehan was given the job of directing and reorganizing the group. Sheehan changed the name of the group from PAX to the Association of Catholic Conscientious Objectors (ACCO) in order to be self-explanatory. By not forbidding the name, the church tacitly recognized the association and with it the right of practicing Catholics to be conscientious objectors.[39] The group received many requests for information about conscientious objection and attempted to keep informed about Catholics who were conscientious objectors and those who had gone to jail for noncooperation with the draft.

The issue of military conscription, like the Spanish Civil War, made apparent to Catholic Workers that there were at least two types of Catholic pacifism operative in the movement—just war pacifism and pacifism based on the Gospel message of peace. In both cases the end result was the same. More importantly, both emphasized the right of the individual in conscience to refuse participation in war. This right had long been part of Catholic teaching and modern popes and traditional defenders of the just war theory professed to uphold individual conscience when the issue of conscription and war were matters of public concern. This right of individual conscience would provide the basis of unanimity among Catholics concerning conscription.

In an exhaustive series of articles in the *Catholic Worker* in 1940, Monsignor Barry O'Toole of Catholic University, developed with scholastic thoroughness the objections of Catholic moral theology to a permanent system of conscription. O'Toole argued that selective service could never be endorsed by Catholics because "the citizen cannot be forced to be free by his government, whether in the form of a totalitarian party or the liberalistic majority." Quoting Aquinas, Vittoria, and Franziskus Stratmann, O'Toole put selective service to the test of the just war and concluded that no war in which men were forced to fight against their will could pass the traditional criteria. O'Toole never mentioned pacifism, but under modern conditions, opposing war fought by conscripts would in effect mean opposing all war.[40] In arguments concerning selective service it was just war pacifism that dominated Catholic thought and writing. Even John Hugo's booklet *The Immorality of Conscription*, originally published in the *Catholic Worker* in 1944, used the just war arguments to oppose the idea of compulsory military service, while adding complaints about family disruption and the possibility of women in combat.[41]

The proposed Burke-Wadsworth Bill in Congress in 1940 confronted the American public in a new way concerning the issue of conscription. The bill favored the use of conscription in a time of peace and to many

Americans this was a complete break with their democratic tradition and an indication of the government's desire to enter the European conflict. In July, the Catholic Worker joined a number of peace groups in carrying the anticonscription message to Congress. Barry O'Toole, Dorothy Day, and Joseph Zarrella, a young draft-age Catholic Worker, testified before the House Military Affairs Committee that conscription was contrary to the church.[42] The church always maintained both the right of an individual to choose a vocation and the duty of every individual to serve one's country. It taught further that when the conscience of a citizen prevented the individual from serving in a military vocation, the individual's conscience would be respected. Monsignor Michael J. Ready, the official spokesperson for the Catholic hierarchy also testified before the committee. Though Ready also maintained the right of freedom of conscience in his testimony, his main concern was stated as follows: "The bishops are opposed to provisions in this bill which include for compulsory military service students for the priesthood and those under vows to serve the works of religion."[43] Dorothy Day's testimony on the other hand pointed out that she was speaking for Catholic lay people. When asked by Senator Burke if the clause in the proposed selective service bill that granted exemption from combat for any member of a "religious sect whose creed or principles forbid its members to participate in war in any form" would protect lay Catholics, Day replied: "It does not protect Catholics, no, it may protect the Quakers, the Mennonites, the Dunkards, but not Catholics. . . . There is nothing in the Catholic Creed which would entitle us to that exemption. It does not deal with Catholics."[44]

A Cleric from the National Catholic Welfare Conference who happened to be at the hearings questioned Dorothy's right to speak for Catholics on the issue. She answered in a few words: 'We are speaking for lay people, and they are the ones who fight the wars.' "[45] On 16 September 1940 after eighty-six days of emotional congressional debate, the Burke-Wadsworth Bill was passed by a narrow margin. When it expired, the House of Representatives passed the Selective Service Extension Act on 18 August 1941 by a single vote—293 to 292.[46]

After the Japanese attack on Pearl Harbor on 7 December 1941, attitudes changed dramatically. Congress quickly responded to the attack by passing within six days an amendment to the Selective Service Act that removed the restriction that limited the service of draftees to the Western Hemisphere and stipulated that their period of military service would continue from the time of induction until six months after the end of the war. [47]

Concern for the rights of individual conscience receded into the background and the obligation of the individual to obey the state and support its just cause now became apparent. Neither the Catholic hierarchy nor Catholic intellectuals denied the right of an individual to be a conscientious objector after World War II was declared, but they did nothing to support such individuals. The next major project the Catholic Worker assumed was direct support for Catholic conscientious objectors. Arthur Sheehan, the founder of ACCO, was the self-appointed Catholic representative who approached the selective service for permission to operate a Civilian Public Service Camp (CPS) for Catholic COs. The federal government approved such camps as the legal alternative service system for individuals who had been granted CO status by local draft boards.

To Catholic Workers, especially Dorothy Day, it became evident that an individual conscience shaped in the just war tradition would not lead to pacifist conclusions for most Catholics. Day acknowledged this, and confessed that "it is a matter of grief to me that most of those who are Catholic Workers are not pacifist, but I can see too how good it is that we always have this attitude represented among us. We are not living in an ivory tower."[48] Most Catholic Workers entered military service. John Cogley, one of this group, later remarked, "Most of us still feel that the war on Nazism was a morally justified enterprise, . . . It was better to have fought that evil, even at the price of slaughter, than to have acquiesced in it."[49] Tom Sullivan, an editor of the *Catholic Worker*, served in the Pacific. Jack English, formerly from the Cleveland House of Hospitality, was a gunner on a bomber that was shot down and he spent a year in a Rumanian prison camp. Day's comment on English was, he "has theologian friends whose opinions keep him away from the extreme pacifist position."[50] Other young men helped at the Catholic Worker as long as the draft board permitted and, as Day put it, "talked the issue over constantly." She maintained that their discussions raised the following questions:

> Can there be a just war? Can the conditions laid down by St. Thomas ever be fulfilled? What does God want me to do? And what am I

capable of doing? Can I stand out against state and Church? Is it pride, presumption, to think I have the spiritual capacity to use spiritual weapons in the face of the most gigantic tyranny the world has ever seen? Am I capable of enduring suffering, facing martyrdom? And alone? Again the long loneliness to be faced.[51]

Neither Dorothy Day nor the *Catholic Worker* was able to supply adequate arguments in response to the evils of Hitler and Japanese aggression; in fact, the pages of the newspaper reflect a conspicuous absence of attempting to deal with these historical realities. Instead what is found in its pages is an undaunted pacifism and advocacy of conscientious objection. "We are still pacifist," the editorial read, "and our manifesto is the Sermon on the Mount, which means that we will try to be peacemakers."[52] Because of its pacifist position, the circulation of the *Catholic Worker* decreased from 130,000 copies a month in 1939 to 50,500 copies a month by November 1944. A wider circulation would not resume until April 1948, when 73,000 copies of the *Catholic Worker* were printed.

In 1943, Dorothy Day decided to absent herself from the Catholic Worker for a year. She had become involved in the Lacouture retreat movement, and under the spiritual direction of John Hugo her faith deepened as she tried to live a more perfect Christian life. In an attempt to evaluate her life, she removed herself from responsibility for the movement and turned over editorship of the paper to Arthur Sheehan; she also took her name off the masthead. World War II was bringing death and destruction to large areas of the globe and desolation to Dorothy Day. Her Catholic pacifist stance had exacted a great toll on the movement, reducing the number of houses of hospitality by 50 percent, and it did the same to the circulation of the paper. The flow of invitations to speak at parishes, schools, and seminaries around the country had ceased. Even Peter Maurin had said that "perhaps silence would be better for a time than to continue our opposition to war." The demands of peacemaking on Dorothy Day were as great as the demands of war. Whatever doubt may have arisen concerning her life at the Worker before her sabbatical, she was back with the Catholic Worker in six months, never to leave again until her death.[53]

Though the *Catholic Worker* would not shift from its position of pacifism during World War II, there was a shift in its theological rationale for pacifism. After the war the Catholic Worker abandoned the just war doctrine. Though Sheehan had argued that the application of the doctrine led to pacifist conclusions in modern warfare, it obviously had not for most American Catholics. Dorothy Day had never embraced the doctrine and had never used it in her writings. When it came to war, Day never gave any consideration to the traditional obligations to render obedience to legitimate authority. She always placed the emphasis on the Gospel message of peace, the core of the Worker ideal, as the reason for its pacifism. Even during World War II, there was no theological development of her Catholic pacifism, which had been foreshadowed by Paul Hanly Furfey. Nonetheless, a significant development had taken place among American Catholics. Pacifism had finally become an option practiced by members of the American Catholic community. Though it would take another twenty years for the church to "officially" recognize pacifism as a legitimate option, Dorothy Day continued to be its most powerful advocate. Her repudiation of war, rather than the search for justifications, has become the dominant thrust of contemporary theology. The Catholic Worker would continue to be the heart of the Catholic peace movement in America to the present day.

# 3

# World War II and the Just War Tradition

WITH THE 1941 ATTACK by the Japanese on Pearl Harbor, the United States became the victim of an aggressor and thus the duty to defend America became paramount. The attack outraged Americans and the American Catholic response was identical to the nation's. Francis J. Spellman, archbishop of New York, reflected this sentiment with great emotion when he said,

> With fire and brimstone came December 7, America's throat was clutched, her back was stabbed, her brain was stunned; but her great heart still throbbed. America clenched the palms of those hands oft-stretched in mercy to the peoples of the nations that struck her. America's brain began to clear. America began the fight to save her life.[1]

This statement summarized the attitude of the Catholic hierarchy and of most Catholics who saw the attack as justifying participation in the war. However, some Catholics challenged the traditional just war doctrine by becoming conscientious objectors. For a few others the just war doctrine provided the rationale to speak out against the obliteration bombing of Dresden and Berlin as well as the atomic bombing of Hiroshima and Nagasaki. But these Catholics were voices in the wilderness. The vast majority of American Catholics supported the nation throughout the course of the war. An important reason for this was that the statements of both the popes and the American hierarchy supported the state.

The reign of Pope Pius XI (1922–1939) coincided with the rise of fascism, Nazism, and communism and the destruction of democracy in Europe. Pius XI at first attempted to work with the new totalitarian

49

governments. In 1933, he accepted the Nazi government's offer of a concordat, but he gradually realized the party's hostility to Christianity. In 1937, he condemned Nazism in his encyclical *Mit brennender Sorge*, and five days later he issued *Divini Redemptoris*, a condemnation of "atheistic communism." "When Pius' response came it was almost too late," wrote historian Ronald G. Musto.[2] At Pius XI's death in February 1939, the college of cardinals, who would elect a new pope, realized that a skillful and experienced diplomat would be needed to direct the church through the coming war.

Eugenio Pacelli, who was dedicated to the internationalist approach of his predecessors, was elected to succeed Pius XI and chose the name Pius XII. With the outbreak of war in Europe in September 1939, he could do little but acknowledge his helplessness. His first encyclical, *Summi Pontificatus* (20 October 1939), summarized his approach to war and peace. He condemned Nazi and Soviet aggression plainly and denounced the evils of the totalitarian state; but once again the state was "the framework for all Pius's thinking."[3] In his 1941 Christmas message, *Nell' Alba*, he continued the papal emphasis on rights, justice, and order and stressed the "rights of minorities, economic equality and justice, and freedom of religion, but he did so 'within the limit of a new order' based on the primacy of the nation-state and the recognition of treaty rights, international agreement, and ruling elites."[4] Never did Pius XII mention conscientious objection in any of his addresses nor did he refer to Scripture or pacifism in the early church. Pope Pius XII relied solely on the just war tradition throughout World War II and granted the state the paramount position in conducting what he viewed as a just war in face of the evils of Nazism and fascism.

Pius XII, however, did use the just war doctrine as the basis for his criticism of the state in three instances during the course of World War II. In 1943, he was highly critical of the bombing of Rome, but his reluctance to protest the obliteration bombings of Dresden or Berlin suggests that his condemnation of Rome's bombing was rooted more in self-interest than in just war principles. In his Christmas broadcast of 1944 the pope acknowledged the will of the people and their role in bringing about peace, "the first time since the Middle Ages that a pope had mentioned the role of the Catholic laity" rather than the state in bringing about peace.[5] When atomic bombs were dropped on Hiroshima and Nagasaki, the pope criticized the actions of the U.S. government.[6] After the war Pius XII began to speak in earnest of the emptiness of new defensive systems and the hollowness of even the most just war fought in the modern world. The horrors of modern warfare were finally beginning to change the pope's attitude toward war itself.

During World War II the American Catholic hierarchy issued five statements on the issues of war and peace that reflected the papal position, but with a distinctively American twist. The framework for their thinking was the just war tradition, but nowhere in their public statements did they condemn the savagery of means used in obliteration and atomic bombing. Despite intense pressure from the Vatican, the American hierarchy refused to condemn publicly the bombing of Rome, although they did attempt to change the government's policy through private correspondence and talks with key officials. It appeared that "the American bishops had to balance their allegiances";[7] they wanted to support the pope's concern over the bombing of Rome, but they would not publicly criticize the government's policies as the Holy See wanted.

The neoconservative George Weigel contends that the American hierarchy's five "remarkable" statements during and immediately after the war have been completely ignored in the contemporary American Catholic debate on war and peace. They have been largely ignored by peacemakers because they reflect the bishops' preoccupation with communism and its impact on them in establishing a new international order after World War II. Their significance is not, as Weigel contends, that they "both challenged the Roosevelt and Truman administrations to make the promises implicit in the origins of U.S. involvement in the war (particularly the program laid out in the Atlantic Charter), and contributed to the further development of the Catholic theory of peace as dynamic political community," but because they explain the basis for the relationship between the American hierachy and the U.S. government in foreign affairs during the Cold War.[8]

In the most important of the five statements, *International Order*, issued in November 1944, the American Catholic hierarchy proclaimed the end of isolationism among its ranks and announced a quickly developed concern for the world beyond the United States. The opening line of the statement: "We have met the challenge of war. Shall we meet the challenge of peace?" clearly reflected the hierarchy's desire to help define the new world order. The hierarchy attempted to enunciate the Thomistic principles for a just peace and remind America of its own ideals of what is right in determining the fate of weaker nations. The enunciation of such principles placed the hierarchy in the forefront of the attempt to prevent the domination of Eastern Europe by the Soviet Union, thus entering "into a whole-hearted alliance with the United States government for the preservation of the world order against international communism."[9] The statement demonstrated that the world government heralded by John A. Ryan and CAIP after World War I and during the isolationist ascendancy of the 1930s was suddenly acceptable to many by 1944. CAIP's plea for an international organization to guarantee the rights of all peoples and to see that nations would abide by international law became the type of peace the bishops wanted.

This vision of an international organization, however, was not totally compatible with the United Nations. In their fifth and final statement, *Man and Peace,* issued in November 1946, the American bishops claimed that the basic issue now was human rights and that the new international order under the United Nations, because of the position of power of the USSR in the UN, was in violation of these basic rights. The hierarchy believed that their battle cry throughout the war was the defense of native freedoms against Nazi and fascist totalitarianism; the aftermath of the war revealed a victorious Soviet totalitarianism just as antithetical to these freedoms.

In the years following the war the American Catholic hierarchy tried to unite the just war tradition with the theory of democratic pluralism in hopes of establishing a new order of peace. They did this through the CAIP, which held observer status in the United Nations. CAIP's anti-communist position fused the objectives of the American Catholic hierarchy with those of the U. S. government. But, unlike Pope Pius XII, the American bishops were uncritical of any U. S. government policy that was performed to stop Soviet aggression. In issues of peace as well as war, the state, not the principles of the just war, were victorious. Thus, more was "rendered unto Caesar" than was consistent with justice and peace.

Despite a concern for the rights of people in communist-occupied countries, the bishops made no mention of the right of an individual Catholic to be a conscientious objector in any of their five statements. The first opportunity for the American hierarchy to address this issue had been occasioned by the Military Draft Bill of July 1940. George Flynn has claimed that the Catholic church took what amounted to an official stand opposing the bill since it initially deferred clergy and did not exempt them as in World War I. This status aroused resistance from the American bishops and as a result of this opposition the final version of the bill granted exemption to Catholic clergy. Flynn states: "The entire episode reveals the degree of unity achievable by American Catholics on a nontheological problem, and deep distrust of most clerics for militarism and foreign adventure, and the effectiveness of Catholic pressure on Congress."[10] Recent research reveals that a deep division within the hierachy prevented it from taking a solid stand for or against conscription before the attack on Pearl Harbor and that they were only concerned about exemptions for priests, brothers, and seminarians; there was no concern for lay Catholics who might be conscientious objectors to the war.[11]

In their annual meeting of 1939, the bishops discussed the possibility of draft legislation coming to the Congress, and voted merely to maintain its opposition to the drafting of priests, religious, and seminarians. Archbishop John Glennon of St. Louis recalled that in 1917 several archbishops had testified before a Senate committee and obtained the needed exemptions. Now, it was decided to leave the defense of their position to Michael Ready who was "recognized by the Government as expressing the mind of the Bishops."[12] At the meeting there was no expressed concern for the Catholic laity. Ready asked for the clerical exemptions when he testified before a House committee and also warned against rushing such important legislation, asking that a one-year, voluntary enlistment program be tried before conscription. Fearing he had gone beyond the mandate of the bishops, he wrote a letter of explanation to the committee. Samuel Stritch, archbishop of Chicago, defended Ready's position and blamed the reason for Ready's excess on "the animosity of much of the Catholic press to conscription and noted that some 'important' ecclesiastics [thought] that the Board should have taken this attitude."[13] The bishops gained their desired exemptions in the final bill, which was signed into law on 16 September 1940. Over the next three years they faced several changes in the law. They were especially concerned when the draft age was lowered to eighteen because this affected minor seminarians. This issue was resolved on local levels between individual bishops and draft boards. The hierarchy's response to conscription reflected a position of total self-interest. They did not hesitate to seek exemptions for their own clergy who were necessary to staff church institutions during a time of war, but they would not exert their influence to defend a lay person's right to be a conscientious objector even though the U. S. government granted such an exemption in the draft law during World War II.

Among Catholics in general, support for conscientious objection before World War II was not impressive. *America,* the Jesuit weekly, in November 1939 published the results of a survey of 54,000 Catholic students of both sexes in 141 Catholic colleges and universities. They were asked to respond to a statement of Francis J. Beckman, archbishop of Dubuque, who had declared, "Catholics should give serious thought to the question of whether or not they should be conscientious objectors if this country should enter the war."[14] The results of the survey showed that 20 percent of young Catholics would volunteer for military service, 44 percent would accept conscription, while 36 percent would conscientiously object.[15] Such statistics illustrated the continued strength of traditional patterns of patriotism among two-thirds of these American Catholic students. Once war was declared the one-third who claimed that they would be conscientious objectors dissipated.

For the men who did choose to be conscientious objectors during World War II, the choice necessitated a direct confrontation with the U. S. government. Everyone eligible for military service was required to fill out a selective service questionnaire. The religious objector was recognized by the Selective Service and Training Act of 1940 since the government exempted from combatant service those who, "because of religious training and belief," were opposed to all war in "any form."[16] In completing the questionnaire the individual was allowed to request a special form for conscientious objectors if he so desired, and this form (DDS-Form 47) became the basis for selective service classification.[17]

Under the operation of the overall conscription program, there were three distinct types of conscientious objection. First, men were classified I-A-O who, on the basis of religious opposition to war, refused all combatant military service or training, but were willing to perform noncombatant military service under military direction within the armed forces. Second, men whose opposition to World War II involved the actual violation of the Selective Training and Service Act by either refusing to register or failing to report for induction or assuming some other posture of noncooperation were imprisoned and considered draft "delinquents." The third group was opposed to war and to all military service, combatant or noncombatant. Nonetheless, they were willing to cooperate with the government and fill out DDS-Form 47. Classified IV-E, these men were assigned to the Civilian Public Service camps, which were under civilian direction.

It is important to note that this complex means of classification applied to but a small percentage of the U. S. population. The highest estimate of the total number of COs during World War II was 2.4 percent of the population. The highest estimate of the number of Catholic COs was 135 out of a church whose membership then numbered 19,913,937, or .0001 percent of that membership. This was a tremendous increase over World War I when, at most four Catholics had been COs.[18] In World War I, 345 different churches were listed by the COs as the source of their religious grounds for objection. All conscientious objectors during World War I were sentenced to twenty-five years imprisonment since the complex classification system for COs did not exist at that time.

Although the selective service system did not keep accurate or complete records on COs during World War II, it estimated that during the life of the Selective Training and Service Act, it ordered the induction of 25,000 men classified I-A-O and 11,887 classified IV-E, and it imprisoned 6,086 COs. Thus, 42,973 of the 10,022,367 males ordered to report for induction into the armed forces were COs. Most striking was the increase in the number of imprisoned COs, which jumped from 450 in World War I to 6,068 in World War II, an increase of 400 percent. Every sixth man in the federal prisons during World War II was a CO.[19]

Because of a lack of accurate records, there is no way to determine the number of Catholics who were classified I-A-O. Statistics are available on the number of Catholics imprisoned and the number of Catholics in the Civilian Public Service camps. The National Service Board for Religious Objectors (NSBRO) compiled a list of sixty-one Catholics imprisoned in sixteen of the twenty-eight federal prisons. The Danbury Federal Prison had the largest number of Catholic COs—eighteen men. These sixty-one men were sentenced for anywhere from eighteen months to five years; the largest number, thirty, were sentenced to three years' imprisonment. Furthermore, on the entire list only one man was cited as being released from a five-year prison sentence to serve in the Army.[20] When the sixty-one Catholic COs in prison are deducted from the total of 135 known Catholic COs the remaining seventy-four COs were classified IV-E and assigned to the Civilian Public Service (CPS) camps.

The idea for founding the CPS camps originated with the historic peace churches. Leaders of the Quakers, Mennonites, and Church of the Brethren, with the support of peace groups concerned about the protection of the rights of COs, met with President Roosevelt on 10 January 1940 to propose a program for COs. They suggested the establishment of an alternative service program under their direction in which COs could perform work of a humanitarian nature.[21]

The actual establishment of the alternative service system, however, forced the pacifist leaders to compromise in a number of ways. First, American law would recognize conscientious objection solely on religious grounds. Second, no exemption would be granted to men who in good conscience could not accept compulsory government service even if it were in the form of labor in the CPS camps. While final plans were being made for the establishment of the CPS camps, certain unwanted conditions were imposed concerning the administration of the camps. President Roosevelt suddenly expressed opposition to the proposed system of camp autonomy and "advocated putting all the men to work under army direction."[22] The leaders of the historical peace churches became fearful and agreed to assume all costs of the alternative service program in order to eliminate military control. This meant that COs in the CPS camps would work without pay. In the end the government granted that old Civilian Conservation Corps camps could be converted into CPS camps with the historical peace churches providing the operational expenses. The government, nevertheless, maintained final supervision over the camps. When Brigadier General Lewis B. Hershey was asked to explain the way funds were provided for the CPS camps, he stated before the Congressional Subcommittee on Conscientious Objection in 1941, "You see, we have three major historical creeds. They underwrite those costs. If the boy has $35 a month, he pays it; and if he has not, his church pays it; if neither has it, the three religious groups pay it."[23] In total the administrative cost to the historical peace churches for the CPS camps amounted to $7,000,000. There were 12,000 pacifists in 151 CPS camps from 1940 to 1946 with a sum of 8,000,000 man-days of free work for the United States.[24]

The leaders of the historical peace churches formed NSBRO to administer the CPS camps. Arthur Sheehan, head of ACCO, which had been formed to help Catholic COs at the Catholic Worker house in New York City, felt a responsibility toward these Catholics and became the self-appointed Catholic representative on NSBRO. The Catholic Worker alone of all the existing Catholic organizations and groups came to the aid of lay Catholics who opposed conscription. Dorothy Day was personally opposed to any form of cooperation with the draft, but she believed individuals had to follow their own conscience in the matter of cooperation. She believed that they needed support from other Catholics for their position and wholeheartedly supported all Catholic Worker endeavors to support Catholic COs regardless of their degree of resistance to the draft.

Arthur Sheehan approached the selective service for permission to operate a camp in the interest of Catholic COs. The government granted a forestry camp at Stoddard, New Hampshire, that would accommodate fifty men, and the Catholic Worker, through small donations, attempted to meet the yearly expenditure estimated to be $12,000. The camp was opened on 15 August 1941, with sixteen men; Dwight Larrowe was camp director, and Joseph Zarella assisted him. Both of these men were from the New York Catholic Worker community and active in ACCO.

The Catholic church, unlike the historical peace churches did not support the CPS camps.[25] This absence of moral and financial assistance inflicted grave hardships on the COs. Since ACCO was a creation of the Catholic Worker movement and financially dependent on it for support, ACCO's source of revenue became as precarious as the Catholic Worker's, which depended on the personal contributions of readers of its paper and people familiar with its houses of hospitality. The CPS camps were never far removed from absolute poverty at Stoddard or later in the other Catholic camp at Warner, New Hampshire.

The opening of the CPS camp at Stoddard was "in a very real sense, the first corporate witness against war and military service in the history of American Catholicism. Indeed, the claim might even be made that it was the first such witness in the entire history of the Church."[26] The irony of this witness, according to Gordon C. Zahn, is that it could not have occurred without the elaborate CO classification system designed by the federal government during World War II. However, he does not give sufficient credit to the Catholic Worker in establishing this Catholic corporate witness.

Zahn's book, *Another Part of the War: The Camp Simon Story*, gives a complete account of the Warner experience based on his own participation as a CO. In the book, he treats the Catholic camps at Stoddard and Warner as two separate phases of one camp experience and calls it Camp Simon. Zahn notes that the Catholic COs were older and more highly educated than their Protestant counterparts in the CPS. Also, 72 percent gave no affiliation with an existing peace organization. Eleven men did mention affiliation with the Catholic Worker, ACCO, or PAX. Zahn believes that a greater amount of maturity was necessary for Catholics to be COs because they were "taking a deviant stand on religious principle *without* the support of the religious community."[27]

The men at Stoddard faced many hardships. Their daily schedule was highly structured and the camp's location—a virtual Siberia— made obtaining supplies and attending Mass difficult.[28] Government trucks were available for work, but not religious purposes, even to travel to Mass on Sundays. The lack of finances for the camp caused additional problems, including the lack of adequate food, especially meat.[29] Dorothy Day told the following story of the camps:

> At first the boys themselves did the cooking. Then began the era of apple dumplings, apple strudel, apple sauce, apple pie. The camps were in the middle of an apple orchard and nothing went to waste. The fellows even sat around at night and sliced apples for drying so that they could be assured of their diet of apple pies for the duration.[30]

The men suffered psychological and emotional strains from doing work for which they were not trained professionally, which they did not believe to be of "national importance," and for which they were not paid. Zahn asserts that the daily schedule at Stoddard was applied to Warner, but it was not kept. He states that very little work was done because CPS was in violation of the two basic principles upon which alternative service was based: "The work was to be of national importance and performed under civilian direction." As a result, the two principles "were distorted and circumvented until they became little more than a grotesque farce."[31]

Conflicts among the men also arose, particularly in the antagonisms caused by the anti-Semitic Christian Front group and by the chapel group (deeply religious men who believed the others were not "Catholic" enough and whose sole aim was to erect a chapel at the camp).[32] Because of the hardships, a few men believed that they could no longer cooperate in *any* way with military conscription and left the camps to assume the extreme position of non-cooperation with the selective service system.[33]

Zahn contends that among the COs at Camp Simon "nothing approaching consensus in principle or application with respect to their opposition to war" existed.[34] Not all the men there were Catholic and the Catholics who were there felt out of place in CPS, "trapped into a situation not of their making, obliged to accept deprivations imposed by a set of concessions and compromises arranged without their approval or participation between the military officers who ran the show and the Protestant peace church leaders."[35]

The absence of consensus on the relationship of Catholicism to the COs' stand against war, is confirmed by Paul Fitzgerald, a Catholic CO who left Camp Simon for the army almost as soon as he arrived. Fitzgerald wrote:

> You must remember that the thinking of most of us, indeed our statuses as COs, was a product of non- war thinking. Few of us were pacifists, except for Dorothy [Day] and a few others. Most of us were products of a time when Thomism was all, . . . when a position on a moral matter was strictly a matter of applying our philosophies to a particular event. And yet, until World War II came about, there was no particular event. So you can see that the actual outbreak of the war threw some of us into an agonizing necessity for making decisions. The circumstances of the war (remember, this was at the time and we had no chance for the 20/20 vision of hindsight) made it most difficult for a moral decision. If we had been pacifists, it would have been a different story. But, again, remember we had no clear-cut theology for pacifism; the years between World War II and the Vietnam war provided that. We had to contend with the murderous attack on Pearl Harbor, Hitler's treatment of the Jews, etc.[36]

In an earlier book, *War, Conscience and Dissent*, Zahn attempted to classify the religious beliefs of these Catholic COs. A major handicap in doing so, he believed, was that there was no definite way of judging the relationship and impact of an individual's Catholic faith on his decision to become a conscientious objector.

> It is hard to generalize about men holding essentially individually deter-mined positions. The source of strength for the conscientious objector in World War II came from personal conviction that he was conforming to the true norms of social living as defined by the great humanitarian thinkers and teachers of the past. True he would still remain a deviant; but his deviation would have something of a supra-social encourage-ment behind it in the identification with certain ideals which for him, at least, transcended temporal and national considerations.[37]

Despite this difficulty, Zahn constructed five categories to explain the theological positions of Catholic COs. The first was "individual" positions, which consisted of Christian Fronters who were scornful of the pacifism of others and believed the United States was fighting on the wrong side, and one or two COs who traced their objection to personal revelations of a presumably supernatural origin. The second category included those who made no religious references, since their position was based on a philosophical or humanitarian ideal. The third position was "evangelical," men who avoided formal theological argu-ments and stated their objections in terms of an antithesis between the "spirit of war" and the "spirit of Christ." Arguments offered by this group were based upon the unifying element they found in Redemp-tion and the doctrine of the Mystical Body of Christ. Somewhat more theological was the "perfectionist" position, which was based upon a literal interpretation of the counsels of perfection as outlined in the Sermon on the Mount. Holders of this view refused to limit themselves to a just war analysis though they would agree to it. They believed the Christian was called to follow a supernatural ethic which went beyond justice to charity. This position was held mainly by the men associated with the Catholic Worker movement. Finally, there was the "tradition-alist" position based on the "just war—unjust war" distinction devel-oped by the writings of St. Augustine, St. Thomas Aquinas, Vittoria and Suarez, Gerald Vann, G. Barry O'Toole, and Franziskus Stratmann. Only nineteen of the sixty-one men at Camp Simon held this position.

In a later book on Camp Simon, Zahn classified the COs in the following manner: the Chapel Group, the Catholic Workers, the Coughlinites, College Boys and Intellectuals, the Artists, the Disrupters, the Workers, the Loners, and the Oddballs. In this study Zahn abandoned his previous attempt at religious classification and concluded that for more than half (thirty-six of the sixty-one) of the men at Camp Simon their Roman Catholic affiliation had no direct relationship or bearing in their decisions to become COs. The importance of both sets of Zahn's categories is that they illustrate both the diversity of positions among Catholic COs in relation to the role religion played in their decision and how difficult it is to determine or define an individual's religious belief.

The Stoddard CPS camp was in existence for one year when its forty-seven members were moved to larger facilites at Warner in October 1942. Two weeks before the Warner CPS camp closed on 17 March 1943, twelve men from the Catholic CPS camp went to the Alexian Brothers' Hospital in Chicago. This was the first instance in which COs were able to leave the camps and work elsewhere as a form of alternative service; the practice became more frequent after 1942. A unique aspect of this program was that living expenses for the COs were not paid by the historical peace churches but by the agency where the men worked.[38] Many reasons explain the closing of the camp at Warner and the cessation of ACCO to attempt to maintain a separate Catholic CPS camp: the men were generally dissatisfied; more meaningful work was opening up in the hospitals; New Hampshire residents wanted the camp removed; and finally, ACCO was not financially capable of meeting the government regulations necessary to keep the camp operating.[39]

After the camp closed, over sixty of the Catholic COs went to Swallow Falls near Oakland, Maryland, CPS camp No. 89. In June 1944, Rosewood Training School in Maryland opened and took many Catholic COs. There the men spent twelve hours a day caring for the mental patients and received an allowance of $15 a month. Other Catholic COs went to Cheltenham, Maryland, and worked in a training school for boys. The chapel group went to a CPS camp for Native Americans sponsored by the American Friends Service Committee in North Dakota and finally realized their dream of building a chapel; Bolton Morris, a member of the chapel group and in later years a well-known Philadelphia architect, designed the building. When the Catholic COs moved from Warner, NSBRO willingly accepted the financing of the men. In NSBRO records, the expense absorbed for the Catholic COs by the Mennonites was $5,975.34 and by the Quakers, $32,707.31.[40]

Besides working in the camps, over five hundred COs, including several Catholics, volunteered as "guinea pigs" for medical research. Two thousand COs served in forty-one mental hospitals and seventeen schools for the mentally deficient.[41] Over fifty Catholic COs served in the hospitals after 1943. The historical peace churches had originally been training some COs for overseas work, but wartime hatred of COs induced Congress to attach a rider to an appropriation bill making this illegal. An offer was made to a group of Catholic COs to go to England to establish a Catholic Worker hospitality house, but passports were refused these volunteers.[42] One intellectual venture of the CPS was a research study program at Columbia University on war relief and reconstruction. Fifteen men, including George Mathues, a Catholic CO, took part in this program even though they had to pay for it out of their own pockets.

In an attempt to keep the now scattered Catholic COs united and informed about one another and thus provide moral support, Arthur Sheehan along with two Catholic COs, Raymond Pierchalski and William Strube, began a quarterly newspaper, the *Catholic CO*, in January 1944. It came out of the Catholic Worker office in New York and sold not as the *Catholic Worker* for a penny a copy, but for twenty-five cents until it went up to fifty cents a copy in 1945. The funds from subscriptions were used to support the publication of the newspaper and to finance the Catholic COs in the CPS camps. After the first edition, the paper was taken over by the responsible men at the Rosewood Training School. The editors who served during the four years of the paper's existence were all Catholic COs: William Strube, Richard Lion, Gordon Zahn, Ray Pierchalski, and Robert Ludlow. Sheehan assisted them in the work. These men felt there was a need for a Catholic newspaper that focused solely on war and peace issues.

The *Catholic CO* took over the peace writings and peace news usually covered by the *Catholic Worker*. The two constant columns in the *Catholic CO* were "In Passing," which contained news about the men in the camps, and a book review. The main feature of each issue discussed conscientious objection, pacifism, or possible alternatives for peace. All the articles attempted to come to grips with the growing militarism in the United States. By 1945, the atomic bomb and the withdrawal issue were discussed in length. In 1946, much space was given to ACCO's withdrawal from NSBRO and Federal Judge James E. Fee's declaration that the CPS camps were illegal. The *Catholic CO* also took time to protest the ultra-nationalism of NCWC and CAIP when they stated that Pope Pius XII was "not in sympathy with a negotiated or compromising peace."[43]

In June 1948, the editors discontinued the *Catholic CO*. They stated their reasons in an article that appeared in the *Catholic Worker's* PAX column. They recognized that members of ACCO had very little in common except their opposition to the war; once that ended there was little else to bind them together. They also felt that the nation no longer needed a separate newspaper to cover war and peace issues; the coverage in the *Catholic Worker* would suffice.[44]

Meanwhile, after the closing of the Catholic camps and the 1944 founding of the paper, ACCO withdrew from NSBRO on 30 October 1945. Arthur Sheehan explained that ACCO had continued its membership in the NSBRO in hopes of working out the difficulties of the CPS and ultimately bringing a fair interpretation of the CO's status, but ACCO now felt at last it was being honest with itself in admitting that CPS was a form of slavery; scarcely any good resulted from the camps and in the end the program proved a failure. Sheehan also urged honesty on the part of NSBRO and hoped as well for its repudiation of CPS. NSBRO soon followed ACCO's act of repudiation.[45]

Robert Ludlow described CPS as "a program of involuntary servitude without compensation, nothing more than a program of slave labor offered by the State as an alternative to outright imprisonment."[46] Though the statement is strong, Zahn contends that it honestly reflected the position of the Catholic men serving in the program. If anything positive can be said about CPS it would be that the hardships, injustices, and wasted talent of the men in the system did not match those endured by the World War I objectors. Nevertheless, with the court system declaring CPS illegal in 1946 there can be no doubt that it was a form of slave labor and imprisonment.

Of the sixty-one Catholic COs who had taken a stand of noncooperation and were sent to prison, Arthur Sheehan managed to arrange parole
talks for eighteen who were incarcerated at the Danbury Federal Prison.
All but two of the seventeen men at the meeting called by Warden
Alexander had one-third of their sentences commuted and were assigned to hospitals in New Haven, Boston, and Baltimore.[47] When
paroled, a CO was assigned to a hospital and required only to appear for
work each day. Thus, these men fared better than the COs in the CPS
camps.[48]

The prison witness was not totally unproductive. Recent peace movement histories point out that these imprisoned COs were responsible for
effective prison reform conducted through hunger strikes, sit-ins, and
other forms of organized nonviolent action. Compared to the COs in
alternative service, these men were more likely to come out of the experience convinced of nonviolence as an effective strategy for peace in the
future, and many made contributions to the postwar peace movement.

Generally speaking, however, Catholic opposition to war was very
feeble, consisting only of the Catholic Worker and 135 known Catholic COs. Most mainstream Catholics viewed the Catholic Worker as
radical and of doubtful orthodoxy; COs in prison went unrecognized.
Nevertheless, the demands of peacemaking on these individuals were
as great as the demands of war.

In assessing the value of the Catholic COs' witness in the CPS
camps, Zahn contends that only those men in CPS offered a corporate
witness in the sense that their witness was for the church and in the
name of the church. He also states that the friendships formed by the
men at Camp Simon were of lasting value and these men have no
regrets about their witness. Zahn cites the following changes since the
end of World War II as proof of the value of their witness: First, the
Catholic Worker and the historical peace churches agreed never again
to cooperate with the government in administering CPS camps as an
alternative service program. Second, the Catholic church has significantly changed its teachings on modern war and conscientious objection, a change in part that can be attributed to the prophetic stance
taken by the Catholic men in the CPS camps:

> If . . . taken to imply that those who refused to serve were directly
> responsible for the crucial changes in theological stance and interpreta-

tion that have developed since, it would be claiming too much. On the other hand, if it refers to nothing more than the recognition that their stand anticipated, and and may even to some extent have prepared the way for, a more unambiguous commitment to peace and nonviolence among important segments of the Catholic community, the Warner witness was a prophetic witness. It met the test of the two characteristic notes of the prophetic tradition; it affirmed, and exercised, the competence of the individual conscience to pass adverse judgment on the acts of principalities and powers; and it insisted that, by doing so, it was fulfilling moral obligations that should have been recognized by all.[49]

Whatever changes occurred in the Catholic church after the war, the fact remains that it was a silent bystander on the issue of conscription throughout World War II. Catholic COs found reasons for their positions in a tradition not encompassed in the normative or popular teaching of Catholicism in the first half of the twentieth century. Although there was little connection between Catholic teaching and the individual's decision to become a CO, the Catholic church in the United States never denied the right of an individual to become a conscientious objector. At the same time the church never articulated its support for this right. The reason for this is not hard to discover— the church had always remained loyal to the nation in time of war. The apparent legitimacy of World War II in face of the evil of Nazism, coupled with the official just war doctrine of the church served to justify such uncritical patriotism.

The means used in the waging of World War II, such as the obliteration bombing of European cities, introduced another challenge to the just war doctrine. Although Pope Pius XII only criticized the bombing of Rome and the American Catholic hierarchy only privately questioned the use of such actions, some segments of the Catholic community, especially pacifists, did criticize the war tactic.

The person most responsible for developing a theological rationale for this moral protest was John C. Ford, S.J., teacher at Weston College. In a scholarly article, "The Morality of Obliteration Bombing," published in 1944, he became the only American Catholic moral theologian during World War II who challenged the bombing of cities as not admissible under traditional just war criteria. In the article Ford defined obliteration bombing in the following terms:

> Obliteration bombing is the strategic bombing, by means of incendiaries and explosives, of industrial centers of population in which the target to be wiped out is not a definite factory, bridge, or similar object, but a large area of a whole city, comprising one-third to two-thirds of its whole built up area, and including by design the residential districts of workingmen and their families. [50]

Ford contended that such bombing was immoral, basing his position in international law, the laws of humanity, and natural law. He pointed out that the question of obliteration bombing leads to the more general one of the possibility of a just modern war: "For obliteration bombing includes the bombing of civilians, and is a necessary practice which can be called typical of total war, and if all modern war must be total, then a condemnation of obliteration bombing would logically lead to a condemnation of all modern war."[51] Ford, however, admitted that he did not intend to go that far and believed that it was possible for modern war to be waged within the limits set by the laws of morality.[52]

While Ford did not accept pacifism and believed that certain wars could be just, he maintained that there were some things, such as the use of poisonous gas and obliteration bombing, which were inadmissible in warfare. He based his argument against obliteration bombing on the distinction between combatants and noncombatants and referred to the writings of many theologians who were firmly convinced of the distinction. One of these writers was the American Catholic theologian, John K. Ryan, author of *Modern War and Basic Ethics*, which was published by CAIP before United States entry into World War II. Ford considered soldiers under arms as combatants, but was not clear about the status of civilian munitions workers, leaving it to international law to decide. However, the rest of the people were clearly seen as innocent noncombatants, and their rights were being violated by obliteration bombing. Ford concluded his argument with a section on "The Mind of the Holy See." Here, Ford cited the condemnation of aerial bombardment of civilians by Benedict XV in World War I, the condemnation of the bombing of cities in Spain during the Spanish Civil War by Pius XI, and the lament of the bombing of Rome during World War II by Pius XII. From such statements, Ford concluded that if the words of the popes "do not contain an implicit condemnation of obliteration bombing as I have described it, then it is hard to see what they do condemn."[53]

Ford was careful to point out that his article was insufficient to impose obligations on the conscience of the individual. "A clear violation of natural law can be known to the ordinary individual soldier in a case of this kind through the definite pronouncements of the Church, or of the hierarchy, or even through a consensus of moral theologians over a period of time. On the question of obliteration bombing we have no such norms."[54]

A few Catholics, as Ford pointed out, had condemned obliteration bombing. James M. Gillis in the "Editorial Comment" in *Catholic World* took such a stand. The editors of *Commonweal* flatly condemned obliteration bombing as murder. The *Catholic Worker* speaking from its pacifist position condemned obliteration bombing and published the statement of Gerald Shaugnessy, D.D., S.M., of Seattle, the only American bishop who spoke out during World War II on the immorality of this tactic.[55] The *Catholic Worker* also printed the words of Monsignor Paul Hanley Furfey's condemnation of obliteration bombing.[56] Thus, there were a few Catholics who protested the United States policy of obliteratiion bombing during World War II. Most Catholics, even the CAIP, never addressed this issue. One Catholic periodical, *America*, urged precautions concerning obliteration bombing.

If the protestations of American Catholics and others had been stronger against the government's policy of obliteration bombing, President Truman would have found it more difficult to drop the atomic bomb on Hiroshima and Nagasaki. As it was, he made the decision to drop the bombs, and one observer noted that "the general American reaction, is one of stunned disquiet. It is not jubilant, yet it contains no real feeling of guilt."[57]

Despite the "stunned disquiet" of most Americans, some did protest the bombing of Hiroshima and Nagasaki. Editors of Catholic publications were spurred on by the pope's criticism of the bombings. Catholics, however, who subjected the American decision to sharp attack were the same ones who had previously challenged the policy of obliteration bombing. The reasons for their protest stemmed from the same reason for their opposition to obliteration bombing; knowledge pertaining to the unique destructive power of nuclear weapons was still unknown. Gillis in the *Catholic World* responded by proclaiming, "I here and now declare that I think the use of the atomic bomb, in these circumstances, was atrocious and abominable; and that civilized peoples would reprobate and anathematize the horrible deed."[58] Dorothy Day in the *Catholic Worker* began her pacifist condemnation of the atomic bomb attack with extreme sarcasm as she talked of the president. "He went from table to table on the cruiser which was bringing him home from the Big Three conference," she noted, "telling the great news, 'jubilant,' the newspapers said. JUBILATE DEO. We have killed 318,000 Japanese." She placed the responsibility for the atomic bomb on "scientists and captains of industry." In her Gospel manner she asserted that Christ had already given his judgment of the act: "What you do unto the least of these my brethren, you do unto me."[59] John J. Hugo's article "Peace Without Victory" also appeared in the same issue of the *Catholic Worker*. Hugo termed the dropping of the atomic bombs "the culminating crime" and attributed it to the United States' capacity to "out-Nazi the Nazis" by using means that do not justify the end, by accepting tribal morality, and by acquiesing in obliteration bombing.

While indignation and dismay at America's use of atomic weapons held the initiative in these Catholic circles many Catholic leaders were not united behind the discontent. This was true among clerical leadership of every denomination in the United States.[60] Catholic groups who abstained from judgment on obliteration bombing, such as *America*, the American Catholic hierarchy, and the CAIP, did the same when the atomic bombs were dropped on Hiroshima and Nagasaki. The principles of the just war doctrine which provided the moral imperative for Catholics to support World War II were insufficient for these same Catholics to criticize the means used by the government to win the war.

After the war in 1947, the CAIP finally spoke out on the issue of the atomic bomb. During the war CAIP, like other peace groups that were advocates of collective security, supported the policies of the government during the war and focused its attention on planning for a postwar community of nations. When the United States helped to build the United Nations, CAIP made many recommendations for a strong UN. It was in this context that the CAIP proposed the UN have "legislative powers . . . to make effective atomic control and inspection and general disarmament."[61] CAIP stated that the use of atomic bombs was illegitimate or unjust when (1) atomic bombing was used to break peoples' will to resist; (2) atomic total war was pursued as an end in itself; and (3) a war was started with a shower of atomic bombs. The use of atomic bombs was just, however, in the following situations: (1) for counteruse by a nation in a defensive war when other means were insufficient and (2) that the United Nations may use atomic bombs against an aggressor nation if the nation's preparations and objective were clearly to enslave the world or a large part of it. CAIP concluded by declaring that "the United States was obliged to stop production of the A bomb and publicly announce this due to suspicion aroused in Russia and the armaments race."[62]

This statement of CAIP probably went beyond dominant Catholic opinion. Though there are no statistics available on exclusively Catholic public opinion, on 8 August 1945, a poll found that only 10 percent of the American population opposed the use of atomic bombs on Japanese cities, while 85 percent approved.[63]

On the question of the use of the atomic bomb, American Catholics evidenced a variety of positions: The majority approved or were silent; the American Catholic hierarchy was silent; CAIP applied the just war doctrine to the new weapon and tried to bring it under the control of the United Nations and develop a rationale that would limit the use of nuclear weapons. For CAIP, the just war theory still provided an ethical rationale that permitted them to support their government in war, even "limited" atomic war if it were necessary for the defense of their nation. *Commonweal*, the *Catholic Worker*, and the *Catholic World* opposed the use of the atomic bomb under any condition. They came to call themselves nuclear pacifists.

The just war doctrine had enabled some few Catholics to become conscientious objectors, to protest obliteration bombing, and to condemn atomic warfare during World War II. Ironically, those who had looked to the just war doctrine for a Catholic justification of their opposition had become increasingly disillusioned with the doctrine in the face of modern warfare. After the war they proclaimed that no modern war, especially nuclear war, could be just. They also became more like the pacifists in the Catholic Worker tradition by looking to the Gospel message in hopes of creating a new peace ethic within Catholicism. The just war doctrine was not dead in the American

Catholic church, but it had been dealt serious blows. Nevertheless, the majority of American Catholics and the hierarchy would continue to view the just war doctrine as the normative teaching of the church on issues of war and peace for the next forty years. During this time Catholic pacifists would continue to gain strength as their Gospel message combined with the theory of nonviolence and nuclear pacifism. The increasing escalation of the nuclear arms race, the growing knowledge of the effects of nuclear warfare, and the unjust war in Vietnam eventually propelled pacifists to a position of parity with just war traditionalists within American Catholicism.

# 4

# The Birth of Nonviolence
## From World War II to Vatican II

FROM WORLD WAR II to Vatican II the main focus of the Catholic Worker, as well as the American peace movement, was the development of the concept of nonviolence as a means of social protest. Among American Catholics concerned about war and peace issues, the Catholic Worker alone moved beyond pacifism into nonviolence under the leadership of Robert Ludlow and Ammon Hennacy. The CAIP had no interest in nonviolence but aligned itself instead with the "realist" school of theologians led by John Courtney Murray, S.J., who attempted to apply just war principles to American nuclear policy. Both CAIP and the Catholic Worker, as well as the entire American peace movement, were greatly influenced during this time period by the Cold War.

After World War II, the Cold War between the Soviet Union and the United States permeated every aspect of American life. The peace movement retreated in face of the issues raised by the Cold War, such as the fear of communism, the arms race, and defensive security. The loyalty-security mania of the early 1950s led to McCarthyism, the domestic counterpart of the nation's foreign policy.[1] Ironically, the Cold War accelerated the very forces the peace movement sought to restrain. Peacemakers continued their struggle by formulating alternatives to American military policies (CAIP) and by serving as prophets of nonviolence (Catholic Worker).

The American peace movement had a long-term interest in Gandhian nonviolence. Nonviolence is "the force which is born of Truth and Love" (satyagraha) and exercises "power or influence to effect change without injury to the opponent."[2] Nonviolent resistance is a technique of action that employs noncooperation and civil

71

disobedience. "Non-cooperation is simply the refusal to cooperate with a requirement which is taken to violate fundamental 'truths' or refusal to cooperate with those responsible for such violations. Civil disobedience is the direct contravention of specific laws."[3] Young pacifists during World War II found these tactics most useful in dealing with the injustices in American race relations, the CPS camps, and the prisons. The use of these tactics to correct injustice achieved the greatest success when performed by the pacifist nonco-operators in the prisons.[4]

After the war many of the COs who had been in the CPS camps and prisons held new ideas about the functions of a peacemaker gained from their experiments with nonviolent resistance. For a time there was a split between traditional pacifists and this young generation, who were termed radical pacifists, as revealed in the two oldest pacifist groups in the United States, the Fellowship of Reconciliation (FOR) and the War Resisters League (WRL). In 1946, however, the radical pacifists who had joined FOR's Congress of Racial Equality sponsored the first Freedom Ride, which was a definite victory for the radical pacifists because it was a tactic of nonviolent resistance. In June 1947, the executive committee of WRL adopted a resolution declaring that it would "adopt its literature and activities to the promotion of political, economic, social revolution by nonviolent means."

Though the radical pacifists had greatly influenced traditional paci-fist groups, they still attempted to form their own peace organizations; the first of any size and permanence being the Peacemakers. The focus of the new group was war resistance. The most unique of their pro-grams called for the nonpayment of taxes to protest war. Recalling the actions of Henry David Thoreau over a century earlier, this tax resis-tance was unique as action performed by a group of people in opposi-tion to war.[5]

Radical and traditional pacifists alike joined in an attempt to secure amnesty for COs imprisoned during World War II. They also cooper-ated in the struggle against the proposal of President Truman to continue complusory military training into the postwar era. In their opposition they again applied the tactics of nonviolent resistance. In February 1947, five pacifists burned draft cards in San Francisco's Union Square. In the same month sixty-three draft cards were burned at a meeting in New York.[6]

By 1950, three government policies brought an end to the American peace movement. The first was the heightening of the Cold War; the second, was President Truman's continuation of tests on the hydrogen bomb; and finally, the outbreak of fighting in Korea. The Korean War came as the final blow because world government organizations almost universally accepted the American role in the conflict.

The American Catholic segment of the peace movement also experienced the effects of these government policies. After World War II, the Catholic peace movement was represented by the relatively few Catholic conscientious objectors who had performed alternative service and their even fewer supporters. "Basically, it dissolved completely until nothing remained to show for it but the Catholic Worker, its principal benefactor throughout the war period."[7] For the most part, Catholic Worker pacifists returned to their roots of social justice concerns and administered the corporal works of mercy to the poor. The pacifist witness remained during the 1950s, however, in the writings on nonviolence by Robert Ludlow in the *Catholic Worker* and in symbolic actions of nonviolent resistance as Ammon Hennacy led Dorothy Day and other Workers in the extension of their pacifism.

The other group of Catholic peacemakers, CAIP, focused attention on the United Nations, where it held observer status.[8] CAIP was directly linked with the NCWC through Rita Schaefer, former secretary of CAIP, who served as the representative of both groups in a consultant position at the United Nations.[9] Her main effort during this period was devoted to the drafting of the International Covenant on Human Rights. Her efforts were also supported by the National Catholic Conference of Women and the National Federation of Catholic College Students, both of which were affiliated with NCWC in America. *The Sword of the Spirit*, a periodical of Catholic peace groups in London and the British Society for International Understanding collaborated with her on this project.[10]

Though CAIP always aimed at combating nationalism and building cooperation among nations for peace, it was particularly unsuccessful at both after World War II. Because of pronouncements by government leaders in America against communism and the pope's condemnation of atheistic communism, CAIP was very conscious of the need to combat it. This fear of communism was most evident in the association's policy toward China. On the one hand, it worked toward bringing to a vote the admission of Communist China into the United Nations, but at the same time it went on record as opposed to Communist China's entrance into the world organization.[11] CAIP also viewed the Korean War as an example of Communist aggression.[12]

During the post–World War II period, the CAIP was also represented at the State Department's "off-the-record" meetings concerning issues before the U.N. At these meetings discussions focused on American foreign policy in relation to the Korean situation and technical assistance to underdeveloped nations of the world.[13]

Through the association's statements, reports, conferences, and pamphlets an attempt was made to reiterate papal teaching on social and international themes such as disarmament, peacetime conscription, and foreign aid. However, this did not result in any significant modification of the Catholic obsession, encouraged by the hierarchy, that the anti-communist crusade was the only real international issue.[14] Even a mild attempt to broaden the discussion during the early Cold War period met with a note of caution from America's most distinguished liberal theologian, John Courtney Murray, as evidenced in his comment on a CAIP paper, "Co-Existing with Communism": "It seems to me that the relations between the Christian concept of man and the Communist concept are better characterized by the word 'war' than by the term 'co-existence.' I mean of course a war that is carried on purely by intellectual and spiritual means."[15] Although American Catholics were sorely anti-communist, many Catholics were at great variance with the views of Catholic Senator Joseph McCarthy and his followers. The anti-communism of most Catholics was rooted in spiritual rather than political concerns. The pope had set the tone with his condemnation of atheistic communism and the American hierarchy had been disillusioned in the peace settlement when Russia took control of Eastern Europe. Catholic prayer books from the postwar era stated that it was a Catholic's duty to resist communism. In their "Prayers After Low Mass," Catholics prayed for the conversion of Russia, a practice which continued until the Second Vatican Council. Because of their religiously ingrained anti-communism, Catholics often transferred the evil of atheistic communism to political issues. Even liberal and radical Catholics preferred to work alone rather than seek a social or political alliance with the Left in America during the early Cold War period.[16] For American Catholics this combination of religious and political anti-communism created a climate of fear and a support of the arms race and defensive security that left the Catholic Worker standing not only isolated, but also subdued in its efforts for peace.

The Catholic Worker movement, though subdued, was not intimidated by the Cold War. In the immediate postwar period, Catholic Workers like all American pacifists concentrated their energies on opposing conscription. In 1946 and 1947, the Catholic Worker joined for the first time with other pacifist groups—the Protestant Fellowship of Reconciliation, the War Resisters League, Peacemakers, and the Committee for Nonviolent Revolution—in a campaign against President Truman's proposed peacetime draft and Universal Military Training (UMT). When the peacetime draft was passed in 1948 without UMT, the *Catholic Worker* continued in its tradition of advocating noncooperation with the draft and offering support to men prosecuted for draft resistance. The case receiving the most attention was that of Larry Gara, a history professor who was imprisoned in 1949 for urging a student to refuse to register if it violated his conscience. The Catholic Worker, however, never performed any actions with the newly formed groups such as the Federation of Atomic Scientists, the United World Federalists, or the World Citizen Movement which had risen to prominence in America and were the forefront of the popular antiwar movement from 1946 to 1949. Though concerned about the issues of atomic arms control and world government, the Catholic Worker was too pacifist, too personalist, and too anarchistic to cooperate with them.

The Catholic Worker was most concerned with continuing its pacifist witness. Experiences in the CPS camps and the dropping of the bomb on Hiroshima and Nagasaki had convinced Workers of the irrelevancy of the just war doctrine, which never appeared again as a basis for their discussion and writing on war and peace issues. From 1948 to 1955 the writings of Robert Ludlow dominated the movement's thought on pacifism and led Catholic Workers to embrace Gandhian nonviolence. Robert Ludlow, a Catholic convert, had just joined the Catholic Worker when he had to confront the prospect of fighting in World War II. He chose not to do so and as a conscientious objector he took his place along with other Catholic COs at the Rosewood Training School in Maryland. During the war he wrote for the *Catholic Worker* and the *Catholic CO* and gained a reputation as the most articulate radical among the Catholic pacifists.

After the war, Ludlow joined the Workers at the House of Hospitality in New York. "Joining" simply meant going to the house and, after a while finding a job that became one's own. Ludlow was an associate editor of the *Catholic Worker* for the next decade and wrote on a variety of topics, but he tended to concentrate on pacifism, anarchism, Gandhian nonviolence, and mental illness. Historian William Miller claims that "Ludlow's contributions to the *Catholic Worker* in this era helped much to make it a distinguished paper."[17] John Cogley described Ludlow as "the predominant intellectual figure of the movement" during this period and credits him along with John A. Hugo and Ammon Hennacy as the main figures who partially reshaped the movement. The reason for the word "partially," Cogley explains, is that "the abiding imprint of the movement has always been that of Miss Day herself, whose genius it has been to cut through all kinds of distractions, abstractions and intellectual complexities to get at the heart of Christianity itself."[18] The first historian, however, to analyze Ludlow's thought and give him his rightful place within the Catholic Worker movement was Mel Piehl.

Piehl contends that Ludlow was "the first Catholic pacifist to understand and to appropriate the Gandhian theory of nonviolence as a comprehensive method of religious peacemaking." He was also "the first to see Catholic pacifism not simply as the witness of a small minority to the counsels of perfection, but as the forerunner of a possibly historic shift in the whole Catholic Church's attitude toward war."[19] Ludlow basically followed the lines of Paul Hanly Furfey's views in the 1930s, but went further in assessing the Catholic Worker's relation to prior Catholic social thought. According to Ludlow, in condemning anarchism, Catholic theologians and philosphers had failed to distinguish between society and the state to the extent that was necessary. Service to the people by the state and coercion and violence against the people by the state were not adequately defined by church doctrine. He believed that an anarchism which preserved social cohesion and authority and at the same time discarded coercive state violence was permissible. Thus, his work consisted of many tirades against the violent actions of the state. In developing a response for the individual in face of the coercive violence of the state Ludlow took Catholic Worker personalism and pacifism and added Gandhian nonviolence. Because Gandhian nonviolence rested on a spiritual vision of life,

Ludlow in the pages of the *Catholic Worker* in 1949 and 1950 hailed satyagraha as "a new Christian way of social change" that would be both politically effective and morally uncompromised. The individual could resist the coercive violent state through the spiritual practices of disciplined social struggle and suffering. In the end nonviolence would remove from pacifism its constant criticism of being individualistic, passive, and sentimental.

Ludlow also provided Catholic pacifists with a more satisfactory interpretation of their own insistent departure from the church's position on just war. While some pacifists saw their position only as a witness of personal conscience, Ludlow argued that war would turn out to be an instance of Cardinal Newman's theory concerning the development of Catholic dogma: the church arrives at many tentative judgments on the way to truth and may even tolerate for a time such unchristian practices as human slavery, which was long permitted but eventually condemned. In such an evolutionary course, Newman had observed, some within the church must risk going beyond the official positions of the time. Ludlow argued that this was true of war and that Catholic pacifists should not fear to differ with leaders of the church on a matter not defined in terms of formal doctrine. "We act in accordance with the belief that war will eventually be condemned" he wrote, "and must try by our actions to add our very small contributions to the time when pacifism may be the norm of society." The moral progressivism of this approach appealed to American Catholic pacifists, who wanted to be not only prophetic but effective. The idea that their pacifist witness was not only a counsel of perfection intended for a few saints, but somehow represented the true "mind of the Church" better than its current voices, gradually shaped the pacifists' self-understanding and relations with other Catholics.[20] Thus, Ludlow's integration of nonviolence into pacifism gave Catholics the means to confront the warmakers and by their example to show how the end of war among nations might be accomplished.

Ludlow's writing on pacifism was featured in the PAX column of the *Catholic Worker* and he often looked back to his CO experiences during the war. One of his main themes was that the Christian pacifist would be considered abnormal or psychotic because of the growing irrationality of modern society which was becoming fragmented by a rapidly expanding technology. This theme increased in significance when President Truman announced that he was sanctioning the testing of the hydrogen bomb. Ludlow's reponse to the announcement was that " 'The whole thing has become unreal and fantastic.' If nothing else nuclear weapons testing would bring man to 'the conclusion that absolute pacifism is the only answer. . . . We live in a world of hate and we can only oppose it by going to the opposite extreme.' "[21]

In the PAX column Ludlow also wrote an occasional report on Catholic conscientious objectors. Once, he thought it necessary to make clear that Catholic Worker COs had nothing to do with Coughlinite COs. In his opinion all Coughlinite COs were anti-Semitic; thus, they were not true pacifists. This return to the past as a source of keeping the issue of pacifism alive during the post-World War II period was also apparent in April 1948, when the paper reprinted the full text of John Hugo's "The Immorality of Conscription." Seventy-five thousand additional copies were printed for handout distribution. This was one of the Catholic Worker's ways of combating the increasing talk in America of establishing universal military training.

Ludlow's contribution to peace after World War II was in promulgating the intellectual and theoretical rationale for a Catholic pacifism that included nonviolence; he combined this with an optimistic view of the moral and political value of such witness. Day herself called him "doctrinaire and dogmatic, and yet the mildest of mortals, meek and disciplined in his personal life."[22]

During the Korean War, the more moderate pacifist groups disbanded or changed their emphasis, the radical groups met much public hostility, and the *Catholic Worker* was more subdued in its antiwar writings than during World War II. In the first issue of the *Catholic Worker* following the invasion of South Korea by the North Koreans, Dorothy Day reiterated her position against all war. "It is heartbreaking once again to see casualty lists in the *New York Times*," she wrote. "We believe that not only atomic weapons must be outlawed, but all war, and that the social order must be restored in Christ."[23] Day focused on the centrality of love in resolving the conflict and not on the actions of the U. S. government. She also talked about the poor whom she identified not only as American soldiers fighting in subzero weather in Korea, but also the Koreans who were the victims of bullets and bombs. During the war the paper constantly featured articles condemning the immorality of conscription, but there was also a warning to objectors not to oppose war "with pride, with condemnation of others, with bitterness."[24] And during the entire Korean War, only one occurrence of direct, protesting action was reported. The one event was when Ammon Hennacy picketed the Phoenix Tax Office to oppose President Truman's declaration of a state of emergency.[25] The Catholic Worker had clearly reached an all-time low in peace activity.

Though the writing in the *Catholic Worker* was more moderate during the Korean War, the pacifist spirit of the Worker remained strong. When Michael Harrington joined the Catholic Worker movement in 1951, he contended that it affected him so that it almost led him to prison as a conscientious objector. His refusal to attend rifle practice as a volunteer for the Army Medical Reserves resulted in several crises with military authorities. Harrington wrote: "What maintained and stiffened my will was that almost primitive Christian sense of mission that pervaded the Worker."[26] There were Catholic COs during the Korean War but their numbers are unknown because the classification forms used did not provide for a religious affiliation category. There were also no CPS camps during the Korean War. From the pages of the *Catholic Worker*, it is known that Catholic conscientious objection to the war was advocated, but how many Catholic COs were assisted by the Worker is unknown.

The impact of the early Cold War period upon the Catholic peace movement was great, but nevertheless, Day and Ludlow kept writing. Day wrote frequently to counteract the increase of anti-communist sentiment. Along with Robert Ludlow and Irene Naughton at the *Catholic Worker*, Day published a statement on anti-Communism:

> Although we disagree with our Marxist brothers on the question of the means to use to achieve social justice, rejecting atheism and materialism in Marxist thought, we respect their freedom as a minority group in this country. . . . We protest the imprisonment of our Communist brothers and extend our sympathy and admiration for having followed their conscience even in persecution.[27]

During this period the *Catholic Worker* opposed the anti-communist Smith and McCarran acts and reacted with horror to the trial of Julius and Ethel Rosenberg and co-defendant Morton Sobell. The writings reflected an attempt to stop the mounting anti-communism among

Catholics. In June 1953, as the Rosenbergs were awaiting their execution, a despondent Ludlow revealed these concerns:

> It is not a just age we live in. It is an age where guilt by association is fast becoming the accepted method of judging. . . . And our patriotic Catholics and our wretched publications do not see this as the leaders of the Church in France did not see it before the Revolution and as the leaders in Spain did not see it. And when they do see it (of course they never really do) then they will envision themselves as the innocent victims of devils. . . . May all Catholics, in union with the Supreme Pontiff who has already asked that clemency be granted the Rosenbergs, send one last plea that these lives be spared.[28]

Many supporters of the anti-communist crusade in America had taken issue with the *Catholic Worker*'s willingness to defend Communists as "our brothers," and to join with them in opposition to certain aspects of capitalism. Senator McCarthy himself took notice of the *Catholic Worker* and his proclamations put some pressure on the movement. "McCarthyites hinted darkly of the paper's communist ties and nicknamed Dorothy Day 'Moscow Mary,' as some reactionaries still call her."[29] FBI agents were sent to interrogate Day and Monsignor Edward R. Gaffney at the chancery in New York City, questioned her about the paper's use of the word "Catholic" in its title.[30] Because of their daily performance of corporal works of mercy to the poor in the name of Catholicism, the Catholic Worker movement was left relatively untroubled by the witch hunt.

By the mid-1950s even liberal Catholics began voicing concern about the mounting anti-communism. John Courtney Murray, wondered whether "we prove our Americanism and our Catholicism simply by being vociferously anti-Communist." He seriously questioned whether Americans were "spiritually and intellectually equipped to meet the communist threat at its deepest level." He called the engagement with Communism on the domestic scene a "basic fiasco."[31] Murray avoided the public debate on communism. His primary concern as a theologian was "to establish the compatibility of American pluralism and Catholicism in the eyes of both the Roman Catholic church and of the American people. Murray's chief legacy to American Catholics was his demonstration that it is possible to be both an

American and a Catholic without being disloyal to either."[32] This Catholic Americanism, more than anti-communism best characterizes the desires and aspirations of the "realist" school of theologians during the Cold War period.

Beginning in the late 1950s, a renaissance of the American peace movement occurred when attention was focused upon thermonuclear weapons. The immediate cause of this was the atmospheric testing of the hydrogen bomb. Despite the sudden commotion at the bombing of Hiroshima and Nagasaki, the American people had never truly appreciated the possibility of wholesale slaughter until the Soviet Union detonated a series of hydrogen bombs during the middle and late 1950s. Although the Soviet breakthrough in thermonuclear weaponry spurred an acceleration of the American "defense effort," it also cut the other way. Prominent political and military leaders now began to talk about the impossibility of victory in a war that rendered survival unlikely.[33]

Catholic concern for peace in face of thermonuclear warfare arose once again from CAIP and the Catholic Worker. CAIP showed its concern mainly through the tactic of lobbying in the United Nations to establish a criteria for the use of nuclear weapons. CAIP, however, refused to embrace nuclear pacifism. Again, Murray's influence on CAIP cannot be underestimated. He provided the justification for CAIP's position on nuclear issues through the just war doctrine by asserting that "the use of nuclear force must be limited, the principle of limitation being the exigencies of legitimate defense against injustice. Thus the terms of public debate are set in two words, 'limited war.' All other terms of argument are fanciful or fallacious."[34] He believed that to say "limited war" could not be created by intelligence, energy, and under the direction of moral imperative was to succumb to some sort of determinism in human affairs.

Murray also countered Catholic opinion that the just war was irrelevant in relation to modern warfare. In his most noted article, "Morality and Modern War," first published in 1958, Murray provided what would become the standard explanation of the relevance of the just war doctrine. He contended that objections are raised not against the doctrine itself but about the usefulness of the doctrine, "its relevance to the concrete actualities of our historical moment."[35] He contended that these questions arise because the doctrine had for so long not been used even by Catholics. And that the indictment should not be placed on the doctrine but on everyone who failed to make the tradition relevant. He argued that the just war tradition is the solvent for the dangerous type of thinking which dichotomizes two extreme positions, "a soft sentimental pacifism and a cynical hard realism." The second false dilemma that the doctrine resolves is the desperate alternative of either universal atomic death or complete surrender to communism, a dilemma which denies moral reason and submits to technological or historical determinism. Murray believed that the strength of the traditional doctrine "is a will to peace, which, in the extremity, bears within itself a will to enforce the precept of peace by arms. But this will to arms is a moral will; for it is identically a will to justice."[36] Thus he rejected the notion that the big problem is to "abolish war" or "ban the bomb." For Murray, the just war tradition's value is that it serves as a standard of casuistry on various kinds of war and has the capacity to set the right terms for rational debate on public policies bearing on the problem of war and peace in today's world of international conflict and advanced technology. Murray believed that the church's just war doctrine still fulfilled its triple function: "to condemn war as evil, to limit the evils it entails, and to humanize its conduct as far as possible."[37] His writing encouraged other Catholics who viewed themselves as "realists" to continue to write about nuclear issues from the basis of the just war doctrine.

In 1955, Monsignor George Higgins was appointed head of the Department of Social Action in the NCWC and automatically became executive secretary of CAIP. Higgins, like Ryan and McGowan, was mainly concerned with the problems of labor[38] and had very little grasp of international affairs.[39] The program of CAIP immediately after World War II changed little under his direction: It continued to play an indirect role in public policy formation by functioning as a Catholic lobbyist group and as an invited observer at the United Nations and the State Department. The committee system still served as the core unit of the association and publication of policy statements, pamphlet reports, and a monthly newsletter, CAIP News, served as the chief means of carrying out the program. Under the directorship of Higgins, CAIP became almost undistinguishable from NCWC. The aim of CAIP, as always, was to make known to its Catholic constituency the "official" position of the Catholic church on the issues of war and peace.[40] The normative position was always the just war doctrine.

The most significant group in the CAIP from 1958 through the Second Vatican Council was the arms control subcommittee of the International Law and Juridical Institutions Committee. Key members were Edward A. Conway, S.J., member of the advisory committee to the United States Arms Control and Disarmament Agency; Alain C. Enthoven, deputy assistant secretary of defense for systems analysis; Charles M. Herzfeld, deputy director, Advanced Research Projects Agency, U.S. Department of Defense; William J. Nagle, director of external research, Department of State; John E. Moriarity, Department of State, colonel, U.S. Air Force and formerly with Weapons Systems Evaluation Group, Department of Defense; James E. Dougherty, St. Joseph's College, assistant director of the Foreign Policy Research Institute, University of Pennsylvania, and professor at the National War College in Washington (1964–65); and William V. O'Brien, professor of international law and chair of the Institute of World Policy, Georgetown University, as well as author of a number of books and articles on the legal and moral aspects of modern war, and an active reserve officer in the United States Army.[41] This committee of one priest and many active laymen in leadership positions in the government wrote CAIP statements on modern warfare and delivered lectures, sponsored symposiums, and compiled literature on the topic.

In 1960, William Nagle edited a book for the CAIP called *Morality and Modern Warfare* on the question of nuclear weapons. Nagle admits in the introduction that since the book "has the character of a pioneer effort fifteen years after Hiroshima indicates something of the failure of the Christian community to come to terms with that event." He attempted to account for the absence of nuclear pacifism and the persistence of the just war criteria in the writings of American Catholics by stating, "[The contributors to the book] are citizens of the nation that has the major responsibility for the defense of the free world. The question here is not one of patriotism but responsibility."[42]

Nagle was careful to point out the noticeable difference between his *Morality and Modern Warfare* and a book published a year earlier in Britain on the same topic. In the British book, *Morals and Missiles: Catholic Essays on the Problem of War Today*, the tone is strongly pacifist.[43] Nevertheless, Nagle concluded his introductory essay with a defense of the just war tradition by quoting the address of Bishop John J. Wright of the Diocese of Pittsburgh at the 1958 CAIP meeting.

Wright said, "It is unfortunately not yet possible for honest theologians to deny that justice may require of us duties from which charity would prefer to shrink."

Several contributors to Nagle's book were members of the arms control subcommittee of CAIP, James E. Dougherty, John E. Moriarity, and William V. O'Brien. All the contributors except for the pacifist, Gordon Zahn, a member of the Sociology Department of Loyola University of Chicago, were just war theorists who were employed by the U. S. government either in the Defense or State departments.

In 1962, CAIP and the Adult Education Centers of the Archdiocese of Chicago co-sponsored a two-day convention in Chicago on "Christian Conscience and Modern Warfare."[44] Most of the speakers were members of CAIP and contributors to Nagle's book: Nagle, Moriarity, Dougherty, and Conway. Zahn was also present to represent the pacifist viewpoint. The most significant address of the conference was delivered by Thomas C. Donahue, S.J., project director of the Center for Peace Research at Creighton University, Omaha. Donahue noted what Catholic moralists in the United States had been saying about nuclear warfare, basing much of his analysis on the scholarship of the men represented in *Morality and Modern Warfare*. He divided American Catholic views on nuclear warfare into the following seven major categories:

> The first theme is that of the theologians who have an *apocalyptic* preoccupation, seeing the most important element of our age as a race to extinction. They believe we are unable to prevent the doom that is sure to encompass us.
>
> The second approach is that of *prevention*. These moralists say we simply have to prevent a major war because it just doesn't make sense to destroy ourselves. No one can win a nuclear war, they believe.
>
> The third theme centers around the idea of *justification*. This school of thought among the moralists holds that we are unable today to justify a war under present circumstances and that the principle of justifying a defensive war is inapplicable here.
>
> Theme number four is that of *innocence*. It notes that too many innocents (noncombatants, civilians) would be killed in any kind of nuclear warfare. Indeed, one writer feels the old theory of a just war is intrinsically altered.[45]

The fifth theme stresses the idea of *public responsibility* and raises
many questions about what the government can do morally in a
situation when force is required if that force is nuclear.

Theme number six is concerned with problems of *policy*. It discusses
the morality of certain aspects of foreign policy and matters such as
the use of war as an instrument of policy.

And, finally, among the moralists who have been writing and speaking
on the Christian conscience in a nuclear world, one group lays stress
on the use of *deterrents*. Many of them seem to feel that the emphasis
on counterforce seems praiseworthy, but they realize there are grave
difficulties involved in the use of effective deterrents for if the deterrents fail to deter, mass destruction on both sides will result.[46]

Thus, in the United States, "the Catholic view" had not established
a position of consensus in 1962. Unlike Nagle, Donahue did not
defend just war theorists, rather, he pointed out that "American
Catholics are not even agreed on two or three major positions of what
moral theologians have been saying."[47] By noting the absence of any
agreement on moral criteria for nuclear warfare at the conference, he
unintentionally launched a frontal assault upon the whole Catholic
tradition of just war in relation to modern warfare.

Despite the results of the conference, the CAIP continued to hold
firm to the normative position of the just war criteria. The next year, in
1963, CAIP and Chicago's Adult Education Centers again cospon-
sored a conference on "Peace and World Order" with emphases on
*Pacem in Terris*, the peace encyclical written by Pope John XXIII, the
role of the United Nations, and the moral and political implications of
the Cold War. Within such a context, the just war criteria remained
the underlying presupposition.

By the time of the Second Vatican Council there was no doubt that
CAIP held as strongly as ever to the just war doctrine. Neither World
War II nor the possibility of nuclear warfare had raised any serious
doubts as to the validity of this normative position within the Catholic
concern for peace. The small liberal membership of the association,
with their key positions in the church, in universities, the State Department, the Defense Department, and the military, believed that they
had done much to apply Catholic moral teaching to public-policy
issues and the just war had served them well. CAIP members believed
that they could look back on the period after World War II and point to

the many accomplishments of which they had been a part: the United Nations as the first international organization chartered to promote world peace and understanding, the nonadmittance of the People's Republic of China into the United Nations, and the Korean War, which had prevented the extension of communism. Above all CAIP believed it had established a just criteria that limited the possibilities of a nuclear war. CAIP's efforts for peace, however, continued its tradition of nonidentification with the American peace movement.

A revival of the peace movement occurred in the late 1950s. The immediate initiator was the atmospheric testing of the hydrogen bomb with the health hazards attached to nuclear "fallout." Around this issue the National Committee for a Sane Nuclear Policy developed. In 1957, they ran their first ad in the November 15 issue of the *New York Times*. The group was open to pacifists and non-pacifists alike. By 1958, the group had 120 chapters representing approximately 25,000 Americans.[48]

The onset of the nuclear-testing issue also caused a renaissance among the radical pacifists. In June 1957, a small group of pacifists committed to nonviolent resistance organized an ad hoc committee, Non-Violent Action against Nuclear Weapons, which reorganized in 1958 as the Committee for Non-Violent Action (CNVA). Perhaps the most successful project of CNVA was the 1958 voyage of the protest vessel *Golden Rule* into a bomb-test area.[49] CNVA also sponsored other actions and became most noted for its peace walks throughout the world.

The revival of the Catholic Worker movement's peace witness during the 1950s can be attributed to Ammon Hennacy, an American radical from the Midwest. He began his "one-man revolution" in 1950 just when most peace action was receding into oblivion. His motivation came from his own vision, the object of his crusade was the state, and his aim was to live apart from any aspect of an institutional life that contributed to the power of the state to do harm to people. He had refused to serve in World War I because as a socialist he would have nothing to do with a capitalist war. In World War II he was a Christian anarchist and would not serve the government.[50]

Hennacy also wrote his autobiography, *The Book of Ammon*,[51] and subtitled it, *The Autobiography of an Unique American Rebel*. Dorothy

Day is quoted on the back of the book jacket as stating that "The story of his prison days will rank with the great writings of the world about prisons." The rationale for his "one-man revolution" is also proclaimed in the book.

The reason that Hennacy's "one-man revolution" merged with the Catholic Worker movement was not because of any deep reflection, but because he admired Dorothy Day and got what he called a "crush" on her.[52] "Ammon had thoughts that perhaps he and Dorothy would marry which annoyed Dorothy. She resented Ammon's suggestions to third parties that something might develop between them, and she let him know it."[53] It was because of her that Hennacy gave seven years of his life to the Catholic Worker and was baptized a Catholic, but it must be pointed out that much of his thought was consistent with the movement and his personal journey paralleled that of Day's. Since the 1950s were the low point of peace activities in America, Hennacy may also have been searching for a community that would provide support and access to the American public.

Like Day, Hennacy had grown up in the Midwest, made radical friends at college, and dropped out before graduating. He was born into a Baptist family in Negley, Ohio, on 24 July 1893. Politics were a central part of his home environment because his father held local elective office as a Democrat in a Republican area. At sixteen, Hennacy joined both the Socialist party and the Industrial Workers of the World. He went off to college in 1913 and attended three different schools over the next three years. At each campus he organized activities on behalf of the Socialist party. He was not yet a pacifist and even took military drill on campus. He left college to provide financial assistance at home for his seven brothers and sisters.[54]

Like Day, Hennacy viewed World War I as an imperialist war. As chair of the local Socialist party chapter, he spearheaded an antiwar and anticonscription campaign. He also refused to register for the draft. He was arrested and stood trial for his leadership role in an antiwar rally and was sentenced to two years in the Atlanta Federal Penitentiary. Still he refused to register for the draft, and an additional nine months in the county jail was added to his term. Midway through his prison term he had his first conversion experience. He wrote of this experience in his prison account:

I had passed through the idea of killing myself. This was an escape, not any solution to life. The remainder of my two years in solitary must result in a clear-cut plan whereby I could go forth and be a force in the world. I could not take any halfway measures. . . . I read Jesus who was confronted with a whole world empire of tyranny and chose not to overturn the tyrant and make Himself king, but to change the hatred in the hearts of people to love and understanding —to overcome evil with good will. . . . Gradually I came to gain a glimpse of what Jesus meant when He said, "The Kingdom of God is Within You."[55]

Upon his release from prison, Hennacy described himself as a "nonchurch Christian." He was met at the gate and immediately arrested for refusing to register for the second draft while in prison. He spent another seven weeks in prison awaiting trial. This time he had a copy of Tolstoy's *The Kingdom of God is Within You*, which led him to believe that bullets and ballots were useless, exchanging one system of power and coercion for another. Hennacy had fully embraced anarchism but brought to it a Christian dimension rooted in himself and his individual relationship with God. Day's religious vision on the other hand saw the church as mediator between time and eternity and the place where the redemption of community occurred. Though Hennacy's life was modeled on Jesus and the Sermon on the Mount, he was individualistic and political in the expression of his belief and rejected all institutions, including an institutional church.

According to his most recent biographer, Patrick Coy, "Hennacy crusaded for one great human value, freedom. At the end of freedom's rainbow was the classical anarchist paradise, where oppression, injustice, and institutional violence were done away with, where no state or church chould divide people and plant seeds of discontent and oppression."[56] Yet, like Day's personalism, the bases for Hennacy's belief were personal responsibility and a heart full of compassion that did not participate in government nor depend on it to correct social injustice. He also embraced poverty and led a life of hard physical labor mainly to avert cooperation with evil institutions so as to remain true to his vision. This quest for personal purity led Hennacy by 1942 to separation from his wife Selma and their two daughters.

World War II led Hennacy to again refuse to register for the draft; at this time he was forty-six years of age and this probably was the reason he was not prosecuted. He notified the government of his refusal and also published in the May 1942 issue of the *Catholic Worker* his statement of refusal to register for the draft. In 1943, he refused to pay income taxes and contended that the position of Dorothy Day and the Catholic Worker had led him to the belief that to pay taxes was un-Christian.

Coy contends that "Hennacy's anarchism and pacifism were two sides of the same coin."[57] His pacifism had always been active and when he studied Gandhian nonviolence it resonated with his personal experience. This led Hennacy to set himself up as the perfect radical and explains his use of the phrase, "one-man revolution." It also accounts for his harsh and critical attitude toward other peace activists and their organizations. Karl Meyer, a Chicago Catholic Worker said, "Ammon was impatient with meetings and seldom went to them. . . . He was unlike Gandhi and A. J. Muste who both made political compromises to build coalitions. . . . He didn't want to be limited. . . . He was not able to work in cooperation or coalition with other people."[58]

Hennacy believed warfare and militarism were the greatest threat to humanity and that pacifists should refuse absolutely in matters of the draft, taxes, and loyalty oaths to the government. The fact that Day's beliefs on these issues were the same as Hennacy's was another reason that he joined the Catholic Worker. In 1952, he moved to the New York Worker House and was baptized a Catholic. His official membership in Catholicism would last fifteen years (1952–1967).

Hennacy was unable to forgive the church for what he perceived as its marriage to corruption and tyranny. His anarchism led him to develop the notion "that it was up to him to show the world—both secular and religious—that one could be a Christian AND an anarchist, indeed, that that was the only way to keep alive the ideals of the Sermon on the Mount."[59] In fact, he began to use the term, "Catholic anarchism" in the *Catholic Worker*, and wrote an unpublished 150,000-word manuscript on the subject. The implication of the term "Catholic anarchism" led Robert Ludlow to disavow its use in the *Catholic Worker*. Because of a personality conflict with Hennacy, Ludlow eventually left the Catholic Worker movement. "The story around the Worker at the time was that Tom Sullivan wanted Bob Ludlow to move out, and that he invited Ammon to come to Chrystie Street knowing that Bob and Ammon would clash, compete for the attentions of the same coterie, argue over personalism and anarchism and that Bob would give up the battle. So it was."[60]

Hennacy argued that "Catholic anarchism" was a valid term even given the hierarchical/clerical nature of Catholicism because the church was not the clergy or the hierarchical structure:

> The REAL Church consists of the Mystical Body of Christ in those who grasp the meaning of the Sermon on the Mount and who do not seek to change the world by ballots or bullets, but by changing themselves daily in that daily communion which the Catholic Church furnishes them. . . . The Catholic Church does offer in daily mass a method of spiritual growth and a world view of brotherhood entirely compatible in method and in ideal to the anarchist dream which envisions a world made different not by wholesale pushing around of crowds but by the individual revolution within the heart of each individual.[61]

With such writing, Hennacy seems very close to Day in her belief in the church, but even Day could not root out Hennacy's anticlericalism and anti-institutionalism. In the end, Hennacy saw his conversion to Catholicism as something of a mistake.

It must be pointed out that within the Catholic Worker movement Hennacy found individuals who shared many of his same concerns. Though the vision of Peter Maurin dominated the movement, it had always been open to the visions of others. Gandhian nonviolence had long been a matter of concern with the Catholic Worker and the movement had always advocated and practiced fasting, picketing, and leafleting as means to correct the evils of social injustice. It had resisted payment of taxes from its inception and had also advocated resistance to conscription. What Hennacy brought to the Worker was the breezy self-confidence of a fighter who possessed a self-discipline and bravery that made him appear invincible. With these personal characteristics he led the Catholic Worker movement into a new level of pacifist activism that was labeled nonviolent resistance. His emphasis was on civil disobedience. The tactic called for the conscientious violation of an unjust law in response to obedience to a higher law that would challenge the public policy of the government and at the same time provide a moral witness to truth. Thus, he integrated both the theory and practice of nonviolence into the existing pacifist witness of the Catholic Worker and led it to a new level of peacemaking.

Hennacy had begun practicing civil disobedience in 1950 in Phoenix, Arizona, where he fasted and picketed the Tax Office for five days to protest tax money being spent on bombs and troops in Korea and in penance for the dropping of the bomb on Hiroshima.[62] He continued to perform this action annually, adding an additional day for each year since the tragedy had occurred. In 1954, he experimented with a variation of this action, which led the Catholic Worker movement into the most widely publicized act of civil disobedience to have occurred in the United States. The focus of the resistance was New York City's air raid drill, participation in which was required by the Civil Defense Act.

In 1954, Ammon Hennacy, Dorothy Day, and a few other Catholic Workers refused to take shelter during the drill. On 15 June 1955, Hennacy, Day, and five Catholic Workers were joined by twenty-three others, mainly members of the WRL and FOR. The following year they repeated their performance and were sentenced to five days in jail. Every year thereafter, a dozen or more practitioners of nonviolent resistance appeared, committed civil disobedience, and served prison sentences for it. A. J. Muste, America's most acclaimed peace activist, expressed their attitude when he told the director of Civil Defense in New York that, "Civil defense, after all, is an integral part of the total preparation for nuclear war. We, on the other hand, are convinced that the only way to a secure defense is for people to refuse to participate in any way in the preparations for war."[63] In response to an article in the *Village Voice* and a letter in the *New York Post*, several newcomers arrived to take part in the 1959 demonstration. When they suggested broadening the 1960 demonstration, the regulars, mostly CNVA members, agreed and organized the Civil Defense Protest Committee to spread the word.

On 3 May 1960, approximately two thousand students and adults throughout New York City resisted the yearly drill.[64] Ten minutes before the sirens were scheduled to blow, about five hundred persons assembled in Central Park, with many more arriving all the time. Among those present were writers Nat Hentoff, Dwight Macdonald, Norman Mailer, and Kay Boyle. It was the largest direct action demonstration against nuclear warfare, and was covered by radio and television as well as the *Village Voice, Nation, Commonweal, New York World*, and the *New York Post*. This demonstration marked the new strategy the American peace movement would use in the 1960s. The tactic of calling together massive numbers of individuals to commit civil disobedience to change the public policy of the U. S. government was a form of nonviolent resistance already being successfully used by the civil rights movement.

The air raid drill demonstration also marked a new spirit of cooperation among Catholics with other peace groups in the United States. The Catholic Worker, Peacemakers, WRL, FOR, and CNVA all practiced the more radical response of nonviolent resistance. These groups also joined with the National Committee for a Sane Nuclear Policy (SANE) in advocating unilateral disarmament.[65] Karl Meyer, a tax resister and member of the Catholic Worker in Chicago, joined the San Francisco to Moscow Walk for Peace sponsored by the CNVA. Dorothy Day helped to lay the plans for the CNVA Polaris action, a Gandhian assault on submarines bearing nuclear-tipped missiles stationed in the town of New London, Connecticut. Ammon Hennacy, Karl Meyer, and Tom Cornell were the only Catholic participants in the project. Cornell contended that "Ammon's involvement made it easier to line up the CW with that kind of experimental nonviolent action early in the game."[66] Catholic Workers also participated in the first General Strike for Peace begun in January 1962, and in many sit-ins and vigils held at the Atomic Energy Commission's office in New York. Fallout shelters were also picketed.[67] Nuclear warfare was the focus of all of these actions: It was not until after the election of President Johnson in 1964 and the escalation of the war in Vietnam that the focus of the peace movement's efforts shifted away from nuclear warfare to the draft.

During these years with the Catholic Worker, Ammon Hennacy had not limited his activity to New York City. He often took his anniversary Hiroshima demonstration to various parts of the United States. In 1957, he went to Las Vegas because the Atomic Energy Commission was conducting a series of nuclear tests near there; in 1958, he was in the nation's capital; and in 1959, he took his "one-man revolution" to Florida to protest another government installation. One of the last episodes in the confrontation that Hennacy had with the federal government in his role as a member of the Catholic Worker was going "over the fence," as he called it, at an Omaha missile base.

This act of going "over the fence" had cost other pacifists six months in jail; one of them had been a Catholic Worker from Chicago, Karl Meyer. He had participated in this act because the construction of missile sites and the continued testing of atom bombs had struck him as a hideous madness that required the most desperate resistance. Hennacy, very attracted to the action, wanted to perform it himself and was also given six months for his act of civil disobedience, which he served in Sandstone, Minnesota's federal penitentiary. He left Sandstone in January 1960.

On 2 January 1961, Hennacy left the Catholic Worker to make his home in Salt Lake City, where he remained until his death on 14 January 1979. However, he did not desert his work. He continued as usual to write his column for the *Catholic Worker*, calling it "Joe Hill House," the name of his own House of Hospitality. The name honored the IWW songwriter who was executed in the state of Utah in 1915.[68]

Though Ammon Hennacy did not leave a lasting impression on the Roman Catholic church in the United States, he did leave his mark on the Catholic Worker movement. By his undaunted actions, he had introduced to the movement the way of nonviolent resistance. Ludlow had said that Gandhian nonviolence and Catholic Worker pacifism were compatible, but Hennacy had demonstrated how to join the two together and how to apply these nonviolent tactics to the issue of peace in America. Thus, practitioners of nonviolence were not left waiting for the state to apply moral principles to nuclear issues, but were able to be the initiators of change in public policy. They were no longer just pacifists saying no to war; they were positing actions for peace. They considered themselves peacemakers.

The radical pacifists in the American peace movement had already begun to perform such actions immediately after World War II. Catholic Workers would begin to collaborate with them as never before after the peace movement's revival in 1957. However, Day envisioned the Catholic Worker movement as much broader than the peace movement. Concern for the poor and oppressed remained a priority as well as did the issues of civil rights and labor. The issues of justice and peace were inseparable. Nonviolent tactics could be used not only to bring the Gospel message to war-and-peace issues but to all areas of social injustice. Day would remain faithful to Maurin's broad vision, but also would incorporate Hennacy's vision into the Catholic Worker. She best described the difference between Ammon Hennacy and Peter Maurin when she wrote, "Ammon is deep and narrow, but Peter was so broad that he took in all the life of man, body, soul and mind."[69]

By the early 1960s, it became clear to many Catholic Workers that the peace issue was of such significance that a Catholic group solely dedicated to peace should be formed. One idea was to reactivate PAX; the other possiblity was to form a Catholic Peace Fellowship (CPF) under the auspices of FOR. The CPF idea was rejected because of the old Catholic suspicion of Protestants. As one *Catholic Worker* editor put it at the time, "All they want to do is use you."[70] Though a high level of cooperation had been achieved among peace groups during the late 1950s, Catholic Workers wanted to maintain their own identity. Self-consciously Catholic, yet critical of the existing militaristic and capitalistic American system, they were ever mindful of the encroachments of other groups, even of other Catholic groups. Stressing autonomy, the idea of reactivating PAX was adopted.

Eileen Egan, a life-long Catholic Worker and close friend of Dorothy Day, was mainly responsible for the organization. She held an executive position in Catholic Relief Services and had also written the book *The Works of Peace*. PAX was affiliated in England with PAX, whose most prominent member was Archbishop Thomas D. Roberts. The archbishop stressed the need for autonomy and told the group to be sure to keep PAX totally free of hierarchical control, especially financially. He pointed to CAIP as an example of what happens if autonomy is not maintained.[71] Sponsors of America PAX included: Thomas Merton, Edward Rice, Marion Casey, Gordon Zahn, Robert Hovda, Dorothy Day, Robert McDole, Anne Taillefer, Robert Fox, Helen Iswolsky, Rosemary Sheed, Dorothy Dohen, and Arthur Sheehan.

Because of financial difficulties, PAX grew slowly, but it succeeded in issuing a valuable quarterly magazine, *Peace*, begun in 1963 under the editorship of Eileen Egan. PAX also observed an annual peace Mass in commemoration of Hiroshima and sponsored an annual conference at the Catholic Worker farm in Tivoli, New York, as well as conducted monthly meetings in a room above the Paraclete Bookstore in Manhattan.

Founders of PAX proclaimed no official position though they themselves were pacifists. Emphasis on the individual as the one who applies the tradition and teaching of the church on issues of war and peace pervaded all of their statements. Ironically, PAX devoted most of its energies not to individuals directly, but to lobbying for peace within the institutional church.

The main reason for PAX's emphasis on the institutional church was that in the same year of its founding, 1962, more than 2,400 bishops from every continent in the world had assembled in Rome for the solemn opening of the Second Vatican Council. Three years previously, 25 January 1959, Pope John XXIII had announced that he would convene the Council. The proposed agenda for the meeting touched on many issues confronting the church in the latter half of the twentieth century, including the issue of peace. This topic came up for debate in 1964 when the council fathers were composing what was ultimately to be one of the council's more significant documents, *The Pastoral Constitution on the Church in the Modern World*. The drafts, proposals, amendments, and debates on the issue of peace centered on Schema 13 of the document during the third and fourth sessions of the council held in 1964 and 1965.

Prior to convening the Second Vatican Council, Pope John XXIII had issued his world renowned encyclical on peace, *Pacem in Terris*, on 11 April 1963. This encyclical was to set the tone for discussion at the council. In it Pope John, like Benedict XV, moved in a pacifist direction and repudiated nuclear war in the modern world, stating that "in an age such as ours which prides itself on its atomic energy it is contrary to reason to hold that war is now a suitable way to restore rights which have been violated."[72] In this statement, John XXIII condemned not just nuclear war but all war in the nuclear age. By repudiating the suitability of war as a means of restoring violated rights he implicitly rejected the theory of the just war. *Pacem in Terris* heralded a new approach to warfare and a revolution in the meaning of Catholic peacemaking.

The reason for this shift in thought can be attributed to Pope John's humanist approach. He built his arguments in the encyclical on the principles of the freedom of the individual and the validity of natural law. John XXIII believed that truth, solidarity, and justice undergirded a universe held together in the harmony and order of peace, and this order was not imposed from above but one that sprung forth from each individual.[73] Each individual was called forth to "observe, judge, act" because it was the individual acting for the common good that would bring forth peace. In *Pacem in Terris* he provided a clear statement of which rights were necessary to preserve the human dignity of each person in society, and he chose to stand with the rights of individual conscience, even over and against the rights of political authority. The pope made clear the priority of the individual conscience and the duty to obey God above human beings.

Consequently, when discussing the authority of the state, Pope John said that "civil authority must appeal primarily to the conscience of individual citizens, that is to each one's duty to collaborate readily for the common good of all."[74] Thus, in *Pacem in Terris* the primacy of the individual right and duty to work for peace is what ultimately informs and judges the actions of governments and organizations.

John XXIII explicitly expressed a hatred of nationalism, repudiated force because it violated the dignity of the person, condemned the arms race and the balance of terror on which the arms race rested, and rejected fear in favor of mutual trust. An emphasis on nonviolence in his writing transcended the old moral categories of the just war and pacifism. Moreover, *Pacem in Terris* called for structural reform of the international political and legal system to deal with the world's problems.

It is important to note that there is no explicit endorsement in this encyclical of the right of self-defense for peoples and for states. Later official documents of the Roman Catholic church, however, continued to assert the right of legitimate defense for states and often made no attempt to reinterpret *Pacem in Terris*. Thus, the door was wide open on the issue of peace when the council convened.

At the Second Vatican Council the positions of the just war and pacifism collided. By 1964 the Cold War, the possibility of a nuclear holocaust, and the pope's encyclical on peace had suggested to a number of bishops throughout the world that a just war was no longer possible.

Thomas Merton, a Trappist monk in Gethsemani, Kentucky, sent an Open Letter to the hierarchy at the Second Vatican Council in 1964.[75] The letter focused on two aspects that he considered to be crucial to the issue of peace in the nuclear age. According to Merton, the moral problems involved in the use of nuclear weapons and the right of a Catholic to be a conscientious objector to war had to be faced by the bishops gathered in Rome. He believed that the writings of Popes Pius XII and John XXIII had already implicitly condemned nuclear weapons and affirmed individual conscience.[76] In his opinion, it was up to the council to make these points explicit. Significantly, Merton's letter pinpointed the two main areas of debate that would emerge at the council.

The first draft of Schema 13 presented at the third session of the council condemned total war, and the condemnation was accepted without debate. The draft, however, also contained a similar condemnation of the use of nuclear weapons, on which point debate flourished.[77] In order to understand what part the American peace groups had in determining the final statements of Vatican II on the issues of war and peace, it is necessary to clarify their different approaches.

In 1963, Harry W. Flannery, president of CAIP, worked closely with CAIP's subcommittee on arms control. Flannery, a firm believer in the just war, urged the members of the subcommittee to prepare a statement to be sent to the bishops at Vatican II. In a letter to a CAIP member concerning nuclear warfare, Flannery said,

> No subject is of more importance today, as you well know, and I am pleased to hear that you are planning to try to get something out to the Council. The European pacifist influence in Rome may need to be offset. Here, too, we need to speak out because of the formation of PAX. Like all extremists, they may have most persistent, devoted and possibly persuasive adherents.[78]

Six active Catholic laymen, Alain C. Enthoven, Charles M. Herzfeld, William J. Nagle, John E. Moriarity, James E. Dougherty, and William V. O'Brien, all members of the subcommittee on arms control of the International Law and Juridical Order Committee of CAIP, prepared a critique of the nuclear war passages in the schema.

The critique was not a formal CAIP statement since the committee believed that there was not time nor need for it to go through the necessary procedures. On 5 August 1964, a copy was sent to Bishop John J. Wright of the Diocese of Pittsburgh. Catholic pacifist lobbyists at the council referred to it as the "secret memorandum." Essentially, the statement declared "the right to have recourse to war in extreme cases is justified by the present defective state of international society, law, and organization."[79] The just war ethic pervaded the entire statement.

Because of CAIP's close relationship with and, by the 1960s, its total financial dependency on NCWC, it is clear that the CAIP statement on nuclear war did not basically conflict with the beliefs of the American hierarchy. Members of CAIP saw no need to go to Rome to lobby for acceptance of their critique of Schema 13. William V. O'Brien in a memorandum, "Morality, Nuclear War, and the Schema on the Church in the Modern World," written in October 1964, perceptively gave the reasons why the Council could not condemn nuclear warfare and would therefore accept the recommendations submitted by CAIP.[80] His main reason was not the threat of Communism but the age-old form of nationalism peculiar to American Catholics known as "Americanism"—if Catholics did not obey their lawfully elected leaders they would be considered disloyal Americans.[81] O'Brien writes, "if the Council were to adopt such a schema [the condemnation of nuclear weapons], it would place close to fifty million American Catholics in an awesome dilemma as to whether to listen to the solemn findings of a Vatican Council or to the hitherto accepted assurances of their government that America's nuclear deterrent is the foundation for international stability and the sine qua non of the defense of the United States."[82] Thus, the only action taken by CAIP in reference to the Second Vatican Council was to prepare and send to Rome a critique of the nuclear war passages in Schema 13.

The pacifist branch of the American Catholic peace movement, however, took a more direct approach. In 1964, some members of the Catholic Worker and PAX went to Rome in hopes of encouraging the council fathers to condemn nuclear weapons and affirm the right of conscientious objection. There were two types of peace witness offered by these American Catholics at the council. The first type consisted of a group of women headed by Dorothy Day who fasted and prayed and discussed the issues with the members of the hierarchy.[83] This type of witness was intensely personal and spiritual. The other type of witness consisted of three members of PAX who self-consciously performed the tasks of a political lobby. Eileen Egan, Gordon Zahn, and James Douglass,[84] a young lay theologian and close friend of Thomas Merton, were tireless in their efforts to produce a positive statement in condemnation of nuclear warfare. They worked simultaneously on two issues in Schema 13, the condemnation of nuclear weapons and the affirmation of conscientious objection.

James Douglass's work on these two issues accounts for the major American contribution to the final statements at Vatican II. Douglass was both a theologian and a lobbyist who worked hard at locating members of the hierarchy throughout the world that were already sympathetic to these two positions. He had done his homework as a theologian and had well-drafted arguments for the positions. On the issue of nuclear warfare he attempted to show the hierarchy exactly how to condemn it within their own traditional framework of the just war ethic. Douglass, greatly influenced by Merton, believed that the just war categories were inadequate in face of the present world crisis, yet he attempted to use the theory with which the council fathers were most familiar. At the same time, Douglass also tried to move them toward a new ethic of peace based on the Gospel, the rights of personhood, and nonviolence.

It is important to note that the inclusion of the subject of nonviolence in the *Pastoral Constitution on the Church in the Modern World* was the result of the tireless lobbying at the council of Jean and Hildegard Goss-Mayr of the International Fellowship of Reconciliation.[85] The document mentions the use of nonviolence as an alternative to war: "We cannot fail to praise those who renounce the use of violence in the vindication of their rights and who resort to methods of defense which are otherwise available to weaker parties too, provided this can be done without injury to the rights and duties of others or of the community itself."[86] The American Catholic peace lobbyists Douglass and Zahn, and Merton who prepared statements for them, would all write books on nonviolence after the Second Vatican Council. Day, of course, had not assumed the role of lobbyist.

At the end of the third session, Bishop John Taylor, the American bishop of Stockholm, Sweden[87] submitted an intervention on Schema 13 that Douglass had prepared.[88] Taylor's statement began with a reference to Merton:

> Thomas Merton, one of the most profound mystical theologians of our times, has written that total nuclear war would be a sin of mankind equal only to the crucifixion of Christ. Modern means of war threaten the very existence of man. Moreover, the Council has a sacred duty to

respond with all its moral power to this threat of mankind's self-destruction.[89]

The intervention changed the technical term "uncontrollability" to the moral term "indiscriminant" based on the rights of non-combatants, supported conscientious objection, and pleaded for nonviolence. Copies of Bishop Taylor's statement were also distributed by the peace lobby to twenty-five council fathers, some of whom used sections of it for their own interventions.

During the third session, the text of Schema 13 was revised and again presented to the council for discussion in its fourth session in 1965. In article 98, "Modern warfare, and in particular so-called 'total' war," the term "indiscriminant" was used rather than "controllability." This was a definite achievement for the peace lobby. Philip Hannan, the auxiliary bishop of Washington, D.C., however, challenged Schema 13's revised text, with the support of nine bishops, three of whom were also Americans—Francis Cardinal Spellman of New York, Bishop Patrick O'Boyle of Washington, D.C., and Lawrence Cardinal Shehan of Baltimore.[90] The challenge claimed that total war had never been condemned in such a manner by "recent popes," as the final draft of the Schema stated. Bishop Hannan also wanted to keep the term "controllability." The Council voted against the challenge and accepted the revision. Article 98 in its final form reads as follows:

> All these considerations compel us to undertake an evaluation of war with an entirely new attitude. The men of our time must realize that they will have to give a somber reckoning of their deeds of war for the course of the future will depend greatly on the decisions they make today.
>
> With these truths in mind, this most Holy Synod makes its own the condemnations of total war already pronounced by recent popes, and issues the following declaration:
>
> Any act of war aimed indiscriminately at the destruction of entire cities or extensive areas along with their population is a crime against God and man himself. It merits unequivocal and unhesitating condemnation.[91]

The exact role of the American hierarchy in the revision of Schema 13 is not clear. After the third session, Gordon Zahn in the March

1965 issue of *Ramparts* charged that some American bishops were circulating a "secret" memorandum and trying to block the condemnation of the use of atomic weapons by the Second Vatican Council. Certainly Bishop Hannan's statements in both sessions and the circulated CAIP critique (secret or not) give some weight to Zahn's charges.

Monsignor George Higgins of CAIP, NCWC, and a council consultant, issued a NCWC news release on 22 February 1965, refuting Zahn's charges. Higgins's release first berated Zahn as a pacifist for having an "infuriating holier-than-thou attitude" and for writing an "outrageously superficial article." Higgins claimed in his article "that the American bishops, with few exceptions, have never even seen the so-called 'secret' memorandum referred to . . . and are certainly not carrying on a concentrated effort, either singularly or collectively to block condemnation."

Higgins's position is supported by several events that occurred during the fourth session. First was the absence of a CAIP lobby in Rome. Second, before Bishop Hannan spoke during the fourth session, there were efforts on the part of other members of the American hierarchy to modify his speech. At the annual NCWC meeting in Rome, Hannan had introduced the topic of nuclear warfare, but Joseph Cardinal Ritter, who was presiding, ruled him out of order and encouraged those interested to stay for discussion after the meeting. Several bishops did remain and tried to persuade Bishop Hannan to modify his position but they were unsuccessful.[92]

The last significant event that supports Higgins's argument was the intervention submitted by Joseph Cardinal Ritter at the council. During the fourth session three British prelates, Abbot Christopher Butler and Bishops Gordon Wheeler and Charles Grant, had spoken against a clause in Schema 13 that upheld nuclear weapons as a deterrent. Ritter then submitted a written intervention asking that the very possession of total-war arms be clearly condemned. Peace lobbyists conjectured that Cardinal Ritter delivered the intervention in writing rather than raising the issue on the floor because he feared provoking a scandalous opposition from some of the more nationalistic American bishops.[93]

Cardinal Ritter represented clearly a very different position from Bishop Hannan at the council. The degree of diversity among the American council fathers is unknown. The fact that there was a compromise position on the part of the bishops on the issue of deterrence illustrated that there was diversity among all council fathers. The final Constitution did not make an "absolute condemnation of the possession of arms which involve the intention or grave peril of total war," as Cardinal Ritter suggested.[94] Nor did the final Constitution affirm the possession of such arms as the more nationalistic bishops would prefer. Instead, the Constitution remained silent on the morality of deterrence since it would not pass judgment on the intention of nations in possession of nuclear weapons.

The council fathers did not transcend the just war criteria. *The Pastoral Constitution on the Church in the Modern World* proclaimed that "As long as the danger of war remains and there is no competent and sufficiently powerful authority at the international level, governments cannot be denied the right to legitimate defense once every means of peaceful settlement has been exhausted."[95] Thus, war could only be condemned if in its execution indiscriminate acts of bombing were committed either by nuclear weapons or traditional methods of warfare.[96] By not explicitly condemning both the intention and execution of modern methods of warfare, the council failed to draw explicit conclusions on deterrence and military defense. Bishop Hannan feared, as had CAIP technical experts' critique, that if the council had acted otherwise, Schema 13 would have meant a wholesale withdrawal of Catholic support from every nuclear arsenal in the world. The council did provide norms on modern warfare, but logical objection and national loyalties could still subject them to the priorities of nations.

The peace lobby was more successful in the council's explicit affirmation of the right to conscientious objection. The thrust for such a provision had come from Archbishop Roberts who spoke at both sessions.[97] After the third session Thomas Merton wrote to Archbishop George Flahiff of Winnipeg suggesting ways of strengthening the provision on conscientious objection. Merton urged that the right to be a conscientious objector had to apply to all wars, not just Vietnam, and that it should not be expressed negatively. Merton suggested that the provision in the draft be changed from "encouraging the consciences of the faithful to submit to the decision of authority in cases of doubt," to a "positive statement using the words of *Pacem in Terris*, 'Those who are morally convinced of the necessity of nonviolent conflict resolution, and who reject war as a solution which will hardly be reasonable in our time.' " He concluded his letter with a plea to get away from the idea of pacifist to the real truth of Christian resistance to evil on a nonviolent basis.[98]

The only American objection on the floor of the council to a provision on conscientious objection came from Francis Cardinal Spellman, the head of the military ordinate for the U. S. armed forces and in effect the bishop of Catholics in the services. Cardinal Spellman asked for a provision in Schema 13 which would make military service obligatory. In a speech before the assembled council fathers he said, "the responsibility for judging the necessity of drafting men for service belongs to civil authorities and individuals cannot refuse their obedience to the state."[99] It is noteworthy that Cardinal Spellman praised the rest of the revised draft on Schema 13.

The final text on conscientious objection adopted by the council clearly upheld the rights and duties of individual conscience and recommended legal provisions for those who resist military commands. The final text also dropped the negative statement that presumed the duty of a person to obey lawful authority until its injustice was clearly manifest.[100]

The peace lobbyists at the Second Vatican Council wanted to shut the door on the scholastic just war doctrine as a viable ethic for modern warfare. They hoped to do it with a condemnation of nuclear weapons and the affirmation of the right of conscientious objection. They were most successful in achieving the latter and the Council's final statements on modern warfare were the result of a series of compromises.

Nonetheless, the door was partially shut on the just war. The development of nuclear warfare and the Cold War had sufficiently influenced the council fathers to attempt to reevaluate the traditional just war doctrine in which they had been trained, but the attempt did not result in the development of a new ethic. This incapacity on the part of the entire assembly had already been experienced by the peace activists themselves, by individual members of the hierarchy, and by theologians throughout the world who had previously made the same attempt. At best, the council fathers opened the way for a new ethic of peace based on their affirmation of the dignity of personhood, the Gospels, and nonviolence. Thus, the very small parts played by all of these participants at the council who desired to see the condemnation of nuclear weapons were only partially successful. The new ethic was yet to be born.

The role of the American hierarchy in working towards the condemnation of nuclear weapons was almost nonexistent except for the intervention of Cardinal Ritter. The statements of other members of the hierarchy throughout the world, particularly of the bishops from England and the solemn and clear condemnation of all nuclear warfare by Patriarch Maximos of Antioch did more for the partial successes achieved on the issue than did the actions of any American. Viewed in these terms, the work of PAX, particularly its representative James Douglass, pales in significance. Yet, he was able to do a great deal, especially in providing the final wording of statements, and was listened to by many members of the hierarchy. This was a great accomplishment since he possessed no power other than the moral power of his message of peace.

After the Second Vatican Council, the just war tradition remained normative in addressing the war-and-peace policies of governments. Pacifism and nonviolence were also recognized as viable positions, but were viewed solely as options for individual Catholics not for nation-states. Vatican II affirmed the right of a Catholic to be a conscientious objector and encouraged all Catholics to work toward the development of a new ethic of peace. The American Catholic who had spent much of his life writing on peace and whose drafts and letters had great influence at the Second Vatican Council was Thomas Merton. Though not a trained theologian, his efforts to develop a new ethic of peace in the face of nuclear warfare and the war in Vietnam would provide spiritual leadership for the American Catholic peace movement during the 1960s and 1970s.

# 5

# Thomas Merton at the Crossroads of Peace

THE PERIOD BETWEEN WORLD War II and Vatican II was a crucible for
the later development of the American Catholic peace movement.
This was the time when the theological rationales for the just war
doctrine and pacifism were being severely challenged and the new
ethic of nonviolence was born. The war in Vietnam would complete
the process in the 1960s when nonviolent resistance became the movement's main means to stop the war. Thomas Merton stood at this
crossroads and attempted to evaluate the Catholic tradition on war and
peace in three areas: just war, pacifism, and nonviolence. His writings
changed once and for all how American Catholics would henceforth
think about peacemaking.

Thomas Merton was born in Praedes, France, on 31 January 1915.
Six years later his Quaker mother died. He spent most of his young
adult life studying in France or England. When he was not in school,
he frequently travelled throughout Europe with his father, who was an
artist and was always in quest of ideas for his paintings.

In 1934, after attending Cambridge for one year, Merton came to
the United States and completed his formal education at Columbia
University, where he obtained an M.A. degree in English. Like Dorothy Day, he had flirted with socialism and communism, but found
them disillusioning because they were too focused on society with
insufficient emphasis placed on personal responsibility. While completing his master's thesis on the religious and mystical elements of the
writings of William Blake, he took the advice of a Hindu monk and
began to read St. Augustine and the early Church Fathers. By the end
of his first year of graduate study, Merton had led himself to a firm
commitment to the Catholic faith.

In November 1938, Thomas Merton was baptized a Roman Catholic at Corpus Christi Church in New York City. In *The Seven Storey Mountain*,[1] an autobiographical account of his spiritual pilgrimage, he wrote that he had been converted from "rank savage paganism, from the spiritual level of a cannibal or of an ancient Roman, to the living faith."

Within two years of his baptism, Merton decided that he wanted to become a priest. This desire to do so was initially frustrated when his application to the Franciscan Order was rejected. Accepting this decision, he went to teach in a small Franciscan men's college, St. Bonaventure, located in Olean, New York. While teaching there, the conviction grew in him that he would dedicate himself to the contemplative life and in 1942 he applied to and was eventually accepted into the Trappist Abbey of Gethsemani in Kentucky.

While making this decision, Merton was faced with the draft. In conscience he knew that he could not kill anyone and would not carry a gun. By personal conviction he was a pacifist. As a new Catholic and older pacifist, Merton decided "the war would have to be defensive, and since the average person could not know whether it was or not, he would simply have to trust the leadership in Washington."[2] In November 1940, he registered for the draft as a noncombatant objector, agreeing to serve in the medical corps. Ironically, after agonizing over this moral dilemma, he failed his physical examination and was not drafted. After the attack on Pearl Harbor, the standards for induction were lowered and he was recalled for the draft. But the military was too late; Merton had already entered the monastery.

On 10 December 1941 Thomas Merton was welcomed into the abbey and given the name Brother Louis. At the monastery he was ordained a priest in 1949 and he became a U.S. citizen on 22 June 1951. During his twenty-seven years as a Trappist monk, Merton wrote, edited, and translated fifty books and three hundred articles, reviews, and poems for periodicals. Because of his writing, he became the most distinguished and well-known Catholic monk in American history. Thus, his writings on peace gave the Catholic peace movement a respectability and wider audience than previously experienced.

Merton himself divided his writings into three periods. The writings of the first period, from his conversion in 1938 to his ordination in 1949, were ascetic, intransigent, and somewhat apocalyptic in outlook.

Written in his "first fervor" days, they represented a rigid, arbitrary separation between God and the world. The second period extended from 1949 to 1959 and was mainly one of transition in which Merton sought to discover ways to integrate God and the world. Readings in depth psychology, Zen Buddhism, and existentialism greatly influenced him and led him to develop a positive view of the individual, which he combined with the theological doctrine of the Incarnation. The integration, however, did not appear until the third period beginning in 1959, when he increasingly focused on contemporary social issues.[3]

It was during the third period that Merton wrote on peace. He was not a systematic theologian like John C. Murray, who followed the logical and linear just war tradition of Augustine and Aquinas. Merton was more literary. He employed a language that was creative, dialogical, and inclusive. In his way of thinking he attempted to raise new questions and present new solutions to peace that challenged the just war tradition. He was the only Catholic writer whose extensive study of the question of peace considered the full variety of approaches: just war, pacifism, and nonviolence. Though by personal conviction a pacifist, Merton attempted to develop a theology of peace that all Catholics could embrace to become peacemakers. In his writings he provided an appreciation of the problems and contradictions of the various approaches to the issues. The focal point of his writings on peace was his belief in the eschatological dimension of the Judeo-Christian vision of a "new heaven and a new earth." According to Merton, the ultimate triumph of the vision would be achieved in the Eschaton. Daniel Berrigan termed Thomas Merton's vision of peace "the long view" and mourned his death because there was no one of Merton's stature who could provide the historical tradition and the eschatological vision of peace to the world.[4]

The international issue of the Cold War and the much discussed issues of the Christian-Marxist dialogue provided the background that eventually led Merton to address the dangers of nuclear war. Most of his writing on nuclear war was completed before the Test Ban Treaty of 1963. Because both the United States and the Soviet Union possessed nuclear weapons, Merton saw the Cold War as the most serious threat to international security.[5] He opposed the extreme nationalism of both the United States and the Soviet Union for fear that technological knowledge might trigger a nuclear war in a time of ideological conflict. His most explicit response to this struggle was written in "Letter to Pablo Antonio Cundra Concerning Giants":

> The two great powers are like sorcerer's apprentices, spending billions of dollars on space exploration and nuclear weapons while failing to feed, clothe, and shelter two-thirds of the human race. They are like the twins Gog and Magog in the book of Ezechiel, each with great power and little sanity, each telling lies with great conviction. . . . If a citizen is not properly classified, Gog shoots him while Magog deprives him of a home, a job, a seat on the bus. In both, life and death depend on everything except who you are.[6]

Merton opposed the Cold War primarily because he feared that an escalation into a nuclear confrontation would destroy the world. He believed that there was no effective control over the use of nuclear weapons and that the Cold War was releasing forces that would eventually lead the great powers into national suicide.

Merton was one of the first theologians to see that the Cold War threat of nuclear war had warped traditional Christian ethics. He held that the normative Catholic teaching of the just war doctrine was inadequate in the nuclear age and required reevaluation. He believed that if there was to be a new theology of peace, Christians had to free themselves of the overpowering influence of Augustinian assumptions concerning war. He was the first American Catholic to proclaim that the only posture that was both reasonable and Christian in the modern world was that of "relative" or "nuclear" pacifism. Such a position, Merton wrote in 1962, "admits the traditional doctrine of a just war by conventional weapons, but . . . insists that nuclear disarmament, or at the very least a completely effective arms control is an absolute moral obligation."[7] A careful reading of all of his writing on nuclear warfare reveals that the term, nuclear pacifism, meant that a Catholic would condemn the use of nuclear weapons by any nation under any circumstances and would refuse to participate in any aspect of a nuclear war from the making of nuclear weapons to the firing of them.

In developing his position, Merton first looked at the just war tradition. He established the historical roots of this tradition in early Christianity with Augustine. He wrote that Augustine imposed many limits on the Christian soldier and that these were not entirely unrealistic in a less destructive age, but he had an excessive naivete with regard to the good that could be attained by violent means.[8] Merton concluded his writing on Augustine with the following analysis: "The twofold weakness of the Augustinian theory is its stress on a subjective purity of intention which can be doctored and manipulated with apparent 'sincerity' and the tendency to pessimism about human nature and the world, now used as a JUSTIFICATION for recourse to violence."[9]

The arguments for the just war were expounded by St. Thomas Aquinas, but Merton, who had been trained in Thomistic philosophy, did not attempt to build a systematic argument against each point of the doctrine. Rather he wrote in a spiritual and literary manner about the qualitative difference between nuclear warfare and traditional forms of warfare. He believed that nuclear weapons had altered the nature of war by bringing instant death to millions of noncombatants and had consequently altered the traditional Catholic doctrine of the just war.

Merton believed that when the Japanese bombed Pearl Harbor "there was no question about the morality of America's entering the war to defend its rights. There was a very clear example of a 'just cause' for war."[10] But the obliteration bombing of cities on both sides, culminating in the massive destruction of Hiroshima and Nagasaki, had completely changed the nature of war. According to Merton, "traditional standards no longer applied because there was no longer any distinction between civilian and combatant. Even the moral principle of double effect was not valid when it 'permitted' the slaughter of fifty-thousand civilians in order to stop production in four or five factories. There was no proportion between the 'permitted evil' and the 'intended good.' "[11] Merton asked how the traditional doctrine of the just war was "so profoundly modified that it is almost ready to permit any outrage, any excess, any horror, on the grounds that it is a 'lesser evil' and 'necessary' to save our nation?"[12]

For Merton the just war theory completed a cyclical process during World War II:

A country begins a defensive "just war." It starts by declaring its firm adherence to the ethical principles held by its Church, and by the majority of its civilian population. The nation accepts unjust suffering heroically. But then the military begins to grow impatient, seeing that its own methods of retaliation are not effective. It is the military that changes the policy. The new, more ruthless policy pays off. The civilian protest is silenced before it begins. Those who might otherwise have objected come to believe what they are told: "This will save lives. It is necessary to end the war sooner, and to punish the unjust aggressor."[13]

In the end, Merton wrote, "the methods of the Allies eventually became as ruthless and as inhumane as those of the enemy."

After World War II, American Presidents Harry S. Truman and Dwight D. Eisenhower relied increasingly on a massive retaliation strategy based on nuclear arms to deter Soviet aggression against the United States and its allies. Under President John F. Kennedy, Secretary of Defense Robert S. McNamara announced a plan to develop the means to strike at Soviet military installations as well as the cities of the Soviet Union. He was attempting to "limit" nuclear warfare. In America prominent Christian "realist" theologians such as John Courtney Murray welcomed McNamara's effort to limit the effects of a nuclear war. Like Merton, Murray stated that an all-out nuclear war would be immoral. But he also argued that to halt the expansion of Soviet Communism, which he considered the primary threat to Western civilization, a limited nuclear war might be necessary and would also be morally permissable under the criteria of the just war doctrine.

In the early 1960s, Merton was one of the first and one of the few Catholics to speak out on the "illogical logic of deterrence." Merton attacked the proliferation of nuclear weapons and the immorality of massive retaliation. In theory Merton admitted that a limited nuclear war could satisfy the just war criteria for a moral war, but in practice it would be impossible to restrict a nuclear war. He wrote:

> It may be quite true that . . . Popes have . . . affirmed a nation's right to defend itself by just means, in a just war. It may also be true that a theological argument for the use of "tactical nuclear weapons" may be constructed on the basis of some of the Pope's statements. But when we remember that the twenty kiloton A-bomb that was dropped on Hiroshima is now regarded as "small" and as a "tactical device" and when we keep in mind that there is every probability that when a force that is being beaten with small nuclear weapons will resort to big ones,

we can easily see how little practical value can be found in these theorizings. [14]

For this reason, he began to attack Murray and the "realists" who were creating a strong and articulate body of theological opinion in the church in America which favored nuclear deterrence as necessary to an "adequate posture of defense." Merton sarcastically censured Murray's position in the following manner: "He takes his stand on the natural law and on the traditional Just War theory. He believes that defensive wars may be necessary and they ought to be fought with conventional weapons or with small nuclear bombs . . . it is adequate on paper, but the 20 kiloton bomb dropped on Hiroshima would be small according to Father Murray."[15] Merton also cited one of Murray's footnotes which seemed to indicate that a preemptive strike could be regarded as "defensive." "One wonders," Merton conjectured, "if this does not after all tend to validate morally everything that goes on at Cape Canaveral or Los Alamos."[16]

Merton concluded his criticism of the "realists" by stating that "the theoretician who splits hairs about 'just war,' and makes nice distinctions in journals for experts is actually supporting the military mind and military policies, which imply no such fine distinctions at all. . . . Men with nuclear weapons will use them when they think the situation is sufficiently critical. And they will not use them with regard for restraints demanded by moral theologians. To cooperate with them now is to share in the responsibility then."[17] Merton believed nuclear warfare was always total and offensive. "In our age," he wrote, "there is essentially a new kind of war and one in which the necessary conditions for a 'Just War' are extremely difficult to maintain. A war of total annihilation simply cannot be considered a 'Just War' no matter how good the causes for which it is undertaken."[18]

Merton also looked for direction in his analysis of the just war in the writings of the popes. He was disturbed that none had formally condemned the use of nuclear weapons, and in various articles he tried to justify this neglect, not only to his readers but also to himself. His writings reflected his own ambiguous feelings on the matter. As Merton viewed it, the popes had not formally condemned the use of hydrogen bombs because to condemn a specific weapon would leave some critics free to make the pope appear to be approving other kinds of weapons.[19]

Another time he contended that the popes had not condemned nuclear weapons because the weapons condemned themselves. Merton also utilized the statements of the popes that condemned certain aspects of war before the discovery of nuclear power to build his case, for example, Pope Pius XII's statement that a weapon is immoral when it becomes so destructive that it cannot be controlled. In the end, Merton contended that Popes Pius XII, John XXIII, and Paul VI had said in so many words that the new means of warfare inherently transgress the permissible limits established by the traditional just war norms of morality and make any resort to nuclear war illegitmate or immoral. Thus, according to Merton, this new kind of war made the concept of a just war impossible to achieve.

Merton also believed that the traditional just war doctrine was irrelevant because the testimony of history is clear in that an attempt to subject the irrationality of war to the rule of reason alone fails miserably. He was convinced that the power of Pope John XXIII's encyclical, *Pacem in Terris*, was that it made clear the key to the meaning of peace lay not in

> a casuistical treatment of the problem of nuclear war but in the profound and optimistic Christian spirit with which the Pope lays bare the deepest roots of peace, roots which man himself has the mission to cultivate. (This necessitates a free commitment to the ethic of Christianity which goes beyond logic to the spiritual and mystical rooted in deep and simple love for God which is also love for His creation and for God's child: man.)[20]

Though he proclaimed the just war doctrine to be irrelevant in the nuclear age, by using it himself, Merton did not break with the doctrine. He had turned to the historical tradition of the just war within the Catholic church to provide legitimacy for a nuclear pacifist position and in the process had ironically reaffirmed the relevancy of the just war doctrine for many Catholics.

According to his biographer, Michael Mott, Merton believed the just war doctrine was irrelevant for three reasons. First, Merton had come to see that to have a "just war" was an ideal as elusive as Aristotle's "perfect ruler" or Plato's "philosopher-prince" in the political theories. Second, the theory of the just war by definition referred to a war of defense and according to Merton almost all war began in defense of something and that this ruled out nuclear weapons because nuclear weapons could only be used to threaten and never as a weapon of defense. And finally, that the just war theory was developed by Augustine to preserve Christianity and the Roman Empire. Yet, the Roman Empire disappeared and Christianity would conquer the conquerors of the empire. Merton's main point here, which he made over and over in the mid-1960s was that "those who tied their faith in Christianity to faith in a single culture and a single political structure served only the structure and had no faith."[21]

It must be pointed out that Merton's writings on nuclear warfare occurred in the first few years of his attempt to address social issues, in the beginning of which stage he looked to the historical tradition within the Roman Catholic church to provide him with a degree of legitimacy. In October 1961, he wrote in his journal:

> I am perhaps at the turning point in my spiritual life: perhaps slowly coming to a point of maturation and the resolution of doubts—and the forgetting of fears. Walking into a known and definite battle. May God protect me in it. The Catholic Worker sent out a press release about my article [on peace], which may have many reactions—or may have none. At any rate it appears that I am one of the few Catholic priests in the country who has come out unequivocally for a completely intransigent fight for the abolition of war and the use of non-violent means to settle international conflicts. Hence by implication not only against the bomb, against nuclear testing, against polaris submarines, but against all violence. Non-violent ACTION, not mere passivity. How am I going to explain myself and defend a definite position in a timely manner when it takes at least two months to get even a short article through the censors of the Order, is a question I cannot attempt to answer.[22]

In 1961, Merton's *Original Child Bomb* was published. It used various accounts of the first atomic bombs dropped on Hiroshima and Nagasaki. In September 1962, *Breakthrough to Peace: Twelve Views on the Threat of Thermonuclear Extermination* was published. Merton admits that he edited the book to counter the written and spoken statements of nuclear "realists." Unable to find American Catholics with a nuclear pacifist position besides Gordon Zahn, Merton drew on other American writers, "faithful to the Judeo-Christian tradition on which our civilization was built." He was inspired to take such action by the influence of Walter Stein in Britain who edited in 1961, *Nuclear Weapons and Christian Conscience.* After publication of *Breakthrough to Peace,* Merton was silenced on writing about war by his religious superiors. He resorted to a mimeograph machine to print his "Cold War Letters," which he circulated to friends until a new abbot general lifted the ban on his war and peace writings in the summer of 1964.

The lifting of the ban carried with it a directive to Merton that he could "write about peace, not war—he was not to show pessimism."[23] Merton believed that this meant he could "radiate sweetness and light but not condemn the bomb." When a letter from the order came, however, saying that Merton's article, "Peace in the Post-Christian Era," could be published in his next book, *Seeds of Destruction,* Merton was jubilant. The book appeared on 16 November 1964 and also contained a selection from the "Cold War Letters." Merton would continue to condemn the bomb and proclaim nuclear pacifism.

The second major theme in Merton's writings on war and peace was pacifism. Merton proclaimed himself a nuclear pacifist and contended that it should be the normative position for all American Catholics to assume in any discussion of nuclear issues. After 1964, Merton left the just war doctrine behind him in his writings on war and peace as he did not believe that it was adequate to address the issues raised by the Vietnam War. He began instead to write of nonviolence. Merton's position on pacifism is the starting point for his writings on nonviolence. Although contradictions may often be found in Merton's writings on pacifism, David W. Givey points out in *The Social Thought of Thomas Merton,* that they were not seen as negative elements by Merton, but as reflective of his life, which he saw as "almost totally paradoxical." Givey contends that Merton's thought was a dialectical process that continued over and over with each step leading him nearer to reality and truth.[24]

Like Day, as a convert Merton had brought his pacifism to Catholicism. On numerous occasions in his writing, he declared that he was not a pacifist, at least in the traditional sense, for fear that readers would reject his writing if he proclaimed pacifism. Personally he had embraced pacifism but his primary concern was creating a new ethic of peace that would replace the existing traditions as the normative position for all Catholics so that they could be peacemakers.

Merton gave four reasons why he did not call himself a pacifist. First, pacifism depended solely upon the conscience of the individual Christian and had no inherent social orientation. The individual witness of the pacifist was not concerned with trying to change public policy. He believed pacifism was inherently passive and a Christian was called to action, to be a "peacemaker." Second, he believed that "the religious ambiguities in the term 'pacifism' gave it implications that were somewhat less than Catholic." A pacifist who believes in peace as an article of his faith, warned Merton, will end up "contending that Christians who are not pacifists are apostates from Christianity."[25] Third, Merton did not like the facile caricature of the pacifist and wanted to disassociate himself from it publicly. Bloom in *Ulysses* best represented this caricature for him.[26] The best explanation of why he did not want to label himself a pacifist was that even though he would not carry a gun nor kill another human being, he believed a Christian could never be forbidden to fight and he refused to admit that a war could never be just.[27]

Concern for the oppressed people of the world was the fourth reason Merton gave for his rejection of unqualified pacifism. Merton affirmed the right of an individual to resort to violence to restore rights wrongfully denied or to reestablish an order necessary for decent human existence. Because of his identification with the oppressed, Merton lamented the hidden violence that masqueraded as just authority in oppressive and highly organized societies. "Those who in some way or other concur in the oppression—and perhaps profit by it—are exercising violence," Merton contended, "even though they may be preaching pacifism. And their supposedly peaceful laws, which maintain this spurious kind of order are in fact instruments of violence and oppression."[28] He summarized his position on this point in the following manner: "If the oppressed try to resist by force—which is their right—theology has no business preaching non-violence to them. Mere blind destruction is, of course, futile and immoral: but who are we to condemn a desperation we have helped to cause!"[29]

By qualifying his pacifism, Merton came into open disagreement with Dorothy Day. Merton had been a contributor to the *Catholic Worker* since the publication of his autobiography, *The Seven Storey*

*Mountain* in 1948. By 1959, the year of their first extant letters, a steadfast friendship had developed. In November 1961, the relationship was tested when Merton wrote for the *Catholic Worker* an article entitled, "The Shelter Ethic." It was in response to an *America* article by L. C. McHugh, S.J., which argued that in a case where a possessor of a backyard shelter was confronted by a less provident neighbor during a nuclear attack, it would be licit for the owner of the shelter to defend against the intruder at gun point.[30] Merton's response was not concerned with the rightness or error of the ethical response of the owner of the shelter. He was willing to grant that an individual did have the right to kill someone if there was no other way to protect self or family. What Merton objected to was seeing the issue completely in these terms. He held that the owner's response was not Christian since it gave the impression that every individual was for self—such an attitude was wrong even on a purely natural level and disastrous to the political interests of the United States. Because of her pacifism, Day took issue with Merton. She could not justify killing another human being under any circumstance. She held that a Christian should not take the life of another even in self-defense.[31] Beyond this single incident there is no evidence of any other disagreement between Merton and Day. Day was grateful for Merton's writings because she believed his was the first voice for peace among the theologians since John Hugo in World War II.[32]

The war in Vietnam caused Merton to shift the emphasis in his writings on peace away from nuclear warfare to limited warfare. All of the distinctions made by him pertaining to nuclear pacifism, the just war, and pacifism seemed ultimately to disappear when he considered the issue of limited warfare in reference to the war in Vietnam.[33] Though Merton had contended that a limited nuclear war could never be just, he had also contended that a limited war without nuclear weapons could be just. This distinction became tenuous in Merton's writings, when he stated that even limited wars (however just) presented an almost certain danger of all-out nuclear war. Thus, it became highly questionable for Merton if any war could be just. He, however, did cite the uprising in Hungary in 1956 as an actual situation where the waging of war was a defensive war and a just war. Merton did not provide any other examples.

The essential evil of the United States in Vietnam for Merton was as Gordon Zahn put it, "the total commitment to violence in utter disregard for the rights of individuals that the war had come to repre-sent."[34] Reflective of his writings on World War II, Merton once again bitterly attacked the ready willingness of the American people to rationalize and excuse acts of large-scale terrorism and a war-making policy that he believed verged on genocide. The American people had entered a psychological state of obsession with the need to "com-pletely wipe out" the enemy. For Merton, Vietnam was also a symbol of the eschatological moment when a nuclear holocaust could result. He wrote in his preface to the Vietnam edition of *No Man Is an Island*, "The War in Vietnam is a bell tolling for the whole world, warning the whole world that war may spread everywhere and violent death may spread over the entire earth."[35]

But the Vietnam War had further implications for Merton. It led him to search for a new theology of peace that would enable the individual to speak against the United States' unleashing of a campaign of destruction upon the Vietnam people. He found it in nonviolence and for the rest of his short life he worked at formulating a Catholic theology of nonviolence.

Merton looked to the doctrine of nonviolence as a means that would provide Catholics with a new social ethic to meet the moral problems of the nuclear age and replace the inadaequate doctrine of the just war. He also hoped that nonviolence would aid pacifists in advancing be-yond a position of conscience, which he saw too closely tied to "passive-ness," to one that would speak more effectively to public policy and the problems of the world. Merton looked to nonviolence as the basis for a new theology of peace.

Merton's solution to the violence in Vietnam was nonviolence. He had arrived at the position by linking the issues of justice and peace. In Merton's writing about racial injustice in America, he had consistently blamed the problem of racial violence at home on the white man and had singled out the work of Martin Luther King, Jr. "as the most Christian and effective plan for achieving racial and national unity at home."[36] The influence of King on Merton can not be overestimated. Mahatma Gandhi was King's inspiration in his nonviolent civil rights campaign in America. Merton's admiration for King led to a study of Gandhian nonviolence that resulted not only in understanding nonvio-lent techniques and requirements, but in believing that only nonvio-lence could break the endless cycle of violence. Thus, "in the field of international affairs he most admired the work of King's guiding spirit,

Mahatma Gandhi."[37] Merton explained Gandhi's significance for Christians:

> One of the very few men of our time who applied Gospel principles to the problems of a political and social existence in such a way that his approach to these problems was inseparably religious and political at the same time. . . . [For Gandhi] political action had to be by its very nature "religious" in the sense that it had to be informed by principles of religious and political wisdom. To separate religion and politics was in Gandhi's eyes "madness" because his politics rested on a thoroughly religious interpretation of reality, of life, and of man's place in the world.[38]

Showing how Gandhian nonviolence was consistent with the Gospel and the Catholic tradition of peace, Merton turned first to Scripture and the writings of the early Church Fathers. He affirmed that, neither blessed nor forbidden by Jesus, war belonged to the world outside the Kingdom which He came to establish. It was the Apocalypse, according to Merton, that presented the eschatological view of peace in its symbolic description of the critical struggle of the nascent church with the powers of the world. War in the Apocalypse was the "Rider of the Red Horse" who, Merton stated, was to prepare the destruction of the civil power structure. Merton asserted that the Holy Roman Empire was clearly understood by the early Christians to possess a demonic power, and this was evident in the Apocalypse where "the battle was non-violent and spiritual, and its success depended on the clear understanding of the totally new and unexpected dimensions in which it was to be fought."[39] There is no indication whatever in the Apocalypse, concluded Merton, that "the Christ would be willing to fight and die to maintain the 'power of the beast,' in other words to engage in a power-struggle for the benefit of the Emperor and of his power."[40]

Merton next explored what Origen and other early Church Fathers such as Clement of Alexandria, Justin Martyr, and Cyprian had written about the Christian's right (or duty) to bear arms. He discovered that the Church Fathers during the first four centuries A.D. taught that Christians should not take up arms in any war. Merton believed he had discovered in Origen, the author of *Contra Celsus*, a theory very different from Augustine's. Origen, said Merton, denied that the early Christians were violent revolutionaries, or that they intended to bring about the overthrow of the empire by force. Origen, himself, did not believe in the need of war because the time would come for all people to be united in the Logos, though this fulfillment most probably awaits the Second Coming of Christ. Origen believed that human society had been radically transformed by the Incarnation, and that, among other things, Christians, who desired the good of all people, should be united against war in obedience to Christ. Because Christians are a "royal priesthood," they did more by their prayers to preserve peace than they could by force of arms. Origen also argued, Merton added, that nonperformance of military service did not free early Christians from their fair share of the responsiblities for maintaining the commonwealth, but their role was primarily spiritual and transcendent. "In a word," Merton explained, "if peace is the objective, spiritual weapons will preserve it more effectively than those which kill the enemy in battle. For the weapon of prayer is not directed against other men, but against the evil forces which divide men into warring camps. If these evil forces are overcome by prayer, then both sides are benefitted, war is avoided and all are united in peace. In other words, the Christian does not help the war effort of one particular nation, but he fights against war itself with spiritual weapons."[41] Merton believed Origen's position was very close to nonviolence and would use the early Church Fathers to show the compatibility between nonviolence and Catholicism. Based on these sources Merton called for a new theology of peace in place of the just war criteria.

At this point, what we have in Merton is the presentation of the Christian myth that provides a vision of the future without any attention to specific means for its achievement. It is focused on the individual and does not address the state as the just war doctrine does, rather it presupposes the existence of a Christian state, which Merton claimed has never existed. All extant ages, according to Merton, have been pre-Christian or post-Christian. He also contended that the New Testament says nothing about politics. Rather than building a new theology of peace whereby the church provides a moral criteria to be followed by the state as in the just war theory, Merton was searching for an ethic not contingent on the actions of the state but based on the actions of individual Christians who could address the political issues of the state. Merton's theology of peace, therefore, began with the conversion of the heart that rejected violence and then subsequently transformed passive ideas of peace into actions that would bring about peace through nonviolence. He realized that he was shifting the responsibility of war and peace away from the state to the individual peacemaker and he found support for his position in the the words of Karl Rahner, who stated:

> Thus the political action of the Christian does not become confused with projects centered around an official and clericalist "party line," nor is it inevitably associated with the propagation of a dogmatic message which the rest of the world is not disposed to hear without challenging it. But on the other hand, this Christian action is concretely ordered to advancing the work of Redemption and deepening the penetration of grace into the realm of society and nature. . . . It is the "action of Christians but not action of the Church."[42]

Accepting Christ's Sermon on the Mount as the basis for ethics, Merton linked the Beatitudes with natural law in his attempt to justify the peacemaker's political action. He stated that "the Beatitudes indeed convey a profound existential understanding of the dynamic of the Kingdom of God, . . . a dynamism of patient and secret growth. . . . This is not merely a matter of blind and arbitrary faith. The early history of the Church, the record of apostles and martyrs remains to testify to this inherent and mysterious dynamism of the ecclesial 'event' in the world of history and time."[43]

Merton, rooted in a Catholic tradition that looked not only to the New Testament but also to its doctrine of natural law for its principles, realized that the church adopted the natural law from pagan philosophy and made it a basis for much of its doctrine and practices. Thus, the natural law became the basis for Christian doctrine concerning the social order. But Merton pointed out that "once the Law of Christ has been promulgated, it is no longer possible to isolate the natural law in a sphere of its own. The natural law itself acquires a Christian perspective from the Sermon on the Mount. It has an aim higher than the mere avoidance of brutality, savagery, and sin. It becomes obligatory for the Christian to orientate all his conduct according to the law of love and to make use of non-violent means of persuasion whenever it is humanly possible. He must do this out of generous love both for his neighbor and for the truth."[44] What Merton was trying to do was move the Christian from passive resistance (a conscientious negative response to participate in a political action by the state that the individual deemed wrong) to a more active resistance (positing direct actions against political decisions by the state which the individual conscience has judged is wrong). It was at this point that Merton proclaimed nonviolence as the Christian's way to peace.

According to Merton, Gandhi provided a means that would involve human beings in the decision-making process and in the discipline of meaningful participation. This means would enable participants in actions of nonviolence to correct the evils of the existing social order without demanding the participants engage in and become part of the evil social structure they were attempting to correct. Thus, Gandhian nonviolent resistance provided a dynamic for social change that was contingent on individuals positing actions to help create the new order. Gandhian nonviolence was consistent with the Catholic faith, according to Merton, because it rested on the Gospel principle of willingness to endure suffering rather than to inflict it upon another and also because its primary goal was truth. Thus, Catholic nonviolence like Gandhi's satyagraha did not seek power but truth. Merton tried to summarize this meaning of Catholic nonviolence in his statement, "It does not say 'We shall overcome' so much as 'This is the day of the Lord and whatever may happen to us, *He* shall overcome.' "[45]

Merton took Gandhian nonviolent resistance and added the eschatological dimension that provided for the ultimate triumph of truth and love only with the Second Coming of Christ. It was Merton's hope that if enough individuals made a free commitment to the love ethic of Christian nonviolence, a new earth would exist and the problem of force-dominated politics of the state would cease. His eschatological vision, which was dependent on personal conversion and nonviolent action, was consistent with Day's and Maurin's concepts of Christian personalism and revolution.

The ethic of nonviolence reconciled with the concepts of eschatology and individual responsiblity constituted the basis of Merton's writings on peace. Merton was plagued by the contradiction between politics and the New Testament and by 1968 in a letter to a friend, said that he was interested in any insights on the problem, but would leave the area alone. He felt himself moving into a kind of "post-political eschatology" which he could not articulate. He hinted that appeals to politics lacked firmness and to accept politics as a religious area of reality would only contribute in the end to the slide into "technical totalism." What Merton called for was a radical rethinking of politics. [46]

Merton himself pointed out his own limitations in attempting an integration of religion and politics. He could add nothing to Gandhian nonviolence in this area. Aware of his lack of political astuteness and removed from participation in direct action in his monastery, he contended that he was not primarily concerned with the tactical strategy of building a peace movement. Rather Merton had come to see the monastery as the model of the nonviolent Christian life of community, conscience, and witness. He summarized the role of Christian monasticism in these terms: "The monastery is not an 'escape from the world.' On the contrary, by being in the monastery I take my true part in all the struggles and sufferings of the world. To adopt a life that is essentially non-assertive, non-violent." [47]

The monastery, however, had not prevented Merton from being a long-standing member of the Catholic Worker. He had joined the Fellowship of Reconciliation, and had lent his name as sponsor in 1962 to the American PAX Association and in 1964 to the Catholic Peace Fellowship. Merton had even desired to become personally involved in the "Peace Hostage Exchange" project and praised and supported the demonstrations of civil disobedience protesting the New York air raid test and the Golden Rule, Phoenix, and Everyman projects. He had also counseled young men seeking conscientious objection status during the Vietnam War. Merton had reservations about the tactic of draft card burning and draft file destruction and was most upset by the self-immolation of Roger LaPorte, a young member of the Catholic Worker. Merton advocated most strongly the need for pastoral and educational work in the area of peace. [48] Practical strategies concerning the means of nonviolence were beyond Thomas Merton. It was nonviolence as a Christian way of life, not as a political strategy, that consumed his thought and writing.

Merton acknowledged that he could not develop what he termed a "systematic theology of love," which, in crisis situations might support actions of resistance. He admitted that, at best, he was only examining "principles and cases which help an individual to see the unacceptable ambiguities of a theology of 'might makes right' masquerading as a Christian theology of love."[49] He was certain, however, that the new ethic required a person to be aware of the dangers posed by the state.

In order for the individual to be a peacemaker in the United States during the nuclear era, Merton believed that the individual must first recognize the predominant myths operative in the country. Merton portrayed America as a "sick nation" where "people are fed on myths" and "are stuffed up to their eyes with illusions" so that "they can't think straight." The two great American myths blinding the individual, Merton asserted, were that "force is the only alternative" and that "power is the only basis for human relationships."[50] Predominant during the Cold War these myths were supported and reinforced by the mass media, according to Merton, and they cultivated a "state of mind" that prevents the individual from grasping the plight of the present situation. This "state of mind," he warned, has taken over the role of morality and conscience and will, and rationalized its prejudices with convenient religious and ethical formulas to condone what has occurred in the United States since World War II.[51] This "state of mind" increases the enslavement of people and the possibilities of personal destruction, because as Merton pointed out, the massive power structures are the only benefactors. As a result, the power structures within that nation exploit the individual and ultimately conscript him into warfare.

After asserting that the individual was in great danger of being swallowed up by the Leviathan state, Merton urged individual Christians to look upon the acts and demands of their nation's leaders with intense suspicion and recognition that there was a high probability of jeopardy to their personal spiritual responsibilities and well-being if they obeyed such leadership. For Merton authority in America was suspect. The reason he gave is that it seeks to compel obedience by increasingly resorting to external force or to the law of fear. Though Merton documents this position by a reference to Pope John XXIII, he gives no concrete examples. "When authority ignores natural law, human dignity, human rights, and the moral order established by God," he concludes, "it undermines its own foundation and loses its claim to be obeyed."[52]

Merton saw this sickness that infected the state reflected in the

Catholic church in America, especially in its stands on the issues of war and peace. In his view this sickness accounted for the ambiguity of so many Catholics on the war question, or worse the frank belligerency of the majority of them. He lamented the failure of his church to inspire its members to be peacemakers and oppose America's militaristic ethos and the arms race, even though it was clear that he did not see the church as an effective agent for social change. His hope for change rested on the actions of individual peacemakers and he viewed spirituality as the basic dynamic in human behavior for durable social change.

Moreover, the "state of mind" which existed in "sick" America, according to Merton, threatened not only the spiritual basis of society but also the democratic process itself. If such a "state of mind" continued among the majority of American people, he feared that America would become the equivalent of Nazi Germany or totalitarian Russia. He compared the spiritually sterile man in America to Adolf Eichmann. In *Raids on the Unspeakable*, Merton noted that Eichmann was considered to be a "sane" man even though he felt no guilt at the extermination of the Jews.[53] The refusal of Eichmann and men like him to accept the imperatives of personal responsibility and oppose Hitler made a Nazi Germany possible.

In contrast to Eichmann, Merton in *Faith and Violence* celebrated such responsible individuals as Alfred Delp, Max Josef Metzger, Franz Jagerstatter, Dietrich Bonhoffer, and Simone Weil, whom he considered authentic Christians. These people defied the totalitarian power of the rulers of Nazi Germany by their acts of resistance and for Merton their nonviolent resistance was a measure of their faith.

Hence, the problem for Merton was not how to change the state, but how to change individuals into peacemakers in America. The question became for Merton how to transform the present "state of mind" into a new consciousness that would result in human liberation and a capacity to act responsibly in face of totalitarian power. Merton gave some impetus and direction to such a process. He insisted that individuals be properly informed, not only about the situation in which they found themselves, but also about nonviolent resistance; moreover, individuals must exercise their rights to protest or resistance. Both of these demanded the recognition of individual conscience. Merton stressed the need for the individual conscience to be based on spiritual principles for the processs to succeed. The means of nonviolence would enable the individual Christian to act in such a way as to have direct relevance to the state and society.

Merton's insistence on a spiritual base as a prerequisite for nonviolent resistance seemingly contradicted some of the statements in his writings on peace where the only prerequsite for the end of war and the unity of humankind was the human response. In the essay "Nhat Hanh Is My Brother" he pointed to the overarching nature of the concept of human solidarity. Nhat, a Vietnamese, deplored war, as did Merton, and for the same reasons: human reasons—reasons of sanity, justice, and love. As Merton put it,

> I have far more in common with Nhat than I have with many Americans, and I do not hesitate to say it. It is vitally important that such bonds be admitted. They are the bonds of a new solidarity and a new brotherhood which is beginning to be evident on all the five continents and which cuts across all political, religious and cultural lines to unite young men and women in every country in something that is more concrete than an ideal and more alive than a program. This unity of the young is the only hope of the world.[54]

In his essay "Taking Sides on Vietnam" Merton says, "The side I take is, then, the side of the people who are sick of war and want peace in order to rebuild their country."[55]

Finally, in what was Merton's most famous statement on the entire issue of peace, first written in a letter to James Forest, and later reprinted and widely circulated by A. J. Muste, the same human dimension is paramount.

> It seems to me of course that the most basic problem is not political, it is a-political and human. One of the most important things to do is to keep cutting deliberately through political lines and barriers and emphasizing the fact that these are largely fabrications and that there is another dimension, a genuine reality, totally opposed to the fictions of politics, the human dimension which politics pretends to abrogate entirely to themselves. Is this possible? I am accused of being too ready to doubt the possibility, though I am as ready as anyone to put some hope in it. At least we must try to hope in that, otherwise all is over. But politics as they now stand are hopeless. Hence the desirability of a manifestly non-political witness, non-aligned, non-labeled, fighting

for the reality of man and his rights and needs in the nuclear world in some measure against all the alignments.[56]

Merton's insistence on the human dimension, however, did not preclude the spiritual. His definition of the "spiritual" or "religious" dimension always presupposed the human which it sought to elevate or perfect. The distinction between human and spiritual is most apparent in Merton's writings when he addressed himself to the eschatological dimension. For him, the inner change in the individual and the consequent change in the social order, which the reign of justice and love demanded, was inextricably bound up with the Second Coming of Christ or the Eschaton. Only at the Eschaton would a revolution that established the primacy of Christian love over force be successful. Only at that time would each individual have undergone the inner change that Merton considered a prerequisite for what he called the "revolution" of society and the reign of justice and peace. Merton's insistence on the inseparable association of personal and social change, and the role of nonviolence in both, was articulated in the following passage: "Never was it more necessary to understand the importance of genuine non-violence as a power for real change because it is aimed not so much at revolution as conversion."[57]

The insistence on the prerequisite of personal conversion together with his long view, which places all of his writings on war and peace within the Catholic tradition and the Second Coming of Christ, defined Merton's concept of revolution. The revolution he called for could not be realized until the Second Coming when all creation would be fulfilled. Therefore, the revolution Merton envisaged is impossible to achieve in human history. Yet, because of his optimistic view of person, where the individual is capable of transcendence and of acting responsibly, the revolution of love that he called for could be realized in human history to the extent that individuals are willing to let Jesus Christ and His Spirit work through them as peacemakers.

In his writings on peace, Merton turned toward Gandhian nonviolence as a way for individual believers to translate their own Christian beliefs concerning peace into a life-style and behavior that would realize, at least partially, his view of revolution. He recognized nonviolence as a viable way for individuals to use their reason, religious faith, and courageous spirit of self-sacrifice to resist the evils of injustice and war and give meaning once again to the ideals of Christianity and democracy.[58]

Merton's optimistic view of the person enabled him to make great demands on the individual as a peacemaker. As he saw it, the crucial link between Christianity and nonviolence as espoused by Gandhi was faith in the meaning of the Cross and the redemptive death of Jesus who instead of using force against his accusers, took all the evil upon himself and overcame the evil by suffering. Merton saw this stance as a basic Christian pattern. It was a realistic theology that

> will give a new practical emphasis to it. Instead of preaching the Cross *for others* and advising them to suffer patiently the violence which we sweetly impose on them, with the aid of armies and police, we might conceivably recognize the right of the less fortunate to use force, and study more seriously the practice of non-violence and human methods on our own part when perhaps, as it happens, we possess the most stupendous arsenal of power the world has ever known.[59]

Merton's major contribution to a Catholic theology of peace was to integrate Gandhian nonviolence into Christianity. In the pamphlet *Blessed are the Meek: The Christian Roots of Non-Violence* Merton sets forth for the peacemaker a list of criteria as touchstones for a relative honesty in the practice of Christian nonviolence. These coincide with many of the points made by him in all of his writings on war-peace issues. They call for a transformation of the present state of the world by a peacemaker who is free from all association with unjust use of power, who stands in solidarity with the poor and underpriviledged, who is free of self-righteous blindness, who avoids the fetish of immediate visible results, who is concerned with manifesting, not obscuring the truth, and who grounds action in Christian hope. For Merton power can never be the hallmark of Christian peacemakers. Rather the "key to non-violence is the willingness of the non-violent resister to suffer a certain amount of accidental evil in order to bring about a change of mind in the oppressor and awaken him to personal openness and to dialogue."

It is evident from his writings on peace that Merton repeatedly stressed that the burden and responsiblity was with the individual. He assured the reader of his own conviction that "the witness of genuine non-violence has been incontestable."[60] He also pointed out that "the non-violent ideal does not contain in itself all the answers to all our questions. These will have to be met and worked out amid the risks and anguish of day to day politics. But they can never be worked out if non-violence is never taken seriously."[61] Finally, Merton offered the peacemaker a bleak promise: "It is the 'men of good will' the men who have made their poor efforts to do something about peace, who will in the end be the most mercilessly reviled, crushed, and destroyed as victims of universal self-hate of man which they have unfortunately only increased by the failure of their good intentions."[62] Indeed, for Merton the demands of peacemaking on the individuals were harder than demands of war.

Thus, Merton's notion of nonviolence affects both the individual and society, for it demands that the ends and means of a peacemaker's action be compatible. Though his work on war-peace issues begins with conscience seen in the light of the history of moral law as both social and individual, both rational and "beyond reason," he argued that when conscience assumed the compatible means offered by non-violence, peacemakers were able to preserve their own integrity and at the same time act with relevance and effectiveness in bringing about social change. Christian peacemakers who have embraced the means of nonviolent resistance, according to Merton, will provide an alternative to, rather than a cooption into, the means of interest-group democracy or power politics. He also believed that Christian nonviolence could open the road to a new policy, more in keeping with the self-interest of the individual and the good of society as a whole.

Merton's primary concern with the role of the Christian against the massive power of the state and his own solitary life as a monk did not enable him to address himself to the question of individuals joining together in building a peace movement. He believed that "Christianity is against all mass movements, for they are intrinsically detrimental to man's well-being. . . . Leaders of movements place their trust in money or technology rather than God."[63] His opposition to such movements extended from Nazism to communism and even in a modified way to the peace movement in later years. For Merton, mass movements mentally portrayed the individual not as a real person but as a part of a group; it labeled people who were part of the group as friends and others outside the group as enemies. Jesus, according to Merton, was mistaken for the enemy and was killed because he did not conform to the pattern of behavior dictated by the dominant group of his day.[64] In no way did Merton promise an effective and successful revolution of love in terms of human history. He offered only the hope that individuals would bring about "a new heaven and a new earth" and he assured peacemakers of Christ's promise of suffering and death and ultimate resurrection. Merton's writing on peace became a source of support to the action of prophetic individuals who embraced Christian nonviolence in America.

In November 1964, Merton conducted a retreat on the "Spiritual Roots of Protest." Six of the men in attendance were later to be in prison for "crimes" of nonviolent resistance. They were Daniel and Philip Berrigan, Robert Cunnane, James Forest, Thomas Cornell, and John Peter Grady. Two other participants were Protestant peace leaders, A. J. Muste and John Howard Yoder. Merton also maintained correspondence over this entire period with American Catholic peace leaders such as Dorothy Day, Daniel Berrigan, and James Forest. He also maintained an extensive correspondence with individuals around the world.

Merton did make a difference by proclaiming the inadequacy of the just war doctrine and pacifism within the Catholic tradition. He was successful at the Second Vatican Council in writing on behalf of the individual's right to become a conscientious objector, but he was unsuccessful in procuring a condemnation of nuclear war and weapons. Yet, Merton would write often that "truth" not "effectiveness" was the criteria of Christian nonviolent action. He spent his years after Vatican II emphasizing the compatibility of nonviolence with Catholicism and urging individuals to practice it in their efforts at peacemaking. He asked his readers not to consider the peace movement as simply another of several new ideologies in a never-ending cycle for power. Like Dorothy Day, he urged each individual to see peacemaking and nonviolence as a completely new way of life, a life that would liberate each individual from the logic of power and power relationships. He also called upon individual Christians to serve the community of humankind, a service that was radical insofar as its aim was to replace a dominating society of force with a society dominated by love. His long view, based on faith, assured a revolution of love.

Thomas Merton provided the spiritual impetus to many American

Catholic peacemakers in their struggle against the American war in Vietnam. He was undoubtedly one of the greatest influences upon the Catholic peace movement in the United States. He gave the movement respectability and he struggled constantly to awaken his readers to their vocation as peacemakers. Numerous Merton Centers for the Study of Peace have appeared across the country. Many colleges and universities have courses on Merton and incorporate his thought into courses dealing with justice and peace. The far-reaching aspects of his influence certainly extended to the bishops, for many of the challenges and statements that he issued were adopted not only at the Second Vatican Council, but also by the National Conference of Catholic Bishops.[65] Individual American Catholics would attempt to embrace nonviolence, if not as a way of life, at least as a strategy for stopping the war. The number of American Catholics involved in working for peace would reach proportions never before experienced in our nation's history. By Merton's death in 1968, the Catholic church in the United States was undergoing an internal revolution that would transform it from a predominantly conservative and patriotic body, whose hierarchy always exhorted its members to obey the nation's lawfully constituted government in matters of war and peace, to a new outlook on peace-making for the rest of the century.

# 6

# The Catholic Peace Movement and Vietnam

IN LESS THAN A year after the adoption of *The Pastoral Constitution on the Church in the Modern World* at the Second Vatican Council, Pope Paul VI undertook a series of pilgrimages for peace. For the first time in American history a pope visited the United States. The highlight of his visit occurred on 5 October 1965, when the pope addressed the General Assembly of the United Nations on its twentieth anniversary. In his address, Paul VI confirmed the teachings of the peace encyclical, *Pacem in Terris*, and the new approach to the issues of war and peace stated in the pastoral directives of the Second Vatican Council.

The pope's message reached its climax when he proclaimed: "No more war, war never again! Peace, it is peace that must guide the destinies of peoples and of all mankind."[1] The pope elaborated on this point by stating:

> If you wish to be brothers, let the arms fall from your hands. One can not love while holding offensive arms. Those armaments, especially those terrible arms, which modern science has given you, long before they produce victims and ruins, nourish bad feelings, create nightmares, distrust and somber resolutions. They demand enormous expenditures, they obstruct projects of union and useful collaboration. They falsify the psychology of peoples.[2]

The pope's message, like that of John XXIII and the council, called for a new approach to the issues of war and peace. In 1967, in his encyclical *Populorum Progressio* he approved conscientious objection and alternative service and connected justice and peace by spelling out the relation between the arms race and the poverty of the Third World.[3] In

131

December 1966, he called for a negotiated settlement of the Vietnam War and in May 1968 he offered the Vatican as a site for peace talks.[4]

During the Vietnam era (1963–1975), Catholicism would pass through the most turbulent period of its short history in the United States. Catholics not only had to cope with changes in American society, they had to contend with changes in their church initiated by the Second Vatican Council. The combination of these events would give birth to the largest Catholic peace movement in American history.

John XXIII opened the Second Vatican Council with a call for *aggiornamento*, that is, to bring the church up to date. At the very first session, some bishops protested the proposed agenda and the people selected for major committee positions. Immediately the papers carried the headlines "Bishops Revolt." "This marked the beginning of an open Council and an open church, in which debate and dissent became accepted. . . . As a result of the Council, . . . Catholics acquired the authority to dissent."[5] The process of implementing the changes unleashed by Vatican II affected the entire hierarchical structure of the church. Vatican II encouraged the role of the laity in the church and the concept of collegiality, or shared authority. The new emphasis on the individual and conscience in the council's "Declaration on Religious Freedom" and the concept that the church was the "people of God" led American Catholics to challenge the authoritative decisions of their church and also the policies of their government.

At Vatican II the bishops also went on to make social justice a top priority and continued the Catholic tradition of linking justice with peace. This tradition would have a profound impact on American Catholics in the 1960s as social changes swept across the land. The civil rights movement, the birth of a women's movement, and a mounting concern with poverty and urban blight involved many Catholics who were committed to establishing a just order in American society. Involvement in these domestic nonviolent struggles for social justice in American society provided a stepping stone for many American Catholics into the peace movement as the United States escalated its role in Southeast Asia.

During the Vietnam War, many Catholics were involved in social justice issues domestically. On the labor front where church leaders had traditionally evidenced support, Cesar Chavez organized the National Farm Workers Association. In 1970, when the association signed the first of several labor contracts with California growers, George Higgins, a priest associated with the United States Catholic Conference was a central figure in the negotiations. The involvement of bishops in these negotiations and in the farm workers' movement was part of a new trend.[6]

Nothing shocked the nation like the civil rights crusade and the racial violence that erupted during the 1960s. The race crisis drew the church into public life to deal with a problem that affected a group who were for the most part not Catholic. Nevertheless, Catholic religious orders like the Josephites had traditionally committed themselves to work solely for blacks. Philip Berrigan, a Josephite, and his brother, Daniel Berrigan, a Jesuit, along with Richard Wagner, another Josephite priest, attempted to join the Freedom Ride in Mississippi led by James Farmer in the summer of 1961 but their religious superiors denied them permission. When one of the most significant marches took place in Selma, Alabama, in March 1965, clergy of all religions took part, including over four hundred Catholic priests, numerous nuns, brothers, and lay people. The American church hierarchy began to encourage priests and sisters to work with the black community and this gave a new prominence to social ministry. In 1967, the Milwaukee priest James Groppi made national news when he led open-housing marches throughout Milwaukee. In 1970, the National Office of Black Catholics was opened and for the first time in over a century, black priests were appointed to the hierarchy.[7]

Race was not the only issue in which many Catholics became involved. Poverty, inadequate housing, and job discrimination in the cities where Catholics lived led many Catholic clergy to become involved in urban affairs. The bishops supported the war on poverty launched by Congress and President Johnson in 1965. John Egan, a Chicago priest, together with social action priests trained in Saul Alinksy's community organizing techniques, founded the Catholic Committee on Urban Ministry (CCUM) in 1967. Within a decade over five thousand men and women had joined the organization. Geno Baroni, a priest in Washington, D.C., who was noted for his work with ethnic groups in the cities, joined Egan to establish the Campaign for Human Development, a national program funded by the bishops in an effort to eliminate poverty.

The parish also took on a new look in the 1960s and 1970s. Many became community institutions committed to serving the needs of all people regardless of race or religion and the church hall became a community meeting place. In New York City, the showcase of this new-style parish was St. Gregory the Great, on the city's West Side. Pastor Henry J. Browne, an important community leader in the 1960s, was aware of the transformation that had occurred and was sensitive to some old-time parishioners who were not pleased with the change. Browne was not surprised when one of them wrote to him: "I would also like to point out at this time that I feel St. Gregory is now a Political Organization and a meeting place for the liberals, hippies, anti-establishment, etc. characters, and since the many incidents of the past year . . . it is with regret that now after more than thirty years, I am no longer a parishioner."[8]

Among this array of social justice activities, the Catholic connection between justice and peace was made and support both directly and indirectly was given to the American Catholic peace movement during the Vietnam era.[9] Many Catholics remained committed to a single issue such as race or community organizing and only indirectly supported the peace movement; other Catholics moved from their social justice work into the peace movement; some integrated the two works. Some Catholics like Mario Savio, leader of Berkeley's Free Speech movement, Tom Hayden, the author of the "Port Huron Statement" which launched the Students for a Democratic Society (SDS), and Timothy Leary, who urged the use of LSD as a sacrament in the counterculture of the 1960s made no connection between their religion and society's problems and left the church. On the other hand, Jack Kerouac, the "beat" novelist and guru of the counterculture, could not abandon his Catholicity.[10] Beyond a doubt, the impact of social changes in American society and the changes within Catholicism after the Second Vatican Council were causing an identity crisis among American Catholics. They were rethinking the meaning of Catholicism in American society and were becoming very visible and vocal in their criticism of the injustices they found.

The connection between justice and peace for American Catholic social justice activists was complicated by the policies of President Johnson. They as well as many other Americans supported the president in his domestic policies of civil rights and the War on Poverty, but many opposed his foreign policy in Vietnam. Others did not want to jeopardize their domestic social gains by opposing the war. Martin Luther King, Jr., more than any other leader, provided the link that enabled the social-justice activists to embrace the peace movement. On 25 February 1967 at an institute sponsored by *Nation* magazine, King delivered his first speech devoted entirely to Vietnam, "one of history's most cruel and senseless wars." In the speech he indicated that the war was limiting the effects of the war on poverty. "The promises of the Great Society have been shot down on the battlefields of Vietnam," he declared. He called for union as a goal for a better America: "We must combine the fervor of the civil rights movment with the peace movement. We must demonstrate, teach and preach, until the very foundations of our nation are shaken."[11]

American Catholics, more than any other group, had a tradition of a conservative and patriotic hierarchy that exhorted its members to obey the nation's lawfully constituted authority, especially during a time of war. As the historian David J. O'Brien has pointed out, "the history of American Catholic responses to international events is more complex than that." He then points to the American hierarchy's opposition to American arms shipments to the Loyalist government during the Spanish Civil War and to the bishops' private conversations during World War II to the president concerning their reservations about war-time policies toward the Soviet Union. O'Brien, however, does not go far enough in his analysis. In both cases the hierarchy was motivated by their anti-communism. This was not sufficient motivation, however, to oppose U.S. entrance into World War II nor obliteration or atomic bombing, but it was the only sufficient rationale for criticism by the hierarchy during that period. O'Brien does make the observation that "For many understandable reasons Catholics were early and active cold warriors, but their anti-Communist militance could and did lead them to become very critical of the government and its policies."[12]

Church leaders favored containment policies in Europe and were concerned about communist expansion in Asia. The victory of communism in China had given rise to a powerful anti-communist lobby in the United States. When the French withdrew from Vietnam in 1954 and left behind in South Vietnam a non-communist government dominated by Catholics led by Ngo Diem, Cardinal Spellman and such Catholics as Senators John F. Kennedy and Mike Mansfield of Montana supported the pro-Diem lobby in Congress. The medical missionary Tom Dooley reinforced this anti-communist position by popularizing a view of Indochina as a battleground between communism and democracy. Thus, the Catholic hierarchy as well as its members along with other Americans were initially sympathetic with American efforts to counter communism in South Vietnam.[13]

The election of the first Catholic president, John F. Kennedy, assured a continuation of these American efforts in South Vietnam. Kennedy's administration established for Vietnam "a political guideline that would be respected by decision-makers for the next thirteen years: in its effort to ensure an anticommunist regime in Saigon."[14] Presidential policymakers disagreed with those on the Right who wanted to use nearly any means in order to maintain an anti-communist regime in Saigon and they also disagreed with the Left who argued that U.S. objectives for Vietnam were unattainable and immoral. Kennedy's choice of a middle course of action gained the support of the majority of Americans who considered themselves neither hawks nor doves, but in the political center.

During Kennedy's administration the American peace movement had been reconstituted on the issue of atmospheric testing. There were basically two wings in the movement. The first was the liberal wing, which used the politics of persuasion and advocacy but experienced frustration in not being able to popularize an agenda of disarmament and a negotiated end to the Cold War. On the other hand, the radical wing emphasized individual acts of moral protest. The only Catholic group identified with the American peace movement was the Catholic Worker, which often joined the radical wing in moral actions of protest against nuclear testing.[15]

The successful passage of the test-ban treaty of 1963 cut through the newly constituted peace movement like a two-edged sword. Since the peace movement proposed a comprehensive test-ban treaty, disarmament and disengagement from the Cold War, the liberal wing was left without its primary issue of atmospheric testing, and liberal groups, like SANE, rapidly declined in membership. The radical wing of the peace movement, however, began to align itself with the student New Left that was emerging out of the civil rights movement and focused on the Indochina policy. Members of the radical wing and the student New Left were often joined by activists in the social and cultural movements. Historians Charles DeBenedetti and Charles Chatfield contend that this realignment signaled the transition from peace advocacy to war opposition in the American peace movement.[16]

The shift of the American peace movement from nuclear issues to opposition to the Indochina policy was also reflected among Catholics involved in the peace movement. The writings of Thomas Merton clearly reflected this change. The year 1963 marked a transition in his writing from a focus on nuclear pacifism to nonviolence as the basis for developing a new ethic for peace as he called for an end to the Vietnam War. This shift within the peace movement became complete after the election of 1964 when President Johnson defined the Vietnam War as "limited" and stated that its escalation excluded the use of nuclear weapons in favor of an air war of obliteration bombing conducted with new electronic and bio-chemical methods.[17] Merton's comment on Johnson's position at the time revealed the hold that the just war doctrine had on him.

> Still Johnson is as much a fire breather as there is when it comes to Vietnam, and that is what is most tragic. There is not a shred of justification for war there. It is a pure power policy, without necessity, a brute piece of stupidity and frustration on the part of people who have no imagination or insight and no moral sense. Because a few people in America want power and wealth, a lot of Vietnamese, Chinese, and Americans have been and will be sacrificed. It is a complete travesty of justice and right and liberty. I do not think it can meet any of the requirements of the traditional "just war."[18]

Official leadership among American Catholics, on the other hand, characteristically continued to support the war for the next five years.

The issue of the draft, however, provided Catholics with a means to address not only the public policy of their government in Vietnam, but also the official stance of the church on conscientious objection and the morality of the war. Some Catholics would protest the Vietnamese policy of the United States by resistance to the draft. Others who were not willing to challenge the war itself, still used the issue of the draft as the focal point for creating change in the teaching of the church in America.

The right of an individual Catholic to become a conscientious objector (CO) had been proclaimed at the Second Vatican Council.

Conscientious objection did not necessitate a judgment against the public policy of government on the part of the individual, it merely required that the individual be opposed to all war. In the case of a selective conscientious objector (SCO) the individual judges the government to be involved in an unjust war and thereby refuses to fight in that particular war. Thus, the same individual could not be both a CO and a SCO. The American Catholic hierarchy would not endorse the right of a Catholic to become a conscientious objector until after the Second Vatican Council. But when it did, the American Catholic hierarchy also recognized selective conscientious objection.

Prior to Vatican II the statements of the Roman Catholic church had been ambiguous on this issue. This ambiguity was reflected as recently as 1954 when Pope Pius XII in his Christmas message had said that "a Catholic citizen cannot invoke his own conscience in order to refuse to serve and fulfill those duties [of combat that] the law imposes." Yet, later in the same address he conceded that, "there are times in which only recourse to higher pinciples can bring peace to consciences. It is therefore consoling," the pope concluded, "that in some countries, amid today's debates, men are talking about conscience and its demands."[19]

The right of a Catholic to be a conscientious objector was invoked by individual Catholics in the United States even before the Second Vatican Council had ended. A few years after Vatican II, the Catholic church came into conflict with the U.S. policy of conscription by supporting the right of an individual Catholic to be a selective conscientious objector, a status that was not recognized by U.S. law. By supporting the right of a Catholic to be a CO or a SCO, church leadership was able to respond in a pastoral manner and on an individual level to its membership in parishes and on college campuses. In this support, church leadership did not have to declare the immorality of the government's policy in Vietnam but it did enable the church to support its members who in conscience had reached such a position. The church hierarchy never advocated or supported noncooperation or resistance to the draft for those acts directly protested the legitimacy of the government's actions by denying its right to draft an individual. The majority of Catholic individuals who refused to be drafted chose to be COs and register their dissent within the law.

Although there are no accurate counts of the number of Catholics who resisted the draft or applied for SCO, records do exist for those who received CO classification: From September 1967 to November 1968, 2.8 percent of men classified for alternative service as COs were Catholic; between November 1968 and September 1969 the percentage of Catholic COs rose to 7.8 percent.[20] This was a larger percentage than of any other single denomination. In addition many others were denied recognition of their SCO position, and some left the country or went to prison for refusing to register for the draft or for burning their draft cards.

Since individuals were powerless to alter directly the means of warfare employed by the U.S. military in Vietnam, the focus for organizing protest against the war became the draft. This opposition enabled individuals to assume personal responsibility and visibly take a stand to reflect their moral commitment. In turn, pressure was applied on the hierarchy as individuals turned to the church for support of their position. Thus, for Catholics the draft became the main organizing tool for peace activists and this constituted their main contribution to the entire antiwar movement during the Vietnam era.

Since for more than thirty years, the Catholic Worker was the only Catholic organization that had provided support to conscientious objectors and advocated noncooperation, it was natural for it to be in the forefront on the draft issue. By the early 1960s, the Catholic Worker in cooperation with other pacifist peace groups had advanced the support of nonviolent resistance with an emphasis on the activist imperative. Symbolic acts of nonviolent resistance against the draft in the 1960s enabled the intense personalism and moral commitment of Catholic Workers to witness against the war in Vietnam. This emphasis on peace pervaded the energies of the Catholic Worker movement after 1964 while other issues such as poverty, labor, and civil rights receded into the background. Houses of hospitality, farming communes, and the paper still continued to flourish. Despite the emphasis on peace in the movement and the formation in 1962 of PAX, a group solely dedicated to bringing a new vision of peace to the institutional church, a significant new Catholic pacifist group directly linked to the broader antiwar movement was formed: the Catholic Peace Fellowship (CPF).

One reason for the formation of the new group was that though it was a pacifist group like the Catholic Worker, its sole focus would be peace and an effort to effect change in the government's public policy in Indochina. CPF would advocate nonviolent direct action and resistance, making it very different from PAX, which continued to focus on institutional changes for peace within the church and basically rejected nonviolent resistance tactics. To reach the hierarchy, PAX embraced not only pacifists but also adherents of the just war theory into its membership. Eileen Egan, friend and traveling companion of Dorothy Day, was mainly responsible for the organization. She directed the energies of the small group increasingly toward achieving institutional changes in the Roman Catholic Church in America on the issue of conscientious objection.

The formation of CPF was the result of the efforts of John Heidbrink, a Presbyterian minister and interfaith director of the Fellowship of Reconciliation (FOR), which had been established in England just after the outbreak of World War I by Henry T. Hodgkin, an Anglican priest. In 1915, he traveled to the United States and established the American FOR. It was a membership organization and individuals could apply for admission on the basis of their agreement with a statement of principles that included the refusal of personal participation in any war. In 1960, Alfred Hassler became the executive secretary of FOR in America and assigned John Heidbrink the task of finding a way to organize the Catholics into a FOR affiliate. Heidbrink went to the Catholic Worker to recruit. There he found James H. (Jim) Forest, "a high school dropout who sought refuge in the Navy, but found the Church and pacifism instead. He was released from the Navy as a conscientious objector and high tailed it to the Catholic Worker. Jim was then nineteen years old and helped in every aspect of the house work and the paper in 1960–1961."[21] Heidbrink persuaded Forest to call together a few people to lay the groundwork for a Catholic Peace Fellowship; but the end result was the formation of PAX. Heidbrink tried again, "incessantly" as Forest says, from 1962 to 1964, when the Christian Peace Conference in Prague provided the occasion for accomplishing his hope. Heidbrink secured a gift from an anonymous donor and organized an American group to participate in the conference. They included Jim Forest, Daniel Berrigan, Hermene Evans, and James Douglass, together with Heidbrink. This group determined to form a CPF within FOR upon their return from Europe.[22]

In 1964, Daniel and Philip Berrigan asked three Catholic Workers, Jim Forest, Thomas (Tom) Cornell, and Martin Corbin to work with them in forming a new peace group.[23] A letterhead listing sponsors was put together, a mailing list compiled from personal Christmas card lists of the organizers and two hundred names from FOR were collated, and an invitational mailing enlisting membership and support for a Catholic Peace Fellowship was sent in August 1964. The organizational membership of CPF was similar to FOR but its daily operation to the Catholic Worker. Those who came to help at the CPF did so on a volunteer basis and directors received only a nominal salary.

The successful formation of CPF under the auspices of FOR was due to the increased cooperation between Catholics and other peace groups in America by the 1960s. Catholic suspicion and distrust of other religions had greatly dissipated since the birth of the ecumenical movement that produced in 1948 the World Council of Churches and later the National Council of Churches in the United States. The Second Vatican Council had also encouraged ecumenism and had devoted one of its sixteen major documents to supporting union rather than separation. The ecumenical spirit affected the American peace movement and CPF became the first Catholic peace group to exist under the auspices of an interdenominational organization—FOR provided financial and organizational support.[24]

The stated purpose of CPF was to affirm life and denounce war: "War has been the way of life of the majority of mankind throughout history, and we only deceive ourselves if we think it is not just as much the life of our times, the impulse of much of our economy, and the preoccupation of our politics. But war is not life, nor even a necessary part of life."[25] The founders viewed their job as that of educating Catholics and others on the issue of peace.

As an educational agency, CPF hoped to address itself to many areas of concern, including building interest in and opposition to the war in Vietnam, raising medical relief for victims on all sides, and providing draft information and counseling services.

Self-consciously Catholic, the founders of CPF also wanted to develop a "theology of peace" with an emphasis on the principles and techniques of nonviolent resistance, and in accordance with the Second Vatican Council, a "vision of a Church that is peacemaking to its very core." Forest was the catalyst, and engaged in lengthy correspondence with Thomas Merton and Daniel Berrigan. He kept in touch with various leaders in the antiwar movement. He wrote and talked and organized Catholics on a day-to-day basis using the talents of each for CPF and also using CPF to assist them in their labors for peace.

The most significant accomplishments during the initial period of CPF were the planting of articles in Catholic journals and the publishing of a booklet by Jim Forest, *Catholics and Conscientious Objection*, with Cardinal Spellman's imprimatur. Free ads offering a criticism of the Vietnam War and written primarily by Gordon Zahn and Jim Douglass were placed in several Catholic journals. Some modest educational activities were undertaken as well as a few demonstrations. Both Forest and Cornell helped to pull together the anti–Vietnam War coalition known as the Mobilization to End the War in Vietnam. But CPF's day-to-day work centered on counseling Catholic conscientious objectors. Implicit in their concern was the desire to build a future constituency for war resistance.

In the fall of 1966, Jim Forest decided to accept an offer to join the FOR staff at Nyack, as special projects coordinator, working two-thirds of the time for FOR and one-third for CPF. Cornell remained in the Manhattan office until 1969. Both operated CPF in the Catholic Worker tradition and utilized the organizational structure and contacts of the FOR for CPF's benefit. Cornell contends that the work of CPF "stimulated the debate on [the Vietnam War's] morality that culminated in the erosion of liberal Catholic support for the war and indeed, in its renunciation by the American Catholic Bishops in 1969."[26]

CPF faced many difficulties due to jail sentences, finances, and personal responsibilities of its leadership. When Tom Cornell was released from prison for burning his draft card in 1969, he decided to accept a paid position for FOR in Nyack, working as the representative at the United Nations on the Non-Governmental Organizations Disarmament Committee where he served on its executive committee. Jim Forest, realizing that he would soon be in jail for his involvement in the Milwaukee 14 destruction of draft files, expressed his concern to Cornell about what his move to Nyack would do to the CPF. Forest wrote to Cornell saying that "Yet, it would be a great blow to the New York scene not to have you here and in it, and to the New York CPF situation. It could conceivably have the effect of moving the CPF into its last days."[27] Cornell had no intention of abandoning the CPF, but as a married man with three children, a paid position offered a little security and the move assured a home in Newburgh for his family. When Cornell moved to FOR in Nyack, the CPF moved to 339 Lafayette Street in New York City. There the office would remain. Since the CPF office was staffed by volunteers its leadership often changed because of the constant turnover in volunteers in the New York City office. Tom Cornell and Jim Forest always maintained control of the organization.

Soon after CPF had been reorganized and Forest was in jail, Tom Cornell received a letter from Alfred Hassler, executive director of FOR, saying that the CPF had a $10,000 deficit with FOR in the last fifteen months.[28] Cornell immediately decided that the best course of action was a fund appeal letter to members of CPF. The financial crisis precipitated a five-page letter from Cornell to Forest after Forest suggested severing any institutional connection with FOR. Cornell's reply provides an assessment of CPF from one of its leaders in relation to FOR and its Catholic Worker tradition.

Cornell first replied to Forest's criticism of the FOR. "The FOR is not what it should be, that emphasis on publications, speaking and 'superficial' contact with individuals coordinated by a top heavy bureaucracy is not what we want. It's not what we have, either. The CPF is quite other as you know and in no way has it been hindered in being quite other by its integration into FOR." Cornell also admitted that he felt at times the religious component in Nyack "is superficial and even fake." Yet, he also admitted that the most positive feature of FOR was its ability to accomodate to different styles and to be a center of communication for the religious groups: Protestant, Catholic, and Jewish. He also believed that the FOR was attempting to meet the needs of the peace movement in general by releasing Ron Young to work on the New Mobilization. Cornell finally did not want to sever his and CPF's financial relationship with FOR. He explained his position to Forest in the following words. "Because I need the security of knowing that the check is coming. Because they do our mailings and take care of bookkeeping that I can not do and you are not here to do. Because it gives CPF more weight in the circles of the movement. Yes, it does. Because it keys us in to other people and is an example of ecumenism. . . . I find that the reason you give for dissolving the ties to FOR are ephemeral, lack substance, even meaning."[29]

Cornell then spent the next few pages attempting to clarify Forest's expectations of the CPF working within the Catholic Worker tradition.[30] He tried to distinguish between the myth and reality of the Catholic Worker. First, he dealt with "community" and stated, "We [CPF] have helped some people to be more aware of each other and more supportive to each other's common longings for some way to work for peace. But if you mean 'community' in the way that we are used to thinking of it, community is a living together, a sharing of resources. This we have not done." Second, he tried to come to grips with the term, "voluntary poverty." Cornell pointed out that after "five years of marriage and two children, now three children, my wife has at last a washing machine! . . . We live with precarity all the time. That is the essence of poverty. Simplicity is the rest. You do not know of another organization or group that works with such precarity or simplicity as the CPF." Third, Cornell dealt with the concept "works of mercy" and said that CPF takes care of that as individuals. And finally he wrote cryptically, "Decentralization. We've got it. Resistance. We started it."[31] In the end Cornell accused Forest of purism and stated that none of these values were antithetical to FOR's values. Unlike Forest and the Berrigans, Cornell was more deeply rooted in the Catholic Worker tradition. Personally, he never went beyond traditional nonviolence and like Dorothy Day, he would never directly confront the church. After Forest was released from prison in 1971, he too continued to work for CPF and assumed a paid position with FOR as editor of *Fellowship*.

CPF remained within the Catholic Worker tradition. The center for CPF remained in New York City, where with a staff of volunteers and a minimal allowance members operated a speakers' bureau, a tape and film library, a publication program, and a production of the bi-monthly *CPF Bulletin*.[32] CPF also collaborated with other peace groups for demonstrations, marches, beg-ins, prayer vigils, and fasting in New York City and in Washington, D.C. The main work of the group on a day-to-day basis was always the providing of free draft counseling for conscientious objectors, sometimes as many as fifty to one hundred a week.[33]

Other CPF groups were founded in major cities throughout the United States. Though each group was autonomous, it could draw on the resources of the New York group. Activities of each CPF group varied greatly and there was no serious attempt made to coordinate

these groups. Some groups devoted their energies solely to draft counseling, others to organizing demonstrations against either the government or the church. The Washington chapter made an effort to
influence the American bishops before their fall national conference
in 1966. The group received most attention when they placed an ad
in the recently founded, *National Catholic Reporter*, a newspaper
independently owned and operated by lay people that was seeking to
keep liberal-minded Catholics up to date on developments in the
church. The CPF ad read:

> When is A
> BISHOPS'
> meeting a
> HAPP
> EN
> ING?
> maybe when
> Pentecost first occurred
> maybe when John
> called a Council maybe when our Bishops
> show they are bothered by the same things we are. The rightness of
> continuing massive civilian casualties in north and south Vietnam—the
> draft—conscientious objectors to unjust wars going to prison—plans for
> universal training—laws against showing love of enemy. As Christians and
> Americans these things bother us. We ask for some concern, some sharing of
> our difficulties. In the problem of war, we ask that Bishops go as far as Paul
> VI and call for an immediate end of the fighting "even at the expense of
> some inconvenience or loss."[34]

Despite the efforts of CPF's public call for the bishops to condemn
the war in November 1966 the bishops issued their pastoral, *Peace and
Vietnam*, which stated, "In light of the facts as they are known to us, it
is reasonable to argue that our presence in Vietnam is justified."[35] In
1966, members of the Catholic hierarchy were recognized for speaking
out in support of the war rather than for speaking critically of it. Most
notable among the hierarchy were Cardinal Spellman and Archbishop
Robert E. Lucey, who as a young priest had worked zealously to build
the CAIP. The cardinal's position on the Vietnam War was no different
than his position on World War II. As the head of the U.S. Military
Vicariate, his annual Christmas messages to the American troops

received wide publicity[36] when he consciously discarded the normative just war tradition by proclaiming his support of "my country right or wrong."[37] In "Peace and Vietnam" the bishops made no mention of other war and peace issues such as conscientious objection, conscription, or efforts to provide medical relief to areas of the world labeled "enemy" by the government.

The New York City CPF issued a statement on the issue of medical aid in 1967 after the *National Catholic Reporter* and the *New York Times* revealed that the Catholic Relief Services provided material assistance to members of the South Vietnamese Popular Forces, yet refused assistance to war victims in North Vietnam.[38] The *National Catholic Reporter*, at a great financial investment it could ill afford, had sent Michael Novak as a correspondent to Vietnam for a few weeks in the summer of 1967, and while on assignment there Novak discovered the Catholic Relief Services' involvement. CPF asked Catholics in their statement to withhold contributions to Catholic Relief Services and to send their money to Caritas Internationalis, the Vatican's relief-coordinating body that provided material assistance to the North Vietnamese Red Cross as well as participating in relief efforts in the South. Since Eileen Egan of PAX worked for Catholic Relief Services, she resented the embarrassment caused by her Catholic pacifist friends in the CPF.[39] Tragically, Catholic Relief Services resolved the conflict by dropping all relief to Vietnam. These efforts gained publicity and gave visibility to those Catholics who opposed the war in Vietnam.

From Vatican II until the end of the war, the Catholic Worker, CPF, and PAX were united in their desires for peace and their opposition to the war. The majority of Catholics and the American hierarchy could not identify with them. Catholics viewed members of these groups as pacifists, radicals, and perfectionists. Most of the bishops dismissed them as a "fringe" group within Catholicism. But as more time passed their prophetic messages concerning the war were recognized as the major contributions of American Catholics to peace and the antiwar movement.

Catholic Worker action in support of traditional nonviolent resistance reached a high point ten days after Pope Paul VI had spoken at the United Nations. On 15 October 1965, a young Catholic Worker named David Miller stepped to the front of a platform and said, "I believe the napalming of villages is an immoral act. I hope this will be a significant political act, so here goes." And then he burned his draft card.[40]

Destroying draft cards was nothing new to the American peace movement, nor was it the first such act performed by a Catholic Worker. At a series of nationwide demonstrations on 2 February 1947, some four or five hundred Americans either publicly destroyed their draft cards or mailed them to President Truman.[41] At a rally in Washington Square at the end of the second worldwide General Strike for Peace in November 1963, Tom Cornell, who was then an associate editor of the *Catholic Worker*, destroyed his draft card along with twenty-five others. He and Chris Kearns, also a Catholic Worker, led a draft card burning at an anticonscription rally in Union Square on Armed Forces Day, 16 May 1964. This rally was sponsored by the War Resisters League, the Student Peace Union, the Committee for Non-Violent Action, and the Catholic Worker.[42]

Also in 1965, a nationwide coordinated National Assembly of Unrepresented Peoples was held in August. *Life* magazine ran a long article on the demonstrations; it contained a picture of Chris Kearns dropping his draft card into a flaming cooking pot. In direct reaction to the picture, Representative Mendel Rivers of the House Armed Services Subcommittee rammed a bill through Congress that made draft card burning a crime punishable by $10,000 fine and/or five years imprisonment. President Johnson signed the bill into law on August 31.[43] Thus, David Miller's action on October 15 became a test case for the act.

Miller had joined the Catholic Worker the previous June following his graduation with a degree in sociology from LeMoyne College. Miller's action acquired unusual visibility since it took place at the largest nationwide antiwar rally to date in New York City. He appeared on the program not as a representative of the Catholic Worker but of draft noncooperators, later to become known as draft resisters. James Peck of the War Resisters League introduced him. Three days later Miller was arrested.

At a rally on 6 November 1965, in front of the Federal Court House in New York City where 150,000 people had gathered to protest the Vietnam War, five more men burned their draft cards. Dorothy Day and A. J. Muste introduced the men. Three of the five were members of the Catholic Worker movement, James Wilson, Roy Fisher, and Tom Cornell.

Cornell, the spokesperson for the group, prefaced his statement by citing the futility of previous protests and the continuing escalation of the war. He claimed that the Rivers Bill outlawing the burning of draft cards was merely an attempt to stifle protest. He summed up the reason for his course of action by quoting a letter from Karl Meyer of the Chicago Catholic Worker to his draft board; it was printed in the October 1965 issue of *Catholic Worker*. Meyer, who was known for his witness of draft and tax resistance, had written: "I am sending to you with this letter, pieces of a Selective Service Registration Certificate and Notice of Classification which I have destroyed by tearing them in half, to signify my resistance to the new law. . . . The mutilation of human beings in Vietnam has become a civic virtue; now, the mutilation of a scrap of paper becomes a grave crime against the state." Cornell added to Meyer's words: "The grave crime, we are told, is not the destruction of life but the destruction of a piece of paper."[44] The five protesters were arrested.

David Miller went to trial on 9 February 1966, claiming that the act of burning a draft card was "symbolic speech" and thus guaranteed by the First Amendment. He was found guilty and a unanimous Court of Appeals later upheld the conviction.[45] Of the five draft card burners who participated in the November 6 rally, one, Jim Peck pleaded guilty and received a two year sentence.[46] The other four pleaded not guilty and based their case on freedom of speech as had Miller. They too were found guilty and were each sentenced to six months in prison.[47]

After these acts of civil disobedience and nonviolent resistance in October and November 1965, many others followed the path of the Catholic Workers. Thus, the draft-resistance movement, later known as "The Resistance" was born. Since over 3,500 draft cards had been publicly destroyed in various ways, the Rivers law was unenforceable and the movement proved to be a success. CPF as well as the Catholic Worker worked closely with the Resistance.

Even more remarkable was the extent to which Catholics who, for reason of sex or age, were not subject to the draft, nevertheless were willing to take risks and make sacrifices in their attempt to stand in solidarity with the young men facing the draft. The most dramatic example of this took place on 17 May 1968, when Daniel and Philip Berrigan together with seven other Catholics removed four hundred draft files from the Catonsville, Maryland, Draft Board office to a nearby parking lot, and burned them with homemade napalm. In a statement released after their arrest, this group called themselves the Catonsville Nine and justified their action on the grounds that "some property has no right to exist." This action began what was to become known as "The Ultra-Resistance."

The Catonsville Nine action began a series of draft board raids from the Milwaukee Fourteen to the Beaver Fifty-five to the East Coast Conspiracy to Save Lives to the Camden Twenty-eight. The exact number of draft board raids is unknown and estimates of their number range from 53 to 250 from the years 1967 to 1971.[48] Often arrests and trials followed. Support groups sprang up around the country. The movement ended when Attorney General John Mitchell announced that a federal grand jury had indicted Philip Berrigan and five others on charges of conspiring both to blow up the heating system of federal buildings in Washington and to kidnap Henry Kissinger. The Harrisburg trial followed.

Rosemary Reuther, a well-known Catholic theologian, and the priest-sociologist Andrew Greeley criticized the Berrigans for their political perfectionism and extremism because it alienated more people than it attracted. The old pacifist groups in the antiwar movement such as the Catholic Worker, the War Resisters League, the Fellowship of Reconciliation, and various Quaker groups, though supportive and sympathetic of the motives of the Catonsville Nine, could not support the destruction of property as a valid nonviolent tactic even in the symbolic violence of draft file destruction.[49] Despite the controversy among Catholics and others involved in the Catholic resistance that resulted, the Berrigan brothers were still acclaimed for their willingness to "pay the price" to stop the war in Vietnam and recognized as the leaders of the American Catholic peace movement.

The issue of the draft was also the catalyst on Catholic college campuses in building support for the antiwar movement. Draft-counseling services were provided as an initial response since there were always a few Catholic priests or lay faculty who believed it was part of their pastoral duty to aid young men facing the draft. As the war escalated, however, a diversity of responses appeared on the college campuses. What happened at the University of Notre Dame provides a good example of how Catholic college students responded to the war in Vietnam.

All college campuses were affected by the free speech movement and the founding of the Students for a Democratic Society (SDS). The most significant events on Catholic college campuses, however, were the 1965 "teach-ins," which were organized by University of Michigan faculty members and spread to the country's leading campuses. These teach-ins legitimized dissent at the outset of the war and their effect was eventually felt on all Catholic campuses.[50] The University of Notre Dame's day-long teach-in took place on 16 October 1965. Faculty, students, and two non-University speakers debated American involvement in Southeast Asia for over twelve hours. The political spectrum of the students represented the nation in microcosm: SDS, Young Americans for Freedom, political realists, conservatives, cold-war liberals, pacifists, and radicals. Two students, Joel R. Connelly and Howard J. Dooley, who wrote about their undergraduate years at Notre Dame in the 1960s, contended that the 1965 Vietnam symposium set the temper of the Notre Dame student protest movement for a decade. They wrote that a pattern emerged on that day which signaled the tone for protest on the campus for the remainder of the antiwar period. "Notre Dame students remained by and large non-ideological in their anti-Vietnam stance, thus avoiding much of the factionalism and irrational one-upmanship which made a shambles of the ideologically committed New Left. Notre Dame students also, for the most part, remained tactical moderates, preferring peaceful demonstrations to bear witness to their concern rather than violent activism."[51] The fact that during the day of the teach-in a Mass for Peace was celebrated on the campus may have been the greatest factor explaining why students preferred peaceful demonstrations, though the student observers made no mention of it. The tradition of celebrating a Mass for Peace also provided a religious dimension to the days of protest on campus and this practice continued during the entire period of campus unrest at Notre Dame. During the homily of every Mass for Peace the ethical and moral issues rather than the political issues concerning the war were constantly being raised. This focused the terms of intellectual debates on moral issues and may account for the absence of political ideology on campus.

After the teach-in, student unrest manifested itself sporadically. In 1967, two hundred students, faculty, and religious demonstrated against the job interviewing that was being conducted at the University

Placement Bureau by Dow Chemical Company, because Dow was producing the napalm used by the U.S. military in the Vietnam War. Then in 1968 the student unrest escalated, but it took various directions. Several different student newspapers appeared on campus protesting the university's administrative policies concerning the lack of a totally open speakers policy, disciplinary regulations and parietal restrictions, the ROTC (Notre Dame had the largest program of any Catholic university), the small number of minorities at the school, campus job interviewing by the Central Intelligence Agency, and the escalation of the Vietnam War. As each issue came to the fore, demonstrations and counterdemonstrations were held. Thoughout 1968 student unrest was creating havoc and when the students returned to campus in 1969 after Christmas break their enthusiasm for such activities persisted.

To avoid future embarrasment and disruption of the university's normal activities, its president, Theodore Hesburgh issued an eight-page letter to the university comunity. This letter set forth what became known in the national media as Notre Dame's "Tough Fifteen Minute Rule." The letter permitted dissent but would not permit disruption of the Notre Dame academic community. Students, faculty, or staff who violated this principle would be given fifteen minutes to reflect on their actions; if they continued their disruption, their identity cards would be seized. In his autobiography, Hesburgh states that "after the letter was distributed, the crisis on campus quieted down, at least temporarily. Resistance to violence, incivility, and boorishness began to stiffen. The letter was at least partially responsible for that. But it had another effect that I never anticipated. It made me a kind of folk hero among the hawks, who saw the solution to the student revolution in terms of truncheons and police action. Maybe that explains why I spent so much time after 1969 trying to get people to understand why the students were legitimately upset and what was good about their concerns. A hawk I was not."[52] Debates on the legal and moral limits of the right to dissent persisted at faculty councils and among the student press. Confrontations also continued to occur. At a national conference on institutional racism sponsored by the National Student Association at Notre Dame, Hesburgh was heckled by students who demanded greater minority enrollment while others called for the withdrawal of academic credit from ROTC programs and an end to the U.S. military involvement in the Vietnam War.[53]

In October 1969, Hesburgh and other U.S. college and university presidents signed an open letter calling on the government to accelerate its withdrawal of military forces from Vietnam, and Hesburgh joined with the students in observing the Vietnam Moratorium Day, which had been announced by the New Mobilization Committee. A peace rally took place on campus and it included a Mass for Peace attended by over 2,500 students, faculty, and staff. Archbishop Thomas Roberts of England spoke of the Christian's obligation to resist immoral behavior by the state and affirmed the action of four students and two assistant professors who destroyed their draft cards during the Offertory of the Eucharistic service when he said, "You may be the only university in the world where the Mass has been connected with the offering of draft cards but when you and I go to daily Mass, more often than not we celebrate the feast of a martyr who was put to death for some form of civil disobedience. We have learned from [the martyrs] that we ought to obey God, not man."[54]

Student protests against the Vietnam War continued when Dow Chemical Company and the CIA tried to recruit on campus again in 1969. Students attempted to take over the administration building and Hesburgh invoked the Fifteen Minute Rule. Five students were expelled and five students were suspended. With the invasion of Cambodia and the killing of students at Kent State University and Jackson State University in the spring of 1970, outrage swept the campus. Mass meetings, memorial liturgies, protest rallies, and Masses for Peace were held. A student strike was also proclaimed. Around-the-clock discussions were held about the university community's proper response to the events. President Hesburgh made provisions for students who felt in conscience that they needed to strike, but he kept the university open for those who did not want to strike. Hesburgh also issued an unequivocal public statement declaring his personal opposition to the war and decrying the paucity of moral leadership in America. Students collected over 23,000 signatures from South Bend residents who agreed with Hesburgh's opposition to the Vietnam War and sent it to Congress.[55] The excellent leadership of Hesburgh during these years of student unrest and the constant incorporation of religion and the message of peace no doubt reduced the level of violence and disruption at the academic institution. In one sense the Catholic college campus looked very much like other college campuses in America during the student unrest period of the 1960s. On the other hand the added religious dimension provided by Masses for Peace that were an integral part of protest demonstrations and the constant structuring of the terms of debate and discussion in moral and ethical language distinguished the Catholic campus from its secular counterparts. The Catholic college campus seemed to be the one institution in American Catholicism that enabled all Catholics, regardless of their beliefs on the Vietnam War, to find a place where they could witness to their convictions.

The college campus was also the place where many young men confronted the issue of the draft. And the proper response to the draft was often a topic of debate. Some students accepted the draft when their number was selected or they were part of the ROTC program on campus. Others received deferments or exemptions from the draft, or left their country for Canada or Sweden to escape the draft, and still others chose the path of resistance. Most students who opposed the war, however, preferred to register their dissent within the laws of American society by applying for CO status. In order for a young man to qualify for CO status a knowledge of the law together with an ability to express beliefs and convictions in a written statement and verbally before a draft board required a certain level of education as well as some counseling. A college student definitely held the advantage in such cases over a high school graduate who went directly into the work force. The position of some of these Catholic men was further complicated by the lack of a legal provision for a selective CO status. Three Catholic groups, CPF, PAX, and CAIP, tried to help the young Catholic men seeking CO status. PAX and CAIP attempted to help them, not directly as CPF did by draft counseling, but by lobbying the church and the government.

The PAX group of the Vietnam era was very different from the first PAX group of the World War II era. The earlier group attempted to offer support to Catholic conscientious objectors. The aim of the new PAX group was to change the positions of both the Roman Catholic church and Congress on conscientious objection.

In *U.S. v. Seeger* in 1965 the Supreme Court extended the privilege of CO status to include as "religious" certain beliefs not identified with conventional religions and thus identified conscientious beliefs with religion.[56] Congress's response was to omit the Supreme Being clause from the 1967 Draft Act. The Seeger decision aided many young men who were not identified with an official church in applying for CO status. It also aroused hopes that the courts or Congress would extend the privilege of COs to selective conscientious objectors. The rationale for SCO was advanced by three theologians who were noted for their work on the just war theory: John Courtney Murray, a Catholic theologian at Woodstock; Ralph Potter, a Protestant theologian at Harvard; and Paul Ramsey, a Protestant theologian at Yale.

Murray developed the Catholic case for SCO. In the mid-1960s, President Johnson had appointed a commission, chaired by Assistant Attorney General Burke Marshall, to consider the question of selective conscientious objection.[57] While serving on the commission, Murray advocated that "the revised [selective service] statute should extend the provisions of the present statute to include not only the absolute pacifist but also the relative pacifist; that the grounds for the status of conscientious objector should be not only religious or non-religiously motivated opposition (Seeger decision) to participation in war in all forms, but also similarly motivated opposition to participation in particular wars."[58] After considerable debate, Murray's position was rejected by the majority of the commission, which was unwilling to extend the right of conscientious objection to include those who dissent selectively. In effect, the commission disavowed the relevancy of the just war tradition for conscientious citizens engaged in public discourse about war. No presidential recommendation was made to Congress on the issue. There was no indication on the part of Congress or the courts that either would extend CO to SCO.[59]

At the time of his death, Murray believed that the issue was not satisfactorily settled and that it should be kept before the country. One of his last acts was to lend his support to the "official" Catholic peace group, CAIP, in planning their 1967 conference on the topic of "Selective Conscientious Objection." The prestige of Murray as a theologian and the fact that he believed the Vietnam War to be justifiable meant that his position on SCO would carry great influence among the just war believers in the Catholic community. This was especially true among the hierarchy.[60] Since Murray used the just war doctrine to develop his position of SCO, for the first time in the twentieth century the just war doctrine was being used not only to measure the actions of the state but also was found to be applicable to the individual. The individual was now being called upon to apply the criteria of the just war theory to an existing war and in conscience make a decision about the morality of that war. Thus, on moral grounds, an individual who had supported World War II could oppose the Vietnam War. Selective conscientious objection has yet to be legally recognized in the United States.

After the Second Vatican Council, PAX's desire to effect change in church and state institutions on the draft resulted in the development of a strategy that would include both pacifists and just war traditionalists. The tactic was the pioneering of a Rights of Conscience Campaign. The campaign had a twofold purpose: "1) to have the Bishops of the United States issue a clarifying statement that a Catholic had the right to be a conscientious objector and further to be one on the grounds of the traditional Catholic teaching of the just war which makes 'selective conscientious objection' a valid Catholic position and 2) to change the draft law so that those who follow the just war tradition should not be discriminated against when they claim the right of conscientious objection."[61]

To help achieve these goals, PAX published *The War That Is Forbidden: Peace Beyond Vatican II*, which was sent free to every bishop in the United States. The organization also sent two memoranda to the bishops before the Selective Service law was extended in 1967. PAX even inserted in *Commonweal* magazine a paid announcement on the rights of conscience campaign and gathered signatures from a wide range of supporters, including theologians, educators, writers, and seven Catholic bishops. The book, the memorandum, and the *Commonweal* statement were also sent to every member of Congress, and Representative Donald Edwards of California read the PAX statement into the *Congressional Record* and urged that Congress take into account the validity of its arguments.[62] Despite the efforts of PAX, Congress remained unfavorable to SCO.

Though the CAIP supported the war in Vietnam and would not work directly with the "too pacifist" PAX, it did work to bring about the same desired change on the issue of conscientious objection in the institutional church. PAX realized this would happen and knew that CAIP was a dying organization after the Second Vatican Council and that as it had not expanded its membership since World War II, it had even fewer resources. Since CAIP was the only "official" peace organization in the church, PAX rightly assessed the need for its support to effect any change in the institutional church.

By the 1960s, CAIP had been totally absorbed into NCWC. Monsignor George Higgins, executive secretary of the CAIP by virtue of his position as director of the Social Action Department, managed to keep CAIP alive by issuing a monthly newsletter, *CAIP News*, and maintaining its annual conferences. Nevertheless, NCWC had refused to allot sufficient funds for a full-time CAIP staff.[63] In 1967, the reorganization of the NCWC into the United States Catholic Conference (USCC) brought along with its new name a new Commission for World Justice and Peace. USCC announced that the duties of the new commission duplicated the work of CAIP. Because of CAIP's total dependence on NCWC and the fact that it had become a very small and inbred group which was out of step with the times, it had no choice but to go out of existence. CAIP's leader and dominant spokesperson, William V. O'Brien of Georgetown University, was the only one capable of keeping it alive, but he did not have the required time, energy, or resources.

The other reason for CAIP's demise was its inability to depart from its conservative political position (what its members called political realism: "more realistic 'power political' approaches to war which emphasized the political and moral responsibilities of the decision maker to use power, but with due appreciation of normative restraints"[64]). CAIP's advocacy of the natural law and the just war doctrine could have attracted the general Catholic population who were looking for a Catholic peace group that would speak to them in those terms as they moved in opposition to the war during the 1960s, but CAIP's inability to depart from political realism precluded that possibility. Thus, CAIP, the first American Catholic peace organization, ceased to exist in 1968.[65] George Higgins stated that his main regret was that it was a lay organization and it died just when lay leadership was being encouraged by the church. Meanwhile, the vision of the new USCC's Commission on Justice and Peace was headed in the opposite direction. It wanted to establish a branch of the commission under clerical leadership in every diocesan office in America.[66] By 1970, these offices began to appear.

Following the Second Vatican Council, the American bishops voted to reorganize themselves and establish the National Conference of

Catholic Bishops (NCCB) as well as the USCC. The NCCB and USCC are separate organizations with the latter serving as the secretariate of NCCB. Generally speaking, the USCC develops policy and programs for approval by the administrative board and the body of bishops. Within the USCC is the Office of International Justice and Peace, which deals with military and political issues affecting other nations, human rights, the arms race, and global economy. It was this office that was responsible for addressing the issues related to the war in Vietnam. Monsignor Marvin Bordelon was appointed the director of the Office of International Justice and Peace at the USCC. The commission itself consisted of Patrick McDermott, S.J., Patricia Ringel, and James R. Jennings.

In the April 1967 bishops' meeting, there was no mention of the Vietnam War. In the November meeting, however, the national conference praised the Johnson administration for "repeated efforts to negotiate peace" and refused to repeat their 1966 endorsement of the war as just. The bishops' next pastoral, the *Resolution of Peace*, criticized the extremism of both left and right but acknowledged that the antiwar protestors represented "responsible segments of our society." Finally, in November 1968 the National Conference issued the important pastoral letter, *Human Life in Our Day*, the American reply to Paul VI's *Humanae Vitae*. The letter tackled two divisive issues in American Catholicism in 1968, the church's position on birth control and Vietnam.[67]

In *Human Life in Our Day*, the bishops recalled Vatican II and explicitly condemned aggressive wars and total war.[68] In relation to America's nuclear capability, the bishops again repeated the message of Vatican II condemning the "indiscriminate destruction of whole cities or vast areas with their inhabitants [as] a crime against God and man."[69] They endorsed the partial test-ban treaty and the non-proliferation treaty, condemned the antiballistic missile (ABM), and the doctrine of nuclear superiority, and escalation of the arms race.[70] This section on nuclear war in the document had not received very thorough discussion because of the attention focused on the first part of the document which dealt primarily with sexual ethics.[71] Turning to Vietnam, the bishops declared their opposition to the peacetime draft and posed several questions about the war in Vietnam. They did not proclaim the Vietnam War to be an unjust war, but stated that valid moral questions could be raised concerning the war effort.[72] The most significant part of the pastoral, however, was its proclamation of the right of a Catholic to be a conscientious objector or a selective conscientious objector to war. In Chapter 2, "The Family of Nations," the bishops not only endorsed the principle of conscientious objection but further recommended that the conscription law be changed to admit selective conscientious objection.[73]

> We recommend a modification of the Selective Service Act, making it possible . . . for so-called selective conscientious objectors to refuse—without fear of imprisonment or loss of citizenship—to serve in wars which they consider unjust.
> Whether or not such modifications in our laws are in fact made, we continue to hope that, in the all-important issue of war and peace, all men will follow their consciences.[74]

It is significant that this statement was only a small section in the larger pastoral that engaged Rome's encyclical reaffirming its teaching on birth control. What the American bishops were doing was attempting to place the issue of birth control within a broader context in which they could affirm the right of conscience in decision making and, by affirming the right of conscience in the broader context rather than in the context of the birth control issue, deflect their criticism of Rome's statement on birth control.[75] This was also the beginning of the bishops linking of abortion and war within a broader context of pro-life issues. Basically, it was all too subtle for anyone (Roman or American) to grasp. Regardless, through the labor of one person, Patrick Mc-Dermott, the bishops recognized the right of a Catholic to become a CO or an SCO.

Patrick McDermott had worked diligently to secure a statement from the American bishops on conscientious objection. After attending a retreat under the direction of Daniel Berrigan, McDermott decided to work at the Office of International Justice and Peace.[76] He was a friend of both pacifists and just war theorists and wrote the drafts for and did the organizing among the American hierarchy on the issue of conscientious objection.

McDermott continued his work on CO and SCO and wrote a pamphlet entitled, *Statement on the Catholic Conscientious Objector*, 15

October 1969, which was issued by USCC a year after the endorsement of the positions in *Human Life in Our Day*. The concluding
paragraph in the pamphlet states:

> We should look upon conscientious objection not as a scandal, but
> rather as a healthy sign. War will still not be replaced by more humane
> institutions for regulating conflict until citizens insist on principles of
> non-violence. John F. Kennedy once said, "War will exist until the
> distant day when the conscientious objector enjoys the same reputa-
> tion and prestige as the warrior does today."

In 1969, Richard Fernandez, the director of Clergy and Laity Concerned About Vietnam, after experiencing frustration at trying to rally
support for war resisters, "voiced his displeasure that a number of
religious bodies, including the National Conference of Catholic Bishops, the Lutheran Church in America, and the Union of American
Hebrew Congregations, had endorsed the concept of selective conscientious objection, but had failed to follow through with supporting actions."[77] In October 1971 the USCC issued a *Declaration on Conscientious Objection and Selective Conscientious Objection* that called on
Catholic organizations to show their support for both COs and SCOs
by hiring them.

> It is clear that a Catholic can be a conscientious objector to war in
> general or to a particular war "because of religious training and be-
> lief." . . . Catholic organizations which could qualify as alternative
> service agencies should be encouraged to support and provide meaning-
> ful employment for conscientious objectors.[78]

This endorsement of support for COs and SCOs from the Catholic
hierarchy during the Vietnam War was radically different from World
War II when, as Dorothy Day said, "I didn't particularly want to help run
a CO camp, but the Quakers, the Mennonites and the Brethren, they
nobly offered the government to go the second mile. . . . The Quakers,
the Mennonites and the Brethren would send the bills [for providing for
Catholic COs] to the Catholic Bishops, none of whom paid. Can you
imagine this? Well, fortunately, some of the Catholic institutions got in

on the deal at the hospital in Chicago and they offered their COs not only to take them in and help with the work but to give them training as male nurses, anesthetists, and laboratory technicans."[79]

James Jennings, reflecting on the USCC Division of World Justice and Peace's work for CO and SCO, believed the greatest influence on them at the time was not the Catholic peace groups but the tremendous amount of mail inquiries and telephone calls from the grassroots: young men, parents, pastors, and draft boards wanting to know what the position of the church was on conscientious objection.[80] It is very doubtful, however, that these individuals would have approached the USCC with such questions if they had not seen or heard the priests, nuns, and laity whose acts of resistance were frequently reported by the press. It is difficult to ascertain how many nuns, priests, brothers, and lay people were involved in the Catholic peace movement. Michael True in *Justice Seekers Peace Makers*, provides portraits of John Leary, a young Harvard graduate, and Kathy Knight, a wife and mother, who were at the center of Catholic peacemaking in Boston.[81] They are representative of Catholics throughout the United States involved in peacemaking.

Whatever the ultimate reason for the American Catholic hierarchy's support of CO and SCO, it reflected PAX's effective strategy of combining the pacifist CO position with the just war SCO position. PAX's choice of the human rights campaign pinpointed the possibilities and limits of the institutional church on the issue of the draft. It failed, however, to change the position of the government on SCO. In 1971, the U.S. Supreme Court announced that it could find in the Constitution no right to exemption from military service for one who claimed to be an SCO.

The general Catholic population, however, which was moving in opposition to the war seemingly in proportion to the war's escalation under the Johnson administration, had no Catholic peace group with which to identify. CPF was a pacifist group whose members were performing nonviolent resistance that seemed very foreign to the teachings of the just war tradition and traditional patriotism. PAX was not so much speaking to the laity but to the hierarchy trying to effect change in the church's teaching on CO and SCO. These Catholics were sought after by the peace movement when the ecumenical thrust among Catholic, Protestant, and Jewish clergymen formed an organization called Clergy (later Clergy and Laity) Concerned About Vietnam (CALCAV). Its initial leadership, Richard Neuhaus, Abraham Heschel, and Daniel Berrigan, held a news conference in the United Nations Church Center on 25 October 1965 to announce the formation of the group. This group wanted to move the churches and public opinion into opposition to the war and maintain a witness to the American tradition of dissent. It embraced both pacifists and just war traditionalists and assumed a middle ground since it did not call for an immediate withdrawal from Vietnam. As the war continued to escalate year after year, however, CALCAV increasingly denounced the war as immoral and moved beyond protest to acts of civil disobedience in its attempt to reverse the U.S. government's policy in Vietnam.

As early as 1963, clerical and lay church leaders had begun moving outside of established organizations to speak against the war in Vietnam. Reinhold Niebuhr, Harry Emerson Fosdick, John C. Bennett, president of Union Theological Seminary, Robert McAfee Brown of Stanford University, and Harvey Cox of Harvard Divinity School were among the first. Also in the summer of 1965, Martin Luther King, Jr., gave indications that he would join other religious leaders in opposition to the Vietnam War.[82] Daniel Berrigan was the one Catholic priest known to these Protestant leaders who was willing publicly to join the new venture. He did not stay with CALCAV very long because his Jesuit superiors sent him to South America early in 1966 to silence him for his public opposition to the war. Upon his return to the United States, Berrigan did occasionally join the group, but his move to Cornell University took him out of the Manhattan area and he lost touch with CALCAV.

Catholics who were not pacifists but were opposed to the war in Vietnam were attracted to CALCAV because of its religious witness. Two Catholics who rose to national prominence as spokespersons for CALCAV were John B. Sheerin, C.P.S., editor of *Catholic World*, and Michael Novak. Sheerin had chastised Catholics for their silence on the war and in the opinion of one historian he "provided a more consistently moral appraisal of the war earlier than most other clergymen. He found the conflict unsupportable when judged by the traditional Catholic doctrine of the 'just war.' "[83] Michael Novak, a writer, became part of CALCAV when in 1967 he collaborated with Robert McAfee Brown and Abraham Heschel on the book, *Vietnam: Crisis of*

*Conscience.* Novak as well as Sheerin later wrote for CALCAV's paper, *American Report,* which began in 1970.

CALCAV wanted a member of the American Catholic hierarchy to join them in their first national mobilization attempt. In December, CALCAV called "American clergymen of all faiths" to meet in Washington, D.C., for two days beginning 31 January 1967 to discuss "Vietnam: The Clergymen's Dilemma." CALCAV spent several weeks attempting to attract at least one Roman Catholic bishop or cardinal. They hoped that Bishop John J. Wright of Pittsburgh would attend, but after his refusal the executive committee sent night letters to all 250 bishops in the United States urging their approval and participation. Only about a dozen responded, a few of them in very hawkish terms. Two thousand five hundred Christian and Jewish clergy attended; not one Catholic bishop was there.[84]

After the mobilization, Archbishop Paul J. Hallinan of Atlanta refrained from endorsing an open letter against the war signed by 800 Catholic priests and laity, Auxiliary Bishop James Shannon of St. Paul-Minneapolis, and ten Roman Catholic college presidents. In February, however, he traveled to New York to speak out at a CALCAV-sponsored ecumenical study conference on "Vietnam and the Religious Conscience." At the symposium Hallinan sided more strongly than ever before with the opponents of American policy in Vietnam. The alternatives that Hallinan suggested in his talk seemed inadequate, for he urged an end to the stockpiling of weapons and support for the peacekeeping efforts of the United Nations. He also linked the civil rights movement in the United States with the war in Vietnam when he called for a "Selma for Peace," that would lead to the end of the Vietnam War.[85] Hallinan's speech was the closest that he had yet come to an outright condemnation of the war; but in the months following the talk he stepped back from his position because the antiwar activists tried to associate him with a project called Vietnam Summer.[86]

It was not Hallinan but James Shannon who eventually became one of the leading Roman Catholic voices within CALCAV. In 1968, Bishop Shannon joined CALCAV for the first time in a silent prayer vigil at the Arlington National Cemetery. Nearly 2,500 people gathered at the foot of the Tomb of the Unknowns and participated in a ceremony led by Martin Luther King, Jr. Shannon concluded the service with "Let us go in peace."[87] Other well-known Catholic clergy, Robert

Drinan, S.J., and Richard McSorley, S.J., supported CALCAV on its various projects. Many Catholic priests like William Hogan of the Archdiocese of Chicago were also involved with CALCAV at the local level.

Catholic involvement in CALCAV was very meager in the beginning years. There had only been five Catholics in the founding group. By 1971, the group's director was still Richard Fernandez, an ordained minister of the United Church of Christ, and its executive committee was still approximately two-thirds Protestant, but in addition to the inclusion of women, over time the most significant change was the proportional decline of Jews and an increase in Catholic participation.[88] In August 1971, when CALCAV sponsored its first national conference in Ann Arbor over four hundred people from thirty-six states attended. "Eighty-four percent claimed some religious affiliation with the same percentage active in at least one peace organization. The largest represented religious groups were Catholic, 21 percent; Methodist, 14 percent, Episcopal, 9 percent; United Church of Christ, 9 percent; Presbyterian, 8 percent; and Quaker, 7 percent. Only 2 percent were Jewish."[89] The increase in Catholic participation is significant for it meant that CALCAV provided a religious organization where Catholics who could not identify with the radical and pacifist organizations like the Catholic Worker and CPF could feel at home in their attempts to stop the war. It had also provided a place for individual members of the American hierarchy to test the waters as they spoke out as individuals against the war in Vietnam. Unfortunately, these same individuals did not speak out against the war before their fellow bishops at the NCCB meetings.[90]

At various times during the 1960s some members of the American Catholic hierarchy while addressing their Catholic constituency did challenge the morality of the Vietnam War. The earliest collective statement of protest concerning the war in Vietnam signed by members of the American Catholic hierarchy appeared in the scholarly journal, *Continuum*, in the summer 1965 issue. The protest came in response to the bombing of Hanoi and was called "A Declaration on the Threat of Bombardment of Civilian Centers." It was written by Justus George Lawler and stated: "Unlike other church issues concerning the war in Vietnam on which there is necessary and justifiable debate, the possibility that either side may bomb any purely civilian center would entail a clear and direct violation of Christian ethics and must be denounced as an immoral action."[91] The following bishops signed the declaration: Henry J. Grimmelsman of Evansville, Marion F. Forst of Dodge City, Hugh A. Donohoe of Stockton, Maurice Schexnayder of Lafayette, Robert J. Dwyer of Reno, Walter W. Curtis of Bridgeport, Mark K. Carroll of Wichita, John J. Russell of Richmond, and Charles A. Buswell of Pueblo.

As opposition grew with the escalation of the war, so did the pressure on the American bishops to take a stand. Not only peace groups like CPF, PAX, and CALCAV were applying such pressure, but as early as 1966 the *New York Times* observed that, unlike most American religious leaders, the Catholic bishops had been largely silent on the question of Vietnam.[92] The *National Catholic Reporter* immediately picked up on the statement and sent a questionnaire about the war to 225 bishops but received replies from only three, Leo Pursley of Fort Wayne-South Bend, Alphonse J. Schladweiler of New Ulm, and George J. Rehring of Toledo, all of whom supported the war in varying degrees.[93]

The earliest written statement by an individual member of the American Catholic hierarchy that raised any doubts concerning the war came in June 1966 when Lawrence Cardinal Shehan issued a pastoral letter, *Vietnam, Patriotism and Individual Conscience*, which was to be read aloud at all Masses celebrated in the Archdiocese of Baltimore. Since this was the first official pronouncement by a prominent Catholic ecclesiastic to give any indication of moral misgivings or reservations regarding the war in Vietnam, it received widespread attention in the American press when it first appeared. The pastoral letter presented a restrained and carefully balanced set of reminders of the traditional limits to be observed in warfare and a cautious endorsement of conscientious objection.

Less than two months later, the cardinal, believing the peace people had gone too far in their claims, explicitly repudiated what he described as attempts "to interpret my pastoral as a condemnation of American presence in Vietnam."[94] In a letter to the national commander of the Catholic War Veterans, he made his position clear. "Our presence in Vietnam and the reasons which have prompted us to involve ourselves there are honorable. The alternative of the withdrawal could well have catastrophic results under the present circumstances."[95] So determined was the cardinal to correct the "distortions" he ordered that the printed copies of the original text distributed by the Baltimore chancery also include the full text of his subsequent clarification.[96]

A few months later Hallinan and his auxiliary bishop of Atlanta, Joseph L. Bernardin, jointly issued a similar pastoral letter. They made it clear in their letter that their continued support for the war depended on the kind of war that the United States was waging in Vietnam. They quoted Cardinal Shehan's warning: "If our means become immoral, our cause will have been betrayed," and then added their own statement: "We must protest, therefore, whenever there is a danger that our conduct of war will exceed moral limits. A Christian simply cannot approve indiscriminate bombing, methodical extermination of people, nuclear arms designed for "overkill" or disregard for non-combatants."[97] Just as with Shehan's pastoral, both hawks and doves claimed it for support. But peace people this time contented themselves with saying that the bishops had not gone far enough. Neither pastoral was effective because a moral yardstick by which to measure the war was not presented. Both pastorals receded into oblivion.

When the number of American troops in Vietnam rose to 475,000 and the casualty figures reached 80,000 during 1967, antiwar demonstrations became larger. The failure of continued American bombing of North Vietnam to hasten military victory in South Vietnam increased the frustrations of many Americans. During this period a few more individual members of the hierarchy critical of the war began to speak out. Fulton J. Sheen, bishop of Rochester, New York, called for the withdrawal of U.S. troops from Vietnam in 1967.[98] Four Catholic bishops, Victor Reed, John Dougherty, James Shannon, and Paul Hallinan, endorsed the group Negotiations Now. In a joint statement, the four bishops said that in conformity with the plea for peace made by Pope Paul VI at the United Nations, they called upon the U.S. government to set a time and place for negotiations.[99] Richard Cardinal Cushing of the Archdiocese of Boston in his 1967 Christmas message pleaded: "For God's sake we must bring this war to an end." Yet, Cushing could not be persuaded in the following year to lend support to efforts to put the National Conference on record in support of selective conscientious objection. He did, however, endorse the Vietnam Moratorium Committee in the fall of 1969.[100]

There was only one American prelate prior to 1969 who consistently spoke out publicly in opposition to the war in Vietnam, James Shannon, an auxiliary bishop in the Archdiocese of St. Paul, Minnesota. It was mainly due to Shannon's persistence that the bishops took a stand in support of conscientious objection in 1968. It was also the frustration which this bishop experienced on the Vietnam issue that partially accounted for his resignation from the priesthood in 1969.[101] Auxiliary Bishop Bernard A. Kelly of Providence, Rhode Island, followed Shannon's opposition to the war and participated in an antiwar demonstration at the naval base in Newport, Rhode Island. He also urged the bishops to take a stand regarding the war at their meeting in the spring of 1971. He was upset that no collective presentation was prepared by the bishops on matters of economic justice or world peace and he too resigned from the priesthood in June 1971.[102] Bishop Thomas Gumbleton of Detroit had made a similar plea at the same meeting. Gumbleton assumed a leadership role among the hierarchy in opposing the war in Vietnam and in working for peace with justice.

By 1968, the bishops were saying that valid moral questions could be raised concerning the war effort and that Catholics could conscientiously object to the war in Vietnam not only because they were pacifists but because they believed the war in Vietnam to be unjust. It was mainly the effort and writing of Bishop Thomas Gumbleton who, with the USCC staff, managed to incorporate the series of questions concerning the morality of the Vietnam War into *Human Life in Our Day*.[103] According to church journalist, Jim Castelli, "It was Gumbleton who ultimately got the U.S. bishops to oppose the Vietnam War."[104] The bishops' pronouncements were not forming but following the lead of Catholic opinion during the Vietnam years. As early as 1965, *Continuum*, a Catholic scholarly periodical, condemned as immoral American plans for the bombing of Hanoi. Two days before Christmas 1966, the Catholic laity's periodical *Commonweal* pronounced the Vietnam War "a crime and a sin."[105] In October 1967, *Commonweal* became the first Catholic publication, excepting of course, the *Catholic Worker*, to take a stand in favor of civil disobedience as a legitimate form of antiwar protest when it editorialized:

> The resistance envisioned is a passive disobedience in the tradition of Thoreau. This might take the form of withholding of taxes, counseling, aiding or abetting young men on avoidance of the draft . . . , or

disruption tactics of various sorts. Such conduct might sound extreme to some, but as Robert McAfee Brown writes in a recent issue of *Look*, the war is so wrong and ways of registering concern about it have become so limited, that civil disobedience is the only course left.[106]

The *National Catholic Reporter* followed *Commonweal* when it called for the immediate withdrawal of U.S. troops from Vietnam and supported draft resistance, conscientious objections, and tax resistance.[107] These periodicals represented the intellectual position of Catholic liberals. There was a significant change not only among the liberal press, but among the Catholic press in general during the Vietnam era as John Deedy, editor of *Commonweal*, points out: "The Catholic press in general shifted from avid support for the struggle to a call for negotiations as a way of ending it [Vietnam War]."[108] The views of the Catholic press in general, like their bishops, grew directly from the traditional doctrine of the just war. As historian David O'Brien points out, it was only the liberal press that regarded pacifism and nonviolent resistance sympathetically. Yet, even these Catholic liberals for the most part remained loyal to the approach and categories of the just war.[109] Catholic liberals and intellectuals clung to the just war doctrine and contributed to maintaining it as the dominant position in the church. The position stated by James O'Gara, one of *Commonweal*'s editors in September 1967, remained typical:

> The war in Vietnam is a tragic and bloody mistake. . . . We have become reckless in our use of power and undercut the goals we seek, so much so that the war cannot be justified morally or politically. If the traditional Christian norms of just means and right proportion mean anything, we should vigorously seek negotiation and get out of Vietnam as quickly as possible.[110]

Thus, despite the image of Catholics as authoritarian, conservative, ultrapatriotic, and militaristic during the days of the Cold War, American Catholics were more critical of the Vietnam War than has often been supposed. According to Gallup Poll data, when the war began, "they were more hawkish than other Americans, when it ended, they were more dovish. And they have remained that way for a generation."[111] In July 1967, a plurality of Catholics for the first time disapproved of President Johnson's handling of the war. "Fifty-five percent of Catholics said it was not a mistake to get into Vietnam to begin with, but, by a 52–36 percent, Catholics opposed Johnson's plans to send another 100,000 men to Vietnam—a larger portion than that among Protestants (47–42 percent) and the general population (49–40 percent). In November 1966, the U.S. bishops issued a statement saying that the Vietnam War met the church's criteria for a 'Just War'; at that point, they were moving in a direction opposite to that of their own people."[112] In November 1969, Catholics described themselves as doves by 60–27 percent. The invasion of Cambodia revealed that Catholics were split, opposing the invasion by 47–44 percent while Protestants supported the move by 54–29 percent. In January 1971, Catholics supported a plan to bring all American troops home by the end of the year by 80–16 percent, Protestants by 68–23 percent. It took the American Catholic hierarchy until November 1971 when they concluded that "Vietnam no longer met the 'Just War' criteria—[that] they had caught up with their people."[113] In fact, the American Catholic hierarchy had almost missed the opportunity to condemn the immorality of the war in Vietnam.

In 1971 the United States Catholic Bishops issued the collective statement entitled *Resolution on Southeast Asia* which concluded that,

> At this point in history, it seems clear to us that whatever good we hope to achieve through continued involvement in this war is now outweighed by the destruction of human life and moral values it inflicts. It is our firm conviction, therefore, that the speedy ending of this war is a moral imperative of the highest priority.[114]

This was the first time in the modern world, not only in America, that during a war a nation's Catholic hierarchy had publicly judged their government's actions unjust.

The question of the significance of the resolution for American Catholics generated much discussion. The conservative press such as the Catholic newspaper, the *Wanderer*, and the journal, *National Review*, considered the resolution a disaster. The liberal press basically said, "Too little, too late." And *Commonweal* observed that the National Council of Churches had condemned the war six years earlier. And as Bordelon pointed out, when the NCCB resolution reached the floor at the November meeting it generated heated debate, and an earlier version had to be softened in order to gain the necessary two-thirds vote. This division among the hierarchy on the issue was evident to the public in a press conference after passage of the resolution when Bishop Gumbleton said anyone who agrees with the bishops "may not participate in the war." And Archbishop Hannan of New Orleans immediately disagreed with that conclusion.[115] For American Catholics the discussion did not end in 1971 nor did the Vietnam War. The condemnation of the war by the American Catholic hierarchy had no more impact on the U.S. government in stopping the Vietnam War than did the nonviolent acts of resistance of Catholic pacifists or the actions and judgments of Catholic just war theorists. Despite President Nixon's effort to discredit the antiwar movement and to continue the war through the air while bringing the troops home, there was peace at last with the fall of Saigon on 1 May 1975. Finally, after thirteen years, the longest war in American history stopped.

Pacifism was the heart of the American Catholic peace movement during the Vietnam era. Introduced into American Catholicism by Dorothy Day and the Catholic Worker movement in the 1930s, by the 1960s it had become a recognized option for Catholics. Tom Cornell attempted to define this Catholic pacifism when he wrote:

> We are opposed to the war in Vietnam not only because it is unjust, but because it is a war. If the United States government were fighting on the other side we would be in opposition also, but we would have different and fewer allies. Catholic pacifists are opposed to war because it is the planned, mass taking of human lives for political purposes and violates God's exclusive dominion over human life. We are opposed to abortion, euthanasia, capital punishment, and economically enforced starvation also, on the same basis.[116]

Nonviolence and nonviolent resistance developed from the concept of pacifism. The draft became the catalyst for the development of nonviolent resistance during the Vietnam era because the draft placed the individual in a position whereby a decisive action had to be taken. The Catholic Worker advocated noncooperation with the draft and when one of its members, David Miller, burned his draft card at a rally in New York City the resistance was born. Catholics beyond draft age identified with these young men who were going to jail because of their convictions and some of them decided to pour napalm over selective service files. These actions gave birth to the Ultraresistance led by the Berrigan brothers. Their commitment and willingness to pay the price of jail placed them in the vanguard of the American peace movement. It also raised the question of "effectiveness" in terms of stopping the war. This led to the question, what will the Gospel message of peace allow in terms of actions necessary to stop the war?

It must be remembered, however, that during the 1960s a far greater number of young Catholics chose to register their dissent against the war within the law as conscientious objection rather than choose the path of noncooperation or resistance. This indicated that the pacifist element was increasing and continued to predominate even though the element of resistance was far more visible because of the publicity generated by the media. Thus, the role of PAX in lobbying on behalf of conscientious objection both at the Second Vatican Council and before the National Conference of Catholic Bishops in America cannot be underestimated.

Finally, although pacifism was the core of Catholic peace activism, the just war doctrine was still the dominant position among Catholics during the Vietnam War. It was the CAIP and the hierarchy that maintained the just war tradition in their peacemaking efforts. John Courtney Murray expanded the just war doctrine so that it not only applied to the state but to each individual in judging the actions of the state during a time of war. Catholics for the first time were using the just war doctrine to condemn their nation's war effort and demanding that their "lawfully constituted authority" end the war.

The leaders in the American Catholic peace movement during the Vietnam era could have been counted on less than ten fingers. Because they all identified with the Catholic Worker tradition there was no claim of leadership by any single individual and there was no one community, or action, or position. Rather, a network of friendship and support developed that sustained all of them. The Berrigan brothers were obviously very close. Tom Cornell and Jim Forest were friends and they kept the CPF together. Forest was also good friends with Daniel and Philip Berrigan and Thomas Merton. Tom Cornell was close to Dorothy Day. Eileen Egan and Dorothy Day were friends and

Eileen Egan and Gordon Zahn kept PAX alive. Zahn also kept close to Tom Cornell at the CPF. Each one of these persons was very independent, and their Catholic faith motivated and sustained them. As a result all were self-consciously Catholic. Every action they posited for peace was religiously motivated and was done for the purpose of bringing peace to American society and persuading the leaders of the Roman Catholic church to adopt a new ethic of peace.

Because its leadership was religiously based, the American Catholic peace movement *was* a peace movement and not an antiwar movement. The Catholic peace movement was alive to the same elements in American culture that affected the antiwar movement. In their study of the Vietnam antiwar movement Benedetti and Chatfield have listed five major components that comprised the movement: changes in liberal thought, the rise of student-led protest, the emergence of the new radical left, the challenge of a nonviolent civil rights campaign, and the growth of the counter-culture.[117] According to their interpretation, politics held these components together. Also, because the American Catholic peace movement came out of the Catholic Worker tradition, there was a basic identification of its leadership with the various analyses of the injustices of American society by both the old and new Left, but the leadership always placed them within a religious context and the solution to the injustices was never in solely political terms. The relationship between politics and religion often left the leadership in a quandary. Members of the Catholic peace movement never used political terms such as liberal or Marxist to identify themselves. Both Dorothy Day and Daniel Berrigan called themselves "personalists" and "fundamentalists," and they also used the term radical, but in a religious sense in terms of living "the radical Gospel message." The leadership in the American Catholic peace movement also saw itself as part of a counterculture, but again in the Catholic Worker tradition where community, poverty, and the Gospel Beatitudes were its trademark. Thus, members of the Catholic peace movement were never particularly attracted to liberal thought, the New Left, or the counterculture. Instead, they tended to work most closely with other pacifist groups such as FOR, WRL, and CNVA or nonpacifist religious peace groups such as CALCAV. They also spent a great amount of energy educating Catholics about peace within existing Catholic institutions by speaking at parishes and schools and working with existing Catholic organizations and groups. Though they were not exclusively, they were self-consciously Catholic.

The most important impact of the American Catholic peace movement was that it helped to persuade large numbers of Catholics to oppose the Vietnam War. Within a few brief years the hawks had turned into doves and this desire for peace has remained a characteristic of American Catholics throughout the 1980s. These Catholics also brought their church hierarchy to a position of declaring the immorality of the Vietnam War. The American Catholic peace movement's most significant contribution to the antiwar movement was in its leadership roles in the Resistance and the Ultraresistance as it attempted to end the war by extending pacifism with new tactics of nonviolent resistance. The American Catholic peace movement also attempted to change the public policy of the U.S. government on the issue of conscientious objection by trying to include SCO in the CO classification. Though this attempt failed with the government, it was successful with the American Catholic hierarchy in its pronouncements of the right of a Catholic to be a CO or an SCO. The American Catholic peace movement also made pacifism and nonviolence a valid option for Catholics. It would take another decade before the American Catholic church would put this in writing, but it would come.

The most important leaders of the American Catholic peace movement during the Vietnam Era were the Berrigan brothers. A look at their personal lives and their quest for justice and peace provides many insights into what it meant to be Catholic and American during this most turbulent time. It also reveals that for the individual the demands of peacemaking are as great as the demands of war.

# 7

## The Berrigan Brothers and the

## Catholic Resistance

On 17 May 1968, nine men and women entered Selective Service Local Board No. 33 at Catonsville, Maryland. The group seized records and burned them outside the building with napalm, which they had manufactured themselves following a recipe in the Special Forces Handbook published by the U.S. government. Within a few minutes the local police arrived and heard Daniel Berrigan, S.J., lead his companions in praying the Our Father as a thanksgiving for the completed action. The police waited until the end of the prayer, then handcuffed the "criminals for peace" and loaded them into a paddy wagon. The Catonsville action symbolized the high point of American Catholic resistance to the Vietnam War in the 1960s. For Catholic peace activists, Catonsville signaled a dramatic move to the Left in their resistance to war. After this action, two of the nine participants, Daniel Berrigan and his brother Philip, emerged as the architects of a new political and theological movement.

The American press labeled this movement the Catholic Left or the New Catholic Left[1] and used these terms consistently and without distinction when describing events related to the Berrigan brothers from Catonsville in 1968 to the Harrisburg Seven Trial in 1972. The press estimated in 1972 that the Catholic Left had grown in size from the Catonsville Nine to several hundred participants and several thousand sympathizers in a church of 47,000,000 American Catholics.[2]

The term Catholic Left or New Catholic Left, however, was a misnomer. Within the antiwar movement there was a coalition of the Left formed by the old Left (Communists and Socialists), the new Left (mainly students led by the SDS who were against those who opposed communists and socialists), and militant pacifists (the radical wings of

173

the traditional peace churches and groups like WRL and CNVA). All of these groups viewed the war in Vietnam as a direct expression of America's military-industrial complex which they felt stood against the social forces of revolution in Southeast Asia. As a result, this coalition viewed American foreign policy as imperialistic and neocolonial. This view was tied to a vision of an American political system that was also considered to be unresponsive to the social-justice demands of its own society. Therefore, instead of relying on electoral politics, this coalition called for resistance to a state that they believed had become illegitimate.

Since the Catholic Resistance also supported many of these same political positions, it is understandable that the press would label them the Catholic Left. It is important, however, to recognize that the Catholic Resistance did not come out of this coalition of the Left. Rather it was a religious group whose aim was not only to stop the war in Vietnam, but to work for justice and peace in both the church and society. Their religious motivation was rooted in a basic revulsion against the secular values of American society that they believed were manifested in a materialistic, racist, and militaristic culture. Communism had little to do with their analysis for, like Merton, capitalism and communism were two sides of the same evil coin. Their journey into resistance first began with their involvement in social-justice issues such as poverty and civil rights. The injustice of the Vietnam War then led them to work for peace. Their resistance escalated as the war continued year after year and the American political system failed to respond to their efforts to bring forth justice and peace. As a result they kept increasing their actions of nonviolent resistance against that system. The term Catholic Resistance rather than Catholic Left makes more sense and is a more accurate term.

The draft board raid at Catonsville marked a new departure in the escalation of resistance on the part of peace activists because the action was planned in secret and destroyed government property.[3] The Catonsville Nine claimed that the raid was a nonviolent direct act of civil disobedience that had both secular and religious implications. By attacking law and property, the bulwarks of a value system the participants believed lay at the roots of exploitation, racism, violence and war, they hoped to expose the evils in the social-value system of America. At the same time they hoped to call the church to heed its message of justice and peace. The participants dramatized the act of civil disobedience by placing it within a theological context of prayer at Catons-ville, thus proclaiming that they had attacked the false values of America, especially the Vietnam War, while affirming human life in a Christian context.[4]

The idea for the destruction of draft files and the organization that led to Catonsville was the work not of Daniel Berrigan, but of his brother, Philip Berrigan, S.S.J. In April 1964 Philip was sent by his religious community to St. Peter Claver parish in Baltimore, where he worked in support of housing for blacks and for peace. In a desire to do more to stop the Vietnam War, Philip Berrigan along with Robert Alpern, Thomas Lewis, Harry Trabold, and James Harney formed the nucleus of a small peace group. They first organized and practiced civil disobedience on several occasions at Fort Myers, Virginia, where most of the Joint Chiefs of Staff resided, but according to Berrigan there were no arrests because too many clergy were present. In the summer of 1967, Philip Berrigan returned to New York City to finish his book *A Punishment for Peace*, and in September he went back to Baltimore to seek a more effective tactic to stop the war. The idea of bombing draft boards was first contemplated by the small Baltimore peace group but it was regarded as too violent. As members of the white middle-class society they maintained that they had no right to resort to violence; other options were still open to them. Finally, Philip Hirchkopf, a Virginia lawyer and head attorney for the Pentagon March in October, came up with the post-Christian era symbolism of pouring blood on the draft files.[5] Daniel Berrigan, of course, was told of the proposed action at the Custom's House in Baltimore, but he did not feel free to join.[6]

Twenty years later, Daniel Berrigan would write in his autobiography *To Dwell in Peace* that when Philip told him of the action "It was all quite simple. It was also unprecedented, calculated to set the head spinning." Daniel wrote to him after the revelation that he "continued to see my [Daniel's] work as standing by the students in their travail; nothing more." Daniel goes on to say that his brother responded with "considerable impatience." He then explains his brother's action:

> Philip's instinct, on the other hand, was to seek out an occasion, at his own time and place, to take the offensive and force the government to respond.

He had come on a way to do this: a moral assault on purportedly sacrosanct territory. An act, he insisted, very much in the spirit of King and Gandhi; but as a tactic, something utterly new. Something, as he must have known, bound to raise towering waves, to erupt in controversy, denunciation, passionate pros and cons, even spite and scorn.

The proposed act was entirely in line with his temperament. His life had been a steady rhythm of improvisation and discipline. He was a surprising spirit; he dug deep and came up with directions, modes, arguments, lights in dark places. And equally of import, he had a capacity to beckon others along; he made virtue attractive. In his presence, as I saw time and again, less hardy spirits such as myself breathed deep, stopped out.[7]

On Friday, 27 October 1967 Philip Berrigan and three others, David Eberhardt, Thomas Lewis, and James Mengel, poured blood on selective service files at the Customs House in Baltimore, Maryland.[8]

It was the combination of the brothers Berrigan that would provide the leadership of the Catholic Resistance. Daniel emerged as spokesperson after Catonsville. Thomas Merton had already articulated the theological rationale for traditional nonviolent resistance, but the monk had never left his monastery to participate. Even Catholic Workers who had limited their actions to traditional forms of nonviolent resistance were not participants at Catonsville, though some of them would follow the example of the Berrigans in subsequent draft board raids. As a writer, a poet, a theologian, and an activist, Daniel Berrigan was able to combine the tradition of the Catholic Worker, the activism of his brother Philip, and the contemplation and writing ability of his friend Merton.[9] Because of his writing and speaking ability, he was able to articulate for the American public a rationale for nonviolent resistance. By conveying sincerity and commitment through his participation, he also brought visibility and a following to the Catonsville action. Thus Daniel, who reconciled the paradoxes of the Catholic peacemaker within his own being, became a symbol of the possibilities and limits of the American Catholic peace movement as it confronted both church and state in resistance to the Vietnam War.

It is difficult to ascertain exactly what led the brothers to take such a daring risk at Catonsville. Some authors attribute it to the authoritarian character of their father or to the authoritarian structure of the Roman

Catholic church and its religious communities; others attribute it to the "supposed sibling rivalry" between the Berrigan brothers. Though these all may have contributed, the best explanation lies in their faith in the Gospel message and the combination of people and events that influenced their thought and action. These experiences led them to new thoughts and actions concerning what it meant to be both Catholic and American.[10]

The Berrigan brothers were not converts to American Catholicism but products of the "immigrant church," sons of a German-born mother and a second generation Irish-American father.[11] Philip was the youngest and Daniel the second youngest of six sons. Their father, Thomas Berrigan, was a strong-authoritarian Irish Catholic who enforced a rigid and often abusive discipline in his home and had no rapport with his sons. He was a great lover of poetry, which he bellowed through the house or silently attempted to write. "His literary rejection over the years soured his heart, and intensified his sense of being a neglected genius."[12] He made his mark in his community in Syracuse with his physical strength, his support of unionism at the light company in Syracuse, and his involvement in social-justice concerns with the poor and civil rights. His home was always open to those who sought relief, and extras were shared with everyone coming to their door during the Great Depression years. Politically he was a Democrat, but he also supported Charles Coughlin during the depression and subscribed to the *Catholic Worker*.

When Daniel tried to evaluate what his father had given him, he attempted to give the answer in terms of faith. "One could console himself in any easy homiletic way—he gave us faith. That would put things simply—and uselessly. That statement would be true, and just as clearly untrue; for what he gave with one hand, he took back with the other."[13] But he went on to say that "he offered something other than faith or a viable or attractive religious sense. Something of persistence, stubbornness, skepticism, a queer kind of gnarled integrity, a sixth sense for the right order of things, thrashing out in all directions. If only this could have been disciplined and directed, what a strength!"[14]

The mother, Frida, was the real spirit in the family. A gentle, fragile, and humble woman of great faith in God and people, she was able to instill confidence and hope in her sons as they confronted each new situation. Daniel's position in the family was different from the other boys; he was pale and delicate, he helped with the work inside the house while the stronger boys, like Philip, did the outside work on their small farm. Daniel and his mother suffered greatly from the physical and psychological strains of the family. As a result a special bond existed between them.[15] Daniel writes of his mother,

> And our faith, as we came to know, had another source than him; it came from our mother. Strangely; for with regard to things religious, she was reticence personified. But in the midst of all, and stuck as she (and we) seemed in a cul-de-sac, her example could not but be noted, even by the blind. It counted for nearly everything, the patience, plain goodness, long-sufferance; and now and then, the right word filling the space, and the religious piety that was never once overbearing or showy, but that carried its burdens, carried others along, and finally carried the day. Oh (as the Irish never conceded), she had a way with her!"[16]

When Philip writes of his parents' influence, he is much less revelatory, but he too stresses the faith they passed on to him. Philip stated, "We were all perfectly aware and deeply pained by the imperfections of Frida and Tom—their marriage was sometimes stormy, contentious, unhappy. But toward others, especially the poor and outcast, they were people of towering compassion and justice."[17] He reiterates repeatedly their background of deprivation and struggle and contends that "Frida and Tom took the Gospel to heart—to a depth unprovided by a lifetime of conventional Catholicism. Their faith was due undoubtedly to experience with desperate need, deprivation, misery, discrimination, oppresssion. Their analysis of social injustice might prove lacking but they understood profoundly the command to care for 'the least of these.' "[18]

All the Berrigan brothers attended St. John the Baptist Academy in Syracuse. Except for Daniel, the boys were average students and participated mainly in athletic activites. During high school Daniel wrote poetry, acted in plays, and learned to dance. His enthusiasm for life even led him to become a cheerleader, for which his brothers relentlessly chided him. Toward the end of his high school years, Daniel applied to the Society of Jesus for acceptance. At first the society would not accept him and told him to go home and improve his Latin. After a year of study, the rejection was rescinded and he entered the Society of Jesus on 14 August 1939.

Daniel underwent the thirteen years of Jesuit training with its emphasis on the intellectual and spiritual life. In these years the training made no provisions for the social apostolate except for three years reserved for teaching. Daniel later wrote of the effect the training had on him:

> We were being asked to accept the truth that the past had something to offer living men. We could accept the truth, abstractly, but we could in fact offer men very little; for our theology, was not a living science. It was a dead one. . . . It was almost entirely an exercise in memory; it ignored living questions on principle; its vernacular was almost as far from man's thoughts as its Latin; it had no urgent need to confront Protestant or Jewish traditions, except as opponents. And in moral questions, it gave a view of the world only as large or liberating as could be gained from the upper storeys of a Roman ivory tower.[19]

He went on to say, however, that it did do one thing, "It made me teachable." It also seems to have provided him with a strong foundation of basic values and a sense of direction that served as a sounding board to evaluate the onslaught of everything new.

After ordination on 21 June 1952, Daniel went abroad for his tertianship. He studied at the Gregorian University in Rome and at the Maison la Colombiere, Paray le Monial, in France. It was during his stay in France that he associated himself with the Worker Priest Movement. The impact of these priests would shape the rest of Daniel's life.

The Worker-Priest Movement was founded after World War II under the guiding spirit of Emmanuel J. Suhard, the cardinal archbishop of Paris. The horrifying experiences of Hitler's atrocities and the incredible inhumanity of World War II in "Christian" Europe, coupled with the moral paralysis of the churches in face of such a disaster, had summoned a few to a rethinking of the social dimensions of Christianity. The worker-priests rejected the Enlightenment notion that religion was a personal private matter and emphasized an involvement in temporal and social spheres. Their political philosophy was largely socialistic and anticolonial. For Daniel the worker-priests combined the personal commitments most emphasized by his parents: a strong support for the workers and a deep faith in God that could translate Christian belief into personal charity. It also showed him an attempt to revitalize Christianity against the encroachments of secularism. Association with these men brought Daniel into contact with the writings of such progressive European theologians as Dietrich Bonhoeffer, Henri de Lubac, Yves Congar, and later Teilhard de Chardin. These contacts were to be among the most important influences on Daniel Berrigan's later writings and actions. The French underground experiences of some of the worker-priests as German prisoners affected Berrigan's theories of civil disobedience; the progressive theologians' concepts of Christianity demanding social involvement confirmed his call to public action, and Teilhard de Chardin's optimistic view of history would contribute to the eschatological dimension that he would attribute to such actions as that at Catonsville.[20]

After returning from Europe in 1954, Daniel Berrigan was not with the workers in America, but with the students. He was assigned to teach high school at Brooklyn Preparatory. His extracurricular interest in these years centered on combating poverty. He first began working with Puerto Ricans in lower Manhattan and later became chaplain for the Young Christian Workers, a Catholic group of high school students involved in social justice concerns. In 1957, he was assigned to teach theology at LeMoyne University in Syracuse. The young liberal college students, especially the activists of the 1960s, shared much in common with Berrigan: Catholicism, gender, higher education, middle-class values, and concern for the oppressed at home and abroad. Besides teaching theology and English, he continued his social-justice involvement by moderating a professional sodality, a group of middle- and upper-class adults whose social action he directed toward housing for the poor and interracial work in the community. He also established an International House on campus after President John F. Kennedy announced his Peace Corps and Alliance for Progress. Such projects brought Daniel Berrigan into a close working relationship with his brother, Philip. This personal relationship would grow during the years and be the most significant and sustaining influence on both men. It would ultimately produce the action at Catonsville and the Catholic Resistance.[21]

Philip Berrigan had taken a different route. Upon graduation from high school, Philip worked for a year scouring soot-caked locomotives at the New York Central Yards to earn college money. He spent a semester at St. Michael's College in Toronto before he was drafted in 1943. The army served as a unique training ground. Philip underwent Field Artillery training in the Deep South, Georgia, Florida, and North Carolina, where he saw black poverty and second-class citizenship. His own account of his army career was written in a brief paragraph to the religious community he later entered. "Went overseas with a field artillery unit as a sergeant. While in Germany volunteered for officer's training in the infantry in the futile and foolish hope of seeing some action. By the time I was commissioned, the war had ended."[22] Philip rarely speaks of his experience in the army and when asked directly, he replies briefly or mentions some account of racial discrimination he witnessed.

After his discharge in 1946, he enrolled at the College of the Holy Cross in Worcester, Massachusetts, where he completed work for his B.A. degree under the G.I. Bill of Rights. Upon graduation in 1950, he entered the Josephite Fathers, whose apostolate is service to African Americans. Philip entered the Society of Saint Joseph because of their apostolate to the African Americans and his own identification with these people and because their period of preparation for ordination was briefer than that of the Jesuits. The final factor in his decision was that his brother Jerome was also a member of the society. Philip had always been closest to this brother. Jerome left the Society of Saint Joseph just before ordination, married and adopted four children, but he continued to help blacks by joining the Catholic Interracial Council and working with his brother Daniel in the professional sodality. Philip continued his studies and was ordained a priest in 1955. From 1956 until 1963, he taught in an all-black high school, St. Augustine, in New Orleans. During these years Philip and Daniel grew closer together as they shared ideas and activities concerning their students, and increased their involvement in the civil rights movement in America and the liturgical movement in the church.

Philip Berrigan spent these years in New Orleans not only in the classroom, but also in outdoor work, maintaining the physical plant of the high school and repairing homes in the black community, where he spent hours of his free time organizing drives for clothes, food, and housing. Obtaining first-class citizenship for African Americans was his top priority. He often read and clipped articles on current events in order to keep abreast of changes in the church and in American society. These years cannot be underestimated in their impact on him as he moved from administering corporal works of mercy to searching for ways to empower the African American community to achieve its own goals.[23] "Phil," as his friend James Forest has said, "looks like an ad for a wheaties boxtop—a Mr. All-American." During these years he was known as a man's man, courageous, strong, direct, fearless, and a man who constantly confronted injustice. In sum, Philip Berrigan spent all his time during these years teaching and working in the social-justice movement for black equality in the South. Daniel Berrigan often sent his LeMoyne students to his brother's high school to work in summer projects for poor African Americans and aided Philip in securing college scholarships for the most able black students.

The impact of the general climate of evolving social protest, especially the civil rights movement, had a profound impact on the Berrigan brothers, as on many thinking Americans. The various church-related, social-action groups had the greatest impact, especially the Southern Christian Leadership Conference under the direction of Dr. Martin Luther King, Jr. This group gave nonviolent direct action and civil disobedience a new dignity by the courage of a conscientious few in the midst of growing awareness of the urgent need for massive social change.

Spurred on by such actions for social justice, the Berrigan brothers confronted the question of civil disobedience for the first time in the summer of 1961. Along with Richard Wagner, another Josephite priest, he decided to participate in the Freedom Ride in Mississippi led by James Farmer. For the first and last time the two asked their religious superiors for permission to follow their consciences in an act of civil disobedience. Daniel Berrigan could not obtain permission, but Philip Berrigan and Richard Wagner received affirmation from their religious superior general, George O'Dea. The two priests got as far as Atlanta, Georgia, where a phone call prevented them from reaching Mississippi. The Congress of Racial Equality (CORE) had released their names to the press two hours before their scheduled arrival. This exploitation of the priests' presence resulted in the bishop of Jackson, Richard Gerow, demanding the removal of the two priests from his

diocese.[24] Obeying their religious superiors, the priests did not participate, but the experience left them no less convinced of the value and
need for priests to give such witness. Since civil disobedience was a
matter of individual conscience, the priests never again asked their
religious superiors for permission to follow their own consciences.

It was also during the period of the late fifties and early sixties that
the Berrigan brothers experienced the changes occurring in the
church. Prior to the Second Vatican Council, the new emphasis on
the emerging laity and the liturgical movement occurred. The liturgical movement viewed the ritual of the earthly church as the visible
expression of Christ's worship, and the mission of the church (including the social apostolate) as the visible expression of Christ's love for the
world. It encouraged full participation on the part of the laity and thus
introduced the vernacular language and a simple and clear liturgy
designed to educate the faithful. Though Daniel Berrigan rose to national prominence in the liturgical movement, it was Philip Berrigan
and not Daniel who had first published a significant article on the topic
in *Worship* magazine.[25] Philip lost interest in the liturgical movement,
however, because he was more interested in work for social justice and
did not have the time or temperment (much like Dorothy Day) to
spend explaining it theologically. He continued to devote his attention
to finding ways to aid the African American community.

Liturgy, on the other hand, greatly influenced Daniel and helped
him to develop a stronger theological basis for his social involvement.
At LeMoyne this enthusiasm for liturgy was reflected in the chapel he
and his family built in the new International House on campus. The
austere lines of the table altar and the stone floor were designed to
emphasize the celebrant, which in Berrigan's case sometimes led to an
excessive use of gestures in his attempt to express the symbolic. The
significance of the liturgical movement resided in its new emphasis on
the Paschal Mystery as an on-going reality at work in the lives of men
and women in their efforts to develop a new world. The sacraments,
expecially the Eucharist, were not merely a remembrance of God's past
activity in Christ, but of God at work in Christ's new body, the community of discipleship, transforming the believing community and
through them the world. Along with all of this was the liturgical
movement's emphasis on salvation-history theology—that in Jesus
Christ the Kingdom was begun, and now history, through the actions

of men and women, moved toward the fullness of the Kingdom and the reign of love, justice, and peace. It was this new emphasis that Daniel Berrigan used to explain the motivation behind acts of nonviolent resistance. He extended the theology outward and not inward on a worshipping community.

Thus, Daniel used these theological emphases of the liturgical movement to move him toward more radical social and political action. The transition from liberal to radical was evidenced in both his theology and politics. By acting with other persons in community against the evils of social injustice and eventually against the evil of the war in Vietnam and his government which perpetrated them and his church which was used to sanction such evils, he believed that he was moving history through such action toward the fullness of the Kingdom—the day of love, justice, and peace.[26]

The ecumenical movement beginning during this period also influenced Daniel greatly. First, it helped to build an increased solidarity among clerics who held similar convictions about theology and action being combined to fulfill the Kingdom. During the early 1960s at Mount Saviour Monastery, Daniel Berrigan and John Heidbrink, the director of church relations for FOR, led Roman Catholic and Protestant retreats for clerics. This ecumenical probing and inquiry established their friendship. John Heidbrink believed he helped "to liberate" Berrigan in the area of ecumenical relations.[27] Heidbrink would often accuse Daniel of legalism in the liturgy and of holding the Apostle Paul in such reverence that he became the fourth member of the Trinity. He also introduced him to the Fellowship of Reconciliation (FOR), which Berrigan joined in late 1962 and which later provided him assistance in the founding of a new Catholic peace organization, the Catholic Peace Fellowship (CPF). Heidbrink commented on the kind of changes Daniel Berrigan was undergoing in the early 1960s.

> Dan was, in the early sixties, a thorough-going artist with a sensitivity for the sensuous which shocked me at times. He was moving into a Hebrew [biblical] grasp of reality in a unified matter-spirit unity. This was before the Teilhard manuscripts were released. But Dan sensed the organic relationship of matter and spirit and would begin soon his efforts to unite these substances so long divided. . . . Dan's ec-

clesiology underwent a massive change and it was then that his often bold and angry iconoclasm began and took such radical forms.[28]

While at LeMoyne, Daniel Berrigan wrote a great deal and his writings reflected the changes in his thought concerning theology and social involvement. Berrigan became most widely known during this period for his poetry and he published two books of poems, *Time Without Number* and *Encounters*. His first prose work, *The Bride: Essays in the Church*, reflected his competence as a biblical scholar and liturgist. In these writings he was concerned with exploring nature, the church, suffering, grace, sin, and the sacraments. His Thomism, legalism, and views about the dichotomy between the spiritual and the natural were quite evident, especially in his defense of the statement "There is no salvation outside of the Church" in *The Bride*. His writing very much paralleled Merton's during this time period. In later years, Dan referred to this prose work as a "sin of his past."[29]

By 1961, however, in his prose work, *The Bow in the Clouds*, and especially in his book of poetry, *The World for a Wedding Ring*, all dichotomy disappeared and the wedding of the sacred and profane was finally achieved. Significantly, this last book of poetry was dedicated to three Catholic social activists: Tony Walsh, Dorothy Day, and Karl Meyer. Suffering was no longer a spiritual agony for Daniel, but a moment of intense anxiety and ultimate rebirth. He found Christ in all nature and in the universe. He began to see the church as a part of a larger movement to serve the world. He saw behind the symbols the realities that the church had betrayed for the sake of acceptance and status. He also altered his view of authority and began to stress service. In his next book, *They Call Us Dead Men*, Daniel attempted to place the individual in a concrete context of social involvement. From this book the person emerges as a sacrament when service is rendered to a brother or sister in need. All issues for Daniel Berrigan were now viewed as religious issues.

At this time he was also publishing in journals such as *Worship*, *Critic*, *Perspectives*, and *Today*. His topics ranged from sacred art, to the Christian in modern times, to the role of the church, to freedom, and to nonviolence. The emphasis in all the writing is on the individual's reaching the fullness of personhood by consciously confronting things as they really are and trying to change them to fulfill the Kingdom of God.

Many of the changes reflected in Daniel's writing were the result of the knowledge he had gained while trying to serve human needs in the social apostolate. But even more important, he was observing, listening, and questioning every person and event that passed before him. He had a series of way stations that provided him these contacts. He maintained his relationship with Tony Walsh at the Benedict Labre House for the poor in Canada,[30] he would stop by the Catholic Worker, he would either make or give retreats at Mount Saviour Monastery in Pine City, New York, and visit or address the Association for International Development (AID) in Paterson, New Jersey.

The years at LeMoyne, however, also supplied negative influences. Daniel experienced increasing opposition from influential people in the Syracuse community because of his activities in civil rights. He was disappointed and angry when the Jesuit censors refused to sanction publication of a book he and his brother Philip had collaborated on. The reason given was that Philip Berrigan's writing was too secular, too hard hitting, and too radical on issues such as civil rights.[31] Despite the anger, Daniel Berrigan accepted the Jesuit censorship of Philip's writing. As a result, Daniel wrote his own book, *They Call Us Dead Men*, and Philip published his own work as *No More Strangers*. Also, and perhaps most difficult to bear, was the inhuman action and constant opposition Daniel received from his rector the last two years at LeMoyne. In 1964, Daniel explained this situation to his provincial while he was on visitation at LeMoyne and asked for a sabbatical. The request was immediately granted.

By 1964, both Berrigan brothers had begun to increase their involvement in the issue of peace, especially opposition to the war in Vietnam. Philip had been concerned about the nuclear issue, but moved to focus his energies on the Vietnam War. One reason for this increase of concern about peace was Pope John XXIII's encyclical, *Pacem in Terris* and the Second Vatican Council's reiteration of Pope John's social orientation. At the time of the council, the church was emphasizing that it is a pilgrim people whose primary task is the transformation of the social order in light of the Gospel message. The Berrigans took this teaching seriously and sought ways or actions that symbolized the ability of Christians to break out of their privatized spirituality and involve themselves with the great social and political questions facing humankind.

By 1963, Philip had become increasingly aware of the issue of peace. He began to see the war in Vietnam as diverting the energies of the American people and government from the struggle for civil rights. He was impatient and dissatisfied with his effectiveness in the civil rights movement while working out of a high school in New Orleans. He was also becoming aware of his own paternalism while trying to assist African Americans. The increased emphasis on black separatism and militancy also persuaded him to realize that he might do more not only for civil rights but for his country as a whole if he devoted his energies to trying to stop the war in Vietnam. Unsure of his feelings and not desiring to leave the struggle for civil rights, he first accepted an assignment as a fund raiser for his religious community in New York City. During this time he arranged for a consulting firm to study the Josephite community and submit recommendations on how the order could better fulfill its mission of service to the African American community. The consultants proposed that $2 million be raised to enable the Josephites to play a more prominent role in the fast developing civil rights revolution. The order's ruling council rejected the proposal, a setback that finally convinced Philip that he could best accomplish his goals on the edge of his community rather than try to change the organization of the religious community itself. [32]

While fund raising, Philip was also serving as a consultant to priests in Harlem who had not yet freed themselves from the attitude of being protectors of the blacks. He often worked with John P. Grady, whose house became the center of many Berrigan meetings in the city. [33] In March 1964, Philip was assigned to teach at Ephiphany Apostolic College in Newburgh. He left the college in April 1965, because the politically conservative community had harrassed the seminary for maintaining him on its staff. They had objected to Philip's positions and activities in civil rights and peace. Philip Berrigan was then assigned to an African American parish in Baltimore, St. Peter Claver. Greatly upset by the fact that his religious superiors had acquiesced to the pressures of the people in Newburgh, Philip asked his brother Daniel to drive to Baltimore with him so they could talk. At that time they made a solemn agreement that regardless of the actions of the church against them, they would not leave the priesthood of their own volition.[34]

Prior to Philip's transfer to Baltimore, Daniel had been revisiting Europe. While in France during 1964, he was again affected by the Worker Priest Movement. This time the question of relevance began to loom large in his thinking. The worker priests taught him that relevance needed to be rooted in being brother to the world—to serving those in need. This was also the time when the memory of France's involvement in Vietnam and Algeria was still viewed as a tragic mistake. The church's role had been mixed, but Berrigan soon learned that all respected European Catholics were pacifists and heavy supporters of the Fellowship of Reconciliation. After his stay in France he concluded that the church in America was not really Christian for it often put him in a position of choosing either for the church or for humankind. "From time to time, it is asked of man to choose between obedience on the one hand, and fidelity to the poor, or the Negro, or the workers, or the Algerians, or the Jews, or a hundred other actual men and situations," he wrote. "But I know, too, that Christ is in His Church; even though silenced, or put to shame, or drowned out by cynicism or politics or cowardice."[35]

More aware than ever of the issues of war and peace, Daniel was asked by FOR to join with twenty other Protestants and Catholics in a new experiment in peripatetic ecumenism through the socialist countries. These men were together for most of the summer of 1964 on a tour that included visits to Prague, Hungary, and the U.S.S.R.. While in Prague, they attended the All Christian Peace Conference. Before leaving the socialist countries, the FOR group decided on a series of resolves. The first and most significant was the "necessity of doing our own part in the peace movement in our churches at home." Another stressed the need for "imaginative and prophetic work at home."[36]

The time abroad had also included a visit to Iona Island off the coast of Scotland and a trip to South Africa. These experiences helped develop Daniel Berrigan's ideas on the church and the individual and provided him with a new vision of America and its role in the world. He also felt that the times had changed enough to permit his ideas a possible area of implementation. In his view the Second Vatican Council had stressed the need to remove the church from the power system and, according to Vatican II's document the *Pastoral Constitution on the Church in the Modern World*, encouraged the Christian to see the church's issues as synonymous with the individual's and to start serving the world by applying the Beatitudes literally. Also, the pressure of world conscience was upon the church, allowing her to remove herself from methods of repression and coercion as evidenced in the Vatican II's *Declaration on Religious Freedom*. This new vision of America and its role in the world would be applied to the war in Vietnam as it continued to be escalated. [37]

In September 1964, Daniel returned to the United States to serve as assistant editor of *Jesuit Missions* magazine, headquartered in New York. He again frequented Mount Saviour, AID, and the Catholic Worker but as a new man fortified by his European experience. The question now paramount in his mind was what should he do in face of the war. Daniel and Philip, at the urging of John Heidbrink, gathered together individuals from the Catholic Worker to begin CPF. Daniel Berrigan and John Heidbrink worked out the structures of CPF and raised enough money for the salary of the first director, James Forest. Convinced by Philip Berrigan to assume the directorship of CPF, Forest and Philip along with Martin Corbin became the national co-chairs. [38] Daniel Berrigan together with Dorothy Day, Archbishop Thomas Roberts, Thomas Merton, and a few others served as national sponsors.

Involvement in the peace issue did not mean the end of other participation. In March 1965, both Berrigan brothers joined the civil rights group in Selma. They also continued their priestly functions of celebrating liturgy and counseling those with personal problems, but most of their energies were spent in working for peace and developing CPF. Both brothers spent as much time as possible writing and speaking on peace. While Daniel Berrigan was the best known nationally, Philip spent more time in the actual running of CPF during its formative period. Both men contributed most of what they earned on the road to the CPF, and it in turn provided a community of conscience for them as for all the others involved. Who was influencing whom at this time is difficult to measure. [39] Jim Forest and Tom Cornell both felt that they had contributed significantly toward Daniel Berrigan's becoming a full-blown activist. Certainly Philip Berrigan always was an activist. [40] In any event, Daniel was beyond the activism of these men as they all attest, for his action was always rooted in the theological, and his vision of the dimensions of each action went beyond history and gave the Catholic peace movement a prophetic, eschatological quality.

In October 1964, a number of clergymen felt compelled to protest the charges which had been lodged against dissenters, particularly against the young people opposed to the draft. About twenty clergymen of the New York area called a press conference. It was Rabbi Abraham Heschel who gave the most definitive assurances to the press when they were asked about continuing activities. So in a sense it might be said that he conceived the idea of forming an organization that later became known as Clergy and Laity Concerned About Vietnam (CALCAV). The group caucused on the question that afternoon and Rabbi Abraham Heschel, Daniel Berrigan, and Richard John Neuhaus were chosen co-chairs. Berrigan was actively engaged in the planning and organization of this ecumenical group of clerics until he was sent on his Latin American journey.[41]

In March 1965, after President Johnson took a crucial escalatory step and ordered retaliatory bombing attacks against North Vietnam, Philip and Daniel Berrigan were the only American Catholic priests to promise total "noncooperation" with the nation's Vietnam policies by signing a "Declaration of Conscience." The statement advocated draft resistance. Among other signers were Martin Luther King, Jr., and Bayard Rustin from the civil rights movement and Benjamin Spock from the peace movement. The repercussions of the act came in October 1965, when David Miller, a former student of Daniel's at LeMoyne and a member of CPF, burned his draft card after passage of the law that made such an act a felony. On 6 November 1965, Thomas Cornell, co-chair of CPF along with four other members of the American peace movement also burned their draft cards. The actions of these men, especially the Catholic Workers and CPF members weighed heavily on the consciences of the Berrigan brothers. Miller and Cornell were risking so much and even going to jail for peace—what were they as priests doing for peace?

In November 1965, Daniel faced a crisis within the Society of Jesus just as Philip had previously met at Newburgh—the only difference was that the disciplinary action taken against Daniel was more severe. It not only meant a transfer, but literally an exile to South America to silence him on the peace issue in the United States. Because of the contradictions in accounts in the *New York Times*, the *National Catholic Reporter*, and *America*, it was evident that there was duplicity on the part of the church authorities concerned. In his autobiography, Daniel was to write about this Jesuit attempt at a cover-up. "Exile? Of course not," he said. "I was sent on a 'routine assignment' to Latin America, as editor of a Jesuit magazine, to file reports on the work of Latin Jesuits. It was contemptible and saddening. For the first time, I had cause to be ashamed of my order, its honorable name, the history of holiness and probity I treasured."[42] At the time when Daniel was exiled, two other Jesuit priests, Francis Keating and Daniel Kilfoyle of St. Peters College in New Jersey, were also silenced because of their activities in the peace movement.[43]

Daniel Berrigan's exile generated a quick reaction. Heschel and Neuhaus issued a joint statement of protest when Berrigan, a co-chair of CALCAV, was exiled. Fifty Fordham students picketed Cardinal Spellman's residence and other people demonstrated at Marquette, St. John's, and Fordham universities demanding Berrigan's return. The Protestant *Christian Century* stated, "These actions appear to be a high-handed exercise of ecclesiastical authority to silence Priests who champion unpopular views."[44] On 5 December 1965, in the *New York Times* an ad appeared entitled an "Open Letter to the Authorities of the Archdiocese of New York and the Jesuit Community in New York." The ad was financed by an ad hoc organization, the Institute for Freedom in the Church, composed of lay Catholics who protest, Daniel said, "if someone gets kicked around." And several hundred young Jesuits threatened to leave the order if he was not recalled. Without this public protest and display of united effort for an individual's freedom of conscience within the church, Daniel would probably never have been permitted to return to New York and to continue his peace activities. The authorities of the church could not silence the conscience of Daniel Berrigan and never again would they attempt to silence or discipline the Berrigan brothers in their quest for peace. This would not be true, however, of the government of the United States.

The exile in Latin America lasted three months. While there Berrigan wrote *Consequences, Truth and . . .* in which he presented the church at the edge of new opportunities. To be successful, he contended, the church must be a revolutionary force in society by rejecting power and prestige and choosing to serve all of humankind by making institutions more humane. The exile served only to radicalize him and intensify his commitment to peace. After Berrigan's return he participated in many peace actions all over the country, but especially in New York City. On 30 March 1966, he participated in the Interfaith Peace March, which included a prayer service at St. Patrick's Cathedral in New York City. On 4 July 1966, he spoke of the need to stop the bombing and to begin negotiations. By June 1966, however, he was working mainly out of the CPF—partly because of his individual style and also because other organizations such as CALCAV were too bureaucratic and concerned about their middle-class constituency.

During this period, Daniel Berrigan continued to write. His poetry received increasing attention and criticism because it was said to have lost its universal quality by alliance with a particular ideology. Even *No One Walks Waters* was criticized in this manner by the *New York Times*. His most unique book, *Love, Love at the End*, a collection of poems, fables, and prayers, received the severest criticism because of its obscurity. Daniel was also finding difficulty locating a place for himself within the Jesuit community. In September 1967, he accepted the offer to become the associate director for service on the Cornell United Religious Work staff. By this time Berrigan felt that the contribution he could make to the specifically Catholic structure was pretty well ended. In an article, "Berrigan at Cornell" he explained his decision and went on to state that the times called for Catholics to integrate and reform themselves and make their values amenable to those who were passionately interested in entering communion with the Catholic tradition, and that humankind was in desperate need of such resources. Yet, he also contended that the church and society were almost at the dead end of their resources and that the moral individual would only take on an understanding of self through the poet, the sacrificial student, the African American, and the inner-city community. This alone, according to Berrigan, would provide the humaneness to which the Gospel offers its widest options.[45]

In his life at Cornell University he was associated with all and closed to no one. His student contact was as wide and diverse as the people at the university. He worked in the resistance movement and still functioned within CPF. Once again he assumed the role of teacher with courses in modern drama and the New Testament.[46]

In October 1967, Daniel Berrigan attended the March on the Pentagon with the Cornell University contingent. At midnight, October 22, he was arrested at the Pentagon for a misdemeanor for "refusing to move on when told" and was placed in jail for the first time. In his "Letter from Three Jails" he wrote that two reflections occurred to him: "1. Why was I so long retarded from so crucially formative a happening? 2. What's the big joke, You there?" On Friday, October 27, just after his release, he heard a radio report of the arrest of Philip and three others for pouring blood on selective service files in Baltimore.

In February 1968, Tom Hayden invited Daniel Berrigan and Howard Zinn to be representatives of the resistance in America and go to Hanoi to obtain the release of three war prisoners: Captain John D. Block, Major Norris M. Overly, and Ensign David P. Matheny. It was again time for Berrigan to witness the horrendous sights of poverty and death. But this time more trauma would result because he would be under the fire of his own country's bombs and witness the war atrocities caused by his countrymen. He was to label Vietnam as the "land of burning children," a recurring theme to be used by the Catholic Resistance. As Berrigan reflected on why he had had this experience he wrote: "I do not as yet know what its import is but I shortly will. . . . To have seen the truth has its price attached."[47]

When Daniel returned home he attended Philip's trial and wrote "My Brother, the Witness."[48] The trial resulted in a conviction of Philip Berrigan and the three others who had joined him. The trial was not widely publicized and Philip's testimony at the trial was direct, simple, and hard-hitting. There was no drama. Philip Berrigan just laid things out as he saw them. By Easter of 1968, he and Tom Lewis were planning a second action drawing on their experience from the October event. Philip Berrigan was doing most of the contact work, approaching people at Cornell, in Mobile, in Boston, and in New York. David Darst was the contact in St. Louis and George Mische was instrumental in getting the Melvilles involved. The idea of napalm came from Tom Lewis and Philip Berrigan, who saw firsthand that the people did not perceive the symbolism of pouring blood, but were convinced that they could not miss the one of napalm. The courage of Philip Berrigan and Tom Lewis and the constant reaffirmation of their presence in the action and of the price they would have to pay strengthened the wills of the others. Daniel decided to be a part of the action only five days before the event occurred.[49] Even the night before, if he did not call his brother Jerome by ten in the morning, it meant that he had decided to act. The final decision was an extremely difficult one for Daniel Berrigan to make.

Many factors entered into the final decision. For years Daniel had lived with the peace movement. He had tried every legitimate means to bring about peace. His friends and followers had even been jailed with no cleric going with them. He had written books and lectured widely on peace and as he told his friend, Paul Mayer, "They slap me on the back and tell me how great I am and nothing happens."[50] All of these things were true of his brother Philip as well, he realized, as he attempted to make the final decision. Daniel Berrigan had also traveled around the world and had seen the poverty and suffering of the majority of people and could not help but compare it to the affluence of America and America's erroneous foreign policy. Though his brother Philip had been limited mainly to sights of poverty in America, especially African American poverty, Daniel knew that he had come to the same conclusions. Next, Daniel Berrigan carried the Society of Jesus with him in his every action. This was an extremely significant factor, for relations with the Jesuits had become increasingly tenuous as his actions for peace escalated. Yet, his brother had similar experiences with the Josephites though they were a less prestigious religious community. Finally, on the eve of the Catonsville action, Philip and Daniel spent the night discussing the pros and cons of the action. With Philip's emphasis on the practical and political and Daniel's emphasis on the ideal and spiritual, it was a soul-searching time for both brothers. The end result was that Daniel joined Philip and the seven others the next morning at Catonsville. After the arrests, the nine were released, each on $2,500 bail. While awaiting the trial on 7 October 1968, the nine began an extensive speaking tour to explain the reasons for their action at Catonsville.

Ironically, the Jesuits did not evict Daniel Berrigan from the community as a result of Catonsville. Rather, a movement began among the rank and file to support him. The Jesuits used the theme: "Our Brother Is In Need," and stressed the right of freedom of conscience. During the week the trial began the Jesuit church and hall of St. Ignatius Parish in Baltimore was used as the gathering place for the nine. Religious services and rallies were held. Peace activists from all over the United States came to participate in a parade to protest the trial of the Catonsville Nine. The trial proceeded for three days during which time the defendants admitted that they had napalmed the files. Just before the verdict was returned, Federal Judge Roszel C. Thomsen engaged in a rather informal discourse with the Catonsville Nine. It seemed to be painful for the judge to arraign people whose intensity of moral passion and accumulated years of service to others rendered them anything but "convicted felons." After all was said, Daniel Berrigan ended the trial the way he had ended the action at Catonsville by praying the Our Father.

The action and the trial of the Catonsville Nine left no doubt to many observers that their moral commitment to peace was so great that it had called them forth to this ultra form of resistance. This commitment revealed to the public that they believed civil disobedience was the required action for those who wanted to follow Christ. It was necessary because the evils in America had become so great. The seriousness of poverty, racial conflict, urban riots, and returning missionaries in reaching negative judgments about U.S. foreign policy combined with the illegality and immorality of the war in Vietnam to create in the Catonsville Nine an alienation from U.S. society. The nine attempted to express this link between injustice and war in their trial. They tried to explain that the evils of injustice and war had extended into every aspect of American life and necessitated an action such as theirs from a moral people. Through civil disobedience these people sought to overhaul the inefficient, cumbersome, and corrupt governmental machinery and its archaic policies of war, racism, and exploitation. Despite their moral plea, a verdict of guilty was returned against each defendant on each of three counts: destruction of U.S. property, destruction of selective service records, and interference with the Selective Service Act of 1967. The convicted proceeded to appeal the decision.[51]

The action itself had been an open and peaceful violation of the law done in obedience to their conscience. It was a so-called "stand-by" action where people openly remained awaiting arrest. These protestors emulated Gandhi, Thoreau, and Martin Luther King, Jr., and other apostles of civil disobedience who were prepared to go to jail for violating the law, even though they thought the law was unjust. Some members of the traditional peace groups believed that they had gone too far by destroying property and breaking and entering. Even though

Dorothy Day was critical of their destruction of property, she continued to support them.

Soon after Catonsville, similar draft board actions occurred in Milwaukee and Chicago, cities with traditionally strong centers of the Catholic Worker from which participants could easily be recruited. These individuals prided themselves on individual acts of conscience and while they admired the Berrigans, they considered neither them nor anyone else to be their leaders per se.

At the time Catonsville occurred, publicity reached a high point and focused on the Berrigan brothers. "Support groups" surrounding the nine began to flourish and a defense committee to raise funds for the trial was also formed. Basically, the nine, the support groups, and the defense committee began to promote themselves as a Christian community. It was a fragile group of volunteers who based their community on love and trust and advocated civil disobedience as the form of protest against the war in Vietnam. Initiation into the inner core of the community was an act of civil disobedience at a draft board. The action was meant to symbolize their unwillingness to allow or permit the uncritical adaptation of Christianity to the society in which they lived. Consequently, the emphasis was on Christianity's conflict with the present war-making policy of their country.

In 1969, the Catholic Resistance underwent significant changes. First, a group calling themselves the D.C.-Nine raided the Dow Chemical office in the nation's capital. This attack on a corporation broadened the targets of the movement to include corporations that produced war materials such as napalm. Second, the members of the New York Eight draft board group did not stand by and await arrest after their action. This group destroyed the draft files at night and later "surfaced." The choice of a night tactic was first used by the New York group to avoid any possible harm to individuals in the selective service office at the time of the raid. The New York Eight's tactic of "surfacing" consisted of calling a press conference and at it Neil McLaughlin, a Baltimore priest, read a statement signed by the eight which claimed moral responsiblity for the draft board action.[52] Surprisingly to the participants, no arrests followed. The reason was lack of evidence. Up to this point most people who had performed draft board actions had come from the Catholic fold: priests, nuns, and lay people who were highly educated and middle class.

The tactic of "night actions" and "surfacing" was adopted by subsequent groups, such as, the Boston Eight, the Beaver Fifty-five, the East Coast Conspiracy to Save Lives, the Flower City Conspiracy, and the Camden Twenty-eight. The exact number of draft board actions to occur between Philip Berrigan's first draft board raid at the Custom's House in Baltimore on 27 October 1967, to the Camden Twenty-eight action on 22 August 1971 is unknown. Theodore Glick, a draft resister and participant in the East Coast Conspiracy to Save Lives and the Flower City Conspiracy, and indicted conspirator in the Harrisburg trial, has estimated that over 250 draft board actions occurred during the time period.[53] Philip Berrigan estimates the number at two hundred actions. And Charles Meconis, a Catholic writer and resister, claimed that altogether some fifty-three draft board actions took place.[54] As the number of actions increased and the members of the resistance became more diverse, the term Catholic Resistance began to lose some of its denominational significance. Many non-Catholics joined the movement and did so from humanitarian and political motivation. Change from the more traditional stand-by action of civil disobedience to night actions and surfacing signalled another departure in the Catholic Resistance. Both represented a decline in emphasis on Christian witness and symbolic action and a greater desire for political effectiveness.

In addition to these actions, one other raid of significance occurred during the time period—a raid on the files of the FBI office in Media, Pennsylvania. This was a night action, but no one ever surfaced to assume moral responsibility, nor was anyone ever prosecuted for the action.[55] The documents taken from the raid were published in the periodical *WIN*. The newspapers carried front page stories on the documents and some excerpts. The documents did detail FBI success at infiltrating college campuses with informers who gathered information on professors as well as students and there was also an internal memorandum that proposed actions to intensify paranoia within the peace movement over infiltration by the FBI.[56]

The man who attempted to build this community of resistance and organize draft board actions was Philip Berrigan. After Catonsville, Daniel Berrigan returned to Cornell University to resume his teaching duties and to write and speak on behalf of the peace movement. Philip, on the other hand, was relieved of any specific duties by his religious superior, and resided at the Josephite Provincialate in Baltimore. From this point of official residence he spent most of his time traveling in hopes of locating people who sympathized with the draft board action and would be possible recruits for future actions. Philip Berrigan believed the draft board community was too elitist and wanted to widen it, but the lack of developing any tactic beyond draft board and corporation raids limited the possibility. Catholicism and the church were central to Philip Berrigan's personal motivation for action, but he did not make this motivation a prerequisite for participation. The only requirement that he had was that participants shared his political analysis and wanted to stop the war in Vietnam through nonviolent direct acts of civil disobedience. With night actions and surfacing even the degree of risk and assumption of personal responsibility was lessened as a prerequisite—there was now a possibility that one would not have to go to jail. The technique used by Berrigan for building such a community of resistance was called a retreat, one or more weekends to discover whether or not an individual would engage in such an action. Philip served as a benevolent facilitator and counselor, being sure that people of like mind were brought together, that people's needs were taken care of, and that precautions and planning had been carried out in full. Philip's long-time friend, John P. Grady, often assisted the participants in the planning of the action. The decision to act and the actual plans of the action were worked out by the members themselves in the group they had formed. Thus, technically, Philip Berrigan was not the leader and not a participant in each action that occurred.[57]

The switch to night actions and surfacing also reflected a change in attitude concerning arrest and jail. Some members were no longer willing to await arrest and go to jail for an action they believed to be morally correct while the draft and complicity of corporations continued unhampered in its perpetuation of an immoral war. This change in the Catholic Resistance also had its effect on the Berrigan brothers themselves.

By 9 April 1970, the appeals of both Berrigan brothers after the Catonsville trial had expired and they were to report to jail on that day. Between October 1967 and April 1970, Philip Berrigan had not spent a full year in jail and Daniel had spent only a few days in jail. Both brothers agreed not to report, but rather to appear publicly first and afterward be hauled away by federal marshals. Daniel Berrigan was to appear at the Cornell Peace Rally on 19 April 1970 and Philip was to appear at the Church of St. Gregory the Great in Manhattan's Upper West Side two evenings later.

On April 19, Daniel Berrigan appeared before ten thousand people at the Cornell peace rally weekend, which was held in his honor and called "America is Hard to Find." At the evening "freedom Seder" Berrigan appeared and gave an impassioned plea for resistance. After the Bread and Puppet Theater had finished its mime of the Last Supper, the lights went out. At that point Daniel was concealed under an immense papier-mache head of an apostle and made his escape. In the darkness of the auditorium he hopped into the figure and walked outside into a truck. In minutes he was transferred to a car and successfully began his four-month underground escapade as a fugitive from justice. The engineer of Daniel Berrigan's underground existence was at the time the relatively unknown Pakistani, Eqbal Ahmad, a fellow at Chicago's Adlai Stevenson Institute for International Affairs. [58]

The FBI agents, embarrassed by his escape, began a series of frantic searches for Daniel. Afraid that Philip would attempt the same type of escape, they sought to capture him before his appearance at the peace rally at 8:00 P.M. at St. Gregory the Great Church. Philip along with David Eberhardt, a fellow fugitive from the Baltimore Four draft board conviction had slipped into the rectory before dawn on April 21. At mid-afternoon the FBI agents entered the rectory and located Philip and David Eberhardt in a closet in the bedroom of the pastor, Henry Browne. The closet was in reality an "inner closet" which had been overlooked by all but one agent. [59] The fugitives were taken to the Federal House of Detention in New York City.

Despite the arrest, over five hundred people assembled at the evening rally. Howard Zinn, a political science professor at Boston University who had accompanied Daniel Berrigan on the trip to Hanoi, Eqbal Ahmad, and Felipe Luciano, a Young Lord, were the featured speakers. Over one hundred FBI agents were also present hoping to capture Daniel Berrigan. The pastor, Henry Browne, presided over the rally and blended together the menagerie of hippies, peace movement people, Black Panthers, Young Lords, professors, middle-class sympathizers, nuns and priests, FBI agents, and even a group of parishioners who staged a counterdemonstration in protest of the church being used as a sanctuary for Philip Berrigan. [60]

The next day Philip Berrigan and David Eberhardt were taken to

Lewisburg Federal Prison and placed in maximum security for the four months that Daniel Berrigan was underground. The two men believed that prison officials unduly punished them in order to put pressure on Daniel Berrigan in the hope that he might give himself up.

Philip Berrigan had never considered the underground as a viable political option for himself, and for the week before they surfaced, Daniel and Philip engaged in heated debates as to its viability. Daniel Berrigan strongly favored it and Philip opposed it.[61] Philip Berrigan's arrest was no shock, but the constant hassle of prison authorities and being placed in maximum security at Lewisburg was. In fact the imprisonment began to affect the psychological stability of both Philip Berrigan and David Eberhardt. On 20 July 1970, Robert Coles, a Harvard research psychiatrist examined both men and found it to be so.[62] Senator Charles Goodell of New York and others were recruited to confront the director of the Bureau of Prisons, Norman A. Carlson, about the harrassment. In July 1970, a demonstration at the prison was held to protest the maximum security confinement. There was no let up on the treatment by prison officials until Daniel Berrigan's capture. On 25 August 1970 Philip Berrigan was transferred to the federal prison in Danbury, Connecticut.

Because of Daniel Berrigan's talents as a writer, he viewed the underground as a means of amplifying—not muting—his propagandizing ability through the media. He believed the media would be more likely to publish the words of a fugitive priest than of a cleric not on the run. He also saw his fugitive status as a way to involve more and more middle-class people in a much deeper commitment to the peace movement by harboring him than they otherwise would make.[63] Thus, Berrigan mainly viewed the underground as an experiment—once there he did not know what would happen. While he was underground, both of these beliefs were realized. On 26 April 1970 the *New York Times* published an interview with him held in a Manhattan walk-up apartment. The following month the *Saturday Review* featured Berrigan writing on the twenty-fifth anniversary of the death of Dietrich Bonhoeffer, a German Lutheran clergyman executed on Hitler's orders for his role in the resistance inside wartime Germany. In August, the premier of his play, *The Trial of the Catonsville Nine*, occurred in Los Angeles. And on Sunday, August 2, John C. Raines, an assistant professor of religion at Temple University, invited Daniel Berrigan to preach at the First United Methodist Church in Germantown, Pennsylvania, where Raines's brother was pastor. Berrigan's sermon lasted twenty minutes, received wide press coverage, and caused great embarrassment to the FBI. During his four months underground, Daniel stayed with thirty-seven families and over two hundred people assisted in making arrangements for his resistance.

But in August, Daniel Berrigan did not follow the advice of his underground organizer Eqbal Ahmad, who had warned him to stay away from life-time friends. Berrigan went to the home of William Stringfellow and Anthony Towne on Block Island, twelve miles off the coast of Rhode Island. While staying there, he spent much of his time working on the manuscript for his *The Dark Night of Resistance*, which he dedicated to his two friends: "To Bill and Tony, for I was homeless and you gave me shelter." On August 11, FBI agents, posing as bird-watchers, arrested him.

The reason for the capture was that Elizabeth McAlister, R.S.C.J., in her letters to Philip Berrigan at Lewisburg prison had mentioned that Daniel Berrigan was going to stay with William Stringfellow. At the time neither Elizabeth McAlister nor Philip Berrigan knew that their smuggled letters were being read by prison officials and FBI agents.[64]

Daniel Berrigan had considered the underground an experiment and from the very beginning he did not know how long it could be sustained. His success at living this form of resistance had serious implications for the future of the Catholic Resistance. First, it considerably escalated and intensified the widening gap between conscience and cooperation with the government. The reason Berrigan gave for his underground experiment was:

Can Christians unthinkingly submit before such powers (war makers)? We judge not. The "powers and dominations" remain subject to Christ; our consciences are in his keeping and no other. To act as though we were criminals before God or humanity, to cease resisting a war which has immeasurably widened since we first acted, to retire meekly to silence and isolation—this seems to Phil and me a betrayal of our ministry.[65]

The resistance and refusal to accept jail on the part of Daniel Berrigan offended not only government authorities but also traditional adherents of civil disobedience who willingly accepted jail for violations of the law.

Second, Berrigan's underground existence encouraged the overreaction of government officials who in 1970 were filled with fear of bombings, political kidnappings, and security leaks in Washington, D.C. The Watergate hearings in 1973 revealed that the threat which the Berrigan brothers posed and the fear that this engendered on the part of government officials was greater than anyone imagined three years earlier.

Third, Daniel Berrigan's writings during his underground experience repeatedly contended that the social institutions in America were corrupt and that idolatry undergirded the value system of America. The writings called no longer for reform, but for revolution. The underground symbolized his radical break with existing American institutions.

By August 25, both Philip and Daniel Berrigan were behind bars in Danbury Federal Penitentiary. Ironically, jail was not to mean silence and isolation for the Berrigan brothers, but rather a new and intensified position of national prominence. This change can be credited to the efforts of J. Edgar Hoover, director of the Federal Bureau of Investigation.

On November 27, before a Senate Appropriations Committee hearing and to the press, Hoover hinted at an East Coast Conspiracy to Save Lives, whose members he alleged were planning to kidnap and bomb to achieve their ends. These people were a great threat to the internal security of the United States. Seven weeks later on 12 January 1971 major newspapers were called to send correspondents to a Justice Department public information meeting. John W. Huske of the department appeared carrying stacks of a four-page press release and an eleven-page indictment. Both handouts made no mention of Hoover's previous statement and his Senate testimony outlining a plot and alleging it to be the work of the East Coast Conspiracy to Save Lives.[66] Six persons were indicted on charges of plotting to blow up heating systems of federal buildings in the nation's capital and also to kidnap presidential advisor Henry Kissinger. The six people who were indicted were: Philip Berrigan, Elizabeth McAlister, Eqbal Ahmad, Anthony Scoblick, and two diocesan priests from Baltimore, Neil McLaughlin and Joseph Wenderoth. The punishment indicated in the indictment if they were convicted of the kidnap conspiracy count was a maximum of life imprisonment and/or a general conspiracy conviction with a five-year maximum in prison. Philip Berrigan and Elizabeth McAlister were also charged with three counts each of attempting to smuggle communications in and out of Lewisburg Penitentiary with a conviction of a single count punishable of up to ten years imprisonment.

The indictment also contained a list of twenty-two overt acts beginning 1 April 1970 and named seven co-conspirators: Daniel Berrigan, Jogues Egan, R.S.C.J., Beverly Bell, S.N.D., Majorie Shuman, Paul Mayer, William Davidon, and Thomas Davidson. Guy L. Goodwin was named the government's attorney. On January 13, Goodwin began a grand jury investigation in which Jane Hoover and Betsy Sandel, Patricia Rom, Zoia Horn, Robert Joynt, his sister Patricia Chanel, and Jogues Egan were subpoenaed to testify. After being granted immunity, all testified before the grand jury except Sister Jogues Egan who was cited with contempt.

The efforts of Egan's attorney, Jack Levine, a young Philadelphia lawyer, resulted in her case being heard by the Pennsylvania Supreme Court.[67] In 1972, the court rejected the stance taken by the Justice Department in the Jogues Egan contempt case. It established the precedent that grand jury witnesses threatened with contempt for refusing to testify could require the government to disclose whether they had been subpoenaed because of information gained from wiretaps. If the government refused to reveal such information, contempt charges would be dropped. It was a choice prosecutors did not make in this case.

The Jogues Egan case became significant not only in legal history and subsequent Senate investigations of Watergate but also to a reconvening of the Harrisburg grand jury. Two weeks after the indictment had been issued, William S. Lynch, the most able prosecutor in the Criminal Division of the Justice Department, was assigned to replace Goodwin as chief prosecuting attorney in the Harrisburg case. The reason for this change was the desperate desire of J. Edgar Hoover, John Mitchell, and Robert C. Mardian, assistant attorney general for the Internal Security Division, to win the case.

Lynch agreed to take the case on the condition that he could issue a "superseding indictment." The new indictment was structured in such a way that the government would not have to prove either the kidnapping or the bombing allegation in order to obtain a conviction on the overall conspiracy charge. Draft board raids would be sufficient for conviction. The new indictment added two defendants, Mary Cain Scoblick and John Theodore Glick, who was already serving time for the Flower City Conspiracy draft board raid. The indictment dropped as coconspirators Daniel Berrigan, Paul Mayer, and Thomas Davidson. Thus, one Berrigan, Daniel, was subtracted from the case, but Glick joined Joseph Wenderoth as the second member of the eleven-member East Coast Conspiracy to Save Lives to be indicted. Before the trial began Susan Davis, S.N.D., another member of the East Coast Conspiracy, and John Swinglish, head of the Catholic Peace Fellowship in Washington, D.C., were added to the list of named coconspirators.

The new indictment also included a maximum of five years imprisonment upon conviction. The irony of the "superseding indictment" was that it was issued without any new evidence being obtained.[68] On April 20, ten days before it was issued, twenty-five persons were subpoenaed to testify before the grand jury in Harrisburg. The people subpoenaed were all linked to the Catholic Resistance through draft board raids or the Harrisburg Defense Committee work. The exception was the in-laws of Eqbal Ahmad, Mr. and Mrs. Abraham Diamond. Of the twenty-five people subpoenaed only the Diamonds testified. Everyone else refused to testify and seven of the twenty-five received contempt sentences. No one was placed in jail pending the Jogues Egan case. As a result, no one cited with contempt, except for Jogues Egan, ever went to jail. Because of the silence of the subpoenaed (unlike Lynch's experience in criminal cases in which individuals talked in exchange for immunity), no new information pertaining to the case was gained by the grand jury. Despite these events, the superseding indictment was still issued on April 30.

Those indicted in the Harrisburg Eight case began meeting weekly at the Danbury Federal Prison to prepare their defense. Three nationally known lawyers were selected by the defendants, Ramsey Clark, Leonard Boudin, and Paul O'Dwyer.[69] Before the trial began Theodore Glick was dropped from the case because he wanted to defend himself. Finally on 25 January 1972 the three-month trial of the Harrisburg Seven opened in the Middle District of Pennsylvania. Judge R.

Dixon Herman, a Nixon appointee and former juvenile court judge, presided. Six of the seven indicted at the time were Roman Catholic clergy—priests and nuns—members of the Catholic Resistance. Central to the case of the Catholic team of prosecutors, William Lynch, John Connally, and John Cattone, were letters between Philip Berrigan and Elizabeth McAlister written during Berrigan's imprisonment. Boyd Douglas, a convict turned informer had been the carrier of the letters. He had copied the letters and turned the copies over to the FBI.[70] In retrospect, since the public announcement of the marriage of Elizabeth McAlister and Philip Berrigan on Memorial Day 1973, the letters can now be viewed in their proper perspective and understood in terms of love, fidelity, duty, and fantasy between a couple dedicated to a cause. These considerations far outweigh the apparent political naivete of the letters. If there had been no love relationship there would not have been any letters. The final judgment of Boyd Douglas's direct relationship with the FBI as an informer, provocateur, and/or entrapper remained unclear even at the end of the trial. The dramatic readings of the letters and the lengthy testimony of Boyd Douglas provided the bulk of the testimony presented by the prosecution.

Ramsey Clark held the privilege of initiating the case for the defense. He surprisingly stood up and declared: "Your honor, the defendants will always seek peace, the defendants continue to proclaim their innocence—and the defense rests." This decision of silence on the part of the defense had been made by a four to three vote on the part of the defendants. Ahmad, Berrigan, and McAlister had voted against it—desiring to confront the government. Ironically, the person who assumed the leadership in this final decision was not the publicly acclaimed Philip nor the intellectual Eqbal, but the small community of four lesser figures, the Scoblicks and McLaughlin and Wenderoth. The four believed that they made the decision by default of leadership. Ahmad had looked to Berrigan as leader and because of Philip Berrigan's ambiguity between his commitment to resistance and his desire to protect Elizabeth McAlister, he was unable to lead.[71]

The concluding arguments by the lawyers were made and the judge charged the sequestered jury, which had been carefully screened for any religious or political bias during their selection. The verdict was a hung jury with a count of ten to two in favor of acquittal. A mother of four sons who were conscientious objectors to the war in Vietnam and a grocery store owner were the only ones who voted for conviction. Berrigan and McAlister were convicted of smuggling communications in and out of a federal prison. The outcome of the trial resulted in a legal and political victory for the defendants, and a setback for J. Edgar Hoover and President Nixon's Justice Department. Ironically, it was also the deathblow to what had come to be known as the Catholic Resistance.

The Harrisburg prosecution showed clearly in its presentation of evidence, actually its lack of evidence, that the case would never have been brought to trial had not J. Edgar Hoover made his accusations against the Berrigan brothers. Four weeks after the trial had ended, Hoover died of natural causes—a seventy-year-old heart giving out. The decision to prosecute illustrated how susceptible the career staff of the Justice Department could be to non-judicial influences of those running the department. The tactic of a political trial to discredit and destroy the antiwar movement under Nixon's administration was not new. It had been used in the conspiracy trials of Benjamin Spock, the Chicago Seven, the Black Panthers, and after the Harrisburg Seven it would be used again in the Angela Davis trial and the Ellsberg trial. Ironically, the government would lose every case in the courtroom. Yet, it would successfully accomplish the goal of eradicating dissident groups in American society. The government seemed to be losing every battle yet winning the war.

By means of pretrial motions, the defense lawyers were able to win victories through the courts to challenge the illegal practices of the FBI and the Justice Department, such as the use of wiretapping, the use of an informer, illegal search procedures, the use of the grand jury as a fishing expedition, and the use of conspiracy laws for political purposes. All such procedures indicated that the Justice Department under President Nixon's administration had become highly politicized in its efforts to eradicate dissent in the name of internal security and the law. [72]

Even the Bureau of Federal Prisons emerged as subject to the Justice Department's pressure. For no given reason, Philip Berrigan and David Eberhardt had been kept in maximum security rather than the usual procedure of putting draft resisters in minimum security. And the special study release program for prisoners, a rare privilege granted by the U.S.

Bureau of Prisons in Washington, D.C., had been granted to an informer, Boyd Douglas, who was paid by the FBI for his information.[73]

All of these factors take on a new significance in American history since the Senate investigations of Watergate. The politicization of American institutions revealed by Watergate was already evident at the Harrisburg Seven trial where the government served as prosecutor and not as defendant.[74]

During the trial the Roman Catholic church offered no official support for the defendants. Since Catonsville, however, there was personal support from some church leaders. Lawrence Cardinal Shehan, archbishop of Baltimore, had visited the men in jail and had designated the archdiocesan lawyer, Francis X. Gallagher, as one of the defense lawyers. There was also bail money provided and character defense testimony given for the defendants by several priests of the Archdiocese of Baltimore. Individual Catholics and some Catholic groups as well as many individual Americans and groups supported the Harrisburg Seven either through financial donations or participation in functions planned by the publicly accountable Harrisburg Seven Defense Committee. Over one half million dollars was raised by the committee and all except $20,000 was spent on trial expenses.[75]

Tragically, the government's use of a political trial to destroy a dissident group in America once again proved effective. But the demise of the Catholic Resistance and the Berrigan brothers efforts had already occurred even before the trial began. The Vietnam antiwar movement in general had declined early in the Nixon presidency, but regrouped to mount massive demonstrations in the fall of 1969. A brief resurgence occurred with the invasion of Cambodia begun on 30 April 1970. At Kent State on May 4 Ohio national guardsmen fired into a milling crowd of students killing four, wounding thirteen, and raising the American crisis to a new level of anguish. Within days, about half a million students left classes and shut down about a fifth of the nation's campuses for periods ranging from one day to the rest of the academic year. On May 14, Mississippi state police and national guardsmen attacked a dormitory at Jackson State University killing two students. On May 9, over 100,000 people on short notice gathered in Washington to protest Cambodia and Kent State, but it dissipated quickly without leadership. A politics of confrontation seemed to have played itself out among a public afflicted with war weariness.[76] Though the Catholic Resistance and the Berrigan brothers had been a separate peace group within the antiwar movement, they relied heavily on the general antiwar atmosphere. Once troop withdrawal began and the promise of peace appeared imminent, the cause of the Catholic Resistance was no longer of immediate concern to the public. The Harrisburg Seven trial kept it before the public, but the end of the trial abruptly signalled the end of a Catholic resistance to the war in Vietnam.

The group itself also contained its own elements of self-destruction. One factor was that it was a voluntary association of highly mobile and widespread people with no day-to-day leader or community to hold it together. Both Philip and Daniel had very independent styles of operation. Another element that weakened the group was that in the face of troop withdrawal the members themselves became increasingly convinced that the tactic of draft board and corporation raids was no longer an effective means of stopping the war. And finally, the high price of long prison sentences was too great for many of its members to withstand. Thus, a retreat from resistance followed.

Philip Berrigan returned to jail after the trial. Daniel Berrigan who was paroled during the trial, refused in any way to assume the role of leader for the Catholic Resistance and sought a new college teaching position. He did, however, continue to make public-speaking engagements and even appeared on the Dick Cavett Show. On national television, he seemed to alienate his audience. The other defendants in the Harrisburg Seven trial also appeared to seek retreat. The Scoblicks bought a small house in Baltimore and so did McLaughlin and Wenderoth. All four of these defendants sought to live normal lives in a changing neighborhood. Eqbal Ahmad returned to his work at the Adlai Stevenson Institute and Elizabeth McAlister returned to her religious community and assumed a part-time teaching position in a small secular college in New Jersey. McAlister did continue to speak publicly about the future direction of the peace movement, stressing the need to keep building small communities of resistance. This would have to have to wait, however, until Philip Berrigan was released from prison. None of the defendants participated in acts of civil disobedience against the war in Vietnam after the trial and all except McAlister wanted to convey to the American public that they viewed the trial as an intrusion on their personal lives.[77]

Ironically, the prosecution of the Harrisburg Seven achieved a national prominence for these defendants in a way that they could never have achieved by themselves. And in the process, the FBI director was revealed as so powerful a man that the president of the United States chose to ignore Hoover's blatant violation of the Bill of Rights. Such actions seemed only to leave a pall of despair rather than hope across the nation. The trial itself confirmed the Catholic Resistance's critical stand against American institutions. This critical position had its roots in the participants' identification with the oppressed in American society and by 1965 extended to the oppression experienced abroad as the result of the Vietnam War. The religious belief of the Berrigan brothers and the Catholic Resistance motivated their actions on behalf of peace and strengthened them as they attempted to confront their own government and bring it to a position of justice and peace. This religious faith made them unique in the Vietnam antiwar movement. Their religious motivation separated them from the political and secular orientation of the New Left. The political ideology of communism held no attraction for the Catholic Resistance though it reached similar conclusions as the New Left in relation to capitalism and imperialism in America.

Despite the Catholic Resistance's efforts to offer an effective peace witness that would awaken the consciences of the public against the war in Vietnam, the power of the U.S. government prevailed. The more it prevailed, the more the resistance escalated. As the resistance escalated the level of personal commitment required for such a peace witness also increased and not many people were willing to pay that price. For this reason the Catholic Resistance was not able to build a broadly based community of resistance. The significance of the Catholic Resistance was that the people involved did offer a peace witness in face of such power and at great personal sacrifice. As Daniel Berrigan wrote: "Peacemaking is hard hard almost as war."[78]

The Berrigan brothers and their witness for peace emerged from the American Catholic pacifist tradition. As they often acknowledged, they together with the Catholic Resistance came out of the Catholic Worker tradition of pacifism and nonviolence. Dorothy Day put it more bluntly when she said, "The Berrigans came and stole our young men away into the peace movement."[79] Like Day, Philip Berrigan addressed the public order by positing actions for peace and in doing so he escalated the level of nonviolent resistance. Daniel Berrigan because of his theological training and writing ability continued more in the tradition of Thomas Merton rather than Dorothy Day. Just as Merton had attempted to provide a theological rationale for nonviolence within Catholicism, Daniel tried to express a new theology of peace from his experiences within the Catholic Resistance. Like Day and Merton, faith was the center of existence for each brother as they embraced poverty and rooted their faith in the Gospel message and an eschatological vision. The combination of Philip's and Daniel's unique strengths and talents enabled them to bring forth the message of peace to their church and country in a way never before experienced in the history of American Catholicism. The impact of their prophetic message and witness for peace is still being experienced as American Catholics struggle more than ever to determine what it means to be both Catholic and American in a nuclear age.

# *8*

# Catholic Peacemaking

In May 1983, the National Conference of Catholic Bishops (NCCB) issued a pastoral letter on war and peace, *The Challenge of Peace: God's Promise and Our Response*. It was a watershed in the teaching of the Roman Catholic church in America on the issues of war and peace. For the first time since the early Christian period, pacifism and nonviolence were officially recognized as part of the Judeo-Christian tradition. The document also emphasized the different levels of church teaching on war and peace and in an unprecedented manner emphasized the role of individual conscience and the right to dissent. Thus, the document permitted individual Catholics to legitimately disagree on various aspects of war and peace and still remain Catholics in good standing.[1] *The Challenge of Peace* was an attempt to create a new vision of peacemaking for American Catholics. The letter concluded with the following injunction: "Peacemaking is not an optional commitment. It is a requirement of our faith. We are called to be peacemakers, not by some movement of the moment, but by our Lord Jesus. The content and context of our peacemaking is set, not by some political agenda or ideological program, but by the teaching of His Church."[2] The efforts of the American Catholic peace movement to build a pacifist constituency solidly within the institutional church contributed greatly to NCCB's pastoral letter. These efforts to influence the institutional church became most effective in the post–Vietnam War period.

The Catholic peace movement maintained its vigor while the broader American peace movement collapsed after the withdrawal of American soldiers from Vietnam and the end of military induction. The most important reasons why the Catholic peace movement grew in strength was the emergence of a resistance community, Jonah

211

House, the founding of a new organization, Pax Christi–USA, and the publication of the bishops' pastoral. Thus, the Catholic peace movement not only continued its witness after Vietnam but even broadened its constituency among mainline Catholics as it shifted its focus from Vietnam to nuclear issues and concern for Central America.

Although the Catholic Resistance stopped its raids on draft boards after the Harrisburg trial, it gained a new life when Philip Berrigan and Elizabeth McAlister founded Jonah House, which began to function in June 1973 when Berrigan and McAlister, together with a few others, rented a house in the inner city of Baltimore and began what they called a resistance community. Here they pledged to share their incomes and hold property in common and to live a life of voluntary poverty. They also set forth a few principles which would guide their new community:

—Nonviolence, resistance, and community are interchangeable— their effects are identical.
—Contemplation (in whatever form—prayer, meditation, reflection, analysis) gives sustenance to spirit and resistance.
—Holding property in common is essential to justice.
—The Scriptures hold the vision of a society faithful to God whose members are loving toward each other, reverent toward all of life.[3]

In September 1973, Philip Berrigan and Elizabeth McAlister also made public their marriage and were subsequently excommunicated from the Roman Catholic church because neither had been dispensed from their religious vows. Jonah House would be their home during the 1970s and 1980s and there their children, Frida, Jerome, and Katy, were born and raised while the two attempted to build and live a resistance community. Jonah House was in the Catholic Worker tradition but it emphasized resistance rather than the corporal works of mercy.

Members of Jonah House continued their resistance while the broader antiwar movement in America was winding down in 1973. They continued their acts of nonviolent resistance against the war— they would not give up. Again, voluntary acts of civil disobedience were performed to make their point against the war effort and jail sentences were served. Moreover, they always tried to link a religious spirit to their acts of resistance. A brief look at some of their actions in 1973 and 1974 provides some understanding of how they attempted to integrate religion and resistance.

In the summer of 1973, a number of Sisters of Notre Dame de Namur, one of whom lived at Jonah House, began the White House Pray-Ins. Each day two to six people were arrested for kneeling and praying during the White House tour. The pray-ins called for a halt to the intense bombing then under way in Cambodia. At Thanksgiving, Jonah House joined with the Community for Creative Nonviolence (CCNV) in Washington, D.C., at the home of Secretary of State Henry Kissinger where they presented him with a world globe into which was plunged a carving knife and fork. At Christmas, Jonah House again joined with CCNV at the White House, where they celebrated the Feast of Holy Innocents in solidarity against the slaughter of innocent lives resulting from the Christmas bombing of North Vietnam. They also performed the morality play, *Herod and the Kings*, which was followed by a liturgy at the Treasury Building.

In 1974, on the January 27 anniversary of the signing of the Paris Peace Accords, a form of theater was staged in front of the White House to protest the Thieu regime. Each Friday during Lent demonstrations were staged at what Jonah House believed were various seats of oppression in Baltimore: the Baltimore City Jail and Maryland State Penitentiary, the Maryland National Bank, the National Security Agency, the Catholic Center and Cathedral, and the Westinghouse plant. In the summer Jonah House participated in the Tiger Cage demonstrations outside the Capitol Rotunda. And in the fall, three members of Jonah House demonstrated at the National Catholic Shrine in Washington, D.C., during the annual conference of the American Catholic bishops. In March 1975, sixty-two people, including Daniel Berrigan and five others from Jonah House, were arrested at the White House for sitting in as a protest to President Ford's amnesty program. These were the type of activities that Jonah House promoted and over 116 such acts of resistance were performed between 1973 and 1988.[4]

The end of the American presence in Indochina in April 1975 coincided with the beginning of Jonah House's antinuclear work. The primary focus of their resistance was a continuing presence at the Pentagon. Disarmament was the aim. Other demonstrations were held at the White House, the State Department, the Congress, the Department of Energy, and the Air and Space Museum. When Philip Berrigan was in jail again in 1977, he began to focus on the "bomb." The issue consumed him more and more. He believed that it threatened not only human life but the planet itself, that he had to do something to prevent a nuclear holocaust. Berrigan searched for ways to respond to the situation and returned to the draft board actions of the Vietnam era. He decided to use the Judeo-Christian symbol of blood, which he would pour over nuclear warheads. Standby actions whereby he would await arrest rather than night actions would be the preferred course of action because it was more in accord with traditional nonviolence.

On 9 September 1980 Philip Berrigan and his brother Daniel along with six others entered a General Electric plant in King of Prussia, Pennsylvania, where the nose cones for the Mark 12A nuclear warheads were manufactured. There they enacted the biblical prophecies of Isaiah 2:4 and Micah 4:3 to "beat swords into plowshares" by hammering on two of the nose cones and pouring blood on documents. Daniel Berrigan has written regarding the action: "We have been at this for years—dramatic events orchestrated, arbitrary but intensely traditional, liturgical, illegal, in every case wrenching the actors out of routine and community life to face the music, face the public, face the jury."[5] In February 1981, the eight underwent a jury trail in Norristown, Pennsylvania. Because the court suppressed individual testimony about the reasons for their symbolic destruction of the warheads in protest of U.S. nuclear war—denied the right to bring forth testimony during the trial—the eight were able to appeal their guilty verdict. The Pennsylvania Superior Court reversed their conviction in February 1984, but the State of Pennsylvania then appealed that decision and the case went to a Superior Court of Appeals panel. The case was finally resolved ten years later. On 11 April 1990, Judge James E. Buckingham of Montgomery County Court of Common Pleas told the eight defendants that they would have to serve twenty-three months in county jail if they were convicted of any more antiwar activity in the next twenty-three months, "a condition that the defendants told the judge they might not be able to fulfill."[6]

Convinced of the significance of the Plowshares actions, three years after the incident at King of Prussia, Elizabeth McAlister and other resisters entered Griffiss Air Force Base near Rome, New York, and damaged some nuclear bomb-carrying equipment in a hangar before being detected by security police. McAlister served two years in prison. Philip Berrigan served as both father and mother to his children during McAlister's imprisonment. From 1980 to 1986 a total of seventeen Plowshares and related disarmament actions were performed. Twenty people who had participated in these disarmament actions were serving prison sentences ranging from one year to eighteen years, while a few others were on probation.[7] By 1990, an estimated total of thirty-five similar demonstrations by other Plowshares groups at nuclear weapons factories and military bases in the United States and Europe had occurred.[8]

In each of the jury trials following the Plowshares actions the participants were denied use of the defense that their actions were legally justified due to the threat posed by nuclear weapons and they were not allowed to present expert testimony. This had not been the case with the draft board actions of the Vietnam era. Moreover, lengthy prison terms applied by the judges in some of the cases were extreme compared to those given to the participants in the draft board actions. The price attached to performing such actions in the 1980s was much greater. Furthermore the absence of testimony in the court rooms denied the drama necessary to attract media coverage.

Daniel Berrigan raised the question of why an individual should perform such actions and answered in the following manner:

> Worth it for ourselves . . . —yes. Such an act must be taken. . . .
> The value of the act is thus measured by the sacrifice required to do it; an old and honored Christian idea. . . . We held our liturgy the night before, broke the bread, passed the cup. Light of head, heavy of heart, we nonetheless celebrated by anticipation the chancey event of the following day; and the trial to come; and the penalty. Our Logic? the body was "broken for you," the cup "poured out for all."

He goes on to try to answer the larger meaning of the Plowshares action and its value for the church and the public:

> Value is created, so to speak, in the breach, in a decision to gather, unite voices in an outcry, to precipitate a crisis that, will strip away the mask of evil.

> But I know of no sure way of predicting where things will go from there, whether others will hear and respond, or how quickly or slowly. Or whether the act will fail to vitalize others, will come to a grinding halt then and there, its actors stigmatized or dismissed as fools. One swallows dry and takes a chance.[9]

The only two people continually living at Jonah House from 1973 to 1990 were Philip Berrigan and Elizabeth McAlister. Daniel Berrigan has always lived with other Jesuits in New York City. This raises the question of how Philip Berrigan and Elizabeth McAlister sustained themselves for so many years in trying to build a resistance community. For them the foremost reason was their marriage. As they put it: "Our marriage was a grace. . . . We were able to keep each other's courage up, to gain new perspectives, new energies."[10] They also had Jerome and Carol Berrigan whose home in Syracuse was a home away from home, as well as Daniel's encouragement, support, and frequent participation in actions. In the attempt to build community at Jonah House many people came and left. Some moved in other directions and some moved out to begin their own resistance communities. Philip Berrigan and Elizabeth McAlister explained the tribulations of trying to form a resistance community when they wrote the story of their lives at Jonah House, *The Time's Discipline: The Beatitudes and Nuclear Resistance.*

> During those early years there was never a question of simple progress in one direction. There were layers upon layers of solitude and loneliness, profound yearning for community, moments when we were blessed with a sense of community, only to undergo a bitter cycle again.[11]

In many ways it was similar to the experiences of Dorothy Day at the Catholic Worker when she attempted to build community. Yet, it was very different—Philip and Elizabeth were married and had children. They were both committing acts of resistance that were often followed by long prison sentences. After both were unexpectedly in prison at the same time in 1977 they agreed that they would not be in jail again at the same time so that one of them would be with the children. Also, since they performed acts of resistance and not corporal works of mercy on a daily basis they could not depend on voluntary contributions for their support. Philip made a living doing carpentry work and painting houses. They did not publish a paper but Philip did write books: *Widen the Prison Gates* and *Of Beasts and Other Beastly Images: Essays Under the Bomb*. Finally, unlike Dorothy Day and the Catholic Worker, they confronted not only the injustices and evil they found in American society but also in the church when they viewed it in complicity with evil and injustice. Their life together is unique in the Catholic Resistance. Formerly, the Resistance had been the preserve of men and even during the Vietnam era only women without the responsibility of children had been involved.

When Daniel Berrigan had been released from prison in 1970 because of a spinal condition he returned to his Jesuit community in New York City. He had decided in prison that he would never again take a permanent position on any college campus. He explained this decision in his autobiography *To Dwell in Peace*: "I liked less and less what I saw there. I would come and go, for a semester at the most, teaching in a way that freed me and the students from the paper chase; and then would depart, no strings, no tenure track, nothing lost."[12]

For the next twenty years, Daniel Berrigan would go where the cause of peace led him. He became a traveling evangelist for peace confronting injustice wherever he saw it and witnessing to peace by his actions. A great preacher, teacher, and writer, he was often in demand. His celibate life-style and membership in the Jesuit community provided him great freedom of movement. His prophetic witness conveyed a consistency that affirmed peace and life over war and death and as a result he often provoked great controversy.

On 19 October 1973 he was invited to speak before the Association of Arab University Graduates in Washington, D.C. A week after the event, an antiwar periodical in New York published the speech, and as Daniel wrote, "the skies fell in."[13] His speech was viewed as vitriolic anti-Semitism. B'nai B'rith, castigated him as did the National Council of Churches. This was true also of the pages of *Commentary*, *Worldview*, *Commonweal*, *Village Voice*, and the *New York Times*. The debate raged for over a year. What Daniel Berrigan had done to merit such a response was to criticize the militarism of the State of Israel and defend the human rights of the Palestinians within Israel. He also urged the Palestinians and their supporters to put aside their reliance on violence and terrorism and adapt instead the practice and spirit of nonviolence.

Jim Forest attempted to come to Daniel Berrigan's defense through his work at Fellowship of Reconciliation (FOR) and the Catholic Peace Fellowship (CPF). He personally wrote a letter to the *National Catholic Reporter* and an article in *Fellowship* over the continuing debate. He also managed to have published a book, *The Great Berrigan Debate*. Forest believed the extreme reaction to "Daniel's speech was rooted in the fact that the Left in general still judges nonviolence and pacifism to be thoroughly counterrevolutionary and indeed reactionary."[14] Forest believed that "pacifist criticism of Israel is certainly no more marked than criticism of Arab and Palestinian groups. But the Press, for whatever reason, had generally ignored pacifist criticism of the Arabs while concentrating heavily on criticism of Israel—and rebuttals to such criticisms."[15] After a month-long, fact-finding trip in Israel, Forest along with Paul Mayer held a press conference on 19 May 1974 on the Palestinian question and supported the need for Israel to recognize the human rights of the Palestinian people in Israel.

Over a decade after the controversy, Daniel Berrigan wrote that he was grateful for having spoken the truth as he saw it. He also linked the situation in Israel with the Nicaraguan situation in the 1980s and contended: "The Nicaraguans are not alone in constructing, by force of brutal necessity, a fortress state. What a cruel necessity, a forensic nightmare, self-fulfilling! Israel is caught in the same cruel web. Inevitably, one might think: because insecurity, danger, and the imminence of terror are hardly conducive to political generosity, an open society."[16] Today, Berrigan is angry with Israelis, Nicaraguans, and Americans for repeating what he terms the oldest sophism of history: "To make peace, prepare for war."[17]

As the Vietnam War was winding down, Daniel Berrigan was again involved in another controversial issue. The issue focused on the human rights of political prisoners held by the government of North Vietnam. This time a split among the pacifists in the antiwar movement resulted. Daniel first expressed his concern on the issue of violence in relation to revolutionary movements and political prisoners when he wrote to Jim Forest in late 1972:

We must make clear to the North Vietnamese and to the Vietcong, that we reject any overt or unlimited violence, any truly military gains won at the price of civilian deaths, or any executions, political or otherwise carried out against the conquered or captured enemy. . . . There is a great unwillingness naturally on the part of all of us to enter into the Vietnamese life and death struggle with some sort of critical treatment of their conduct. On the other hand, I know that history is going to judge not only the crimes of the American military and political leaders; we also are going to be judged if we have "taken sides" on death, without making clear, even to our friends across the other line, that we object to death for no matter what pretext of what kind of gain.[18]

Forest sent a copy of Berrigan's letter to Alfred Hassler at FOR with a letter of his own expressing his agreement and concern for future direction on the matter.

On the other hand I do think the antiwar movement has become dangerously superficial, as Dan says in his own way in the letter, and that the widening enthusiasm for violence, so long as it is supposedly revolutionary, does have to be challenged. The question is how to do it in a way that contributes to the purpose of nonviolence, that being— in the most radical sense—reconciliation.[19]

In April 1973, Daniel and Philip Berrigan wrote a letter to Pham Van Dong of the delegation of the Peoples' Democratic Republic of North Vietnam asking him to respond to the allegations of the torture of American prisoners of North Vietnam.[20] Their concern for political prisoners was a result not only of their own experience in prison, but also of reports of such torture from the pacifist Unified Buddhist Church in Vietnam which worked during the war for the organization of a coalition government with the National Liberation Front and the North Vietnamese Communists. Alfred Hassler had always placed great hope in the Buddhist presence in Vietnam and in 1966 he had been instrumental in arranging a lecture tour in America for Thich Nhat Hanh, a leading Buddhist monk and poet who became a member of FOR. It was at that time that Daniel Berrigan and Thomas Merton became friends with Nhat Hanh. Berrigan supported Nhat Hanh and kept in close contact with him through the Unified Buddhist Church in Paris. In May, a letter from Tren Trong Quat on behalf of Pham Van Dong in Hanoi refuted the charges of the treatment of prisoners by simply stating it was nothing but a "campaign of slander" on the part of the United States government against the government of North Vietnam.[21] Unsatisfied with the response, the Berrigan brothers, who were also dissatisfied with the way other peace activists had responded to the allegations made by returned prisoners and the Buddhists, criticized the peace movement's admiration for an admirable enemy that had gradually turned into idolatry of that enemy. "A kind of human manifesto: that we would not countenance, or ourselves inflict, physical torture or moral degradation, on any other human. Whatever the provocation whatever the crime."[22] Daniel Berrigan then wrote to Jim Forest on the day of Rabbi Heschel's death asking Forest to call on world religious communities to ask the pope to visit North and South Vietnam and speak there in the name of all religious traditions about the bombing and suffering and make a plea for human rights, especially for those of political prisoners. Daniel said that Eqbal Ahmad would be in charge of the project and Jim Douglass would help organize it.[23] The idea, however, never worked.

From his position as editor of *Fellowship*, Jim Forest attempted to address the issue. In the summer of 1973, he published an appeal on behalf of imprisoned Soviet dissidents. Some critics called the article a revival of the cold war. In the article Forest quoted in length a letter by Aleksandr Solzhenitsyn in which the Nobel laureate pleaded for a more forthright condemnation of violence committed by the communist countries. In the article Forest also referred to the thousands of Vietnamese allegedly tortured and incarcerated by the Saigon government. He wrote, "But there is a mandate to respond to prisoners of conscience elsewhere as well, including those in the USSR. Our first allegiance is, after all, to the planet, not to any state or political group."[24] Besides continuing to write on the issue of political prisoners in *Fellowship*, Forest along with Tom Cornell organized "An Appeal to North Vietnam to Observe Human Rights."[25]

This appeal coincided with the final withdrawal of U. S. troops from Vietnam and was a result of Forest's fears that the new Vietnam might merely substitute a new, even more ruthless tyranny for the old system of arbitrary power. Forest believed the pacifist Buddhists would be among the first victims. After the fall of Saigon, the Unified Buddhist

Church had gone out of its way to demonstrate its good will toward the new regime. Uninvited, nine hundred monks and nuns had participated in the victory celebration held in Saigon 15 May 1975. A few days later, on May 19, twenty thousand Buddhists had gathered in front of the An Quang Pagoda for a tribute to President Ho Chi Minh in celebration of his birthday. Yet little justice was to be forthcoming, and the communists soon demonstrated that they had no use for these would-be allies. Pagodas were seized or destroyed, religious statues smashed, orphanages confiscated, and social service centers closed. Thich Tri Quang, the monk who had led the Buddhist movement of protest against Ngo Dinh Diem and who as recently as 31 May 1974 had participated in a demonstration calling for the resignation of President Thieu, was arrested on August 12 after giving a sermon that queried the new government in Vietnam about its promise of concord and reconciliation. Concerned about the information they were receiving from the Buddhists about the disregard for human rights in North Vietnam, Jim Forest and Tom Cornell initiated the appeal.

In the fall of 1976, Richard Neuhaus, a former antiwar activist associated with CALCAV, joined Jim Forest, a representative of both FOR and CPF, in drafting and circulating an "Appeal to the Democratic Republic of Vietnam to Observe Human Rights." In the appeal they mentioned reports of widespread violations of human rights, including the detention of large numbers of people in so-called reeducation camps. They also wrote to the Vietnamese observer at the United Nations, asking for a response to these charges. Forest followed the announcement of the appeal with an article, "Vietnam: Unification without Reconciliation," in the October 1976 issue of *Fellowship*. Because of the names of Neuhaus and Forest, CALCAV and CPF and FOR became indirectly involved in the appeal.

The timing of the Forest-Neuhaus appeal split the pacifist wing of the peace movement apart. In June 1976, the American Friends Service Committee (AFSC) board had approved a campaign to collect one million signatures on a petition calling for normalizing of relations and reconstruction aid for the Democratic Republic of Vietnam. The petition also made reference to amnesty for American draft-law offenders and rehabilitation support for veterans. Supporters of this appeal believed the Forest-Neuhaus appeal would contribute to the hostile atmosphere in the United States towards Vietnam. Dave McReynolds of the

War Resisters League (WRL) would also have nothing to do with the appeal and spoke adamantly against it. The FOR staff was also split over the appeal. Regardless of the intentions of its sponsors, many pacifists believed it played into the hands of the U. S. government and others who opposed UN membership for Vietnam and normalization of relations between the United States and Vietnam. Forest was accused of being too pure in his quest for human rights and in turn was hurting the broader aims of the movement.

Forest, however, would not relent in his pursuit of protecting the rights of political prisoners. In December 1976 he resigned as editor of *Fellowship* and assumed the post of coordinator for the International Fellowship of Reconciliation (IFOR) headquartered in Holland. Forest continued his efforts on behalf of human rights from that position though he knew it was causing a factional split within the peace movement. From Holland, Forest remained focused on the issue of political prisoners whether it was those in detention camps, or the persecution of Buddhists in Vietnam, or the boat people arriving in the United States. These three groups documented for Forest the violence of the North Vietnamese and justified his continued attempts to stop it.

Forest would often forward letters written by Daniel Berrigan to Pham Van Dong asking "for release of religious peoples, and an international team to go in," always advocating that Amnesty International organize such a team.[26] In 1975, Daniel Berrigan collaborated with Thich Nhat Hahn on *The Raft if Not the Shore*. In Holland in 1978 Forest published a pamphlet on *The Unified Buddhist Church of Vietnam: Fifteen Years of Reconciliation*. Then in 1978, Daniel Berrigan threatened to resign from FOR because it refused to support a vigil at the Vietnamese embassy on behalf of Buddhist monks who were being held as political prisoners. The issue was never resolved to Forest's or Berrigan's satisfaction, but the Catholic peace movement had made a significant contribution to the human rights effort that would continue around the world. When Forest left for Holland, Daniel Berrigan was to lose his main organizer for peace in the United States. Through Forest's new international position, however, he was often able to include Daniel Berrigan in various international peace projects.

During these years, Daniel Berrigan also lent his name and voice to many other causes. In the 1970s and 1980s he was attempting to integrate every issue into his position of nonviolent resistance and to develop a consistent message of peace and life, not war and death. In conjunction with the Center for Constitutional Rights in New York, Daniel and Philip worked for the improved welfare of federal prisoners. On 24 September 1973, Daniel Berrigan and fifty other religious among several hundred U. S. and Canadian citizens signed a public advertisement in the *New York Times* condemning the military takeover in Chile; it asked the U. S. government not to recognize the new regime in Santiago and urged the United Nations to guarantee the human rights of all persons in Chile.

As the keynote speaker at the 27th Annual New England Congress of Religious Education at the University of New Hampshire, Daniel Berrigan turned his attention from foreign policy to the homefront and talked about the family as an "Instrument of Violent Society." He strongly attacked the family when he said that "the family has allowed itself to be reduced to a tool of the materialistic economy, so that it is little more than a 'consuming unit, a tax paying unit, a biological unit, for the next war—producing sons for the cannons.' " And on 3 May 1974 he was a featured speaker with Paulo Freire, Richard Barnett, and Harvey Cox at Marygrove College for a week-end seminar "Is Peace Possible" sponsored by the Archdiocese of Detroit's Commission for World Justice and Peace. In private correspondence with Jim Forest in April 1975 Daniel Berrigan raised the issue of abortion when he wrote "Is the dignity of the women's movement served by an (essentially western, war ridden, itchy, competing, mechanistic) position like control of our bodies? . . . Maybe the most crucial and hopeful statement of the seventies is a nonviolent statement 'Everyone should live.' "[27] It would not be until the late 1980s that Daniel would join a pro-life group and commit civil disobedience in opposition to the abortion laws in the United States. He received many awards at colleges and from peace groups. Promoting Enduring Peace, Inc., gave him the 1974 Gandhi Peace Award and in the same year the WRL presented him their annual peace award.

Daniel Berrigan also continued to accept visiting professorships in the 1970s and 1980s in Europe, Canada, Detroit, Berkeley, and the Bronx. But again, his prophetic witness for peace provoked controversy. When he was at the Jesuit seminary in Berkeley, Daniel could not abide the fact that degrees were granted by the University of California that he believed "provided cover for the malignant Livermore

Laboratories, a vast nuclear weapons research center some thirty miles distant from Berkeley."[28] While teaching in Berkeley, Berrigan led hundreds of people on Ash Wednesday to the administration building where a request was made to meet with the president of the university concerning Livermore Laboratories. Around midnight the campus police cleared everyone out. The Ash Wednesday action as well as other demonstrations against Livermore Laboratories continued through the 1980s. But as Daniel Berrigan says of the action, "With the exception of a small number of students, no one was troubled at Berkeley."[29] And perhaps Daniel's greatest disappointment while teaching at Berkeley was when his fellow Jesuits did not welcome him as a peer.[30]

In the early 1980s, Daniel Berrigan taught three successive summers at Loyola University in New Orleans. While there he was confronted with another moral dilemma. Once again living with his fellow Jesuits at a Jesuit institution of higher learning, he believed he had to resign his teaching position because the university supported an ROTC program. This time the experience for Daniel was to prove positive, for in 1987 the ROTC program was removed from Loyola and Daniel returned to teach there in the summer of 1988.

Teaching at universities, however, was not Daniel Berrigan's main work. He often joined Jonah House in their demonstrations at the Pentagon and, of course, joined his brother Philip in the King of Prussia Plowshares action. He also spent a great deal of time writing and by 1987 had published thirty-seven books. Attempting to comprehend as fully as possible the meaning of life and death, Daniel Berrigan decided to do volunteer work first with dying cancer patients and later with dying AIDS patients in New York City. Rather than volunteering at a soup kitchen or a homeless shelter, he found that his hospital work became his way of administering the corporal works of mercy. Many of his books written in the 1980s reflect his experiences with the dying.

His efforts on behalf of with AIDS victims inspired a renewal of his work with homosexuals, which had begun at Cornell University. A brief look at some of this work reveals again the consistency of Daniel's message of peace and life. First, the issue brought him into direct conflict with the Jesuits and his church. Whenever conflict with his religious order occurred, Daniel Berrigan always experienced great pain and suffering. Drawing on his past experience of being silenced and exiled for his work for peace, Daniel offered to help his fellow

Jesuit John McNeill, who had published his book *The Homosexual and the Church* in 1977 and had been silenced by church authorities from writing and public speaking on the topic of homosexuality. Daniel Berrigan with the assistance of McNeill published an article on the whole matter, but it did not help and John McNeill was dismissed from the Jesuits. Daniel wrote of the experience:

> John appears as yet another courageous victim of the attempt underway to ravel the seamless robe of the Second Vatican Council. Precious gains must be set back, the personal and social freedom of Catholics reduced to tatters. . . . McNeill's predicament was my own, it was simple as that. My own freedom was assailed when McNeill's was.[31]

Second, his work with homosexuals like all work for Daniel was viewed in terms of peace and life. This was obvious when he was asked to address the gay fellowship of the Unitarian-Universalist church in San Francisco. Daniel told his audience that if the gay rights movement were to be taken seriously, it had to have a vision that included the larger suffering of the world. Berrigan offered them his own vision and pointed out to them the nuclear arms race, epitomized a few miles from Berkeley in the Livermore Laboratories. Daniel then pleaded with them to connect their own lives with the lives of the poor, the powerless, and the homeless. In other words, to link the many injustices they experienced as gays with the injustices experienced by other Americans under the larger umbrella of peacemaking.[32] As this incident suggests, Daniel Berrigan's words and actions were always rooted in peace and life. Again, the issue did not change Berrigan's message. Homosexuality, abortion, the Middle East, Nicaragua, political prisoners, and every other issue that Daniel Berrigan confronted he linked to peacemaking and an affirmation of life.

In practice both Daniel and Philip Berrigans' approach to peacemaking remained essentially the same from the 1968 Catonsville draft board raid. Following the ancient Judeo-Christian prophetic tradition, they hoped to offer themselves as moral witnesses to their brothers and sisters in the church and the world with the hope that the consciences and concerns of enough people might alter the destructiveness that injustice and war wrought. Unable to devise a new action that would answer their critics' protestations against the destruction of property, they were able to reject the controversial night actions in attempting to keep within the guidelines of traditional nonviolence. Their antinuclear Plowshares protest in King of Prussia continued in the same tradition and their protest was "one of the best-known antiwar incidents in this country since the Vietnam War."[33] But more important was the daily witness of peacemaking these two men have offered over the past twenty-five years. Again, Philip was more focused and limited in his resistance. He wanted to stop the production of nuclear weapons as he had wanted to stop the war in Vietnam. Philip served as the convener of Plowshare actions and organizer of demonstrations at the Pentagon from Jonah House. Daniel, the traveling peace evangelist, tried to link all that he experienced into a consistent peacemaking ethic. Both have tried to break through encrusted public apathy and penetrate the country's larger sense of fatalism with a new spirit that has sparked many Americans in popular outcries over the years. Their message of peace and life over war and death has affirmed the dignity of the individual and the right of conscience and human rights. They have courageously stood up to the U.S. government when evil was being perpetrated and also to their church when it seemed to be in complicity with the government. They have not been able to resolve the tensions between religion and politics to the satisfaction of their critics, but this has not prevented them from attempting to be prophets of peacemaking within the American Catholic peace movement.

By looking at their lives what is found is an increasing alienation from American society and a radicalization of their political views, especially of the U.S. government, which they came to believe had lost all legitimacy because of its policies of militarism, racism, and exploitation. This position has been complicated by their position as priests in the Roman Catholic church. Dorothy Day had experienced alienation and radicalization before her conversion to Catholicism and brought her pacifism with her. Because the Berrigan brothers were born and raised within traditional American Catholicism, they wanted to correct the evils they found not only in their country but also in their church. Thus, their journey to reach the same conclusions as Dorothy Day took much longer.

The CPF, founded by Daniel Berrigan in 1964, was the main vehicle for organization and support of his actions until his friend, Jim

Forest, left CPF and FOR to assume a position with the IFOR in Holland in 1976. During the last years of the Vietnam War, CPF spent a great deal of time and energy working with the Berrigans. In 1972 CPF wrote in behalf of Daniel and Philip Berrigan for the Nobel Peace Prize. In 1973, CPF assisted the Harrisburg Defense Committee and began work on the series of appeals for political prisoners.

CPF has always been a membership organization. At its peak in 1974, it had a membership of 3,000 people. Control of CPF had always been in the hands of its co-chairs, Jim Forest and Tom Cornell, who ran CPF from their FOR offices in Nyack. The main office for CPF was in New York City and was staffed by volunteers who received direction from Nyack. Forest and Cornell never attempted to democratize CPF. The main focus of CPF was always draft counseling and the publication of the *CPF Bulletin*. The volunteers in the central office kept these two aspects functioning and then organized or participated with other groups in campaigns and demonstrations against the Vietnam War.

CPF always had local chapters throughout the United States, but most often with no help from the central office in New York City. The work of each chapter varied greatly. For example, the Northern California CPF under the direction of Vincent O'Connor, and with the cooperation and the thanks of administrators and counselors, entered every Catholic high school in several counties of the state to bring teams of draft resisters and COs to the students. The rate of conscientious objection to the Vietnam War increased significantly wherever this was done. The New England CPF established an annual conference that attracted hundreds every spring, most of whom were not members of CPF. Chapters ebbed and flowed around the country.

After Forest left for Holland, Tom Cornell remained committed to CPF and continued to chair the organization. Forest's influence on CPF continued, however, through correspondence. Jim Forest would write to Cornell about significant international peace issues and request that Cornell organize support for these efforts in America. In addition, when Forest went to Northern Ireland in support of the Peace People in Belfast and organized a small conference on nonviolence, he wrote an article on the Peace People for the *CPF Bulletin*. The same was true when he went to Latin America to promote nonviolence and to South Africa for a conference on apartheid. At Forest's request,

Cornell successfully coordinated the Catholic Worker, CPF, WRL, CALC (Clergy and Laity Concerned—they dropped "About Vietnam" after the war), and FOR in a support for Aldolfo Perez Esquivel and his nomination for the 1977 Nobel Peace Prize. Forest also placed the Mobilization for Survival in contact with Cornell. Cornell in turn kept Forest informed of events in America, for example, the work of Cesar Chavez and news of the Catholic Worker in New York and the activities of the peace movement. Basically, the friendship of the two men within CPF under the larger umbrella of FOR enabled them to bring forth CPF support for international issues. Forest provided the information and network while Cornell did the organizing in New York.

By June 1977, however, Forest was expressing dissatisfaction with the *CPF Bulletin* when he wrote to Cornell: "Finally, wasn't much impressed with the last Bulletin—can't remember why, except I thought it could have been published by the World Humanist Association. No Catholic scent to it, or did I miss something?"[34] By August 1977, Forest was suggesting to Cornell to close down CPF at the 339 Lafayette address. Cornell, however, was determined to keep the CPF in existence.

In September 1979, Tom Cornell was fired from his position with FOR. This was a result of restructuring within FOR, budget cuts, and the arrival of new leadership within the organization. For the next two years Cornell attempted to keep CPF alive at 339 Lafayette and directed its activities from his home in Newburgh, New York, while he sought employment and a new direction for his life. A few people did send support money to Cornell after he lost his job at FOR.[35]

The issue of Central America consumed most of his energy during the fall of 1979. In the name of CPF, he lobbied Congress against the intervention in Nicaragua. Along with John Quigley of USCC he tried to organize local assistance for the U.S. Support Committee for Central America. In January 1980, at the request of Forest and the Goss-Mayrs at IFOR, Cornell organized in America the International Days for Justice and Peace in Central America. About thirty groups across the United States participated in the observance. Cornell sent the money collected at the New York service to San Salvador Archbishop Oscar Arnulfo Romero.[36] In June, he sent letters in the name of CPF opposing aid to Central America to the President of the United States and ten congressmen.

In December 1979, the Red Army invaded Afghanistan to shore up a faltering communist government under siege by Moslem rebels. President Carter shelved SALT-II, suspended shipments of grain to Russia, initiated an international boycott of the 1980 Summer Olympics in Moscow, and proposed a reinstitution of the draft in America. It was the reemergence of the draft issue that gave Cornell the idea of offering draft-counseling seminars through church diocesan offices. Since Cornell had always maintained that draft counseling was the top priority of CPF and he had over twenty years experience in the work, he believed it would be a way to keep his family and CPF alive. After consulting with Gordon Zahn, he wrote to Bryan Hehir, the director of the Office of International Justice and Peace at USCC, enclosing a letter of recommendation from Zahn and asking Hehir to write a letter of support for his draft-counseling program to all the diocesan offices. Cornell also had the support of Patrick McDermott at the USCC, who promoted his program. Hehir wrote the letter. By July 1980, Cornell had given draft counseling training seminars in the dioceses of Davenport, Richmond, Bridgeport, and Peoria. Within one year he had educated seven hundred people on the draft and had made a total of $3,500.[37] In November 1980, Cornell went to press with Jim Forest's revision of his pamphlet, *Catholic Conscientious Objection*, and acquired the imprimatur for the pamphlet from the Archdiocese of New York.

Cornell could not continue without a more adequate means of support for his wife and children and so in 1981 he left New York for Waterbury, Connecticut, where he took a job with the World Council of Churches running a soup kitchen serving three hundred people a day. He remained in this work through the 1980s. CPF continues in the old office at 339 Lafayette Street with Bill Ofenloch as coordinator and Tom Cornell's name remains on its letterhead as national secretary. This existence continues at a minimal level of operation waiting for the next crisis with the draft to occur. Befittingly, Tom Cornell's last organizing effort before his departure from New York was the memorial service for Dorothy Day held at St. Patrick's Cathedral in January 1981.

The main reason for the decline of CPF was the unexpected growth of a new Catholic peace organization, Pax Christi–USA. Just as PAX and CPF had its origins in the Catholic Worker, so too did Pax Christi–USA. In 1971, a critical moment for PAX occurred when the British PAX Society merged with Pax Christi International and left the American PAX without an international link. Eileen Egan and Gordon Zahn, the founders and cochairs of PAX, explored the feasibility of bringing Pax Christi to the United States. In Europe, Pax Christi worked closely with the Roman Catholic hierarchy and a bishop was president of each national section. Bernard Cardinal Alfrink was the international president and Carel ter Maat was the international secretary. But Egan and Zahn did not want the new organization under the control of the American hierarchy either financially as CAIP had been or in terms of decision making as it was in Europe. Thus, they agreed on an episcopal moderator rather than a president for the new group and approached Thomas Gumbleton, auxiliary bishop of Detroit, because of his leadership on the peace issue in NCCB.[38] In November 1971 he accepted the role of moderator. At Pax Christi's International Council meeting in April 1972, Eileen Egan proposed that PAX be the basis for the U.S. branch of Pax Christi. At the meeting, Pax Christi International formally recognized the existence of Pax Christi–USA.

In June 1972 at Oakridge, New Jersey, an organizational meeting was held. At the meeting Tom Cornell represented the CPF, Dorothy Day and Patrick Jordan were there from the Catholic Worker, Jim Forest and Harriet Godman came from Emmaus House, and Edward Guinan, a Paulist priest, and Rachelle Linner were there from the Community for Creative Nonviolence (CCNV). Egan explained that the new organization would appeal not just to pacifists but to a broad range of American Catholics concerned about peace. The aim of the new group would be to "lay stress on peace education through a nationwide 'Peace Week' on a given theme, and through the publication of a bulletin giving news of European Pax Christi programs and peace developments throughout the world. The activism of demonstrations would be the work of other peace organizations."[39] Cornell supported Egan's idea because it would further clarify CPF as a pacifist organization. Thus, Pax Christi–USA was born that weekend. Edward Guinan was named general secretary, Clare Danielsson was the treasurer, Eileen Egan and Gordon Zahn were named co-chairs of an eight-

member directing committee, and Bishop Gumbleton was the moderator. Later that year, Egan invited Carroll T. Dozier, bishop of Memphis, to join Bishop Gumbleton as episcopal comoderator of Pax
Christi–USA. Dozier, a newly appointed bishop in January 1971, had
issued a pastoral letter, *Peace: Gift and Task*, that December. In the
letter he advocated the strongest position on peace ever taken by an
American bishop when he said that "we must stop the war in Vietnam," which he called "sinful" and "not justified."[40]

Edward Guinan returned to CCNV where he established the secretariat of Pax Christi–USA. CCNV was a community that ran a soup
kitchen, a hospitality house, a shelter for the homeless, and a legal aid
program for the needy in Washington, D.C. CCNV viewed itself as a
community called to give a prophetic witness to the world and this
ultimately meant activism and demonstrations. Thus, from the very
beginning the aim of Pax Christi–USA—peace education for mainline
Catholics—was in opposition to the vision of CCNV, but this fundamental conflict was not anticipated in the beginning. Another planning meeting was held at the Catholic Worker in New York on 23 June
1973, where it was decided that a fall national assembly would be held
at George Washington University and a regular publication containing
Pax Christi–USA news and articles of peace interest would be published. The publication would be called *Pax Christi Thirdly*. Ed
Guinan was responsible for both projects.

In the summer, Guinan and CCNV became involved in the protest
actions at the White House with the prayer-ins supported by Jonah
House. Eileen Egan who did not want Pax Christi–USA's first public
event, the October national assembly, to be characterized by such
activism in which the CCNV was involved wrote to Guinan, "In
confidence, I feel we have to open many doors, to bring to the peace
movement many Catholics hitherto alienated from it. That means to
me no Berrigans since their drama . . . would drown the Pax Christi
message and twist the whole message out of context."[41] Guinan ignored the letter. He and CCNV worked hard on the national assembly
and it was a success. A few days after the assembly, however, CCNV
continued to attract national attention by its demonstrations. At a
peace conference in Washington, D.C., commemorating the tenth
anniversary of *Pacem in Terris*, Guinan and several CCNV members
equipped with laughing boxes disrupted Henry Kissinger's talk and

were removed from the gathering. Bishop Dozier who was present at the gathering let it be known to Pax Christi–USA's board that he was upset.[42]

Guinan's next demonstration occurred when the new archbishop of Washington, William Baum, purchased a $500,000 home. Guinan began a "fast to death" in opposition to what he believed was the scandalous posture of the archbishop toward justice and the poor in the city. Guinan had identified himself to the press as Pax Christi–USA's general secretary. Again, Bishop Dozier was upset.[43]

Despite time spent demonstrating, Guinan successfully conducted the daily operations of Pax Christi. He responded to all phone calls and mail inquiries and helped to set up Pax Christi–USA groups in different cities.[44] Guinan also made available for $5. to Pax Christi–USA members a "peace packet," which contained *The Nonviolent Cross* by James Douglass, *Kill for Peace?* by Richard McSorley, S.J., *Catholics, Conscience and the Draft*, edited by Eileen Egan, six Thomas Merton essays, and an annotated bibliography on peace. He also published three issues of *Pax Christi Thirdly*. The first issue focused on "Conscience," the second on "Liberation in Latin America," and the third on "Women in the Church." Guinan was also planning the next general assembly to be held in 1974 and had secured Cesar Chavez, William Stringfellow, and James Douglass as keynote speakers for the event. To prepare for the assembly Guinan had arranged for John McKenzie, S.J., the scripture scholar, to come to Washington to speak with the Pax Christi–USA officers to prepare them for the assembly. After McKenzie's presentation there was a business meeting at which time Egan told Guinan to "dis-invite" Douglass.

After lobbying for peace at the Second Vatican Council, James Douglass became well known in the American Catholic peace movement following the publication of his books *The Non-Violent Cross* (the first statement on Christian nonviolence to issue from an American Catholic) and *Resistance and Contemplation*. He assumed a teaching position at St. Mary's College, Notre Dame, and later became a director of the Program in Nonviolence at the University of Notre Dame. After a divorce and remarriage, Douglass left Notre Dame for a professorship at the University of Hawaii. Imitating the draft board actions of the Berrigans, he destroyed files at Hickham Air Force Base in resistance to the Vietnam War. Douglass was arrested and convicted for his act of resistance; then he travelled to Canada in violation of his parole. Since he would be on a speaking tour in the eastern part of the United States at the time of the Pax Christi–USA assembly, he accepted the invitation. Since Guinan did not want to "dis-invite" Douglass, he sent a letter to the episcopal moderators and cochairs of Pax Christi–USA which stated that "The problem if we can speak in such terms, is not with Jim Douglass, but with reactionary attitudes within Pax Christi. Have we not matured enough to embrace those who have jeopardized themselves within the Gospel context, and who provide the most articulate, real commitment to Pacifism and Nonviolence in the North American Church? I believe that it is imperative that we reinstate the invitation with full force of Moderators and Officers. . . . My continuation as the General Secretary of Pax Christi and the Secretariat's continuation here in Washington, D.C. would depend upon this decision."[45]

Almost immediately, "An Open Letter to Pax Christi," was drafted and circulated to the press. *Commonweal* printed it in full. The letter was in support of Guinan's position at Pax Christi–USA and was signed by Daniel Berrigan, Jim Forest, Ned Murphy, S.J., Judy Peluso, S.N.D., Phil Berrigan, Elizabeth McAlister, Robert Hoyt, Rick Gaumer, and Bill Ofenloch. Both Jonah House and CPF were responsible for the letter. This public display of infighting among American Catholic peace movement groups only served to alienate the officers and moderators of Pax Christi–USA even further from Guinan. Eileen Egan, who was employed by Catholic Relief Services, which was the target of a similar open letter organized by CPF during the Vietnam War, was particularly furious. On 22 August 1974 Edward Guinan resigned. The October assembly was canceled and Pax Christi–USA was back to the organizational drawing board.[46]

There was no way that Eileen Egan and Gordon Zahn would relinquish control of Pax Christi–USA. From the beginning they had stated that they wanted to educate mainline Catholics about peace and that demonstrations would be left to other groups. They wanted a "respectable" American Catholic peace group in Pax Christi–USA and they wanted to keep it on course. Guinan's style was too extreme for them. Nevertheless, over the next ten years, Pax Christi–USA's umbrella would extend far enough to embrace even a Guinan as well as many other Catholic antiwar activists of the Vietnam era. But these activists never assumed a leadership position at the national level.

Bishop Dozier and Eileen Egan were most responsible for rebuilding Pax Christi–USA. Dozier wanted a sound organizational structure and a clear statement of purpose. The restructuring began with the naming of a fourteen-member executive committee.[47] Joseph Fahey, a professor at Manhattan College in New York and director of its Peace Studies Program, agreed to do the administrative work and serve as the organization's general secretary. The new executive committee resolved that Pax Christi–USA would be committed to its role in the institutional church, respectful of the church's traditions, and sensitive to the majority of Catholics. Its mission was to convert individual Catholics to peace and through them to make the Roman Catholic church in the United States an instrument of peacemaking. Both pacifists and just war traditionalists would be welcomed in the organization, but the focus would be "to move into the mainstream of Catholic life with a realistic approach to nonviolence."[48] There was no confusion as to the purpose of Pax Christi–USA when its new general secretary, Joe Fahey, said that he saw its aim as reaching in two directions—"up" to the hierarchy, and "down" to the people in the parishes.[49] The executive committee also agreed that Pax Christi–USA would focus on four areas of concern: disarmament, amnesty, selective conscientious objection, and the United Nations.

In less than ten years, Pax Christi–USA achieved its goals. Under the secretariat of Joseph Fahey the foundations of the organization were firmly put into place. To secure its ties with Pax Christi International, representatives of Pax Christi–USA attended the yearly meetings of the executive committee of Pax Christi International and Joe Fahey and later Bishop Gumbleton became very involved in the international committee work. At home, a national assembly was held annually. A *Pax Christi Newsletter* was started by Gerald Vanderhaar in Memphis. Annual elections were held for the executive committee in order to keep the organization democratic. When the level of individual membership reached 365 in 1976 a regional structure was put in place. Memphis, New York, Boston, and Chicago were the centers of the four regions and each one had its own coordinator and annual assembly. Pax Christi–USA also sent representatives to such national church gatherings as the Eucharistic Congress and the Call to Action. At these meetings it was successful in witnessing to the church's role in peacemaking. Conscious of its aim to reach "up," it also sponsored three annual Bishops' Masses for Peace after which Bishops Dozier and Gumbleton invited their fellow bishops to join Pax Christi–USA. It also attempted to reach "down" when Mary Evelyn Jegen, S.N.D., prepared a Lenten educational program on peace and justice for the National Federation of Priest Councils to be used in local parishes. Bishop Gumbleton also received a small grant to pay for the publication of a slim blue booklet *The Church and the Arms Race* written by Mary Lou Kownacki, O.S.B., which was made available to the membership and for use by local discussion groups and was one of its most successful publications.

During Fahey's secretariat the basic elements of Pax Christi–USA's organizational structure and focus were in place, and by March 1976, fifteen bishops had become members.[50] In the same year it restated its purpose in its newsletter and proclaimed that "Pax Christi seeks with the help of its episcopal members to establish peacemaking as a priority for the American Catholic Church. To accomplish this, Pax Christi–USA will work with various Catholic communities and agencies, and will collaborate with other groups committed to nonviolent peacemaking." In 1977 the name of the Bishop of Richmond, Virginia, Walter Sullivan, was added to the group's letterhead as episcopal moderator along with that of Dozier and Gumbleton. By the end of 1977, the organization had 970 members from forty states and it had grown from four regions to eight regions. The budget for that year was $6,954.49, the bulk of which came from voluntary contributions.[51] There was so much administrative work that Joe Fahey had to hire a part-time staff associate, Kathleen Kramer, C.S.J., to assist him. By March 1978, the task had become so great that the executive committee decided to make the secretariat a paid full-time position. At the same meeting the main priorities for Pax Christi–USA were reshaped into the following categories: disarmament, primacy of conscience, a just world order, education for peace, and alternatives to violence.

On 1 January 1979 Mary Evelyn Jegen, assumed the full-time position of national coordinator of Pax Christi–USA. She served in that capacity for three years and maintained a delicate balance between all segments of the Catholic peace movement. Under her leadership the organization experienced phenomenal growth. By 1982, it had 5,500 members, forty-six of whom were bishops, and a $90,000 yearly operating budget with six paid staff members.[52] Under Jegen's leadership it maintained the internationalist perspective and the tactic of lobbying Congress and the church that had characterized the no longer existing CAIP and PAX. Pax Christi–USA also expanded its pacifist core membership. Like the CPF and the Catholic Worker, Pax Christi–USA reached out to the broader peace movement and formed coalitions with groups committed to nonviolence. It also publicly supported and worked with the Catholic Resistance spearheaded by the Berrigans and Jonah House and, while maintaining this delicate balance, attracted mainline Catholics and individual bishops to its organization.

Jegen hired staff people to work in regional development and to encourage Pax Christi–USA groups in parishes throughout the country. Policy decisions were confined to the national executive council, which included Jegen, as national coordinator, the episcopal moderators, and the elected representatives from the membership. The primary means of communication with its membership continued to be the *Pax Christi Newsletter*. Under Jegen it was given a professional look, assuming a magazine format, and was called *Pax Christi–USA*. The magazine covered major peace issues and activities nationally; there were feature articles and, like the newsletter, it had a section on regional news and the activities of Pax Christi International.

Jegen also established a Pax Christi–USA press service that distributed two articles a month on peace to sixty diocesan newspapers and Catholic newsletters. She made available peace supplements for parishes to insert in their Sunday bulletins. She increased the organization's publications by issuing a disarmament package and a *Book of Prayers for Peacemakers*. Jegen encouraged the formation of reflection/action groups concerned about the links between the Bible, international systems, and poverty to come together for the stewardship program and those interested in the link between armaments and poverty to join the Swords into Plowshares project. She enabled others to offer workshops on spirituality and nonviolence and seminars in nonviolent training. She promoted and handled Zahn's film, *The Refusal*, on the life of Franz Jaegerstaetter. She also annually promoted the planning of liturgies and vigils and demonstrations in conjunction with Hiroshima Day and the Pope's World Peace Day. Jegen organized the annual national assembly and through all of these means kept the organization's aim of education for peace its paramount goal.

By maintaining close contact not only with other Catholic groups, but with the broader peace movement, especially pacifist groups with a religious identification, Jegen was able to establish Pax Christi–USA as an integral part of the peace movement in the United States. Her work on FOR's national council assisted her greatly in forming coalitions with other peace groups. While maintaining the delicate balance of attracting all Catholics concerned about peace under the Pax Christi–USA umbrella, Jegen gradually moved the organization away from the just war tradition and toward pacifism and nonviolence as the most viable Catholic attitude toward peacemaking.[53]

The major reason for Pax Christi–USA's popularity during Jegen's administration was the awakening that many Catholics experienced in their attitudes toward the state. The reason for this was the government's policy on issues of war and peace. In 1980, the agenda set forth by the new Reagan administration differed greatly from that of the hierarchy, especially on social issues. At the November 1980 meeting in Washington, D. C., the American Catholic bishops voted to go forward with proposals for two pastoral letters. The first, on nuclear war, was entrusted to Archbishop Joseph L. Bernardin of Cincinnati and the second of these, on the economy, was given to Archbishop Rembert Weakland of Milwaukee to oversee. At the meeting, the bishops had just completed a *Pastoral Letter on Marxism* and the combination of these three letters would set the hierarchy on a collision course with the Reagan administration.[54] It would be the pastoral on nuclear war that directly challenged the U.S. government's policies on the issues of war and peace. Pax Christi–USA's criticisms of these policies were more vociferous and extreme than that of mainline Catholics and the hierarchy. Its criticism focused on three main areas of concern: the draft, Central America, and nuclear warfare and disarmament.

After the Soviet invasion of Afghanistan and a political campaign that sought to use the draft as a test of loyalty and anti-communism, Pax Christi–USA opposed registration for the draft and established a bank that would store the written statements of COs and SCOs. The statements were crucial as evidence of an individual's claim to conscientious-objector status since the new computerized draft registration forms, unlike those of old, did not provide a place for individuals to declare themselves COs. Pax Christi–USA also issued new materials on conscientious objection for Catholics: a pamphlet by Eileen Egan, *Catholic Conscience and the Draft: The Right to Refuse to Kill*, and a reprint of a *National Catholic Reporter* article by M. Evelyn Jegen, "Conscience Doth (Not) Make Cowards." The organization also supported and promoted Tom Cornell's draft-counseling program being offered in various dioceses. A $50,000 grant for the development of a "national draft program" was received from an anonymous donor. Cornell wrote that "I voted to accept [the grant], although I would much have preferred that the anonymous donor had given CPF the dough. We can do a better job, finally, this Draft Counseling Training Program is my family's principal means of keeping a leaky roof over our heads."[55] Gordon Zahn administered the grant and established the Center on Conscience and War in Boston. Pax Christi–USA also supported the bishops' *Statement on Registration and Conscription for Military Service* issued 14 February 1980, which again affirmed the Catholic right of CO and SCO. The bishops approved the general idea of draft registration, but they declared that the state must show convincing reasons for its particular action. And despite the approval, the bishops affirmed their opposition to the draft at the time, condemned a draft of women, and recommended that draft counseling be available in Catholic schools and agencies.[56]

Pax Christi–USA's national council took the most extreme position on the draft when it passed a resolution on 8 October 1982 which stated: "Although we neither advise nor encourage such action, Pax Christi–USA recognizes non-registration for the draft based on conscientious objection to conscription and opposition to growing militarization of this nation as a valid Christian witness deserving the respect and support of the entire Christian community."[57] With this resolution the organization placed itself in the pacifist and nonviolent resistance tradition of the Catholic Worker and CPF on the issue of the draft, but on other justice and peace issues remained open to other perspectives. In June 1983, Pax Christi–USA joined other religious groups in calling for an end to draft registration.[58]

Another area of concern was Central America. Political and social turmoil in this region had intensified during Jegen's tenure as national coordinator. Central America was the one issue on which Pax Christi– USA followed the bishops rather than trying to lead them. As early as

1977, it had become involved in Latin America at the request of Miguel D'Escoto, M.M., director of communications at Maryknoll. Bishop Gumbleton along with six other Pax Christi–USA bishops wrote to Bishop Obando y Bravo of Managua expressing support for the Nicaraguan church in the difficult struggle the country was experiencing in the overthrow of Anastasio Somoza. The dictatorial Somoza family had ruled Nicaragua since 1936 and were long-time allies of the United States. The revolutionaries called themselves Sandinistas after the Nicaraguan who had fought American marines in the early 1930s. Joe Fahey wrote to President Carter and three congressional leaders in the name of Pax Christi–USA urging an end to aid for Somoza.[59] One of Pax Christi–USA's first actions of support of the hierarchy on Central America was to respond to the call of the secretariat of the Bishops Conference of Central America and Panama to "unite with us in a campaign for a deeper understanding of the Gospel and the vindication of human rights."[60] In 1980, Pax Christi–USA joined CPF and John Quigley at the USCC in support of the International Days for Justice and Freedom in Central America. It also recommended that its members write to the president, Congress, and State Department "urging withdraw of aid, especially arms transfers to dictatorial and repressive regimes in Central America."[61]

In November 1981, the USCC issued its *Statement on Central America*.[62] Gone was the just war approval of the early stages of the war in Vietnam. Instead, the bishops affirmed the Second Vatican Council, and the statements from the general conferences of Latin American bishops held at Medellin in 1968 and Puebla in 1979 that confirmed the tradition of liberation and peace. They mourned the martyrdoms of Archbishop Oscar Romero and the four American churchwomen in El Salvador and confirmed their solidarity with the members of the church in Central America. The bishops called for an end to U.S. military intervention in Central America and stated that the problem was not communism, but the internal condition of poverty and the denial of basic human rights. Pax Christi–USA urged Catholics to support the bishops who called on the U.S. government to "stop military aid to El Salvador."[63] It asked members to write to the Coalition for a New Foreign and Military Policy, the Interreligious Task Force on El Salvador, and/or the Religious Task Force on El Salvador. In the fall of 1982, Pax Christi–USA established an ad hoc committee to help respond to the current situation in Central America and stated that "Nicaragua is struggling to overcome its own interior divisions at the same time it is faced with massive military pressure and economic destablization from the U.S. Educated action is urgently needed to stop the escalating U.S. involvement."[64]

The major problem that confronted Pax Christi–USA in the Central American crisis was not the institutional church's response to public-policy issues in Central America but the question of theology. Liberation theology, which had developed from the Latin American experience, permits violent actions on behalf of the oppressed. Pax Christi–USA promoted a theology and spirituality of nonviolence. Such opposing views forced many of its members to ask if the organization allowed room for violent actions or did it restrict its political options to nonviolent ones? Jegen did not accept this simplistic interpretation of liberation theology and answered such questions by stating that as a U.S. organization it was permitted only nonviolent actions, but in relation to the revolutionary situation in Central America and liberation theology it would continue to support the efforts of the oppressed peoples of the world. Thus, despite the theological tension, Jegen and Pax Christi–USA stood with the poor and oppressed of Central America while they attempted in a nonviolent manner to stop U.S. military aid to Central America.[65] Its attempts to stop U.S. involvement in Central America would become the main focus of Pax Christi–USA's work for peace after the demise of the antinuclear movement in the mid-1980s.

The third area of concern was nuclear warfare and the antinuclear weapons protest movement. This consumed the greatest part of the energies of the organization during the Jegen years. The reason for this was the flourishing of the nuclear weapons freeze campaign. In the early 1980s, Ronald Reagan, the new president, kept his campaign promise to direct a massive buildup of American military forces. Despite Reagan's popularity, support for the freeze increased dramatically: by 1982 it was active in all fifty states. By 1983, 140 Catholic bishops had endorsed the freeze. This was a dramatic change not only for the bishops, but for all Catholics in the United States when these actions are compared with the antinuclear-weapons movement of the 1940s and the Ban-the-Bomb movement of the 1950s and 1960s, which only Catholic Workers and a few individual Catholics like Thomas Merton supported. The success of the freeze campaign was short-lived, however, and by 1984 it was in decline and faded into the background when it merged with SANE in 1987.[66]

Pax Christi–USA first became involved in the antinuclear weapons issue on 16 May 1978 when the UN hosted its first Special Session on Disarmament to which religious leaders from all over the world were invited. Pax Christi International presented to the preparatory UN Special Session on Disarmament, a statement which called for the banning of nuclear weapons, the condemnation of indiscriminate warfare, and the abstention from war and claimed that the funds spent on the arms race killed the poor.[67] After the close of the disarmament session, Pax Christi–USA had its own Mass at Holy Family Church near the UN. Bishop Thomas Kelly, O.P., general secretary of the USCC, came from Washington to take part in the Mass. Such a sign of support for Pax Christi–USA from the USCC made Fahey comment, "I really felt we had made it, that one of our key goals was met."[68]

On 18 October 1978 Bishop Gumbleton, Joe Fahey, and Gerald Vanderhaar were invited to attend the Conference on SALT II for Religious Leaders at the State Department in Washington, D.C. After listening to three testimonies on why the treaty would not weaken the defense of the United States, all three Pax Christi–USA representatives believed the treaty should not be supported.[69] This decision proved to place the group in the difficult position of calling for nuclear arms reduction yet rejecting a nuclear arms reduction treaty because it was too minimal. Pax Christi–USA wanted more and for this reason it supported the Hatfield amendment for a nuclear moratorium.

The debate on the ratification of SALT II wrecked havoc not only in the broader peace movement, but also among the bishops. Bishop Gumbleton spoke strongly against ratification in NCCB. USCC believed that Gumbleton's position threatened to unravel all that they had done to persuade the bishops to address the public policy issue on control of nuclear weapons. Debate on the issue flourished and Bishop Gumbleton and Pax Christi–USA modified their position by supporting SALT II with an amendment. In 1979, the bishops supported SALT II, but their collective statement of support for the treaty was made only after a highly unusual session of the bishops' administrative committee, an elected body that acts in the name of the entire conference between general meetings. "SALT II A Statement of Support" was delivered by John Cardinal Krol, archbishop of Philadelphia, before the U.S. Senate Foreign Relations Committee on 20 September 1979.[70] Krol's support of SALT II did not rest solely on the minimal accomplishments of the treaty, but also reflected concern about the morality of deterrence:

> As long as there is hope [of meaningful and continuing reductions], Catholic moral teaching is willing, while negotiations proceed, to tolerate the possession of nuclear weapons for deterrence as the lesser of two evils. If that hope were to disappear, the moral attitude of the Catholic Church would almost certainly have to shift to one of uncompromising condemnation of both use *and* possession of such weapons.[71]

Pax Christi–USA's moral position condemned both the use and possession of nuclear weapons which went beyond the point reached by the bishops. This position had been spelled out by Pax Christi International at the first UN Special Disarmament Session in 1978. At that time, Pax Christi International unequivocally accepted the nuclear-pacifist position and said no to nuclear war and to nuclear weapons of any kind. The 2 August 1979 issue of *Commonweal* announced that Pax Christi–USA was launching a "Campaign to Help Stop Nuclear Weapons," calling for "an end to all research, development, testing, manufacturing and development of any new nuclear weapon that is not yet fully developed."[72] That same year a local Pax Christi–USA group led by Bill Hogan, a Chicago priest, "sat-in" at the Commonwealth Edison nuclear plant in Zion, Illinois, and the local in Washington, D.C., led by Richard McSorley, S.J., joined the Nuclear Moratorium.[73]

In early 1980, Pax Christi–USA's executive council wrote a "Call to Conversion" and invited individuals and groups to sign its pledge, which stated "I am prepared to live without the protection of nuclear armaments. As a Christian, I wish to take a stand in our country for the political development of peace without nuclear arms."[74] At the same time, it announced that Daniel Berrigan would be its keynote speaker at its national assembly in the fall, And in March 1981, it was among the 275 participants invited to attend the national strategy session on the freeze in Washington, D.C.

Pax Christi–USA continued to increase its disarmament efforts in the early 1980s by applying pressure on corporations, the government, and the church. It called for a boycotting of nuclear weapons manufacturers and listed the responsible companies in its magazine. It also pledged itself to work with other groups on disarmament. It joined with sixty groups in sponsoring, "Ground Zero," a week of educating Americans on the nuclear issue, which had been modeled on Earth Day activities. Pax Christi–USA was also one of the founding groups along with FOR of a New Call to Peacemaking, Sojourners, and World Peacemakers in launching the New Abolitionist Covenant, which attempted to coordinate efforts among the churches to get a "freeze" on any new nuclear weapons. The New Abolitionist Covenant explained its purpose in the following manner:

> The purpose of the covenant is to place before the churches the abolition of nuclear weapons as an urgent matter of faith. The nuclear threat is a theological issue, a confessional matter, a spiritual question, and is so important it must be brought into the heart of the church's life.[75]

Pax Christi–USA viewed the formation of the group as a continuation of its position during the SALT II debate, when it pressed for the Hatfield amendment for a nuclear moratorium.

The freeze drew strong support from the religious community, particularly Catholic bishops. At the suggestion of Bishops Gumbleton and Sullivan a statement on the freeze was sent to all the bishops in the United States along with a card on which to indicate support. At this time Pax Christi–USA had fifty-seven bishops in its ranks. The mailing drew an amazing response.[76] At the Nuclear Weapons Freeze national press conference held in Washington, D.C., on 26 April 1982, Bishop Joseph Francis of East Orange, New Jersey, announced that over 138 bishops of the Roman Catholic hierarchy had endorsed the Nuclear Weapons Freeze.[77]

Pax Christi–USA also participated in the second UN Special Session on Disarmament from June to July 1982. Joe Fahey had assumed primary responsiblity for drafting Pax Christi International's statement for the session. He had consulted theologians and met with the military vicariate about the document.[78] The core of the statement reflected a nuclear pacifist position, which differed, however, from the Vatican's position at the session. On June 11, the Vatican secretary of state,

Agostino Cardinal Casaroli, delivered an address to the session in the pope's name. His talk echoed Vatican attacks on the arms race and contained the following statement on deterrence that was to be quoted endlessly during the ensuing debate: "Under present conditions, deterrence based on balance—certainly not as an end in itself, but as a stage on the way to progressive disarmament—can still be judged to be morally acceptable."[79] Pax Christi International's nuclear pacifist position went beyond Pope John Paul II's position by calling for a bilateral freeze. In order to try to accelerate the process toward a position of nuclear pacifism at the UN some Pax Christi–USA members joined the antinuclear activism, which ranged from liturgies to civil disobedience surrounding the disarmament session.

Within Pax Christi–USA the effort to educate mainline Catholics on the disarmament issue had resulted in a popular nuclear disarmament movement among Catholics that was well connected with the broader peace movement in America and was symbolized by the efforts of Helen Caldicott of Physicans for Social Responsiblity and Carl Sagan of the Union of Concerned Scientists. Pax Christi–USA had successfully popularized for Catholics an issue that was previously confined to government circles. The organization's emphasis on local and regional development provided a network that combined spirituality, intellectual debate, and a call to nonviolent action in support of nuclear pacifism.

A new ingredient was added to the antinuclear movement when Catholic pacifists tried to develop a pro-life argument linking abortion with the nuclear arms race. At the outset, a group of women at the PAX Center in Erie, Pennsylvania, started an organization called Prolifers for Survival.[80] Jonah House picked up on the linking of abortion with the nuclear arms race and sponsored a "Prolife Week at the Pentagon." Both Prolifers for Survival and Pax Christi–USA supported the event. The purpose of the event was to make obvious to mainline Catholics and the hierarchy that consistency in the church's teaching was necessary. Since the church condemned abortion because it killed human life, it should also condemn nuclear war and the arms race which could kill not only all human life, but the entire planet.[81] In 1981, Pax Christi–USA issued its statement "The Unborn Child and the Protection of Life."

The linking of antinuclearism and antiabortion gained considerable momentum in the mid-1980s when Joseph Cardinal Bernardin, the archbishop of Chicago, presented his consistent ethic of life speech in the William Wade Lecture at St. Louis University on 11 March 1985. Since Bernardin was the chief architect of the peace pastoral and in 1986 would chair the Pro-Life committee of NCCB, he attempted to link the issues of abortion and nuclear warfare into part of a total pro-life position by the Roman Catholic church. Bernardin would insist that the

> systemic vision of a consistent ethic of life will not erode our crucial public opposition to the direction of the arms race; neither will it smother our persistent and necessary public opposition to abortion. . . . A consistent ethic of life does not equate the problem of taking life (e.g., through abortion and in war) with the problem of promoting human dignity (through humane programs of nutrition, health care, and housing). But a consistent ethic of life identifies both the protection of life and its promotion as moral questions. It aims for a continuum of life which must be sustained in the face of diverse and distinct threats. . . . It is not necessary or possible for every person to engage in each issue, but it is both possible and necessary for the Church as a whole to cultivate a conscious explicit connection among its several issues.[82]

The key figure in helping Bernardin to develop his consistent ethic of life was J. Bryan Hehir.

A Boston priest with a doctorate in theology from Harvard University, Hehir became the director of the Office of International Justice and Peace at USCC in 1973, and he remained in that position until 1984, when he was promoted to secretary of the more comprehensive USCC Department of Social Development and World Peace.[83] Hehir officially left USCC in 1987, but he continues to act as a consultant. During his years at the USCC Hehir created a framework for foreign-policy analysis that many bishops followed.

While with USCC, Hehir spent a great amount of time giving talks to Catholics across the nation informing them that justice and peace were "constitutive" parts of their faith and calling them to live out the church's teaching on these issues in their daily lives. Bryan Hehir also cooperated with Pax Christi–USA from the time of its reorganization under Bishop Dozier. Though Hehir was never a member, he remained in dialogue with this organization since he believed it represented the post-Vietnam Catholic activists and intellectuals concerned about peace.

Hehir worked with the hierarachy, with mainline Catholics, and with Pax Christi–USA because he viewed himself as a mediating force in the American Catholic debate on war and peace. Like John Courtney Murray he believed in and worked out of the just war tradition, but on nuclear issues he departed from Murray's call for the evolution of nuclear weapons that would meet the just war standards. As regards nuclear issues, Hehir believed there was an absolute moral imperative of non-use for weapons of indiscriminate effect, speaking more in the tradition of Merton than Murray.

He was a nuclear pacifist.[84] But unlike Merton, he worked systematically within the just war tradition, never abandoning it for nonviolence. He viewed nuclear pacifism as an alternative for Catholics that would serve as a point of convergence between traditional pacifists and just war theorists. As a result, many individuals from all segments of the church viewed Hehir as a friend and ally in their opposition to nuclear war and the arms race. In the early 1980s, however, while working on *The Challenge of Peace*, Hehir came to believe that the position of nuclear pacifism was not tenable because the split between use and deterrence was too absolute. He therefore rejected nuclear pacifism as a viable moral position for the official church in America to promulgate. Thus his position and the one of the pastoral letter on peace are the same. As Hehir states, "Close to nuclear pacifism but not quite."[85] Because of his influential position in the church, he has had a very significant impact on the development of American Catholic thought on the nuclear issue.

Before Hehir arrived at the USCC in 1973 the bishops had already issued a statement that discussed the nuclear issue.[86] The 1968 pastoral letter *Human Life in Our Day* had included a lengthy discussion of arms-control issues and noted that nothing suggested the anti-life direction of technological warfare more than the neutron bomb. The bishops did not again address nuclear issues until 11 November 1976 when to commemorate America's bicentennial anniversary, the bishops issued a lengthy pastoral on moral life called *To Live in Christ Jesus: A Pastoral Reflection on the Moral Life*. Though only one section of the pastoral dealt with war and peace issues, it did contain a significant paragraph on nuclear weapons:

> With respect to nuclear weapons, at least those with massive destructive capability, the first imperative is to prevent their use. As possessors of a vast nuclear arsenal, we must also be aware that not only is it wrong to attack civilian populations, but it is also wrong to threaten to attack them as part of a strategy of deterrence. We urge the continued development and implementation of policies which seek to bring these weapons more securely under control, progressively reduce their presence in the world and ultimately remove them entirely.[87]

The declaration that it is wrong to threaten to use nuclear weapons against civilians was the most dramatic change in the NCCB/USCC teaching on nuclear war since the Second Vatican Council; ironically it was adopted without any substantive discussion. The concept originally came from the pen of Russell Shaw, the USCC secretary for public affairs. "I felt honestly at the time it was a new step for the bishops," Shaw said. "It was logically consistent with things individual bishops and the conference itself had said. It was another step forward in a logical progression."[88] Hehir incorporated Shaw's paragraph in the final draft of the pastoral which spoke of "the need to control rigorously nuclear weapons" and closed with a few words on human rights in foreign policy.[89]

Hehir again addressed the nuclear issue in the first collective statement of the bishops since the Vietnam War devoted solely to the issue of war and peace, *The Gospel of Peace and the Danger of War*, issued 15 February 1978. The statement focused on disarmament and the SALT II negotiations and the upcoming UN Special Session on Disarmament and said "the primary moral objective is that the arms race must be stopped and the reduction of armaments must be achieved."[90]

While Hehir was working within USCC alerting bishops to the moral significance of the nuclear issue, Pax Christi–USA was encouraging bishops to join their organization. The buildup of the Nuclear Freeze Movement and increased press coverage of the issue across the nation also influenced the bishops. As a result, an increased activism on the nuclear-disarmament issue by individual members of the hierarchy occurred. Between 1980 and November 1981 over forty bishops had spoken out on the issue.[91] The two bishops who attracted the most attention during this period followed their statements with a public action that fostered a new consciousness among other members of the hierarchy and mainline Catholics about what their faith demanded in response to nuclear disarmament.

The most notable member of the hierarchy to address the issue was Raymond Hunthausen, archbishop of Seattle.[92] In a series of statements in 1981 and 1982 he publicized his nuclear pacifist position and dealt directly with the issue of Trident nuclear submarines that were located in Puget Sound, an area under his episcopal jurisdiction. Hunthausen was challenged to speak because the construction of the Trident was in conflict with the church's "first-strike nuclear doctrine."[93] In a pastoral letter to his archdiocese dated 28 January 1982, he went beyond letter writing when he announced that "after much prayer, thought, and personal struggle, I have decided to withold fifty percent of my income taxes as a means of protesting our nation's continuing involvement in the race for nuclear supremacy."[94] He did not urge such action for the members of his diocese, that was a matter of individual conscience, but meant his action to be a means to awaken them to a better path of peace than through nuclear deterrence.

Pax Christi–USA kept its members well informed of Archbishop Hunthausen's words and deeds and in 1983 the national executive council approved the proposal that it "recognizes tax resistance as an important and valid Christian witness at this time"[95] Though it had always supported the World Peace Tax Fund Bill in Congress, this was the first time Pax Christi–USA had supported tax resistance. Among Catholic peace groups, the Catholic Worker Movement alone advocated and practiced collective and individual tax resistance as a form of nonviolent resistance to the state. Until Archbishop Hunthausen, no member of the hierarchy had ever advocated, much less practiced it.[96]

Like Archbishop Hunthausen, Leroy T. Matthiessen, bishop of Amarillo, addressed the nuclear disarmament issue in relation to the effect it was having in his own diocese. Matthiessen was particularly angry at the Reagan administration's decision to deploy the neutron bomb. The Pantex plant, located fifteen miles from Amarillo, was the final assembly point for U.S. nuclear weapons, including the neutron bomb. On 21 August 1981, Matthiessen issued his statement, "Nuclear Arms Buildup." His condemnation of neutron warheads was a logical progression from statements in the 1968 pastoral *Human Life in Our Day* and a statement by Archbishop John Quinn of San Francisco issued in 1978 in support of President Carter's decision to defer production of neutron warheads.[97] The conclusion of Matthiessen's statement set forth a new precedent when he said: "We urge individuals involved in the production and stockpiling of nuclear bombs to consider what they are doing, to resign from such activities and to seek employment in peaceful pursuits."[98] Bishop Matthiessen followed up on this when he created a Solidarity Peace Fund to financially assist employees who in conscience resigned from their arms-production jobs at the Pantex Plant. Pax Christi–USA immediately solicited contributions for the fund and encouraged its members not to work for arms-production industries.[99]

Ironically, it was not only the Catholic Resistance but also the actions of individual members of the hierarchy who moved Pax Christi–USA further away from a just war position toward a pacifist position. The nuclear-disarmament issue illustrated its best efforts during the Jegen years. It always supported members of the American hierarchy and united them in Pax Christi–USA with the old core pacifists of PAX and CPF; it managed to support and work with the Catholic Resistance and still attract mainline Catholics. From this position in the center of the Catholic peace movement in the 1970s and 1980s Pax Christi–USA was able to link Catholics with the broader peace movement in the United States.

The most publicized Catholic action for peace and against nuclear warfare and nuclear weapons was the aforementioned pastoral letter, *The Challenge of Peace*, issued collectively by the 350 bishops who comprised the American Catholic hierarchy. The institutional church's pastoral, however, would not have been possible without the threat of nuclear annihilation and the peace witness of Catholic laymen and women that began with the founding of the Catholic Worker fifty years earlier.

The immediate impetus for *The Challenge of Peace* was a proposal for new business submitted to Bishop Thomas C. Kelly, general secretary of the NCCB/USCC, in the summer of 1980 by P. Francis Murphy, an auxiliary bishop of Baltimore. Murphy proposed that the bishops consider a statement on the Catholic teaching on the morality of war and peace and urged educational efforts to make that teaching more widely known. At the November 1980 NCCB meeting discussion on the proposal focused on the subject of nuclear weapons and the bishops formally agreed to address the issue. Two months later Archbishop John Roach of St. Paul-Minneapolis, president of the NCCB, appointed an ad hoc committee on war and peace to draft the bishops' statement. The chair of the committee was the highly respected Archbishop Joseph L. Bernardin of Cincinnati, who was known for his ability to build consensus. The four other committee members were Auxiliary Bishop Thomas Gumbleton of Detroit, Auxiliary Bishop John J. O'Connor (of the military ordinariate), Bishop Daniel Reilly of Norwich, Connecticut, and Auxiliary Bishop George Fulcher of Columbus, Ohio. Neither Reilly nor Fulcher had been previously identified with the nuclear issue.[100]

The USCC staff who worked with the committee were Bryan Hehir and Edward Doherty. The principal outside consultant and the individual who actually drafted the final text of the 1983 pastoral was Bruce Russett of Yale University, editor of the *Journal of Conflict Resolution*. The committee staff was completed with the appointments of Richard Warner, Indiana provincial of the Congregation of the Holy Cross, as representative of the Conference of Major Superiors of Men, and Juliana Casey, of the religious community of the Immaculate Heart of Mary, as representative of the Leadership Conference of Women Religious.[101]

The committee heard testimony from thirty-six formal witnesses on all aspects of the issue. They ranged from Tom Cornell and Gordon Zahn of the Catholic peace movement to Defense Secretary Caspar Weinberger and Arms Control and Disarmament Agency head Eugene Rostow. Biblical scholars, military officers, a physician, a conflict-resolution specialist, and two former defense secretaries also gave testimony. The most important testimony, due to its influence on Reilly and Fulcher, came from former Defense Secretaries James Schlesinger and Harold Brown. Reilly recalled that the two were "so forceful in resistance to nuclear war, in saying that nuclear war has to be avoided at all costs as unthinkable madness. They were very affirming of the committee's work."[102]

The four key figures throughout the writing of the letter were Bernardin, Hehir, Gumbleton, and O'Connor. Bernardin had announced at the first committee meeting that the group's one ground rule would be that "it would not, under any circumstances, support unilateral nuclear disarmament"[103] and he continually urged the committee to move "back toward the center."[104] Hehir's role was different. According to Gumbleton, Hehir determined the agenda and what issues had to be resolved. Bernardin also constantly looked to Hehir for clarification.[105] The two extremes on the committee were Gumbleton and O'Connor. Gumbleton, who had experienced a conversion to pacifism, represented the prophetic and personal peace elements in the church. He wrote the sections of the pastoral on pacifism and nonviolence. O'Connor represented the just war tradition and support for the military in America. According to Gumbleton, no single individual was responsible for writing the pastoral; as he put it, "he could personally point to each paragraph and name the member responsible for it."[106] Because Hehir determined the agenda and was intellectually committed to the just war doctrine as were O'Connor, Bernardin, and the other members of the committee, the just war doctrine would provide the moral principles and framework for the document.

The pastoral went through three drafts, which were made public, and extensive debate and compromise took place before the final letter was passed by the bishops. On 2 July 1982 a major portion of the first draft appeared in the *National Catholic Reporter*. Jegen reflected the disappointment of many members of the peace movement when in response to a letter to Gordon Zahn she wrote:

> I see no way of avoiding a split over the pastoral. The important thing is to handle it with charity and a desire for continuing dialogue and eventual consensus. I simply cannot praise the overall thrust of the piece, as you sincerely can. . . . I certainly agree that Tom Gumbleton should not bear the brunt of our criticisms. He is, after all, only one member of the committee.[107]

Like Jegen many other Catholics wanted a more prophetic statement and criticized the hierarchy's accommodation to power and the just war tradition. They also wanted a condemnation not only of the use but also the possession of nuclear weapons.

Other Catholics condemned the pastoral for going too far in the direction of pacifism. Philip Lawler, director of studies at the Heritage Foundation, formed a group of lay Catholics to "call public attention" to the church's traditional teachings on war and peace. Michael

Novak, author and lay theologian, organized a group of fifty prominent Catholic laymen to be called the American Catholic Committee to counter the move of the bishops toward pacifism and return them to the teachings of St. Augustine, St. Thomas Aquinas, and the Catholic just war tradition. Ed Marciniak, a Catholic lay leader in Chicago, who had formed a National Center for the Laity for Catholics, thought the bishops have gone too far on the nuclear issue.[108]

Between the second and third drafts, a consultation was held at the Vatican on 18–19 January 1983. American participants in the consultation were Bernardin, Roach, Hehir, and Monsignor Daniel Hoye, general secretary of the NCCB/USCC. The meeting involved other bishops and specialists from France, West Germany, Great Britain, Belgium, Italy, and the Netherlands. Vatican participants included Joseph Cardinal Ratzinger and Agostino Cardinal Casaroli and other representatives of pontifical commissions. The proceedings were confidential, but insights into the meeting can be gleaned from a synthesis prepared by the priest Jan Schotte, secretary of the Pontifical Justice and Peace Commission, and published as "a point of reference and a guide to the U.S. bishops in preparing the next draft of their pastoral letter." The text of the Schotte synthesis was released to the NC News documentary service, *Origins*.[109] The synthesis characterized the consultation as "centered on five main themes: the precise teaching role of a bishops' conference; the application of moral principles to the nuclear weapons debate; the use of scripture; the relationship between just war theory and pacifism in Catholic tradition; the morality of deterrence."[110] On each of these points alterations were made in the third draft.[111] It must be remembered, however, that the consultation raised issues needing to be clarified and it was the American hierarchy, not Vatican authorities, that clarified them.

A major issue of concern was the application of moral principles to concrete situations. The Vatican raised the question of how morally binding the pastoral letter of the American hierarchy was on individual members of the church. The American bishops resolved this in the opening page of *The Challenge of Peace* when they claimed that the letter was "an exercise of our teaching ministry" and "that not all statements in this letter have the same moral authority. At times we state universally binding moral principles found in the teaching of the Church; at other times the pastoral letter makes specific applications, observations and recommendations which allow for diversity of opinion on the part of those who assess the factual data of situations differently."[112] The implications of this resolution were clearly assessed by Jim Castelli in his book *The Bishops and the Bomb: Waging Peace in a Nuclear Age,* when he commented on the unprecedented, almost dramatic, emphasis on the role of individual conscience and the right to dissent on matters of contingent, prudential judgment:

> If people may legitimately disagree over whether or not it is moral to start a nuclear war and still remain Catholics in good standing, the mind boggles at the implications for less cosmic issues like contraception, sterilization, abortion, divorce. The church will, no doubt, try to draw a line between issues like those and issues of war and peace; but many American Catholics, including many bishops, won't accept that. A conscience, once awakened, doesn't easily go back to sleep.[113]

*The Challenge of Peace* called for a critical examination of nuclear war, its strategies, the concept of first use, and deterrence. The pastoral emphasized the qualitative difference between nuclear and conventional weapons and emphasized the destructive power of nuclear weapons which "threatens the human person, the civilization we have slowly constructed, and even the created order itself."[114] The bishops also became convinced of the "overwhelming probability" that a major nuclear exchange would be unlimited and stated explicitly that "under no circumstances may nuclear weapons or other instruments of mass slaughter be used for the purpose of destroying population centers or other predominantly civilian targets."[115] This condemnation applied to retaliatory second strikes as well. The bishops concluded that "this condemnation, in our judgment, applies even to the retaliatory use of weapons striking enemy cities after our own have already been struck. No Christian can rightfully carry out orders or policies aimed at killing noncombatants."[116] In their argument the hierarchy invoked the just war principles of noncombatant immunity and proportionality first applied by John C. Ford, S.J., to World War II. The bishops also opposed any preemptive first strike when they declared that they did "not perceive any situation in which the deliberate initiation of nuclear warfare, on however restricted a scale, can be morally justified." The bishops again repeated their "extreme skepticism" that a nuclear exchange could be controlled, no matter how limited first use might have been and thus the bishops supported a "no first use" policy.[117] The bishops then concluded that the "first imperative" was to prevent any use of nuclear weapons.

On the issue of deterrence, the bishops accepted Pope John Paul II's formula for deterrence that Casaroli announced at the UN Special Session on Disarmament on 11 June 1982. According to Casaroli deterrence was not as an end in itself, but a temporary transition to true disarmament.[118] The significance of the Vatican consultation became most evident on this issue. By accepting the pope's position, the bishops had to keep their argument for deterrence within those limits. As Bryan Hehir has stated, the only opening left by the bishops on which to accept the pope's position was that the bishops did not explicitly reject the possible retaliatory use of small-yield nuclear weapons against clearly definable military targets. On this "centimeter of ambiguity," the positive support of deterrence rested.[119]

Even though they accepted deterrence, the bishops tried to stop the arms buildup by endorsing several arms control treaties and plans backed by the Nuclear Freeze Movement.[120] They also called for international controls on arms and the arms race, the substitution of conventional weapons for nuclear forces as a means of disarmament, and cast doubt on the validity of civil defense as a defensive option.[121] It was clear that the bishops were saying no to the use of nuclear weapons at a time when new technological possibilities and the Reagan administration's rhetoric had convinced millions of people that the use of nuclear weapons was not only possible but inevitable. The bishops never proclaimed a nuclear-pacifist position because like Bryan Hehir they maintained a "centimeter of ambiguity," in order to support Pope John Paul II's position on deterrence and follow the directive of Bernardin not to support unilateral disarmament and to keep on "center." As a result, the bishops, despite their intense criticisms, never unequivocally condemned nuclear warfare and the possession and use of nuclear weapons. Thus, it was not the bishops but the small community of resisters at Jonah House and Pax Christi–USA who remained the prophets in the church and stood at the cutting edge of the national conscience on nuclear issues.

The most significant factor in determining the ultimate outcome of the bishop's pastoral was the "traditionally" Catholic position taken by the Bernardin committee by using the just war doctrine as the mediating language of the document. Though the bishops proclaimed the qualitative difference between nuclear and conventional warfare, they were unable to address nuclear issues with an ethic that was qualitatively different from that of the just war. The staff at USCC believed that only the just war doctrine spoke to both Christian witness and public policy. They clung to the dominant just war doctrine and Hehir finely crafted its arguments. At best, the just war ethic as presented in *The Challenge of Peace* stressed the new weight given to the protection of the rights of conscience. At worst, the just war ethic could not provide the bishops with an ethic that would unequivocally condemn what they had proclaimed as the supreme crisis of nuclear warfare: "The whole human race faces a moment of supreme crisis in its advance toward maturity. We agree with the [Second Vatican] Council's assessment; the crisis of the moment is embodied in the threat which nuclear weapons pose for the world and much that we hold dear."[122] It was not the failure of the moral norms presented in the just war ethic, but as John Courtney Murray contended, the failure of those who do not make the just war tradition relevant. Merton had used the just war ethic to reach a position of nuclear pacifism; Pope John Paul II, Bernardin, and the staff at the USCC had not.

Indeed, the pastoral did question and criticize the legality and morality of the national-security policies of the U.S. government in relation to nuclear issues, but it left the burden of peacemaking to the individual. *The Challenge of Peace* stated that peacemaking was no longer an option for the Christian, but it failed to deliver the same message to the U.S. government.[123] Though the pastoral rejected pacifism, even nuclear pacifism, as a viable position for the government, it affirmed pacifism and nonviolence as a viable option for the Christian peacemaker.[124] As a result, the pastoral did establish pacifism as well as the just war as valid positions within the Catholic tradition but relegated pacifism and nonviolence to the individual and the more prophetic Parts I and IV of the pastoral. Whenever pacifism or nonviolence was mentioned, it was tied to conscience, individual conversion, suffering, and even martyrdom. The pastoral's message for the individual peacemaker who embraced pacifism and nonviolence was that peacemaking was hard, indeed harder than war. But there is little acknowledgment of the capacity of pacifism and nonviolence to address public-policy issues. At best, the tactics of nonviolence were affirmed as a means of national defense against enemies.

A significant part of the pastoral was the call for a new world order which the bishops described in accordance with the traditional lines of Catholic internationalism. This was the same idea that CAIP and John A. Ryan endorsed in the 1920s. Then, according to the church's approach since Pope John XXIII and Vatican II, the bishops stressed the pressing reality of world interdependence and development in the Third World. The pastoral broke new ground when it called for a new world order based not on the American-Soviet conflict nor on world government, but on the obligations of the United States to share its wealth and resources with the rest of the world. An emphasis was also placed on the moral question raised by the "massive distortion of resources" for armaments when so much of the world remained poor and helpless.[125] The absence of Cold War rhetoric in the document and the emphasis on the link between arms production and the poor of the world was also present in the 1980 pastoral letter on Marxism and would also be present in the economic pastoral issued in 1986. The emphasis on the new world order section acquired a new validity with the dismantling of the Berlin Wall.

What *The Challenge of Peace* did for the American Catholic peace movement was to validate its existence. The message to Catholics was that peacemaking was not a virtue limited to a few "saints," but an essential commandment to be followed by all. The need to "build a new theology of peace" was acknowledged, but the course of action to be followed was now no longer limited to the just war tradition, but pointed to pacifism and Gospel nonviolence as the base upon which individual conscience and conversion to peacemaking rested. Though many have heralded the pastoral as a revolution in peacemaking marked by the reconciliation of opposing views and the synthesis of a new theology of peace, no such revolution occurred. The just war ethic still dominated the message of the church in its attempt to address public policy; pacifism and Gospel nonviolence dominated its message when the church attempted to defend individual conscience and promote human rights. Though the pastoral recognized opposing views within the Roman Catholic tradition of peacemaking, a new synthesis was not achieved. Nuclear pacifism based on the just war ethic was not the "middle road" toward a new theology of peace. The just war ethic reached its apotheosis when the institutional church would not proclaim nuclear pacifism. Although the just war ethic did not fail when it was applied to the individual in the matter of SCO, it did fail when applied to the state on nuclear issues. At best, the just war ethic did condemn the use of nuclear weapons (and conventional weapons) of indiscriminate effect even in self-defense, but it did not condemn the production and possession of nuclear weapons even with the realization that the use of such weapons could result in the annihilation of humankind.

Though *The Challenge of Peace* received more press coverage than any other Catholic pastoral in American history, many American Catholics remained completely unaware of its message. The bishops provided very little follow-up on the pastoral. Members of the hierarchy, church leaders, journalists, and intellectuals continued to cling to the just war doctrine as the dominant ethic in the church on issues of war and peace. Some just war adherents, as Murray had advised, were applying the principles of the just war in their peacemaking attempts and in conscience arriving at the conclusion that the extent of damage wrought by both conventional and nuclear weaponry all but ends the prospect that any war could be deemed just. Many Catholics, however, continued to believe that a just war was possible.

The bishops wrote their next pastoral (1986) on capitalism and focused their energies almost exclusively on the abortion issue for the rest of the 1980s. Though the peace movement linked both abortion and nuclear issues to their pro-life position, the efforts on the part of the institutional church consistently to make the same link has been limited mainly to the efforts of Bernardin, who has repeatedly emphasized the consistent ethic in his speeches on abortion.[126] Again, it was the work of the American Catholic peace movement, especially Pax Christi–USA that attempted to continue to educate the mainline Catholic on their responsibility of following Jesus's call to peacemaking, "Peace I leave with you; my peace I give to you."

Since the publication of *The Challenge of Peace*, the American Catholic peace movement has continued its religious witness and quest for a new theology of peace. Since 1983, members of the peace movement have worked within a church that recognizes the legitimacy of their positions. Pacifists, nuclear pacifists, practitioners of Gospel nonviolence and resistance, conscientious objectors and selective conscientious objectors are now at home in the church. The American Catholic peace movement also continues to attempt to change the public policies of the U.S. government from the direction of militarism and war toward a policy based on peace and the affirmation of life. But the government has not embraced the peacemakers. Instead it has closed the door to their message as well as to the bishops' "preferential option for peace," offered by the pastoral. In 1990, the greatest obstacle confronting the American Catholic peace movement is not the church but the U.S. government. Thus, the challenge of peacemaking still remains harder than war.

# Note on the Sources


In an attempt to locate the origins of the American Catholic peace movement I was able to identify two possible antecedents: the Catholic Association for International Peace (CAIP) and the Catholic Worker movement. Though the latter proved to be the leaven within American Catholicism that fostered the phenomena to emerge in force during the Vietnam era and continue to the present day, both groups had to be presented in order to provide a full understanding of the various approaches to peace-making.

## The Catholic Worker Movement
The principal sources used in the preparation of this study were Dorothy Day's published writings about her life in the Catholic Worker Movement: *From Union Square to Rome* (Maryland: Presentation of the Faith Press, 1939), *Houses of Hospitality* (New York: Sheed & Ward, 1939), *The Long Loneliness* (New York: Curtis Books, 1952), and *Loaves and Fishes* (New York: Harper & Row, 1963). Ammon Hennacy's *The Autobiography of a Catholic Anarchist* (New Jersey: Libertarian Press, 1952), was also very helpful. The latest edition of the book appears under the title, *The Book of Ammon* (Salt Lake City: n.p. 1965). Most essential to any study pertaining to the Catholic Worker is its newspaper, the *Catholic Worker*. I first used the copies of the newspaper located at St. Charles Borromeo Seminary Archives in Philadelphia. Significantly, issues published during World War II were missing. The complete newspaper is available on microfilm at the University of Notre Dame. The manuscript collection of Catholic Worker papers, correspondence, and so on, is in the archives at Marquette University. Dorothy Day named William D. Miller her official biographer. His two books, *A Harsh and Dreadful Love: Dorothy Day and the Catholic Worker Movement* (New York: Liveright, 1973) and *Dorothy Day: A Biography* (San Francisco: Harper & Row, 1982) have been a valuable aid. It must be pointed out that when asked, Day and Miller both contended that there is no pertinent information on peace in the collection at Marquette University.

## The Catholic Association for International Peace
The principal source for a study of this group is the CAIP collection located in the archives at Marquette University. Although these papers are open to the public, the

material has rarely been consulted. The Catholic University of America possesses the John A. Ryan papers, a limited portion of which were pertinent to this study.

## Conscientious Objection

The newspaper, *Catholic CO*, published during World War II by the Association of Catholic Conscientious Objectors (ACCO) is available on microfilm from the University of San Francisco. The Peace Collection at Swarthmore College contains material related to the ACCO, the CAIP, the Catholic Worker; it also has the complete files of the National Service Board for Religious Objectors (NSBRO) as well as the U.S. Selective Service System report published in 1950 as *Conscientious Objection*, Vols. I and II. A copy of Gordon Zahn's unpublished Ph.D. dissertation from Catholic University in 1953, *A Descriptive Study of the Sociological Backgrounds of CO's during World War II*, is also there. The writings of John Courtney Murray on Selective Conscientious Objection (SCO) are located in the archives of Woodstock College at Georgetown University. Arthur Sheehan, director of the ACCO, and Gordon Zahn, a Catholic CO during World War II, provided significant information through interviews and correspondence.

## Thomas Merton

For the Thomas Merton section of this study the main sources were Merton's writings on peace and these are found in the endnotes of Chapter V. There is also correspondence between James Forest and Thomas Merton during the last ten years of Merton's life which Forest gave me permission to use; the letters are located at Regina Laudis Monastery in Bethlehem, Connecticut. Also contained in the collection are some of Merton's unpublished writings on peace that he mimeographed and circulated among friends. The definitive biographer of Thomas Merton is Michael Mott, *The Seven Mountains of Thomas Merton* (Boston: Hougton Mifflin, 1984). Mott had access to all of Merton's writings, even his restricted journals. Merton's materials are located at the Thomas Merton Studies Center at Bellarmine College in Louisville, Kentucky.

## The Second Vatican Council

The most valuable sources for this section were the writings and correspondence of James Douglass during his intervention at the Second Vatican Council. Douglass lent this collection to me and it proved to be very helpful. I have referred to this correspondence and writings as the "JD Collection" in the endnotes.

## PAX

There is much valuable material, especially correspondence, in the possession of Eileen Egan, cofounder and codirector of PAX and Pax Christi–USA. In November 1990 she decided to send her papers on these two organizations to the archives of the University of Notre Dame. Gordon Zahn's papers are also in the archives at the University of Notre Dame.

## The Berrigan Brothers

The main sources for Chapter VII were the published writings of the Berrigan brothers and their conversations and writings to me. Jerome and Carol Berrigan provided me with hospitality and access to their personal archives on Daniel and Philip Berrigan. The Berrigan Collection is located in Special Collections, Olin Library, Cornell University. Both Daniel and Philip have placed their writings and documents in the collection.

## Catholic Peace Fellowship (CPF)

The CPF Collection is located in the archives at the University of Notre Dame. Thomas Cornell and most recently Bill Ofenloch have submitted material for the collection.

## Pax Christi—USA

The Pax Christi Collection is located in the archives at the University of Notre Dame. Mary Lou Kownacki, the national coordinator, has collected and submitted the material. It is very extensive. There are many limitations in the first years of the organization, but the unpublished history of that period, *Pax Christi USA: the Early Years, 1972–78*, written by Gerard A. Vanderhaar in 1988 completes the story for those years. Vanderhaar's papers and material are located in the archives at the University of Notre Dames as well as the "unofficial" papers of Bishop Thomas Gumbleton. His official papers are located in the archives of the Archdiocesse of Detroit.

## Oral Interviews

My first interview for this study took place almost twenty years ago when I approached Dorothy Day after she had spoken at a rally at St. Ignatius Hall in Baltimore in support of the Catonsville Nine. I still vividly remember my enthusiasm as I rushed up to her and asked her about the relationship of Daniel Berrigan to the Catholic Worker. Her reply was sharp. "Dan isn't a Catholic Worker, he came to us and stole our young men away into the peace movement." I was shocked and confused. Fortunately I was able to talk to her several other times before she died. Since I was privileged to interview many of the people mentioned in this study, I will just name the few whom I found to be most helpful: Daniel and Philip Berrigan, Henry Browne, Thomas Cornell, James Forest, Gordon Zahn, Paul Hanley Furfey, John Peter Grady, Patrick McDermott, James Jennings, George Shuster, Archbishop Thomas Roberts, Monsignor George Higgins, and Bishop Thomas Gumbleton.

Secondary sources of relevance to this study have been cited in the endnotes.

# Notes

### Preface

1. National Conference of Catholic Bishops, *The Challenge of Peace* (Washington, D.C.: United States Catholic Conference, 1983), par. 121.
2. William D. Miller, *A Harsh and Dreadful Love: Dorothy Day and the Catholic Worker Movement* (New York: Liveright, 1973), 3.

### 1: Origins of the Catholic Peace Movement

1. John Tracy Ellis, "American Catholics and Peace: A Historical Sketch" (Washington, D.C.: United States Catholic Conference, 1970), 25, reprint from James S. Rausch, ed., *The Family of Nations* (Huntington, Ind.: Our Sunday Visitor, Inc., 1970).
2. Henry J. Browne, "Catholicism in the United States," in James Ward Smith and A. Leland Jamison, eds., *The Shaping of American Religion* (Princeton, N.J.: Princeton University Press, 1961), 77.
3. John Higham, *Strangers in the Land: Patterns of American Nativism, 1860–1915* (New Brunswick, N.J.: Rutgers University Press, 1966), 218.
4. Browne, "Catholicism in the United States," 77.
5. Richard P. McBrien, *Catholicism*, vol. 2 (Minneapolis, Minn.: Winston Press, 1980), 938.
6. Ibid.
7. Ronald G. Musto, *The Catholic Peace Tradition* (New York: Orbis Books, 1986), 169.
8. Ronald E. Powaski, *Thomas Merton on Nuclear Weapons* (Chicago: Loyola University Press, 1988), 8.
9. John Tracy Ellis, *American Catholicism*, 2d ed., rev. (Chicago: University of Chicago Press, 1969), 141.
10. Musto, *Catholic Peace Tradition*, 240.
11. Ellis, *American Catholicism*, 144.
12. Jay P. Dolan, *The American Catholic Experience: A History from Colonial Time to the Present* (New York: Doubleday, 1985), 342.
13. Joseph M. McShane, *Sufficiently Radical: Catholicism, Progressivism and the*

*Bishops' Program of 1919* (Washington, D.C.: Catholic University of America Press, 1986), 27.

14. Dolan, *American Catholic Experience*, 343.
15. Ibid., 346–369.
16. David J. O'Brien, *American Catholicism and Social Reform: The New Deal Years* (New York: Oxford University Press, 1968), 42.
17. John A. Ryan, *Social Doctrine in Action, a Personal History* (New York: Harper & Brothers, 1941), 137.
18. McShane, *Sufficiently Radical*, 41.
19. Musto, *Catholic Peace Tradition*, 171.
20. Harry W. Flannery, "CAIP Fights for International Peace," *U.S. Catholic* (September 1963): 25 and 26. See also John A. Ryan's autobiography, *Social Doctrine*, 140, 141, 145.
21. Francis L. Broderick, *Right Reverend New Dealer John A. Ryan* (New York: Macmillan, 1963), 104.
22. Flannery, "CAIP Fights," 25. The correspondence received by Flannery while researching CAIP is located in the CAIP Collection in the archives at Marquette University, hereafter referred to as AMU.
23. Ibid., 25, 26.
24. Broderick, *Right Reverend New Dealer*, 135.
25. Ibid., 160.
26. Ibid., 136.
27. Ibid., 77.
28. Ibid., 138.
29. AMU, CAIP Collection, "Notes on CAIP" by Raymond McGowan, 4 August 1958.
30. Ibid.
31. Ibid.
32. Broderick, *Right Reverend New Dealer*, 138.
33. AMU, CAIP Collection, "CAIP Constitution," Section 2.
34. O'Brien, *American Catholicism and Social Reform*, 121.
35. AMU, CAIP Collection, letter dated 1 March 1963, Mrs. R. M. Patterson to Harry W. Flannery.
36. Dennis Robb, "Specialized Catholic Action in the United States, 1936–1949: Ideology, Leadership, and Organization," Ph.D. diss., University of Minnesota, 1972, 32.
37. Flannery, "CAIP Fights," 27.
38. This point about type of membership is similar to the thesis of Sondra R. Herman, *Eleven Against War: Studies in American International Thought, 1898–1921* (Stanford, Calif.: Hoover Institution Press, 1969), ix.
39. AMU, CAIP Collection, letter dated 2 February 1963, George Shuster to Harry W. Flannery.
40. Flannery, "CAIP Fights," 27.
41. AMU, CAIP Collection, "Summary of CAIP Committee Work," Section 1, 6.

42. AMU, CAIP Collection, "A History of the Catholic Association for International Peace 1927–1953," by Clarence L. Hohl, Jr., 22; see John A. Ryan's *International Ethics* (Washington, D.C.: Paulist Press, 1928).
43. AMU, CAIP Collection, letters to Ms. Elizabeth Sweeney.
44. AMU, CAIP Collection, letters during 1930s, Anna Dill Gamble to Elizabeth Sweeney.
45. AMU, CAIP Collection, letters during 1930s, Mary Workman to Elizabeth Sweeney.
46. AMU, CAIP Collection, "Minutes of the Executive Committee," 27 December 1928, and 22 April 1930.
47. AMU, CAIP Collection, letter dated 5 April 1935, Sister Rose de Lima to Elizabeth Sweeney.
48. AMU, CAIP Collection, letters dated 9 May 1935 and 28 October 1936, Sister Rose de Lima to Elizabeth Sweeney. Also a typed page announcing the two meetings on November 20 at St. Elizabeth College in New Jersey and at Rosary College in River Forest, Illinois.
49. *Congressional Record*, 71st Cong., 3rd Sess., 1931, 74: 2263–2267.
50. Norman Krause Herzfeld, "Working for Peace," *Voice of St. Jude* (December 1954), n.p.
51. AMU, CAIP Collection, letter dated 19 April 1933, Patrick J. Ward to Elizabeth Sweeney.
52. George Q. Flynn, *American Catholics and the Roosevelt Presidency 1932–1936* (Lexington, Ky.: University of Kentucky Press, 1968), 150.
53. Ryan, *Social Doctrine*, 214, 215. Broderick in his biography of Ryan, *Right Reverend New Dealer*, states that Ryan resigned from NCPW because it was too pacifist.
54. Ryan, *Social Doctrine*.
55. AMU, CAIP Collection, letter dated 26 June 1929, Franziskus Stratmann, O.P., to Elizabeth Sweeney.
56. AMU, CAIP Collection, "Summary of CAIP Work 1927 to 1952," 7.
57. Ibid.
58. Broderick, *Right Reverend New Dealer*, 233, 234.
59. *New York Times*, 16 October 1939, cited in Charles J. Tull, *Father Coughlin and the New Deal* (Syracuse, N.Y.: Syracuse University Press, 1965), 217.
60. Ryan, *Social Doctrine in Action*, 216, 217.
61. George Q. Flynn, *Roosevelt and Romanism: Catholics and American Diplomacy 1937–1945* (Westport, Conn.: Greenwood Press, 1976), 189.
62. AMU, CAIP Collection, Hohl, "A History of the Catholic Association . . . ," 55.
63. In this chapter I have presented a general interpretation of Coughlin's relationship to the Catholic peace movement. To achieve this interpretation I have consulted a number of studies on Coughlin. See O'Brien, *American Catholicism and Social Reform*; Tull, *Father Coughlin*; David H. Bennett, *Demagogues of the Depression: American Radicals and the Union Party, 1932–36* (New Brunswick, N.J.: Rutgers University Press, 1969); Aaron Abell, *American Catholicism and Social Action*

(1960, reprint Notre Dame, Ind.: University of Notre Dame Press, 1963); Sheldon Marcus, *Father Coughlin: The Tumultuous Life of the Priest of the Little Flower* (Boston: Little, Brown, 1973); Alan Brinkley, *Voices of Protest: Huey Long, Father Coughlin, and the Great Depression* (New York: Knopf, 1982); Craig A. Newton, "Father Coughlin and His National Union for Social Justice," *Southwestern Social Science Quarterly*, 41 (December 1960): 341–349; and James P. Shenton, "The Coughlin Movement and the New Deal," *Political Science Quarterly*, 73 (September 1958): 353–373. I have also consulted twenty pamphlets written by Coughlin and his newspaper, *Social Justice*, 1937–1942. Pamphlets and newspaper are located in the archives at the University of Notre Dame.

64. *Catholic Worker*, September 1933, and April 1935, cited in O'Brien, *American Catholics and Social Reform*, 195.
65. Dorothy Day's books are mainly autobiographical: *From Union Square to Rome* (Silver Spring, Md.: Presentation of the Faith Press, 1939); *Houses of Hospitality* (New York: Sheed & Ward, 1939); *The Long Loneliness* (New York: Harper, 1952); and *Loaves and Fishes* (New York: Harper & Row, 1963). There is no autobiography by Peter Maurin. There are two biographies, however, Arthur Sheehan, *Peter Maurin: Gay Believer: The Biography of an Unusual and Saintly Man* (New York: Hanover House, 1959), and Marc H. Ellis, *Peter Maurin: Prophet in the Twentieth Century* (New York: Paulist Press, 1981).
66. Day, *The Long Loneliness*, 166.
67. Herman, *Eleven Against War*, ix.
68. The major influences were Benedictine Virgil Michel, Monsignor Paul Hanley Furfey, Tolstoy, Berdyaev, and Emmanuel Mounier.
69. *Catholic Worker*, October 1939 and June 1940.
70. A complete study of American Catholics' reaction to the Spanish Civil War is found in the works of J. David Valaik: "American Catholic Dissenters and the Spanish Civil War," *Catholic Historical Review* 53 (January 1968): 537–546 and "Catholics, Neutrality, and the Spanish Embargo, 1937–1939," *Journal of American History* 54 (June 1967): 73–85.
71. *Catholic Worker*, May 1935.
72. Interview with Dorothy Day, 24 June 1971: Dorothy stated that there was never any significant cooperation with other peace groups until the 1950s.
73. *Catholic Worker*, April 1934, January 1936, and March 1937.
74. Ibid., July–August 1939.
75. Ibid.
76. Ibid., December 1934, also cited in O'Brien, *American Catholicism and Social Reform*, 202.
77. *Catholic Worker*, May 1934.
78. Ibid., July–August 1935, July 1936, May 1937, and January 1938.
79. Ibid., May 1936.
80. Ibid., January 1938.
81. Ibid., October 1938.
82. Charles Chatfield, *For Peace and Justice: Pacifism in America, 1914–1941* (Knoxville: University of Tennessee Press, 1971), 325.

83. "War," *Catholic Encyclopedia*, vol. 15 (New York: Encyclopedia Press, 1913), gives Charles Mackey's definition of the just war criteria and presents it as normative. "War," *New Catholic Encyclopedia*, vol. 19 (New York: McGraw-Hill, 1967), quotes Paul Ramsey: "It has been observed that according to recent papal teaching (Pius XII and John XXIII) there is no longer any just war theory, because these popes have withdrawn the right of war in the situations to which these tests or conditions had reference, i.e., offensive war. This means that contemporary moral teaching represents both a continuation and a radical adjustment of traditional teaching on just warfare."

84. "Dorothy Day Describes the Launching of the *Catholic Worker* and the Movement Behind It, May 1933," cited in John Tracy Ellis, ed., *Documents of American Catholic History*, 2 (Chicago: H. Regnery, 1967), 629.

## 2: Dorothy Day

1. Chatfield, *For Peace and Justice*, 7.
2. Dwight Macdonald, "The Foolish Things of the World—II," *New Yorker*, 17 (11 October 1952): 40.
3. Ibid., 38.
4. William D. Miller, *Dorothy Day: A Biography* (New York: Harper and Row, 1982), 1.
5. Dorothy Day as quoted in Eileen Egan, "Dorothy Day: Pilgrim of Peace," in Patrick G. Coy, ed., *A Revolution of the Heart: Essays on the Catholic Worker* (Philadelphia: Temple University Press, 1988), 71.
6. Ibid., 49–50.
7. Mel Piehl, "Politics of Free Obedience," in Coy, *A Revolution of the Heart*, 179.
8. Macdonald, "The Foolish Things," 40.
9. As quoted in Macdonald, "The Foolish Things," 40–41.
10. Quotation in Day, *Long Loneliness*, 149–150.
11. Robert Coles, *Dorothy Day: A Radical Devotion* (Reading, Mass.: Addison-Wesley, 1987), 71.
12. Ibid., 62.
13. Piehl, "Politics of Free Obedience," 199.
14. William D. Miller, *A Harsh and Dreadful Love*, 56
15. Miller, *Dorothy Day*, 247.
16. Egan, "Dorothy Day: Pilgrim," 73.
17. Interview with Eileen Egan, 29 November 1990. Egan stated that Day's use of the term Catholic anarchist always upset her. She asked Day why she did not use the term Catholic personalist and Day's response was that she called herself a Catholic anarchist to wake people up and make them think.
18. Coles, *Dorothy Day: A Radical Devotion*, 96.
19. Miller, *A Harsh and Dreadful Love*, 14.
20. Miller, *Dorothy Day*, 247.
21. Dwight Macdonald, "The Foolish Things of the World—I," *New Yorker* 27 (4 October 1952): 46.
22. Miller, *A Harsh and Dreadful Love*, 3.

23. Mel Piehl, *Breaking Bread: The Catholic Worker and the Origin of Catholic Radicalism in America* (Philadelphia: Temple University Press, 1982), 198.
24. Marc H. Ellis, *Peter Maurin*, 24.
25. John C. Cort, "Dorothy Day at 75," *Commonweal* 97 (23 February 1973): 476.
26. Dorothy Day, *Long Loneliness*, 206 as quoted in Egan, "Dorothy Day: Pilgrim," 77.
27. Piehl, *Breaking Bread*, 191–193.
28. Miller, *A Harsh and Dreadful Love*, 139.
29. *Catholic Worker*, September 1936, as quoted in Nancy L. Roberts, *Dorothy Day and the Catholic Worker* (Albany: State University of New York Press, 1984), 119.
30. Piehl, *Breaking Bread*, 194.
31. Marc H. Ellis, *Peter Maurin*, 89, 90, 91.
32. As quoted in Miller, *A Harsh and Dreadful Love*, 166.
33. Ibid., 168.
34. Ibid., 174.
35. Gordon Zahn, "Leaven of Love and Justice," *America*, 127 (11 November 1972): 383.
36. *Catholic Worker*, April 1938.
37. Swarthmore College Peace Collection (hereafter referred to as SCPC) ACCO Collection, PAX Manifesto.
38. Dorothy Day, *Loaves and Fishes*, 60.
39. *Catholic Worker*, May 1943. Perhaps the reading here is too beneficent toward church authorities.
40. Piehl, *Breaking Bread*, 195.
41. Ibid.
42. U.S. Congress, House Committee on Military Affairs, Report of the Hearings anent H.R. 10132, 30 July 1940, 152–160.
43. Ibid., 299–323.
44. Egan, "Dorothy Day: Pilgrim," 79.
45. Ibid.
46. Leslie S. Rothenberg, *The Draft and You* (Garden City, N.Y.: Anchor Books, 1968), 11.
47. Ibid.
48. Day, *The Long Loneliness*, 304.
49. Ibid.
50. Ibid.
51. Ibid., 305.
52. "Editorial," *Catholic Worker*, January 1942.
53. For more about Day's sabbatical, see Egan, "Dorothy Day: Pilgrim," 85–87.

### 3: World War II and the Just War Tradition

1. Cardinal Spellman as quoted in Lawrence S. Wittner, *Rebels Against War: The American Peace Movement, 1941–1960* (New York: Columbia University Press, 1969), 36.

2. Musto, *Catholic Peace Tradition*, 175.
3. Ibid., 176.
4. Ibid., 177.
5. Ibid., 185.
6. "Atomic Bomb," excerpt from *l'Observatore Romano*, 10 August 1945, in *Tablet*, 18 August 1945, 78.
7. Earl Boyea, "The National Catholic Welfare Conference: An Experience in Episcopal Leadership, 1935–1945, Ph.D. diss., Catholic University of America, 1987, 179. See pp. 159–179 for his complete coverage of the "Bombing of Rome."
8. George Weigel, *Tranquillitas Ordinis: The Present Failure and Future Promise of American Catholic Thought on War and Peace* (New York: Oxford University Press, 1987), 58.
9. Musto, *Catholic Peace Tradition*, 246.
10. Flynn, *Roosevelt and Romanism*, 77, as quoted in Boyea, *National Catholic Welfare*, 123.
11. Boyea, *National Catholic Welfare*, 123.
12. Ibid., 124.
13. Ibid., 130.
14. Paul Comly French, *We Won't Murder* (New York: Hastings House, 1940), 157.
15. "National Catholic College Poll," *America* 62 (11 November 1939): 116–119, and 62 (18 November 1939): 144–147.
16. Lillian Schlissel, *Conscience in America* (New York: E. P. Dutton, 1968), 219.
17. Ibid.
18. Paul Riley, a graduate student in the Department of Religion at Temple University while doing research for Dr. Elwyn Smith on the subject of American Catholicism and conscientious objection from 1776 to 1924, found only four Catholics who were COs in World War I: John Dunn, Francis X. Hennessy, Christian Lellig, and Benjamin Salmon. Ammon Hennacy, a CO during World War I, later converted to Catholicism.
19. U. S. Selective Service System, *Conscientious Objection*, 1950, vol. I, 53, 60, 105, 117, 263, 320,
20. SCPC, NSBRO Collection, Box G-76. Dorothy Day in an article, "Women and War," *Catholic C.O.*, Fall 1946 (also cited in Egan, "Pilgrim," 85), wrote that there were two Catholic COs during World War I and during World War II, 154 Catholic COs in jail and 200 Catholic COs in CPS.
21. Wittner, *Rebels against War*, 70.
22. Clarence Pickett as quoted in Ibid.
23. Schlissel, *Conscience in America*, 225.
24. SCPC, NSBRO Collection, Box G-76.
25. Arthur Sheehan visited Paul Comly French, director of NSBRO, who told him to observe the American Friends CPS camp at Cooperstown, which had a budget of $50,000 a year. Sheehan believed that the Catholic Worker could run a camp for $15,000 annually. Archbishop John T. McNicholas of Cincinnati gave $300 and the American Civil Liberties Union gave $500. Four other bishops helped

financially: Karl J. Alter, bishop of Toledo; Francis J. Beckman, archbishop of Dubuque; John B. Peterson, bishop of Manchester; and Gerald Shaughnessy, S.M., bishop of Seattle. Other sources of revenue came in small donations of $25 or less.

26. Gordon C. Zahn, *Another Part of the War: The Camp Simon Story* (Amherst: University of Massachusetts Press, 1979), xiii.

27. Ibid., 260.

28. *Catholic Worker*, December 1941.

29. SCPC, ACCO Collection, letter from Dwight Larrowe to Miss E. S. Brenton dated 22 July 1942, for an appeal for funds. Larrowe stated that thirty-nine men were at Stoddard and that he was running the camp at $16 a month per man rather than the prescribed $35. He had spent $5,000 in the past year and needed two to three times that amount for the next year.

30. Day, *Loaves and Fishes*, 64.

31. Zahn, *Another Part of the War*, x.

32. Interview with Richard Leonard of LaSalle College, Philadelphia, a Catholic CO at Stoddard, Warner, and Rosewood, on Tuesday, 4 November 1969.

33. Theodore Pojar, Robert Lindorfer, and Francis Bates were three such Catholic COs. See the *Catholic Worker*, May 1942.

34. Zahn, *Another Part of the War*, ix.

35. Ibid., xi.

36. Ibid., 219.

37. Gordon Zahn, *War, Conscience and Dissent* (New York: Hawthorn Books, 1967), 152.

38. *Catholic Worker*, May 1943.

39. Telephone conversation between Arthur Sheehan and the author on 21 October 1969: Mr. Sheehan indicated that the decision to close the CPS camp at Warner was not simply a matter of finances as Wittner in *Rebels Against War* (54) contends.

40. SCPC, NSBRO Collection, Box A-44.

41. Wittner, *Rebels against War*, 60.

42. SCPC, ACCO Collection, Memorandum.

43. *Catholic CO*, October 1944. This newspaper is available on microfilm at the University of San Francisco.

44. *Catholic Worker*, June, 1948.

45. Mulford Q. Sibley and Philip E. Jacob, *Conscription of Conscience* (Ithaca, N.Y.: Cornell University Press, 1952), 468–475.

46. *Catholic CO*, January–March 1946.

47. J. F. Powers, the noted American author of *Morte D'Urban*, is an example of such a Catholic CO.

48. *Catholic Worker*, April–June 1944, and letter from Arthur Sheehan to author dated 30 October 1969.

49. Zahn, *Another Part of the War*, 251–252.

50. John Courtney Ford, S.J., "Morality of Obliteration Bombing," *Theological Studies* 5 (September, 1944): 267.

51. Ibid.
52. Ibid.
53. Ibid., 305.
54. Ibid., 268–269.
55. Ibid., 271.
56. *Catholic Worker*, October 1944. See also Paul H. Furfey, "Bombing of Non-Combatants Is Murder," *Catholic CO*, July–September 1945, and *The Mystery of Iniquity* (Milwaukee: Bruce, 1944), 165–166.
57. "Atomic Bomb," *Commonweal* 43 (31 August 1945): 468.
58. J. M. Gillis, "Editorial Comment," *Catholic World*, 166 (September, 1945): 449–450.
59. *Catholic Worker*, September 1945.
60. Wittner, *Rebels against War*, 126–28.
61. AMU, CAIP Collection, "Summary of CAIP Committee Work—End of War to 1952," 21.
62. Ibid.
63. Wittner, *Rebels against War*, 128–29.

### 4: The Birth of Nonviolence

1. Wittner, *Rebels against War*, 213.
2. Joan V. Bondurant, *Conquest of Violence: The Gandhian Philosophy of Conflict* (Berkeley: University of California, 1969), 8 and 9.
3. Ibid., 36.
4. Wittner, *Rebels against War*, 62–96. He gives a detailed account of the acts of nonviolent resistance performed by radical pacifists during the war.
5. Ibid., 156, 157.
6. Ibid., 163.
7. Gordon C. Zahn, "The Future of the Catholic Peace Movement," *Commonweal*, 99 (28 December 1973): 338.
8. AMU, CAIP Collection, Memorandum entitled "Organizations to be Represented at Paris," dated 9 July 1948. Other peace groups that held observer status within the United Nations were the Carnegie Endowment for International Peace, Women's Action Committee for Lasting Peace, and the pacifist group, Women's International League for Peace and Freedom.
9. AMU, CAIP Collection. Miss Rita Schaefer represented not only NCWC and CAIP, but also the National Catholic Conference of Women.
10. AMU, CAIP Collection, letter dated 13 April 1948, John Eppstein to Miss Rita Schaefer. John Eppstein, author of *The Catholic Tradition of the Law of Nations*, was director and editor of the British Society for International Understanding.
11. AMU, CAIP Collection, "Summary of the CAIP Committee Work, 1927 to 1952," 25.
12. AMU, "CAIP Collection," Annual Report, 30 June 1949–30 June 1950, 2.
13. Ibid., 25.

14. Michael O'Neill, "The American Catholic Bishops and Foreign Policy—Vietnam and Latin America," Ph.D. diss., University of Edinburgh, 1974, 84.
15. As quoted in ibid., 85.
16. Anne Klejment, "In the Lion's Den: The Social Catholicism of Daniel and Philip Berrigan, 1955–1965," Ph.D. diss., State University of New York at Binghamton, 1980, 106.
17. Miller, A Harsh and Dreadful Love, 219, 220.
18. John Cogley, "A Harsh and Dreadful Love," America 127 (11 November 1972): 395.
19. Piehl, Breaking Bread, 205.
20. Ibid., 206–208.
21. Miller, A Harsh and Dreadful Love, 225.
22. Piehl, Breaking Bread, 205.
23. As quoted in Roberts, Dorothy Day, 140.
24. Ibid., 141.
25. Ibid.
26. Harrington as quoted in ibid., 146, 147.
27. Catholic Worker as quoted in Miller, A Harsh and Dreadful Love, 229.
28. Ibid., 234.
29. Bruce Cook, "Dorothy Day and the Catholic Worker," U.S. Catholic (March 1966): 29, as quoted in Roberts, Dorothy Day, 143.
30. Roberts, Dorothy Day, 143–145.
31. John Courtney Murray as quoted in Donald E. Pelotte, John Courtney Murray: Theologian in Conflict (New York: Paulist Press, 1975), 28.
32. Ibid., 2.
33. Wittner, Rebels against War, 254.
34. John Courtney Murray, S.J., Morality and Modern War (New York: Council on Religion and International Affairs, 1959), 18.
35. Ibid., 15.
36. Ibid., 17.
37. Ibid.
38. In 1962, George Meany received CAIP's Annual Peace Award.
39. Letter dated 17 August 1972, George N. Shuster to author.
40. AMU, CAIP Collection, untitled typed memorandum by Harry W. Flannery.
41. James Douglass Collection (hereafter referred to as JDC), a copy of CAIP critique and cover letter dated 5 August 1964, William V. O'Brien to Most Rev. John J. Wright, D.D. JDC is all the written material of James Douglass from his lobbying efforts at the Second Vatican Council. The collection is in his possession.
42. William Nagle, ed., Morality and Modern Warfare: The State of the Question (Baltimore: Helicon Press, 1960), 6, 7.
43. Charles S. Thompson, ed., Morals and Missiles: Catholic Essays on the Problem of War Today (London: J. Clarke, 1961). This book includes essays by Canon F. H. Drinkwater, Dom Bede Griffiths, O.S.B., Christopher Hollis, Sir Compton Mackenzie, Archbishop Thomas D. Roberts, S.J., Franziskus Stratmann, O.P., and E. I. Watkin.

44. In July 1961, the Institute of World Polity at Georgetown University published the papers presented at the Second Annual Conference on Christian Political and Social Thought. The topic of the conference was "Christian Ethics and Nuclear Warfare." William V. O'Brien was one of the editors of the compendium. The conference noted that much of what had been accomplished through the centuries by way of the just war doctrine in providing limits to warfare collapsed in the nuclear age and that technically "aggressive" modern war became unjustifiable as Pius XII said in his Christmas address of 1944.

45. John C. Ford in "The Hydrogen Bombing of Cities," in Nagle, *Morality and Modern Warfare*, 98–103, bases his argument against the use of nuclear weapons as he did in his arguments against obliteration bombing on the rights of noncombatants. This position is adopted by the Second Vatican Council.

46. Donald J. Thorman, "The Christian's Conscience and Nuclear Warfare," *New City* (15 November 1962), reprint found in AMU, CAIP Collection. Thorman's article provided Donahue's definitions of the major approaches given in this summary.

47. "The moral or political principles on which our most critical decisions are to be made may, in themselves, be relatively simple, but the assumptions on which they are based are immensely complicated. It is not difficult to appeal to traditional norms of justice and law, and apply them to our present situation in such a way as to come up with logical and plausible conclusions. But the very plausibility of the conclusions tends to be the most dangerous thing about them, if we forget that they may be based on premises which we take to be axiomatic and which, in fact have been invalidated by recent developments of weapons technology. . . . There is a very serious danger that our most critical decisions may turn out to be no decisions at all, but only the end of a vicious circle of conjectures and gratuitous assumptions in which we unconsciously make the argument come out in favor of our own theory, our own favorite policy." Thomas Merton, *Breakthrough to Peace: Twelve Views on the Threat of Thermonuclear Extermination* (New York: New Directions, 1962), 219.

48. Wittner, *Rebels against War*, 244.

49. Ibid., 154–55; 247, 248.

50. Miller, *A Harsh and Dreadful Love*, 279.

51. Ammon Hennacy, *The Autobiography of a Catholic Anarchist* (New Jersey: Libertarian Press, 1952). Edition used by author.

52. Miller, *A Harsh and Dreadful Love*, 279.

53. Archives at University of Notre Dame, hereafter referred to as AUND, CPF Collection, letter dated 30 April 1980, Thomas Cornell to Professor William Miller.

54. Patrick G. Coy, "The One-Person Revolution of Ammon Hennacy," in Patrick G. Coy, ed., *A Revolution of the Heart: Essays on the Catholic Worker* (Philadelphia: Temple University Press, 1988), 134–136.

55. Hennacy as quoted in Coy, "The One-Person Revolution," 139.

56. Coy, "The One-Person Revolution," 141.

57. Ibid., 151.

58. As quoted in Coy, "One-Person Revolution, " 142.
59. Coy, "One-Person Revolution," 161.
60. AUND, CPF Collection, letter dated 30 April 1980, Thomas Cornell to Professor William Miller. Cornell goes on to state in the letter that when Ludlow announced his reevaluation of anarchism at the annual Labor Day weekend Pacifist Conference at Peter Maurin Farm on Staten Island, it caused quite a commotion and that the conference was suspended until 1963 when Cornell revived it. Ludlow published his reevaluation in the *Catholic Worker* in June 1955. Cornell agreed with Ludlow's reevaluation and disliked the use of the term anarchism and believed it should not be used since no one affiliated with the Catholic Worker knew what it meant or how to apply it. Cornell preferred the term personalism.
61. Hennacy, "Why I am a Catholic Anarchist," 3, as quoted in Coy, "One-Person Revolution," 162.
62. A spur to Hennacy's decision was a two-week fast in Glen Gardner, New Jersey, begun by Dave Dellinger and others, against the sending of troops to Korea. Hennacy wrote to Dellinger that he too would fast, but was unsympathetic to Dellinger's World Citizen emphasis. See Hennacy, *Autobiography*, 163.
63. A. J. Muste as quoted in Wittner, *Rebels against War*, 265. Wittner gives a very detailed description of the demonstration.
64. *Catholic Worker*, June 1960. A similar event occurred in London's Trafalgar Square where 75,000 people turned out in support of unilateral disarmament of nuclear weapons.
65. Ibid., April 1960.
66. AUND, CPF Collection, letter dated 30 April 1980, Thomas Cornell to Professor William Miller.
67. *Catholic Worker*, January 1962. Jean Morton, Nelson Barr, Bob Kaye, Charles Butterworth, Elain Paulson, Mark Samara, Carol Kramer, and Jim Forest were Catholic Worker participants. Thomas Merton wrote a letter of support that was published in the same issue.
68. Miller, *A Harsh and Dreadful Love*, 300, 301. Much of Miller's information on why Hennacy left is obtained from Dorothy Day's chapter on Hennacy in *Loaves and Fishes*.
69. Dorothy Day as quoted in Miller, *A Harsh and Dreadful Love*, 266.
70. James H. Forest, "No Longer Alone: The Catholic Peace Movement" in Thomas E. Quigley, ed., *American Catholics and Vietnam* (Grand Rapids, Mich.: Eerdmans Publishing Co., 1968), 144.
71. Address given by Archbishop Thomas D. Roberts, S.J., to a small group at Pendle Hill, Pennsylvania (a Quaker center), in the fall of 1970, attended by author.
72. William J. Gibbons, ed., *Pacem in Terris: Encyclical Letter of His Holiness Pope John XXIII* (New York: Macmillan, 1968), par. 127.
73. Ibid., par. 5.
74. Ibid., par. 48.
75. JDC, letter dated 13 August 1965, Thomas Merton to Archbishop George Flahiff states that Merton sent a copy of the letter to *Commonweal* for publication but it was rejected.

76. Thomas Merton, "In Acceptance of the PAX Medal, 1963" in Gordon C. Zahn, *Thomas Merton on Peace*, (New York: McCall, 1971), 257 and 258.

77. The original text in the first draft read as follows: "Although after all helps to peaceful discussion have been exhausted, it may not be illicit, when one's rights have been unjustly trammeled, to defend those rights against such unjust aggression by violence and force. Nevertheless, the use of arms, especially nuclear weapons whose effects are greater than can be imagined and therefore cannot be reasonably regulated by men, exceeds all just proportion and therefore must be judged most wicked before, God and man." See Floyd Anderson, ed., *The Council Daybook*, Session III (Washington, D.C.: National Catholic Welfare Conference, 1966), 243.

78. AMU, CAIP Collection, letter dated 14 March 1963, Harry W. Flannery to Victor C. Ferkiss.

79. JDC, copy of CAIP critique, p. 2 of alternative text section.

80. AMU, CAIP Collection.

81. Ellis, *American Catholicism*, 120–122.

82. AMU, CAIP Collection, Memorandum, "Morality, Nuclear War, and the Schema on the Church in the Modern World."

83. A text of a leaflet issued to explain the purpose of the fast is found in "Appeal to Rome," *Reconciliation Quarterly* (Fourth Quarter, 1965): 612–614.

84. James Douglass attained an M.A. degree in theology at Bellarmine College, and while at the school he became friends with Thomas Merton. After lobbying at the Council, he wrote *The Non-Violent Cross* (New York: Macmillan, 1966). In 1969, he was co-director of the Program in Non-Violence at the University of Notre Dame. In 1971, he wrote his second book *Resistance and Contemplation*. He has remained committed to a life of nonviolence.

85. James Douglass, *The Non-Violent Cross*, 134.

86. *Pastoral Constitution on the Church in the Modern World* (Huntington, Ind.: Our Sunday Visitor, 1968), 85.

87. JDC, copy of the intervention. The intervention was also signed by Archbishop George Flahiff of Winnepeg and English Bishops Gordon Wheeler and Charles Grant.

88. JDC, letter dated 28 November 1964, James Douglass to Philip Scharper. Douglass based much of the final version of the text on the suggestions of Philip Scharper, another member of PAX. Douglass had also consulted many theologians on the wording of the intervention. Fathers Bernard Haring, Yves Congar, and Gregory Baum expressed virtually complete agreement with the text. Father Karl Rahner was reluctant to condemn the concept of a total war deterrent for mainly political reasons and Father Charles Davis wanted more on the responsibilities of the heads of states rather than the emphasis on conscientious objection.

89. JDC, Intervention of Bishop John Taylor (Stockholm, Sweden).

90. JDC, copy of Challenge dated 2 December 1965.

91. *Pastoral Constitution*, 87, 88.

92. JDC, letter dated, 2 February 1966, Donald Quinn to James Douglass. Donald

Quinn at the time was editor of the *St. Louis Review*, the official newspaper of the Archdiocese of St. Louis.

93. Douglass, *The Non-Violent Cross*, 117.
94. Ibid., 118. For a complete text of Cardinal Ritter's Intervention, see pp. 118 and 119.
95. *Pastoral Constitution*, 87.
96. The accepted compromise is very similar to the arguments developed by the American theologian John Ford, S.J., in response to obliteration bombing and the dropping of the atomic bomb on Hiroshima. See Chapter III.
97. JDC, contains copies of both interventions. In the intervention during the third session, Archbishop Roberts called attention to the fact that Catholics have been denied this right. In the fourth session he devoted his intervention to the case of Franz Jagerstatter. See Gordon Zahn, *In Solitary Witness: The Life and Death of Franz Jagerstatter*, (New York: Holt, Rinehart & Winston, 1964).
98. JDC, letter dated 13 August 1965, Thomas Merton to Archbishop Flahiff.
99. *The Council Daybook*, 37.
100. *Pastoral Constitution*, 86.

### 5: Thomas Merton at the Crossroads of Peace

1. The original unexpurgated manuscript of *The Seven Storey Mountain* is located in the Boston College library.
2. James Thomas Baker, *Thomas Merton: Social Critic* (Lexington: University Press of Kentucky, 1971), 13.
3. This paragraph is a paraphrasing of a letter, dated 17 June 1968, written by Thomas Merton to a student working on her master's thesis in order to assist her in organizing his writings.
4. Letter from Daniel Berrigan to author, dated 12 June 1969.
5. For the best account of Merton's writings on the Cold War and Marxism, see Baker, *Thomas Merton: Social Critic*, 66–97.
6. For accounts of Merton's use of Gog and Magog, see ibid., 70–89, and Gordon C. Zahn's introduction to *Thomas Merton on Peace*.
7. Thomas Merton, *Peace in the Post-Christian Era* (unpublished, mimeographed copy, 1962), 71, 72. A copy is at the Thomas Merton Studies Center at Bellarmine College in Louisville, Kentucky. The author used James Forest's copy.
8. David W. Givey, *The Social Thought of Thomas Merton: The Way of Nonviolence and Peace for the Future* (Chicago: Franciscan Herald Press, 1983), 54. Merton felt that very little was actually known about what really took place in the thinking of the church as this time, the time when he believed "Christiandom went into business." The author is grateful to James Forest, who provided access to his personal correspondence with Merton over a ten-year period. This correspondence was located at Regina Laudis Monastery, Bethlehem, Connecticut, when the author consulted it.
9. Thomas Merton, *Seeds of Destruction* (New York: Macmillan, 1964), 151.

10. Thomas Merton in Gordon C. Zahn, ed., *The Nonviolent Alternative* (New York: Farrar Strauss & Giroux, 1980), 94, 95.
11. Ibid., 95.
12. Ibid.
13. Merton as quoted in Powaski, *Thomas Merton on Nuclear Weapons*, 15, 16.
14. Merton, *Peace in the Post-Christian Era*.
15. Thomas P. McDonnell, ed., *A Thomas Merton Reader* (New York: Harcourt Brace & World, 1962), 291.
16. Ibid., 295.
17. Merton in Zahn, *The Nonviolent Alternative*, 92.
18. Ibid., 93.
19. Merton, *Breakthrough to Peace*, 108.
20. Merton, *Seeds of Destruction*, 129.
21. Michael Mott, *The Seven Mountains of Thomas Merton* (Boston: Houghton Mifflin, 1984), 375, 376.
22. Merton in his *Restricted Journals* as quoted in Mott, *The Seven Mountains*, 374.
23. Ibid., 400.
24. Givey, *The Social Thought of Thomas Merton* 5, 6.
25. Merton, *Seeds of Destruction*, 91.
26. Thomas Merton, "Peace and Revolution: A Footnote from Ulysses," *Peace*, 4 (Fall/Winter, 1968–1969).
27. Merton, *Seeds of Destruction*, 90.
28. Ibid., 123.
29. Thomas Merton, *Faith and Violence* (Notre Dame, Ind.: University of Notre Dame Press, 1968), 8. It is interesting to note that the Catholic peace activists are often admonished for refusing to criticize the use of violence by "revolutionary" groups or to impose restrictions upon others whose leadership they do not share.
30. L. C. McHugh, S.J., "Ethics at the Shelter Doorway," *America*, 105, no. 27 (30 September 1961): 824–826.
31. Interview with James Forest, 3 December 1972.
32. Ibid.
33. Zahn in his introduction to *Thomas Merton on Peace*, reduces and dismisses Merton's qualifications of pacifism as merely a matter of semantics.
34. Ibid., xxvi.
35. Ibid., xxvii.
36. Baker, *Thomas Merton: Social Critic*, 116.
37. Ibid.
38. Merton as quoted in Powaski, *Thomas Merton on Nuclear Weapons*, 94.
39. Merton, *Seeds of Destruction*, 132.
40. Ibid.
41. Ibid., 140, 141.
42. Ibid., 136.
43. Merton, "Blessed are the Meek: The Christian Roots of Non-Violence," in Zahn, *Thomas Merton on Peace*, 210.
44. Ibid.

45. Merton, "Peace and Revolution: A Footnote from Ulysses," 75.
46. Zahn, Introduction, *Thomas Merton on Peace.*
47. Preface to the Japanese edition of *No Man Is An Island,* quoted in James H. Forest, "Thomas Merton's Struggle with Peacemaking," in Gerald Twomey, ed., *Thomas Merton: Prophet in the Belly of a Paradox* (New York: Paulist Press, 1978), 21.
48. For details on these specific events refer to Zahn, Introduction, *Thomas Merton on Peace.*
49. Merton, *Faith and Violence,* 7.
50. Thomas Merton, "The Christian in World Crisis," in Zahn, *Thomas Merton on Peace,* 25.
51. Thomas Merton, *Life and Holiness* (New York: Herder and Herder, 1963), 114.
52. Merton, *Seeds of Destruction,* 122.
53. Thomas Merton, *Raids on the Unspeakable* (New York: Farrar, Straus and Giroux, 1961).
54. Merton, *Faith and Violence,* 108.
55. Ibid., 110.
56. Copy of statement given to author by James Forest.
57. Merton, "Peace and Revolution," 10.
58. Thomas Merton, Preface to Pierre Regamey, *Non-Violence and the Christian Conscience* (London: Herder and Herder, 1966), 12–14.
59. Merton, *Faith and Violence,* 10.
60. Merton, Preface, in Regamey, *Non-Violence and the Christian Conscience,* 13.
61. *Ibid,* 14.
62. Thomas Merton, *New Seeds of Contemplation* (New York: New Directions, 1961), 115.
63. Thomas Merton, *Disputed Questions* (New York: Farrar, Straus and Cudahy, 1960), 115.
64. Thomas Merton, "Christianity and Mass Movements," *Cross Currents,* 14 (Summer 1969): 203, 204.
65. Givey, *The Social Thought of Thomas Merton,* 107.

### 6: The Catholic Peace Movement and Vietnam

1. "Address of Pope Paul VI to the General Assembly of the United Nations," *Catholic Mind,* 63 (November 1965): 7.
2. Ibid., 8, 9.
3. Musto, *Catholic Peace Tradition,* 193.
4. David J. O'Brien in "American Catholic Opposition to the Vietnam War: A Preliminary Assessment," in Thomas A. Shannon, ed., *War or Peace?* (Maryknoll, N.Y.: Orbis, 1980), contends that "the Vatican did not succeed in detaching itself completely from the Cold War or from association with the Western powers. . . . In Vietnam, the Pope's desire to play the role of peacemaker, flawed at the start by the diplomatic approach, could only appear hypocritical to those who believed not simply that the war was evil, but that the primary responsibility for that evil lay with the governments of South Vietnam and the United States." 124.

5. Dolan, *American Catholic Experience*, 426.
6. Ibid., 446.
7. Ibid., 447.
8. Henry J. Browne, "Groping for Relevance in an Urban Parish: St Gregory the Great, New York, 1968–70" (unpublished paper), 5 as quoted in Dolan, *American Catholic Experience*, 449.
9. See David J. O'Brien, "Styles of Public Catholicism," in O'Brien, *Public Catholicism* (New York: Macmillan, 1989), in which he delineates three styles: evangelical, immigrant, and republican.
10. James Terence Fisher, *The Catholic Counterculture in America 1933–1962* (Chapel Hill: University of North Carolina Press, 1989), 205–248.
11. Dr. Martin Luther King, Jr., as quoted in Mitchell Kent Hall, "Clergy and Laymen Concerned About Vietnam: A Study of Opposition to the Vietnam War," Ph.D. diss., University of Kentucky, 1987, 79.
12. O'Brien, "Catholic Opposition to the Vietnam War," 120.
13. O'Brien, *Public Catholicism*, 238, 239.
14. Charles DeBenedetti and Charles Chatfield, *An American Ordeal: The Antiwar Movement of the Vietnam Era* (Syracuse, N.Y.: Syracuse University Press, 1990), 86.
15. Ibid., 52.
16. Ibid., 68.
17. Mark Clodfelter, *The Limits of Air Power: The American Bombing of North Vietnam* (New York: Free Press, 1989). The United States dropped 6.3 million tons of bombs and other aerial munitions on Indochina in the seven years beginning in 1965. As Clodfelter points out after the greatest amount of bombing and shelling in the history of warfare, peace without victory was the result.
18. AUND, CPF Collection, letter dated 22 July 1964, Thomas Merton to Jim Forest.
19. Musto, *Catholic Peace Tradition*, 185.
20. "1970: A Year of Concern for all CO's," *The Reporter for Conscience's Sake* 27 (January 1970): 2. This coincides with the report dated 11 May 1970 sent to author from NSBRO which gives the number of Catholic COs as of February 1966 as 17, as of November 1968 as 69, and as of September 1969 as 175.
21. AUND, CPF Collection, Thomas Cornell, "The First 10 Years of the CPF," *CPF Bulletin* (February 1975).
22. Ibid.
23. In my first interview with Dorothy Day, I asked her about Daniel Berrigan and his role in the Catholic Worker movement. Dorothy's immediate response was sharp when she contended that she hardly knew Dan. All she knew was that he dedicated a book to her, invited her to speak at LeMoyne College, and took all her men away from the Catholic Worker into the peace movement. Interview occurred at a rally at St. Ignatius Church in Baltimore two days before the opening of the trial of the Catonsville Nine, 1969. Day was at the rally to speak and support the Catonsville Nine.

24. AUND, CPF Collection, *CPF Bulletin* (June 1965). The first list of sponsors appeared as follows: Baron Antoine Allard, Daniel Berrigan, S.J., Dorothy Day, Leslie Dewart, James W. Douglass, Rev. William H. DuBay, Hermene Evans, Edward T. Gargen, John Howard Griffin, Dom Bede Griffiths, Rev. Robert W. Hovda, Edward M. Keating, Robert Lax, Justus George Lawler, Rev. Robert McDole, Rev. Thomas Merton, Rev. Peter J. Riga, STD, Archbishop Roberts, S.J., Karl Stern, Anton Wallach-Clifford, Gordon Zahn. The co-chairs were listed as James H. Forest, Philip Berrigan, SSJ, and Martin J. Corbin. The education advisor was listed as Thomas Cornell and the field secretary as John Lee.

25. AUND, CPF Collection, The Catholic Peace Fellowship, membership pamphlet.

26. AUND, CPF Collection, Cornell, "The First 10 Years."

27. AUND, CPF Collection, letter dated 4 November 1968, Jim Forest to Tom Cornell.

28. AUND, CPF Collection, letter dated 2 July 1969, Alfred Hassler, executive secretary of FOR, to Tom Cornell. In 1975, Tom Cornell recorded that the $10,000 debt of CPF to FOR was paid in full, AUND, CPF Collection.

29. AUND, CPF Collection, letter dated 22 September 1969, Tom Cornell to Jim Forest.

30. Tom Cornell remained very close to Dorothy Day and visited the Catholic Worker at least once a week until her death. Jim Forest had fallen from Day's good graces in 1967 when he divorced his wife and married Linda Hassler, the daughter of Al Hassler, executive director of FOR.

31. AUND, CPF Collection, letter dated 22 September 1969, Tom Cornell to Jim Forest.

32. AUND, CPF Collection, Cornell, "The First 10 Years." Volunteers were Abraham Bassord, a Presbyterian seminarian; Paul Velde, once of *Commonweal*; Maggie Geddes; Ken Curtain and Joanne Sheehan, members of the Christian Appalachian Project in Kentucky; and many others such as Jack Doyle, Paul Frazier, Janet Gallagher, Beth Gregory, Mary McCarthy, Bob Oliva, Jack Riles, Mike Murphy, Walter Hanns, Mary Sheehan, Rick Gaumer, Bill Ofenloch, Brendan Coyne, Bill Dorfer, Steve Kurzyna, and Lyle Young.

33. Forest, "No longer alone," 146.

34. As quoted in ibid., 147.

35. *Peace and Vietnam*, 18 November 1966, *In the Name of Peace: Collective Statements of the United States Catholic Bishops on War and Peace, 1919–1980* (Washington, D.C.: U.S. Catholic Conference, 1983), 25–29.

36. Forest, "No longer alone," 147.

37. Gordon C. Zahn, "The Scandal of Silence," *Commonweal* 95, no. 5 (22 October, 1971): 81, and Musto, *Catholic Peace Tradition*, 255.

38. Forest, "No longer alone," 147.

39. Interview with James Forest, 3 December 1972.

40. Catherine Swann, "Burning a Draft Card," *Catholic Worker*, November 1965. For this section on burning draft cards, most of the factual data is taken from John L.

LeBrun, "The Role of the Catholic Worker Movement in American Pacifism, 1933–1972," unpublished Ph.D. diss., Case Western Reserve, 1974.

41. Michael Ferber and Staughton Lynd, *The Resistance* (Boston: Beacon Press, 1971), 3, 4, 9, 10; and Dwight Macdonald, "Why Destroy Draft Cards?" *Catholic Worker*, November 1965.

42. Edward Forand, "Christie Street," *Catholic Worker*, December 1964.

43. *New York Times*, 11 August 1965, p. 14 and 1 September 1965, p. 17.

44. Tom Cornell, "Life and Death on the Streets of New York," *Catholic Worker*, November 1965; Cornell, "Not the Smallest Grain," in Ferber and Lynd, *The Resistance*, 39, 40. Cornell's statement printed in full as "Why I am Burning My Draft Card," *Commonweal*, 73 (19 November 1965): 205.

45. Schlissel, *Conscience in America*, reprints United States v. Miller, District and Circuit Court Decisions, 1965–66, 275–84.

46. The complete statement was printed in the *Catholic Worker*, March 1966. See also Jim Wilson, "Chrystie Street," 12 January 1966, and the *New York Times*, 12 January 1966, p.8 and 5 March 1966, p.21.

47. "Draft Card Burners Convicted," *Catholic Worker*, December 1966; "CPF Head Found Guilty in Draft Card Case," *Fellowship* 32 (October, 1966): 1; "CPF Head Appeals Six-Month Sentence," *Fellowship*, 33 (February 1967): 3; and *New York Times*, 25 October 1966, p. 11 and 19 July 1967, p. 42.

48. James H. Forest, "In Time of War," in *Delivered into Resistance*, (New Haven, Conn.: The Catonsville Nine-Milwaukee Fourteen Defense Committee, 1969), 5–7. There is no way to document the exact number of draft board raids by the ultra-resistance.

49. DeBenedetti and Chatfield, *The American Ordeal*, 296, 297.

50. Ibid., 108.

51. As quoted in Thomas J. Schlereth, *The University of Notre Dame: A Portrait of Its History and Campus* (Notre Dame: University of Notre Dame Press, 1976), 215. For this section on student unrest during the Vietnam War, the factual data is taken from Schlereth's book, pp. 215–220.

52. Theodore M. Hesburgh, C.S.C., *God, Country, Notre Dame* (New York: Doubleday, 1990), 118.

53. Ibid., 216.

54. Ibid., 216, 219.

55. Ibid., 219, 220.

56. U.S. v. Seeger, 380 U.S. 163 (1965) is reprinted in Schlissel, *Conscience in America*.

57. For a complete transcript of the report of the 1967 President's Advisory Commission on Selective Service, "In Pursuit of Equity: Who serves when not all serve?" see, the John Courtney Murray, S.J., Collection located in the Woodstock Archives at Georgetown University.

58. John Courtney Murray, *Selective Conscientious Objection* (Huntington, Ind.: Our Sunday Visitor, 1968), 5.

59. John A. Rohr, *Prophets Without Honor: Public Policy and the Selective Conscientious*

*Objector* (Nashville: Abingdon Press, 1971). Rohr more explicitly than any other writer points out the limitations of the just-unjust war theory. According to him, the SCO cannot base his position on the just war theory since it places all responsiblity for war on the state and the individual bears no responsiblity. Therefore, the individual had no obligation to become a SCO; he is free in conscience to comply with the state since the just war theory has made it the decision maker for all individual consciences. He also considers the three cases which were presented for SCO before the Supreme Court during the 1970–1971 term: Negre v. Larsen, U.S. v. Gillette, and U.S. v. McFadden. None of the cases was successful.

60. Interview with Patrick McDermott, S.J., 21 June 1971.
61. "Catholic Conscience and the Draft," *Peace* 5 (Special Draft Issue with n.d.): 31. (PAX did a brief summary of their activities in the campaign).
62. Ibid.
63. AMU, CAIP Collection, Monsignor Higgins made unsuccessful attempts to secure foundation funding for CAIP from 1963 to 1965. See letter dated 27 September 1963, Richard M. Catalano, assistant to George Higgins, to Howard G. Kurtz of the Ford Foundation; letters dated 16 December 1964, Charles J. McNeill to William E. Moran, Jr., president of CAIP and to George Higgins. There are also letters expressing discontent with the committees, for example, letter dated 15 January 1964, Alba Zizzamia to James L. Vizzard on the defunct Cultural Relations Committee and letters to James L. Vizzard dated 15 November 1963 from William Glade, 11 November 1963 from T. J. McDonagh, and (n.d.) from Charles F. Johnson on dissatisfaction with the Economic Life Committee.
64. William V. O'Brien, *War and/or Survival* (Garden City, N.Y.: Doubleday, 1969), 42.
65. Interview with Patrick McDermott, 21 June 1971.
66. Interview with George Higgins, 8 May 1990 at the Catholic University of America.
67. Musto, *Catholic Peace Tradition*, 255.
68. *Human Life in Our Day* (Washington, D.C., U.S. Catholic Conference, 1968), pars. 98 and 99 and as quoted in Musto, *Catholic Peace Tradition*, 255.
69. Ibid., par. 105.
70. Ibid., pars. 106–113.
71. Jim Castelli, *The Bishops and the Bomb: Waging Peace in a Nuclear Age* (Garden City, N.Y.: Doubleday, 1983), 79. Also according to Castelli, Ed Doherty, who was working in the State Department at the time, wrote the draft for Part II at the request of Bordelon. Bordelon used most of the draft verbatim.
72. *Human Life in Our Day*, pars. 144–145, 15–51.
73. Interview with Patrick McDermott, 21 June 1971.
74. *Human Life in Our Day*, pars. 142 and 153.
75. Interview with Thomas J. Gumbleton, bishop of Detroit, at the University of Notre Dame, 26 April 1990.
76. Interview with James Jennings, 8 May 1990.
77. Hall, "Clergy and Laymen," 154.

78. "Declaration on Conscientious Objection and Selective Conscientious Objection" (Washington, D. C.: U.S. Catholic Conference, October, 1971), par. 11. Copy of set of quotes from document given to author by James Jennings, 8 May 1990.
79. AUND, CPF Collection, Doug Lavine, "Interview with Dorothy Day," (n.d. and unpublished).
80. Interview with James Jennings, NCCB/USCC Headquarters on 8 May 1990.
81. Michael True, *Justice Seekers Peace Makers: 32 Portraits in Courage* (Mystic, Conn.: Twenty-Third, 1985), 3–7, 14–18.
82. Hall, "Clergy and Laymen," 16, 17.
83. Ibid., 76.
84. Ibid., 65.
85. Thomas J. Shelley, *Paul J. Hallinan: First Archbishop of Atlanta* (Wilmington, Del.: Michael Glazier, 1989), 275.
86. Ibid.
87. Ibid., 122.
88. Ibid., 219.
89. Ibid., 224.
90. Taped interview with Bishop Gumbleton dated 1 July 1990. The author has placed the tape in the AUND, Pax Christi Collection.
91. "A Declaration on the Threat of Bombardment of Civilian Centers," dated 13 July 1965, *Continuum* (Summer 1965). Copy at AUND, CPF Collection.
92. *New York Times*, 15 February 1966.
93. *National Catholic Reporter*, 30 March 1966.
94. Zahn, "The Scandal of Silence," 8, 9.
95. Ibid.
96. Ibid. The CPF had immediately issued a reprint of the text for sale at 5 cents per copy before the clarification had been added.
97. Paul J. Hallinan and Joseph L. Bernardin, *War and Peace: A Pastoral Letter to the Archdiocese of Atlanta*, October 1966, as quoted in Shelley, *Paul J. Hallinan*, 274.
98. DeBenedetti and Chatfield, *An American Ordeal*, 186.
99. Shelley, *Paul J. Hallinan*, 276, 277.
100. Ibid., 253.
101. Bishop Shannon's name is never mentioned in the memorandum issued by the USCC.
102. O'Brien, "American Catholic Opposition to the Vietnam War," 129.
103. Taped interview with Bishop Gumbleton dated 1 July 1990.
104. Castelli, *The Bishops and the Bomb*, 69.
105. "Getting Out," *Commonweal* 85 (23 December 1966): 335.
106. John G. Deedy, Jr., "The Catholic Press and Vietnam," in Quigley, *American Catholics and Vietnam*, 130, 131.
107. Musto, *Catholic Peace Tradition*, 256.
108. Deedy, "The Catholic Press and Vietnam," 121–132.
109. O'Brien, "Catholic Opposition to the Vietnam War," 136.

110. As quoted in ibid.
111. George Gallup, Jr., and Jim Castelli, *The American Catholic People: Their Beliefs, Practices, and Values* (New York: Doubleday, 1987), 82.
112. Ibid., 78.
113. Ibid., 79.
114. "Resolution on Southeast Asia," Paragraph 13 as quoted in Marvin Bordelon, "The Bishops and Just War," *America* (8 January 1972): 17.
115. Ibid.
116. AUND, CPF Collection, Cornell, "The First 10 Years."
117. Benedetti and Chatfield, *An American Ordeal*, 68.

## 7: The Berrigan Brothers and the Catholic Resistance

1. Klejment, *In the Lion's Den*, 35, states that "Although I have not conducted an exhaustive search of the origin of the word [New Catholic Left], William O'Rourke, a writer covering the Harrisburg trial was one of the first to use the term. William O'Rourke, *The Harrisburg 7 and the New Catholic Left* (New York: Thomas Y. Crowell, Apollo, 1973), 263.
2. Jack Nelson and Ronald J. Ostrow, *The FBI and the Berrigans: The Making of a Conspiracy* (New York: Coward, McCann & Geoghegan, 1972), 14.
3. It was not the Berrigans who launched the first draft board raid, but a nineteen-year-old Minnesotan named Barry Bondhaus. His eleven brothers and machinist father helped him prepare for the 1966 action by collecting material he would use. Bondhaus dumped two buckets of human feces into a Selective Service filing cabinet. Although the protest, known as The Big Lake One, drew little press notice, it was credited as "the movement that started the movement." See Nelson and Ostrow, *FBI and the Berrigans*.
4. Interview with Robert A. Ludwig, 28 July 1972. At that time Ludwig was a doctoral candidate at the Aquinas Institute of Theology and was completing his dissertation on the theology of Daniel Berrigan. He was most helpful in systematizing the influences on and development of Daniel Berrigan's "political theology."
5. Philip Berrigan, letter to author dated 21 October 1968.
6. All three brothers, Phil, Jerry, and Dan, when asked by the author in 1973 why Dan did not participate responded the same way: "He (I) did not feel free to do it."
7. Daniel Berrigan, *To Dwell in Peace: An Autobiography* (New York: Harper & Row, 1987), 200, 201.
8. For the best account of the Customs House action, see Philip Berrigan, "Blood, War and Witness" in John O'Connor, ed., *American Catholic Exodus* (Washington, D.C.: Corpus Books, 1968).
9. In a letter to Representative William R. Anderson of Tennessee, Daniel Berrigan cited Dorothy Day and the late Thomas Merton as having shaped his nonviolence. Recalling that he and Philip had attended a 1964 retreat conducted by Merton on the "spiritual roots of protest," Daniel Berrigan said: "I wrote him once that I could still remember the article of his in the *Catholic Worker* that turned me

from damp straw to combustible man. . . . He got us started, after Dorothy Day. The consequences are not theirs, but ours."

10. The best-known biography of the Berrigan brothers is that of Francine du Plessix Gray, *Divine Disobedience: Profiles in Catholic Radicalism* (New York: Knopf, 1970). See pp.130–210; The chapter entitled "Berrigans" was reprinted from the *New Yorker*, 14 March 1970.

11. Jay P. Dolan, *The Immigrant Church: New York's Irish and German Catholics, 1815–1865* (Baltimore: Johns Hopkins University Press, 1975).

12. Daniel Berrigan, *To Dwell in Peace*, 42.

13. Ibid., 43.

14. Ibid., 43, 44.

15. Interview with Mrs. Frida Berrigan, 2 November 1968 in Syracuse, New York. Interviews with Mr. and Mrs. Jerome Berrigan on the family were also conducted.

16. Daniel Berrigan, *To Dwell in Peace*, 43.

17. Philip Berrigan and Elizabeth McAlister, *The Time's Discipline: The Beatitudes and Nuclear Resistance* (Baltimore: Fortkamp, 1989), 7.

18. Ibid., 6.

19. Daniel Berrigan, "Reflections on the Priest as Peacemaker," *Jubilee* 12 (February 1966): 25.

20. Interview with Robert A. Ludwig, 18 July 1972.

21. Daniel Berrigan, *The World Showed Me Its Heart* (St. Louis, Mo.: National Sodality Service Center, 1966), 11; an interview with Jerome Berrigan on 2 November 1968, and visit to International House on LeMoyne campus, 2 November 1968.

22. Interview with Matthew O'Rourke, S.S.J. and use of the file on Philip Berrigan, in the archives of the Josephite Provincialate in Baltimore, Maryland, on 5 October 1968. The quotation is cited in Nelson and Ostrow, *The FBI and the Berrigans*, 40.

23. From 1968 to 1972, the author was personally involved in the Catholic Resistance. Many statements and motivations attributed to Philip Berrigan came from conversations and correspondence with him through the years. The author's relationship with Daniel Berrigan was limited to two interviews, three letters of correspondence, and a proofreading by him of the author's M.A. thesis on Daniel Berrigan entitled "The Evolution of a Conscience."

24. Interview with Richard Wagner, S.S.J., on 6 October 1968.

25. Philip Berrigan, "The Challenge of Segregation" *Worship* 35 (November, 1960): 597–603.

26. Interview with Robert A. Ludwig, 28 July 1972.

27. Cornell University, Special Collections, Olin Library, Berrigan Collection, a copy of Letter dated 14 October 1968 from John Heidbrink to author.

28. Ibid.

29. Cornell University, Special Collections, Olin Library, Berrigan Collection, letter from Daniel Berrigan to his family from Eastern European trip in 1964.

30. Interview with Tony Walsh on 31 October 1968.
31. Interview with Daniel Berrigan, on 17 November 1968. The author read many letters of correspondence between Daniel and his religious superiors in the Society of Jesus. Upon Daniel's request these are not quoted directly and are paraphrased.
32. Nelson and Ostrow, *The FBI and the Berrigans*, 45.
33. Interview with John P. Grady on 6 October 1968. Grady, a Catholic layman and father of five children had spent much of his time since the mid-1950s working with Daniel and Philip in their many projects and very closely with Philip in developing the Catholic Resistance.
34. Interview with Beverly Bell, S.N.D., on 8 April 1973. Philip Berrigan had told her this when they were discussing the viability of religious life.
35. Daniel Berrigan, *The World Showed Me*, 25, 26.
36. Cornell University, Special Collections, Olin Library, Berrigan Collection, letter from Daniel Berrigan to his family from Eastern European trip in 1964.
37. Many of Daniel's essays during this time reflect this attitude.
38. Later Thomas Cornell also became a co-chair.
39. Cornell University, Special Collections, Olin Library, Berrigan Collection, a copy of letter dated Monday, 21 October 1968 from Philip Berrigan, at the Baltimore County Jail to author.
40. Interview with Thomas Cornell in summer of 1968.
41. Reverend Richard J. Neuhaus, letter to author dated 21 October 1968.
42. Daniel Berrigan, *To Dwell in Peace*, 182.
43. Interview with Francis Keating, S.J., and Daniel Kilfoyle, S.J., on 6 October 1968. These men along with Daniel Berrigan agreed that the best reporting was done by John Leo from the *National Catholic Reporter*. James Hennesey, S.J., who was the executive assistant to the provincial superior of the New York Province of the Society of Jesus at the time of Berrigan's transfer, said that the Archdiocese of New York and Cardinal Spellman as the press contended had nothing to do with it. It was the Jesuits who initiated the action. James Hennesey, *American Catholics: A History of the Roman Catholic Community in the United States* (New York: Oxford University Press, 1981), 374.
44. " 'Peace' Priest Muzzled," *Christian Century* 82 (8 December 1965): 1500 and 1501, as quoted in Hall, *Clergy and Layman*, 26.
45. Daniel Berrigan, "Berrigan at Cornell," *Jubilee* 15 (February 1968): 29.
46. Daniel Berrigan, *To Dwell in Peace*, 186–214. The chapter, "Cornell: Poison in the Ivy," provides his reflections on the period.
47. Daniel Berrigan, *Night Flight From Hanoi: War Diary With 11 Poems* (New York: Macmillan, 1968).
48. Daniel Berrigan, "My Brother, the Witness," *Commonweal* 88 (26 April 1968): 181.
49. Philip Berrigan, letter to author dated 21 October 1968.
50. Interview with Paul Mayer, 4 October 1968.
51. Daniel Berrigan, *Trial of the Catonsville Nine* (Boston: Beacon Press, 1970).
52. Interview with Neil McLaughlin, 10 April 1973.

53. Interview with Theodore Glick, 3 February 1969. Estimates of the number of draft board raids that actually occurred varied with different members of the Catholic Resistance. Glick gave the highest estimate.

54. Anne Klejment, "The Berrigans: Revolutionary Christian Nonviolence," in Charles DeBenedettii, ed., *Peace Heroes in Twentieth Century America* (Bloomington: Indiana University Press, 1988), 246.

55. William Hardy, the informer of the Camden Twenty-eight draft board raid, told the FBI that John P. Grady had confessed to him that he had engineered the raid at Media. *Philadelphia Inquirer*, 16 March 1972, p. 1.

56. Nelson and Ostrow, The *FBI and the Berrigans*, 188.

57. These were the author's impressions after attending several such retreats.

58. Nelson and Ostrow, *The FBI and the Berrigans*, 60, and author's eyewitness account.

59. Interview with Jay P. Dolan on 8 January 1972; at the time of the search he was in residence at St. Gregory the Great rectory.

60. Observations of the author, who attended the rally.

61. Interview with John P. Grady on 21 April 1970. Grady stayed with Philip much of the time that he was underground.

62. Robert Coles and Daniel Berrigan, *Geography of Faith* (Boston: Beacon Press, 1971). The Introduction provides Coles's analysis.

63. Nelson and Ostrow, *The FBI and the Berrigans*, 56.

64. No one knew exactly how the FBI found out about Daniel's existence at Block Island. After the letters were released by the prosecution at the Harrisburg Seven Trial, it was assumed that the letters provided the FBI with the knowledge.

65. Daniel Berrigan, "Notes From the Underground; or I was a Fugitive from the FBI," *Commonweal* 92 (29 May 1970): 263–265.

66. Nelson and Ostrow, *The FBI and the Berrigans*, 17, 18.

67. Interview with Jack Levine on 22 April 1971.

68. Nelson and Ostrow, *The FBI and the Berrigans*, 303.

69. The process of selection of lawyers was tedious. For example, the Berrigan brothers met with Ramsey Clark who offered his services in the case. Personal and political motivations between them were discussed and not found to be in conflict. Interview with Neil McLaughlin at the University of Notre Dame, 15 October 1971.

70. Nelson and Ostrow, *The FBI and the Berrigans*, 111–128, presents lengthy excerpts from the letters. Nelson also treats Boyd Douglas on the witness stand in great detail, pp. 237–281. His book contains great detail, more factual material, and more political analysis of the trial than does the more impressionistic character portrayals of the book by William O'Rourke.

71. Interview with Neil McLaughlin and Joseph Wenderoth on 17 February 1973.

72. Nelson and Ostrow, *The FBI and the Berrigans*, 303–306.

73. Ibid., 302, 303.

74. See John C. Raines, ed., *Conspiracy* (New York: Harper & Row, 1974). The various contributors attempt to evaluate the significance of the Harrisburg trial.

75. Nelson and Ostrow, *The FBI and the Berrigans*, 215.
76. DeBenedetti and Chatfield, *An American Ordeal*, 3, 278–280.
77. Interviews with Neil McLaughlin and Joseph Wenderoth and Anthony and Mary Scoblic, 17 February 1973.
78. Daniel Berrigan, *To Dwell in Peace*, 215. First two lines of his poem, "Catonsville: The Fires of Pentecost."
79. Interview with Dorothy Day at St. Ignatius Hall in Baltimore at a rally in support of the Catonsville Nine, 1968.

### 8: Catholic Peacemaking

1. Castelli, *The Bishops and the Bomb*, 182.
2. *The Challenge of Peace: God's Promise and Our Response*, (Washington, D.C.: USCC, 1983), par. 333.
3. Philip Berrigan and McAlister, *The Time's Discipline*, 13.
4. Ibid., 226–232. Appendix B, The Chronicle of Hope, lists the actions.
5. Daniel Berrigan, "Swords into Plowshares," in Arthur J. Laffin and Anne Montgomery, eds., *Swords into Plowshares: Nonviolent Direct Action for Disarmament* (New York: Harper & Row, 1987), 60.
6. *New York Times*, Wednesday, 11 April 1990, p. A10.
7. Laffin and Montgomery, *Swords into Plowshares*, 3. A description of each action and each person involved in the actions is given in the book.
8. *New York Times*, Wednesday, 11 April 1990, p. A10.
9. Daniel Berrigan, "Swords into Plowshares," 61.
10. Philip Berrigan and McAlister, *The Time's Discipline*, 16.
11. Ibid., 17.
12. Daniel Berrigan, *To Dwell in Peace*, 300.
13. Ibid., 17.
14. AUND, CPF Collection, letter dated 21 May 1974 from Jim Forest to Kathleen Keating.
15. Ibid.
16. Daniel Berrigan, *To Dwell in Peace*, 284.
17. Ibid., 285.
18. AUND, CPF Collection, letter dated 15 September 1972, Daniel Berrigan to Jim Forest.
19. AUND, CPF Collection, letter dated 21 September 1972, Jim Forest to Al Hassler.
20. For the full text of the Berrigans' letter and Hanoi's reply, see *Win*, (6 September 1973): 16.
21. Guenter Lewy, *Peace & Revolution: The Moral Crisis of American Pacifism* (Grand Rapids, Mich.: Eerdmans, 1988). Lewy covers the issue of political prisoners and human rights in great detail.
22. Daniel and Philip Berrigan, "On the Torture of Prisoners," *Fellowship*, 35 (September 1973): 4.

23. AUND, CPF Collection, letter dated 23 December 1973, Daniel Berrigan to Jim Forest.
24. James H. Forest, "Solzhenitsyn and American Pacifists," *Fellowship*, 35 (August 1973): 2.
25. AUND, CPF Collection, Memo on Appeal had been signed by Dorothy Day, Jim and Shelly Douglass, Arthur W. Clarke, and Bishop John J. Dougherty.
26. AUND, CPF Collection, letter dated 24 August 1977, Jim Forest to Daniel Berrigan.
27. AUND, CPF Collection, letter dated April 1975, Daniel Berrigan to Jim Forest.
28. Daniel Berrigan, *To Dwell in Peace*, 303.
29. Ibid., 305.
30. Ibid.
31. Ibid., 318.
32. Ibid., 281.
33. *New York Times*, Wednesday, 11 April 1990, p. A10.
34. AUND, CPF Collection, letter dated 23 June 1977, Jim Forest to Tom Cornell.
35. AUND, CPF Collection, Hermene Evans sent $10,000. Zahn continued his pledge of $1,000 a year to CPF, and the Goss-Mayrs sent enough to purchase a woodburning stove.
36. AUND, CPF Collection, letter dated 15 January 1980, Tom Cornell to Hildegard Goss-Mayr.
37. Telephone conversation with Tom Cornell, Tuesday, 22 July 1990.
38. For Gumbleton's own story of how he became involved in the peace issue, see "The Bishop as Social Activist," *Origins* 12, no. 18 (30 September 1982): 249–256.
39. AUND, Pax Christi Collection, Gerard A. Vanderhaar, "Pax Christi USA: the Early Years, 1972–78,"(unpublished history, 21 June 1988), 1–5. Direct quote from p. 6. There is also a collection of the letters and writings of Gerard A. Vanderhaar at the AUND.
40. Carroll T. Dozier, Bishop of Memphis, *Peace: Gift and Task—Pastoral Letter to the People of the Diocese of Memphis*, December 1971. Pamphlet reprint from the diocese of Memphis.
41. AUND, Pax Christi Collection, letter dated 5 September 1973, from Eileen Egan to Ed Guinan; also quoted in Vanderhaar, "Pax Christi," 15.
42. AUND, Pax Christi Collection, Vanderhaar, "Pax Christi," 15.
43. Ibid., 15 and 16.
44. AUND, Pax Christi Collection. In the third *Pax Christi Thirdly* twelve local peace groups were identified in Boston, Erie, Washington, Pittsburgh, Richmond, Norfolk, Kansas City, Milwaukee, Dubuque, Davenport, New Orleans, and Portland.
45. AUND, Pax Christi Collection, Bishop Dozier's Files, letter dated 7 August 1974, Ed Guinan to Bishops Dozier and Gumbleton, Eileen Egan and Gordon Zahn as quoted in Vanderhaar, "Pax Christi," 18.
46. AUND, Pax Christi Collection, Vanderhaar, "Pax Christi," 18–20.

47. AUND, Pax Christi Collection. The first members of the executive committee were Bishop Carroll Dozier, Memphis; Bishop Thomas Gumbleton, Detroit; Alden Brown, Queens College, Flushing, New York; Clare Danielsson, Beacon, New York; Edward Cripps, S.J., *America* magazine, New York; Dorothy Dohen, Fordham University, New York; Jean Eckstein, National Council of Catholic Laity, Iowa City; Eileen Egan, New York; Joseph Fahey, Manhattan College, New York; Mary Evelyn Jegen, S.N.D., Catholic Relief Service, New York; Paul Mc-Laughlin, Regis College, Boston; Gerard Vanderhaar, Christian Brothers College, Memphis; Mary Rae Waller, O.P., Network, Washington, D.C.; Gordon Zahn, Boston. List of people taken from Vanderhaar, "Pax Christi," 28.
48. "Current Comment," *America* 131 (14 December 1974).
49. Ibid., 30.
50. AUND, Pax Christi Collection. The membership file for 1973 to 1977 lists the following bishops as members of Pax Christi in March 1976: Joseph J. Donnelly, John J. Dougherty, Daniel Hart, James Rausch, Kenneth J. Povish, Marion Forst, Walter Schoenker, Walter F. Sullivan, William Johnson, Carroll T. Dozier, Thomas Gumbleton, Joseph L. Howze, Daniel E. Sheehan, J. Francis Stafford, and Ernest L. Unterkoefler.
51. AUND, Pax Christi Collection, Financial Records, Budget 3/31/77 to 1/15/78.
52. AUND, Pax Christi Collection, Membership and Financial files.
53. See M. Evelyn Jegen, S.N.D., "The Pacifist Vision," *Fellowship* 42 (10 May 1980).
54. The irony of the differences between the two agendas was that Reagan had appointed many Catholics to key positions in his administration: Alexander Haig, John Lehmann, and William Clark. The military services included Catholics in the highest ranks of command, Admiral James Watkins and General Paul X. Kelley. Edward Hickey had major responsibilities in the Secret Service detail. And General Vernon Walters, a State Department appointee later became ambassador to the United Nations. See Eugene Kennedy, *Cardinal Bernardin: Easing Conflicts—and Battling for the Soul of American Catholicism* (Chicago: Baners Books, 1989), 201, 202.
55. AUND, CPF Collection, letter dated 27 September 1980, Tom Cornell to Daniel J. Corcoran, Winona State University.
56. *In the Name of Peace*, 83–86.
57. AUND, Pax Christi Collection, Minutes of National Council meetings.
58. *Reporter for Conscience Sake*, 30, no. 6 *(June 1983)*: 27, as referred to in Musto, *The Catholic Peace Tradition*, 325.
59. This is a summary of Pax Christi–USA activities described in Vanderhaar, "Pax Christi," 30–36, and a reading of the *Pax Christi Newsletter* published by Vanderhaar during this time period. Copies of the newsletter are in the AUND, Pax Christi Collection.
60. AUND, Pax Christi Collection, *Pax Christi–USA Newsletter*, December 1979.
61. Ibid.

62. *Statement on Central America* dated 10 November 1981, published Washington, D.C., as cited in Musto, *The Catholic Peace Tradition*, 325.
63. AUND, Pax Christi Collection, *Pax Christi–USA Newsletter*, January 1982.
64. AUND, Pax Christi Collection, *Pax Christi–USA Newsletter*, January 1983.
65. AUND, Pax Christi Collection, Correspondence of M. Evelyn Jegen, S.N.D.
66. Frances B. McCrea and Gerald E. Markle, *Minutes to Midnight: Nuclear Weapons Protest in America* (Newbury Park, Calif.: Sage Publications, 1989), 15, 16.
67. AUND, Pax Christi Collection, *Pax Christi Newsletter*, May 1978.
68. Vanderhaar, "Pax Christi," 37.
69. The debate among Catholics on the ratification of SALT II is presented in *Commonweal* (2 March 1978) in an article by Bishop Thomas Gumbleton against ratification and in another article by J. Bryan Hehir supporting the treaty. Joseph Fahey in *America* (24 February 1978) wrote an article advocating a third position between active support and opposition of SALT II.
70. Castelli, *The Bishops and the Bomb*, 23
71. John J. Cardinal Krol, "SALT II: A Statement of Support," testimony before the Senate Foreign Relations Committee on 6 September 1970, reprinted in *Origins* 9, no. 14 (20 September 1979): 197.
72. AUND, Pax Christi Collection, *Pax Christi–USA Newsletter*, September 1979.
73. AUND, Pax Christi Collection, *Pax Christi–USA Bulletin*, April 1979.
74. AUND, Pax Christi Collection, *Pax Christi–USA Newsletter*, March 1980.
75. AUND, Pax Christi Collection, "New Abolitionist Covenant" pamphlet.
76. Castelli, *The Bishops and the Bomb*, 60.
77. AUND, Pax Christi Collection, *Pax Christi–USA*, May 1982.
78. AUND, Pax Christi Collection, *Pax Christi–USA*, December 1981.
79. Castelli, *The Bishops and the Bomb*, 95.
80. The PAX Center was run by Benedictine nuns who were the first to make a corporate witness to peace by giving $100 a month and 10 percent of their profits from fundraisers to Pax Christi–USA. In 1985, Pax Christi–USA would name Mary Lou Kownacki, a Benedictine nun, its national coordinator and locate its headquarters in Erie.
81. Castelli, *The Bishops and the Bomb*, 95.
82. Eugene Kennedy, *Cardinal Bernardin: Easing Conflicts*, 255.
83. See Weigel, *Tranquillitas Ordinis*, 314–324 for a comprehensive analysis of Hehir's thought. In conversation with Bryan Hehir in the summer of 1989, Hehir stated that Weigel is the first author to attempt an analysis of his thought and that basically it is an accurate assessment, but Weigel's point of view must be taken into account.
84. This was true of Hehir's position in the early years of the formation of Pax Christi–USA. The author directly questioned Hehir on his just war position in relation to nuclear warfare. Hehir responded that he was a nuclear pacifist. Annual Pax Christi–USA conference, University of Dayton, 1976. Hehir explains his nuclear pacifist position in J. Bryan Hehir, "The New Nuclear Debate: Political and

Ethical Considerations," in Robert A. Gessert and J. Bryan Hehir, *The New Nuclear Debate* (New York: Council on Religion and International Affairs, 1976), 35–76.

85. Letter to author from J. Bryan Hehir dated 12 April 1991. For clarification of Hehir's new position, see J. Bryan Hehir, "Moral Issues in Deterrence Policy," in Douglas MacLean, ed., *The Security Gamble Deterrence Dilemmas in the Nuclear Age* (Totowa, N.J.: Rowman & Allanheld, 1984), 53–71.

86. Ed Doherty, who was on Hehir's staff, was responsible for many of the initial drafts on the nuclear issue. Castelli, *The Bishops and the Bomb*, 22, 23.

87. *To Live in Christ Jesus: A Pastoral Reflection on the Moral Life*, as quoted in Castelli, *The Bishops and the Bomb*, 22.

88. Castelli, *The Bishops and the Bomb*, 23. Castelli also contends that "Doherty argued in the conference—without much reaction—that the statement meant Catholics could not serve in the nuclear branch of the military."

89. *In the Name of Peace*, 63.

90. In Robert Heyer, ed., *Nuclear Disarmament: Key Statements of Popes, Bishops, Councils and Churches* (Ramsey, N.J.: Paulist Press, 1982). This book also contains the statements of eighteen North American Catholic bishops who spoke out against nuclear disarmament.

91. Castelli, *The Bishops and the Bomb*, 39. Castelli contends that "Reporters ask the local bishops, 'And what do you think?' and another statement is made."

92. Weigel, *Tranquillitas Ordinis*,, 170–173, presents a distorted view of James Douglass's influence on Archbishop Hunthausen. Certainly Douglass was an influence, but insufficent credit is given to the archbishop himself and his own conversion experience and the influence on him caused by the actions of other bishops on the issue.

93. Castelli, *The Bishops and the Bomb*, 27.

94. Archbishop Raymond G. Hunthausen, Pastoral Letter to the Archdiocese of Seattle, 28 January 1972.

95. AUND, "Pax Christi Collection," *Pax Christi–USA*, March 1983.

96. The subsequent investigation of Hunthausen by the Vatican was not related to his position and action on the nuclear issue. Interview with Bishop Thomas Gumbleton, 26 April 1990 at the University of Notre Dame. Gumbleton stated that he had never been under investigation because of his position on peace. For a complete account of the investigation, see Kennedy, *Cardinal Bernardin: Easing Conflicts*.

97. Archbishop John Quinn, "Remarks as President of NCCB, on President Carter's decision to defer production of neutron warheads," 14 April 1978, in Heyer, *Nuclear Disarmament*, 95, 96.

98. Castelli, *The Bishops and the Bomb*, 28, 29.

99. AUND, Pax Christi Collection, *Pax Christi–USA*, January 1982.

100. Castelli, *The Bishops and the Bomb*, chaps. 1, 5. Also see Weigel, *Tanquillitas Ordinis*, 267.

101. Weigel, *Tranquillitas Ordinis*, 267, 268.

102. Castelli, *The Bishops and the Bomb*, 81.
103. Ibid., 79.
104. Ibid., 135.
105. Interview with Bishop Thomas Gumbleton, 26 April 1990 at the University of Notre Dame.
106. Ibid.
107. AUND, Pax Christi Collection, letter dated 20 July 1981 from Mary Evelyn Jegen, S.N.D., to Dr. Gordon Zahn.
108. *Wall Street Journal*, Wednesday, 9 June 1982.
109. "A Vatican Synthesis," *Origins* 12, no.43 (7 April 1983): 691, 692.
110. As quoted in Weigel, *Tranquillitas Ordinis*, 275, 276.
111. Weigel, *Tranquillitas Ordinis*, 275–280. Weigel places too much emphasis on Vatican intervention. In terms of the NCCB's challenging the authority of the pope as Hehir points out in his article, "From the Pastoral Constitution of Vatican II to *The Challenge of Peace*," in Philip J. Murnion, ed., *Catholics and Nuclear War: A Commentary on "The Challenge of Peace" The U.S. Catholic Bishops' Pastoral Letter on War and Peace* (New York: Crossroad, 1983), 71, the pastoral does go beyond the moral teaching of the pastoral constitution.
112. *The Challenge of Peace*, "Summary," par. 3.
113. Castelli, *The Bishops and the Bomb*, 181.
114. *The Challenge of Peace*, par. 123.
115. Ibid., par. 147.
116. Ibid., par. 148.
117. Ibid., par. 153.
118. Ibid., pars. 172–177.
119. As quoted in Weigel, *Tranquillitas Ordinis*, 271.
120. *The Challenge of Peace*, pars. 188–191.
121. Ibid., pars. 221–225.
122. Ibid., "Summary."
123. *The Challenge of Peace*, pars. 332 and 333.
124. All the sections of the pastoral pertaining to pacifism and nonviolence were the results of the labor of Bishop Thomas Gumbleton.
125. *The Challenge of Peace*, pars. 234–279.
126. Interview with Monsignor George Higgins, 8 May 1990, at the Catholic University of America,

# Index

abortion issue: and antinuclear issue, 244–245; and Daniel Berrigan, 223; as focus of American Catholic hierarchy in 1980s, 157

Afghanistan, Soviet invasion of, and draft, 237, 329

African Americans: advice from consulting firm to Josephites on, 187; and Berrigan brothers, 181–182; and Black Panthers, 206; and militancy and separatism in civil rights movement, 187; priests, appointed to Catholic hierarchy, 133

Age of Constantine, and pacifism of primitive Christian church, x, 29

Ahmad, Eqbal, 199, 201, 204; and draft, 237; and Harrisburg Seven trial, 205, 208; and human rights issue, 220. See also Harrisburg Eight case

air raid test demonstrations, 91–92, 122

Alfrink, Bernard, 230

Alinsky, Saul, 133

America, 32, 54, 116, 191; attitude toward obliteration and atomic bombing, 67, 68

American Catholic bishops: aid to Civilian Public Service camps, 269n25; and Catholic Peace Fellowship ad, 145; conflict with Reagan administration, 237; joining Pax Christi—USA, 235, 236; and Jonah House demonstrations, 213; and League of Nations, 7; and nuclear freeze, 243; reorganization after Second Vatican Council, 156–157; Statement on Registration and Conscription for Military Service, 238; support for Franco, 17–18; and Vietnam War, 142, 145, 157–160. See also American Catholic hierarchy; National Conference of Catholic Bishops

American Catholic hierarchy: and abortion issue, 244–245, 257; annual meeting of 1939, 53; and anti-communist crusade, 74;

appointment of black priests to, 133; attitude toward Catholic peacemakers, xiii, 146; attitude toward obliteration and atomic bombing, 68; attitude toward United Nations, 52; and bombing of Rome during World War II, 51; and CAIP, xi, 98; and CALCAV, 162; and Catholic immigrants, 1–2; and Catholic participation in civil rights movement, 133; and Catholic Worker call for draft resistance during World War II, 43; and Catholic Worker movement, 22; on causes of World War II, 40; and Central America, 239–240; and Challenge of Peace, 211, 212, 249–258; and Cold War, 51–52; Committee on Reconstruction, 6; and conscientious objectors, 43, 46, 52–54, 138, 159–160, 165, 166; and conscription during World War II, 45, 65; and debate on ratification of SALT II, 241–242; and draft legislation during World War II, 53–54; focus on domestic concerns, 1–2; as focus of PAX during Vietnam War, 139, 140; and formation of National Catholic War Council, 4; and Harrisburg Seven trial, 207; impact of American Catholic peace movement on, 172; influence of anti-communism on foreign policy positions of, 135–136; influence of Catholic peacemakers on, xiii; influence of Hehir on, 246–247; influence of PAX on, xii, 160; involvement in urban affairs, 133–134; and isolationism, 51–52; and just war doctrine, x, 69–70; and National Catholic Welfare Council, 4–6; and nuclear weapons freeze campaign, 240; and obliteration bombing, 65; pastoral letter after World War I, 4; pastoral letters on social problems in 1983, ix; and Pax Christi—USA, 230, 234–235; and PAX lobbying at Second